Capture the Magic

Jack Dykinga

Capture the Magic

Train Your Eye, Improve Your
Photographic Composition

rockynook

Editor: Joan Dixon
Copyeditor: Theano Nikitas
Layout: Petra Strauch
Cover Design: Helmut Kraus, www.exclam.de
Printer: Tara TPS, Ltd. through Four Colour Print Group
Printed in Korea

ISBN: 978-1-937538-35-4

1st Edition 2014 (2nd printing, February 2015)
© 2014 Jack Dykinga

Rocky Nook, Inc.
802 E. Cota Street, 3rd Floor
Santa Barbara, CA 93103

www.rockynook.com

Library of Congress Cataloging-in-Publication Data

Dykinga, Jack W.
 Capture the magic : train your eye, improve your photographic composition / by Jack Dykinga. -- 1st edition.
    pages cm
 ISBN 978-1-937538-35-4 (softcover : alk. paper)
 1. Composition (Photography) I. Title.
 TR179.D96 2013
 770.1--dc23
                        2013023613

For Nicholas
May his world be filled with beauty and magic

Table of Contents

Decisions

What is it that piques our interest? Why do we stop, pull out the camera, and decide to photograph?

In order to answer these questions, we need to look at photography as a form of communication. It's a marvelous language—universal, powerful, and one that crosses linguistic borders. We see something that we find interesting and we simply want to share it.

My journalistic background taught me to go a step further, by emphasizing that images require content that both affects and enlightens the viewer. Since much of my work is related to environmental causes, I want my work to take the viewer to places less traveled and even less seen.

The problem is: not everything we wish to photograph is visually pleasing. In order to communicate effectively, we must learn to compose and craft our images.

Why do some images cause us to linger for a more contemplative study? Often it's not apparent, but in successful images the photographer has organized the visual elements in the image to direct our focus and our emotional reaction. Through the careful use of composition, photographers share their personal visions and create pathways for a shared vision.

We all love to use the camera to record unusual events. Imagine driving through a parched landscape with only the strongest plants surviving. Then imagine my reaction driving through the same desert after an unusually wet spring when the harsh Sonoran Desert poured forth color. My pulse raced and I inhaled the scent of spring. My overpowering urge to share this scene demanded that I photograph it.

There seem to be many factors that draw us to capture particular images; certain primal human biases that we collectively respond to: things like color, fire, water, movement, chaos, or perfect order. Photographers who recognize and exploit this commonality increase their potential to reach viewers with their images.

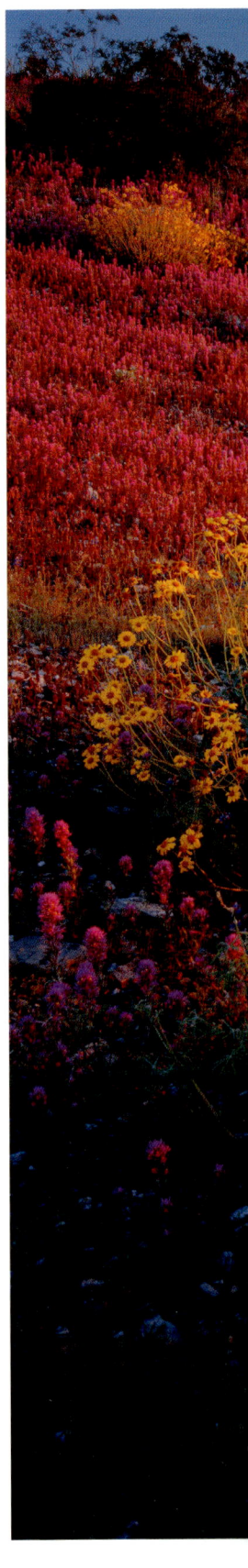

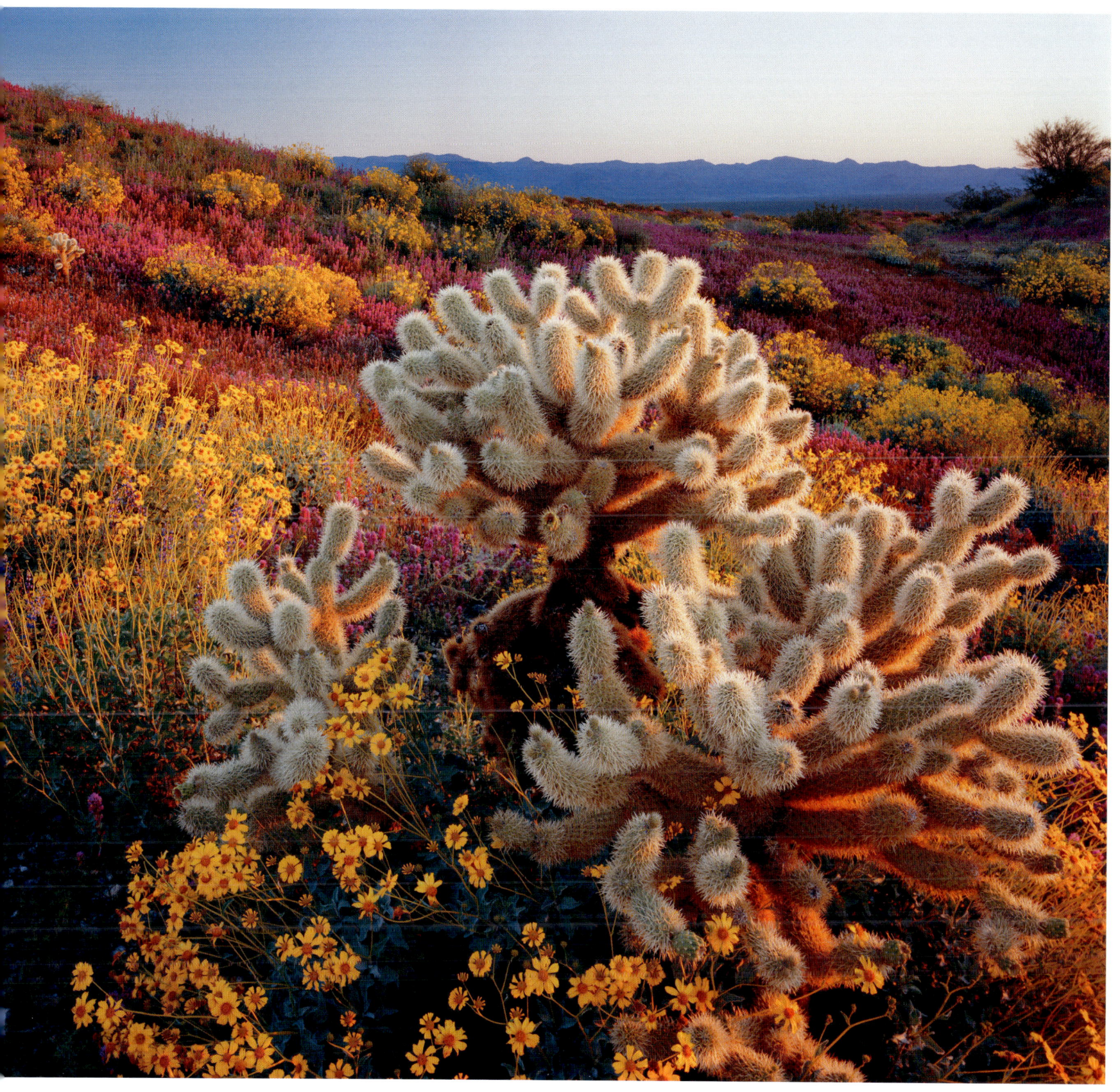

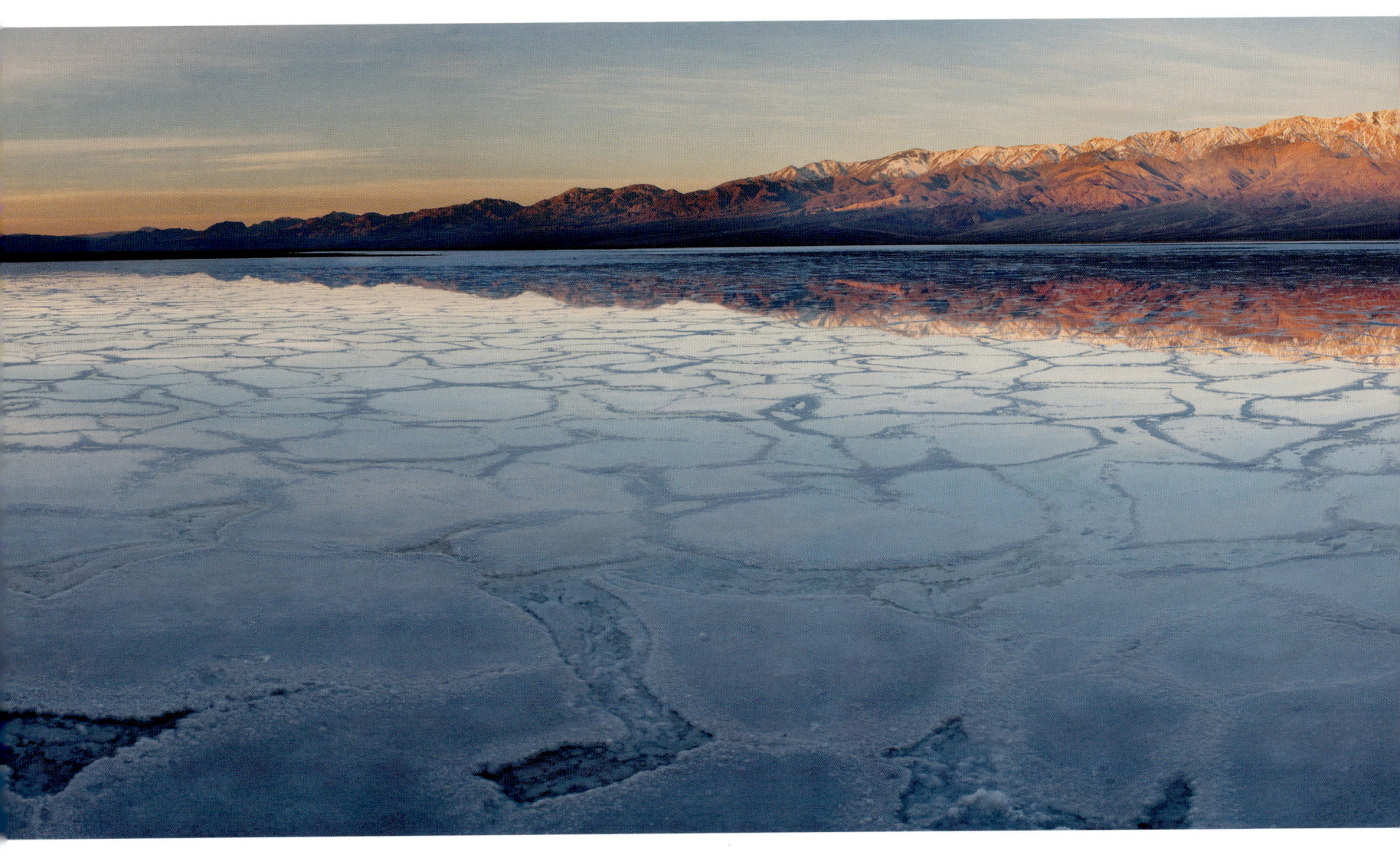

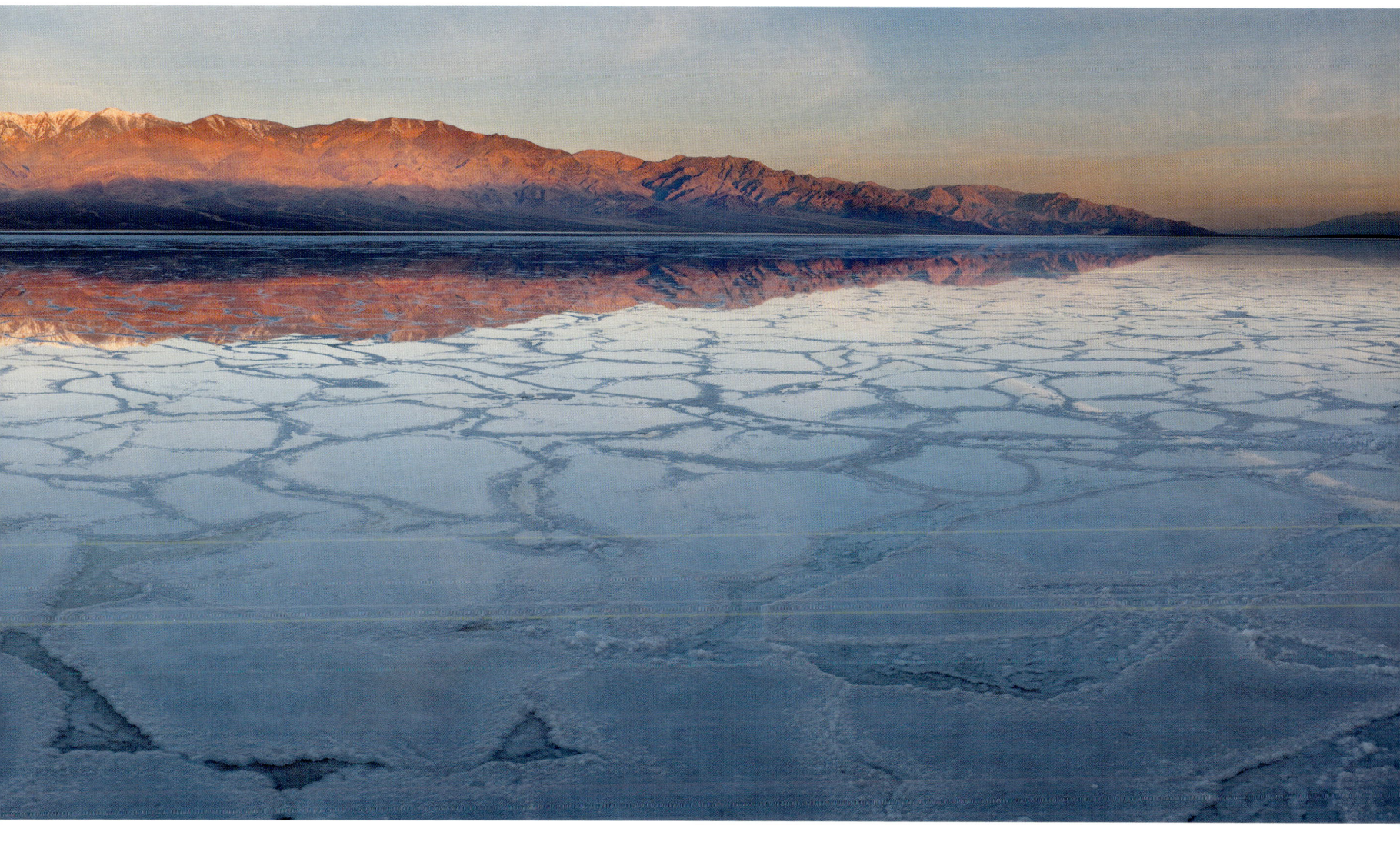

Images are ubiquitous and we can learn and profit from those who have gone before us. The giants of photography have laid down paths to follow, and they have provided stirring examples of their visions and approaches to photography. During the learning process we all borrow styles and techniques as we expand our own capabilities. However, meaningful photography is also deeply personal. It must reflect our personal visions. How we respond to visual stimuli is where it all begins.

Once I've decided to make a photograph, my first goal is to get to know the subject or area. I make visual inventories of what I observe and I search for potential images that help create a narrative that will describe my subject. I make basic decisions concerning each potential image, a process that I refer to as "honoring the subject." At the most basic level, if it's a tall mountain I will think vertically, or with the dry saltpans in Death Valley, I'm likely to think horizontally or, as in this image, even panoramic.

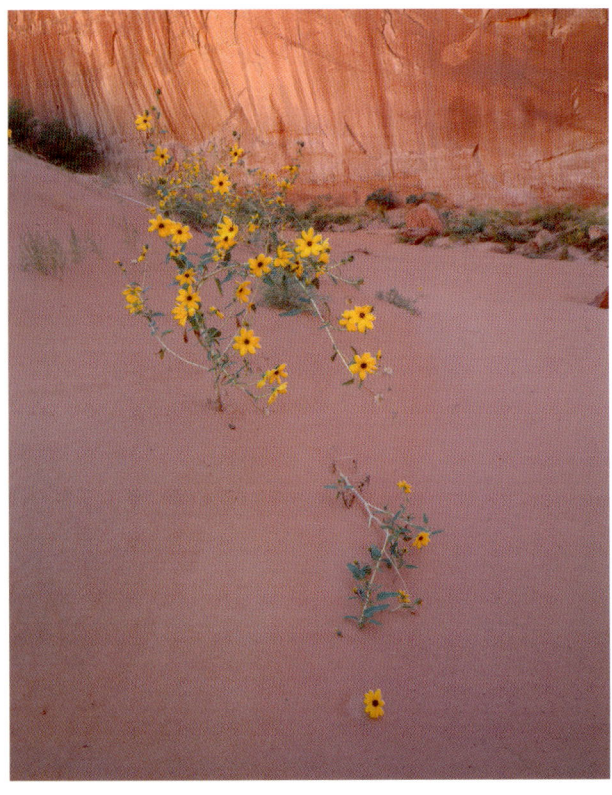

Problems can arise quickly when we're confronted with a new and strange landscape. It's easy for visual overload to occur. That's perfectly normal. When I'm on an assignment and the clock is ticking down to a deadline, I've been known to panic about needing to be creative on demand. I believe this happens to us all.

But how do I begin? My technique is quite simple. I start small. While making my visual inventory, telling details within the grand landscape often grab my attention. For me, they are the most important. They provide the flavor of a place. I also look for designs, colors, or biological significance. I take my time, rejecting many situations until the perfect combination of light, form, and moment come together. A photographer is defined as much by what he or she decides not to photograph as by what is photographed.

The key to successful photography is taking time to really *see*. It may sound simple, but this is the hardest thing we do—training the eye to see nuances in colors, compositions, and imperfections.

I can easily find compositions from a speeding car; however, when I actually walk the land and carefully observe, the imagined images evaporate.

My friend, Jay Dusard, likes to say: "We're imposing a rectangle on a scene." We control what's in and what's out of the rectangle. It's our personal canvas on which to create our masterpiece. There's always one thing that makes us decide that a scene is worthy of a photograph. We decide the point of interest and how best to emphasize it.

An example of this was when I was in southern Utah, deep in the chaotic canyon complex on the Escalante River drainage when an amazing scene of sunflowers emerging from the pink sand lay before me. I loved the desert-varnished cliffs rising above the dunes. I loved the struggle for life taking place in the shifting sands. In fact, I loved everything. So I composed a scene that reflected that vision, as seen in the image on this page.

But I knew at once the real reason I stopped was that I was drawn by the struggle for survival of a half-buried sunflower. By showing everything in the scene, I was giving equal weight to all the elements. If I couldn't decide what was important, how could I expect the viewer to know what moved me to photograph the scene?

I changed the angle, got closer, and simplified the image. I emphasized the diagonal line of the sunflower stem and consequently strengthened the composition. "Simplicity is the ultimate form of sophistication," said Leonardo da Vinci.

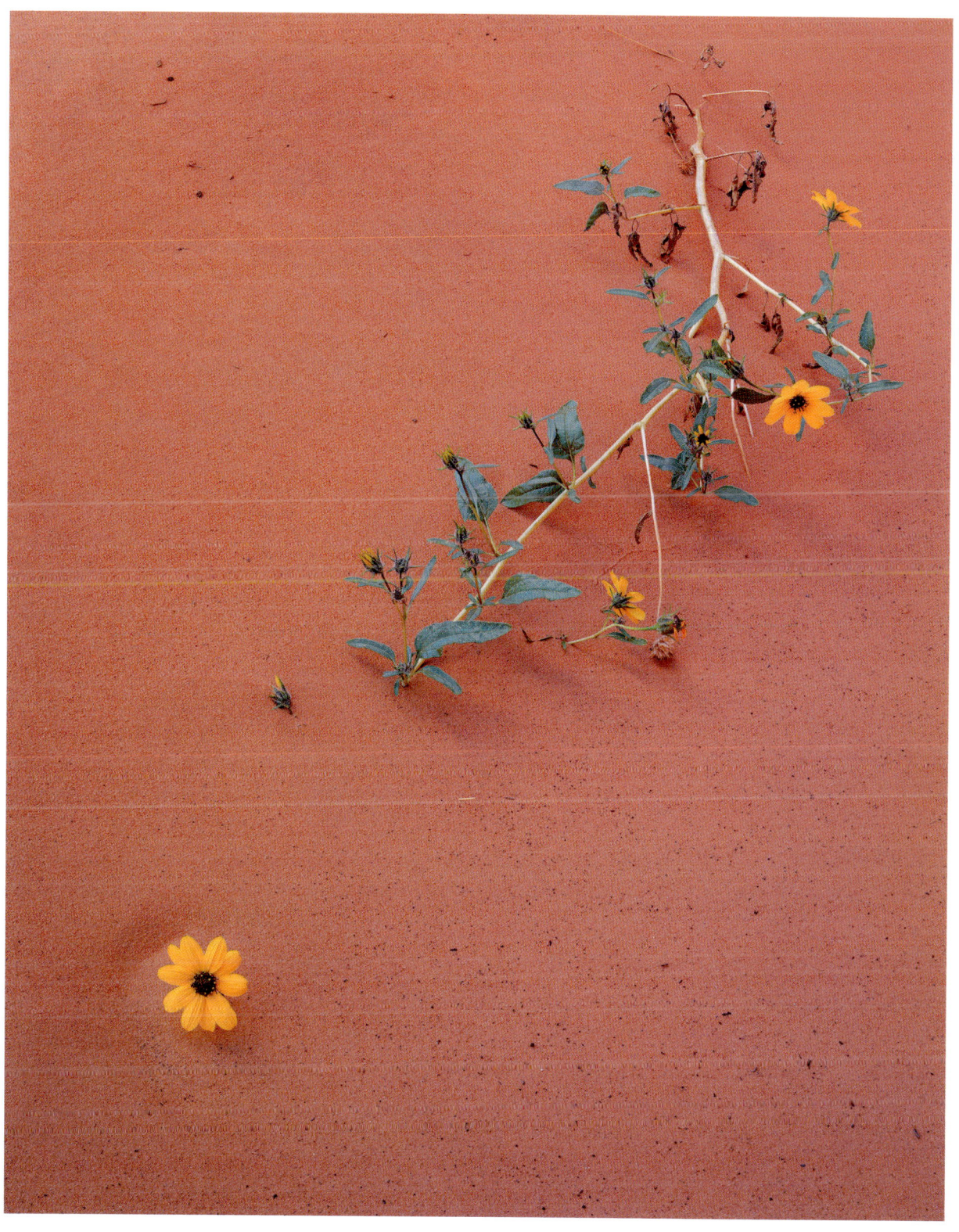

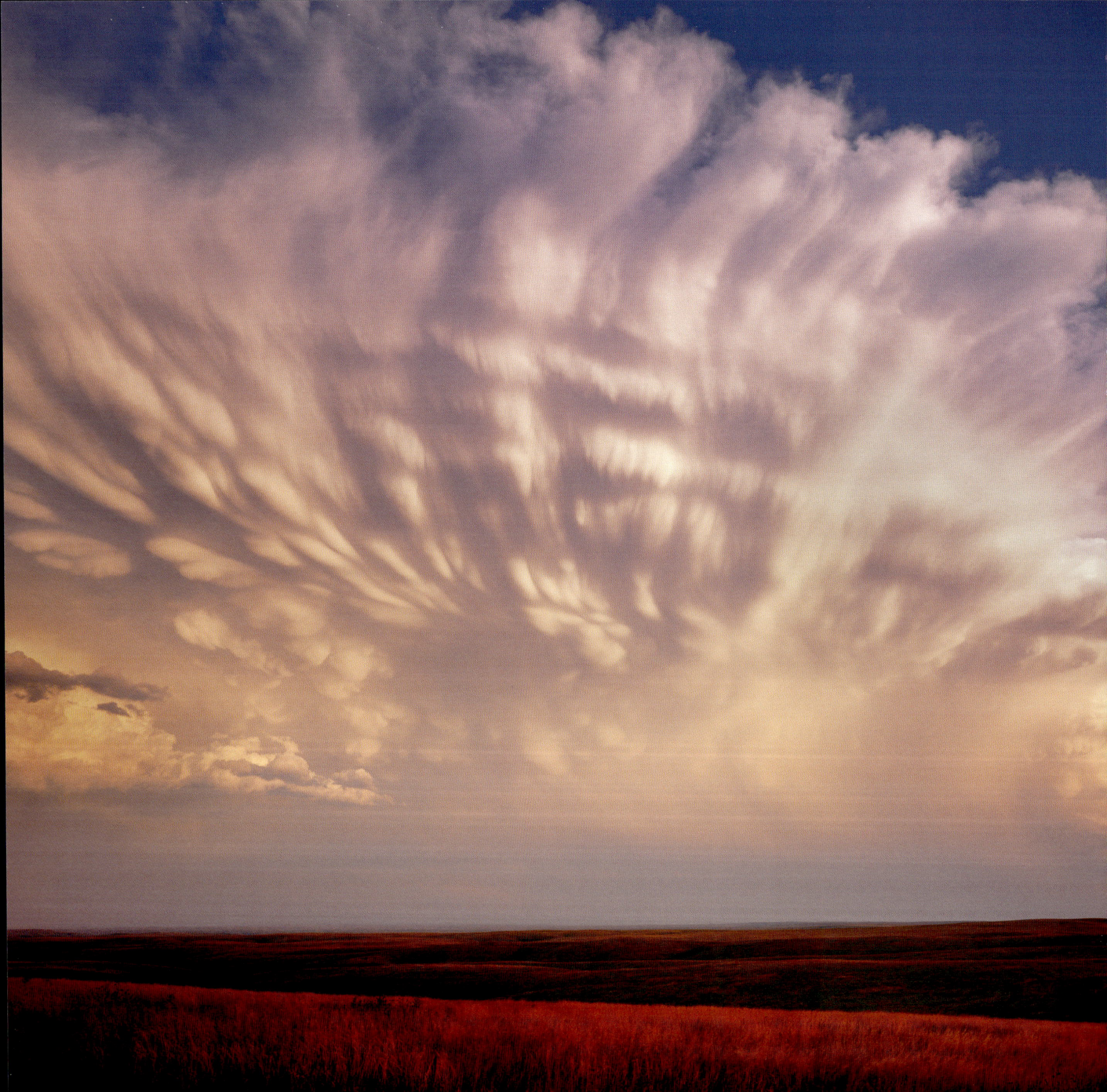

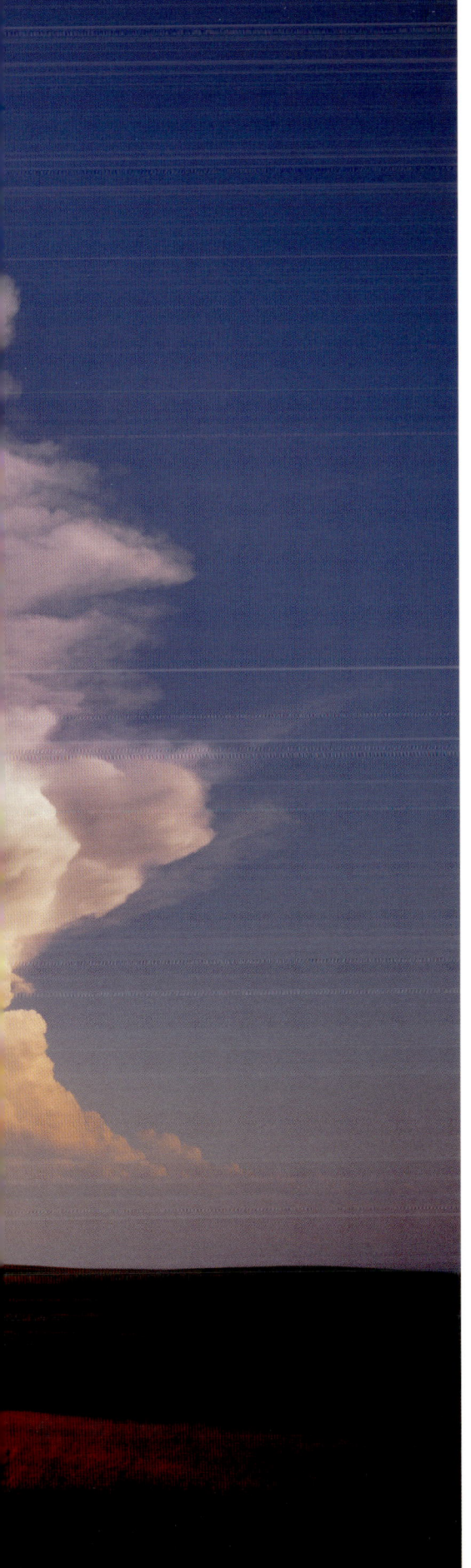

Asking ourselves simple questions like, "Are we photographing the land or the sky?" can help us decide what is important. Indecision produces boring images such as those with a horizon line at dead center. Of course, decisions on whether or not photography is even possible due to weather, light, or safety are also in the mix. But, when the wild afternoon storm cells of Wyoming's high plains create threatening cumulus clouds, I'm going to aim the camera skyward to emphasize the cloudscape.

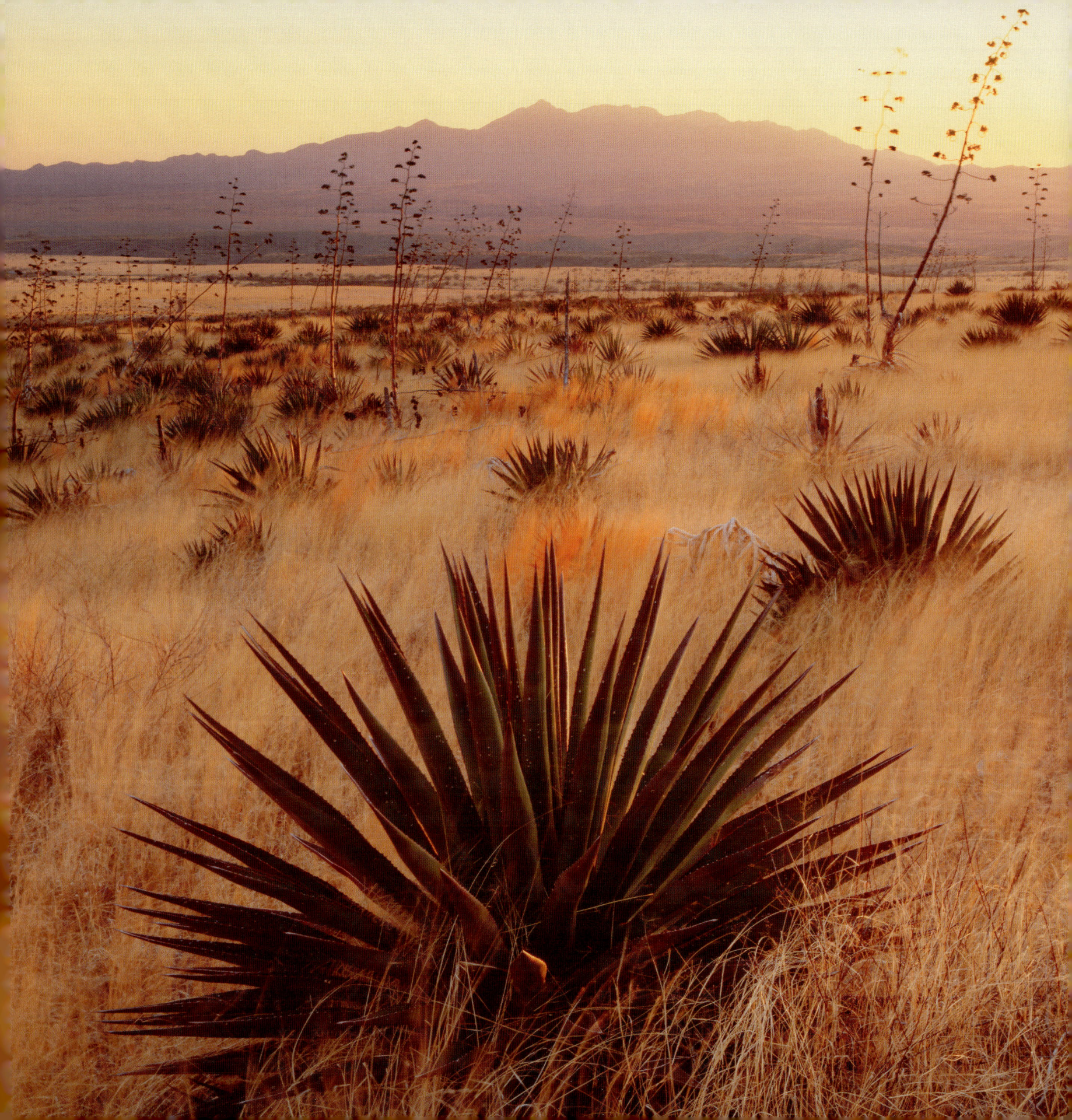

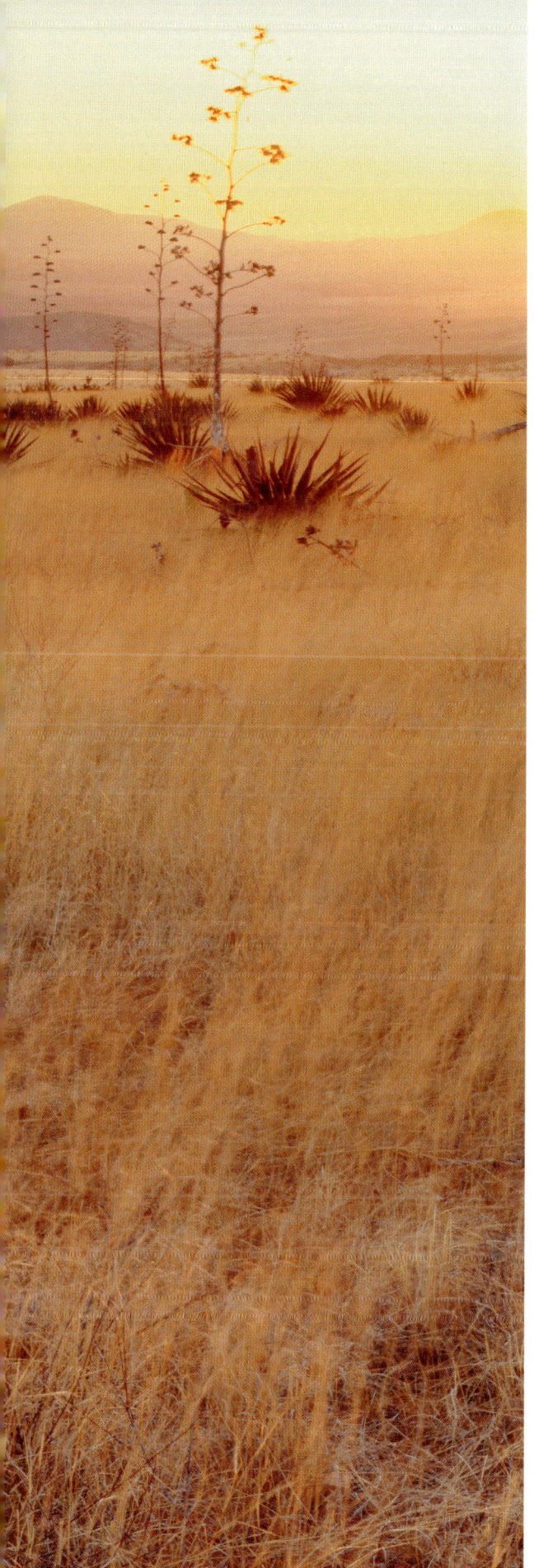

Sometimes, when faced with a challenge, a new approach is called for. For example, I was in a grassland dotted with agave plants. I wanted to illustrate the delicate nature of the landscape by showing the fine details in the sinuous grasses. But the wind was blowing. Like the song says: "You can't always get what you want."

I set about solving the problem, not by fighting the wind (I'd lose). Instead, I decided to go with the wind and photograph using slow shutter speeds to emphasize the motion. I identified a specific problem and found a way to solve it

This was an epiphany for me. Solve the problem ... capture the magic.

Design

I photograph to create truly satisfying images. I feel complete when I craft images that are compelling, informative, beautiful, and sometimes troubling. This is what Joseph Campbell called "following my bliss."

I cannot *not* photograph, and I can't stop the internal movie. I see images all the time; even in my dreams.

What do I look for when creating a composition? What are the building blocks? Often, I find a visual element in the landscape that reminds me of something else. For example, this swirl in hardened lava reminded me of a coiled nautilus shell. The design rotates around the center of my frame, and that's not an accident. I balanced the upper-left and lower-right corners to reinforce the symmetry.

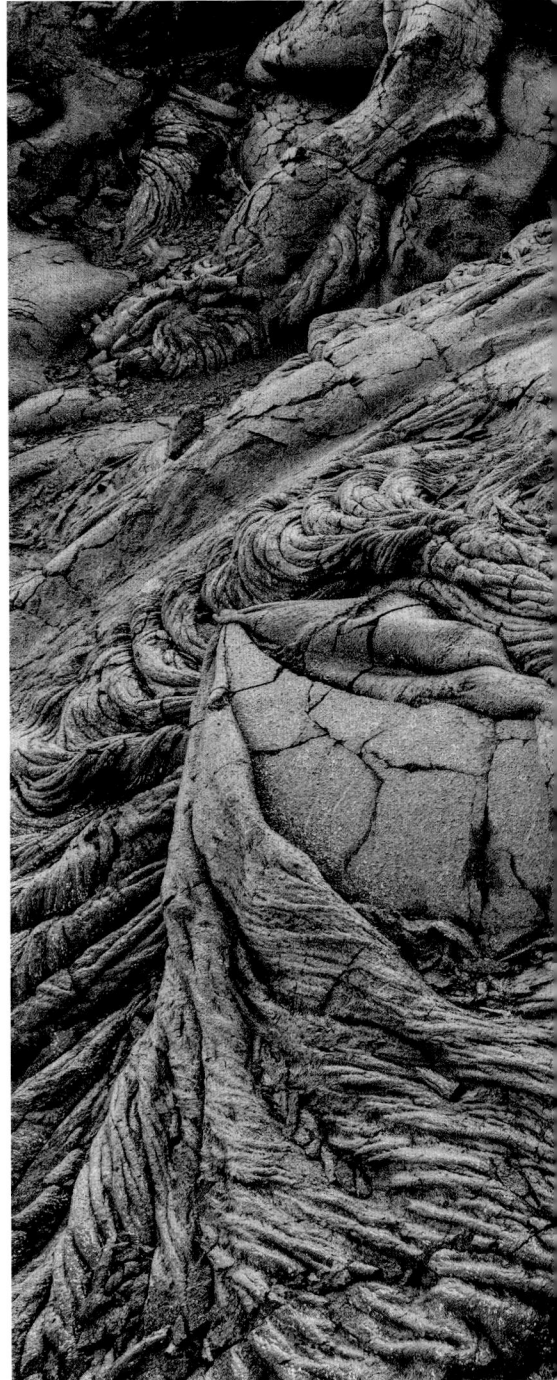

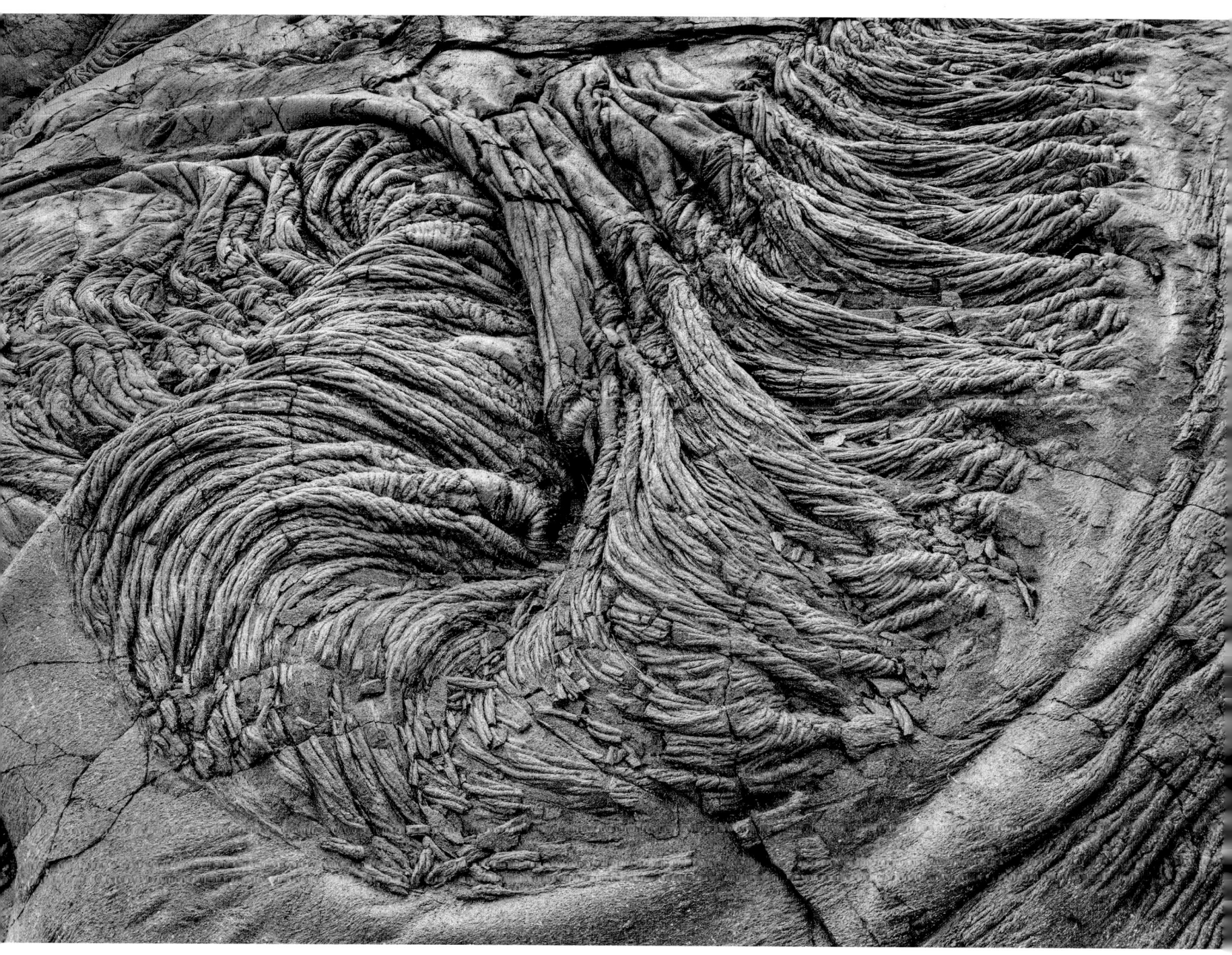

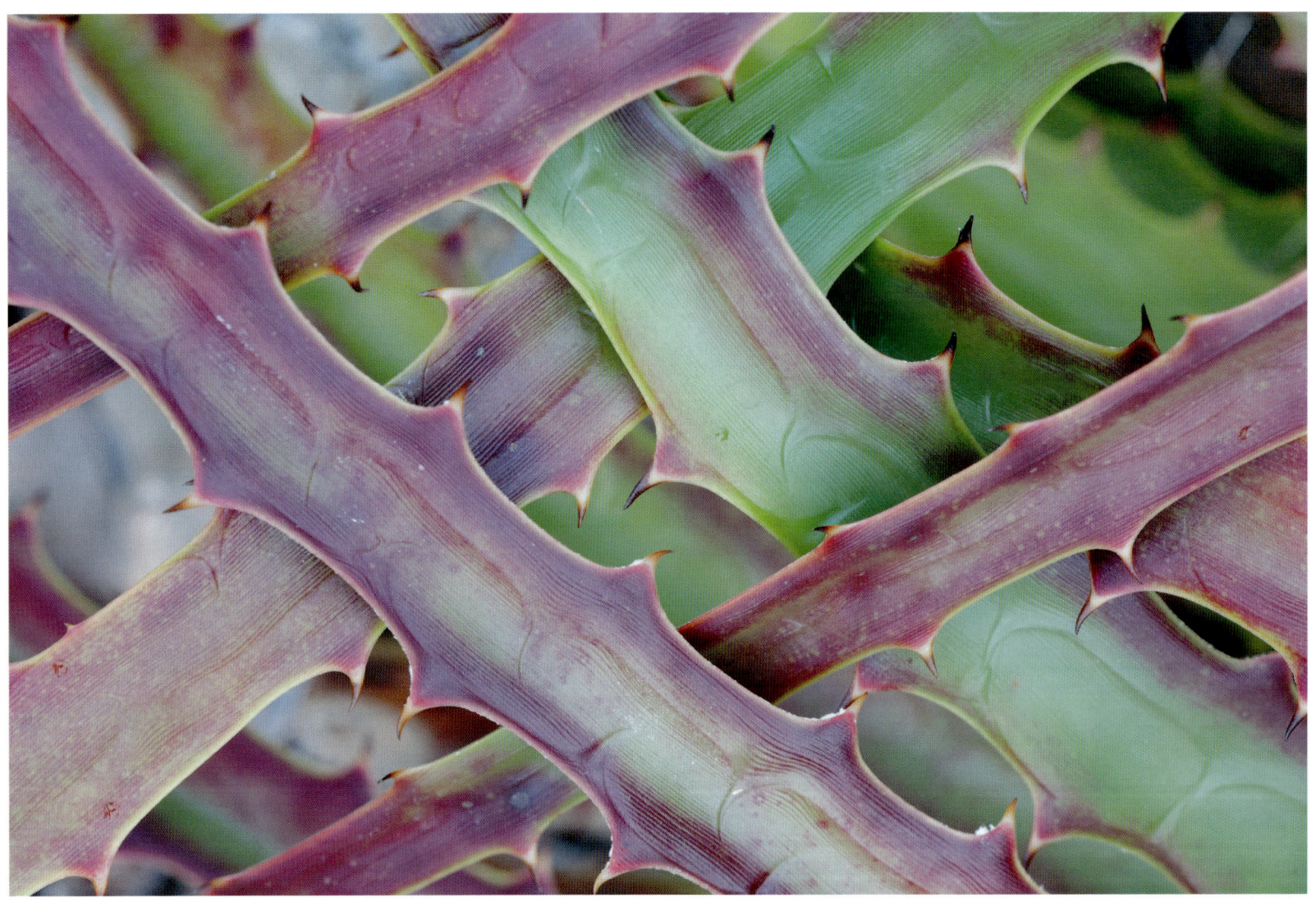

Other times I might be drawn to spiny plants with blades that appear like the strands of a woven basket. In this case, I was first drawn by the subtle contrast in colors. I then selected a composition that concentrated on the jagged blades and I noticed how they had grown together. By adjusting the camera position to emphasize the strong lines crisscrossing the composition, I created an image that felt complete.

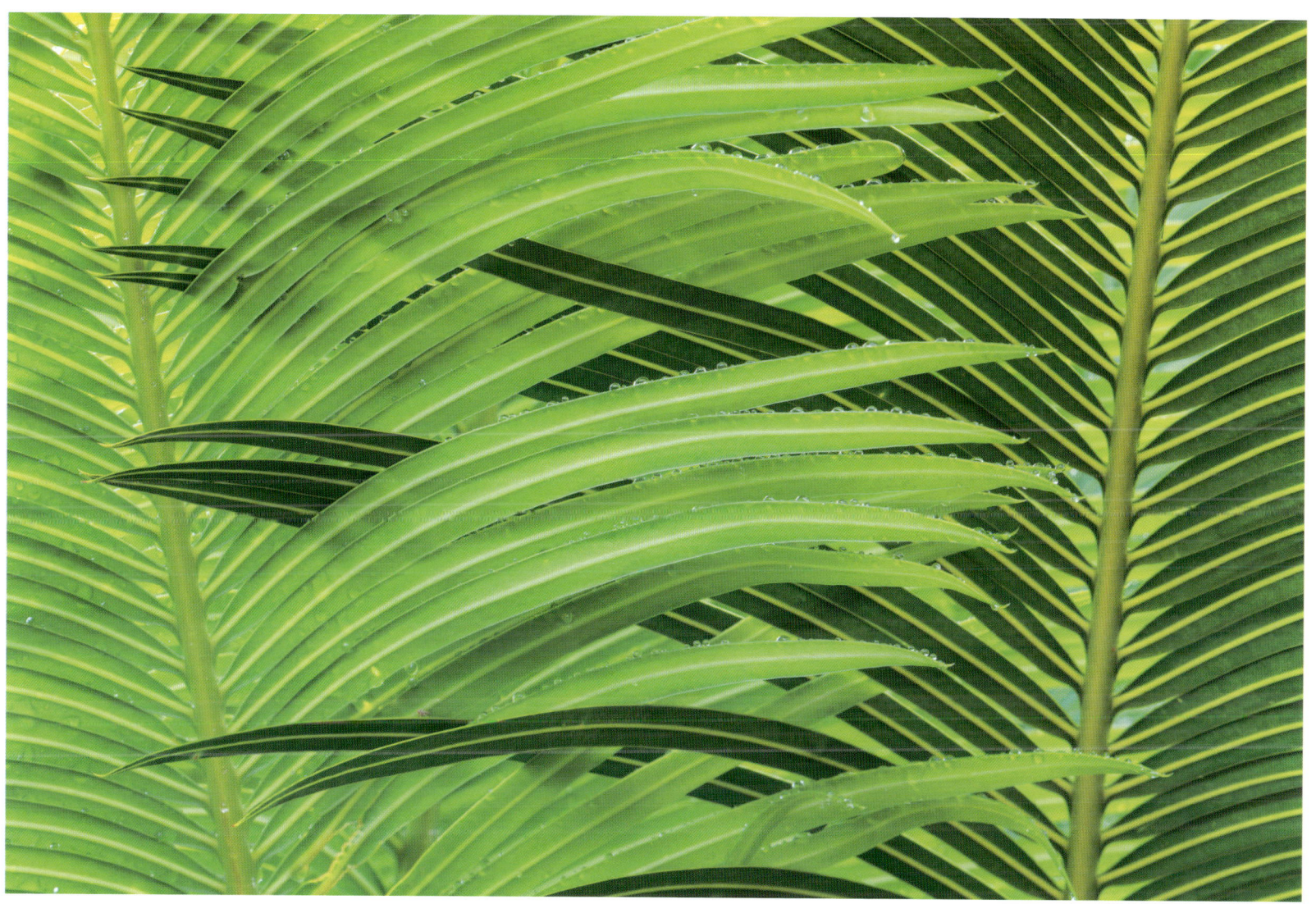

An image's borders frame my subject. Within that frame lies the workspace in which I craft a composition. I can balance distance and weight of subject matter by making tiny adjustments. I problem solve the composition by carefully examining the entire frame, paying special attention to the corners. The power of my images radiates from strong corners. If I choose to make a passive statement, subjects are centered.

Here, the equalized space between the two palm fronds fits perfectly within the frame, creating a balanced design. The interwoven shades of green and the water droplets complete the scene.

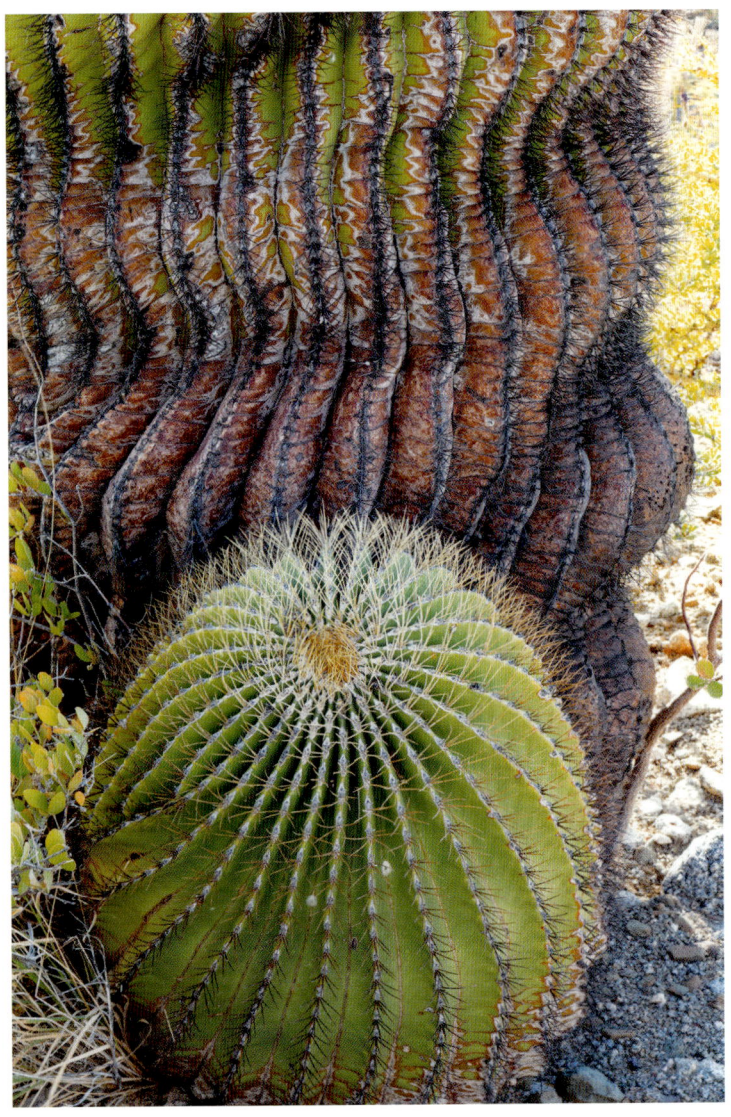

Once I select my subject, I get close enough so the subject itself becomes my canvas.

As we can see in the image to the left, the sunlit background is a distraction.

I solve that problem by getting close enough so that the cactus in the background becomes the backdrop, while eliminating the distracting highlights. In the next image (right), the simplicity of the closer cactus's circular design in the spines is contrasted against the sunbaked convolutions in the background cactus, now without the strong highlights at the frame's edge.

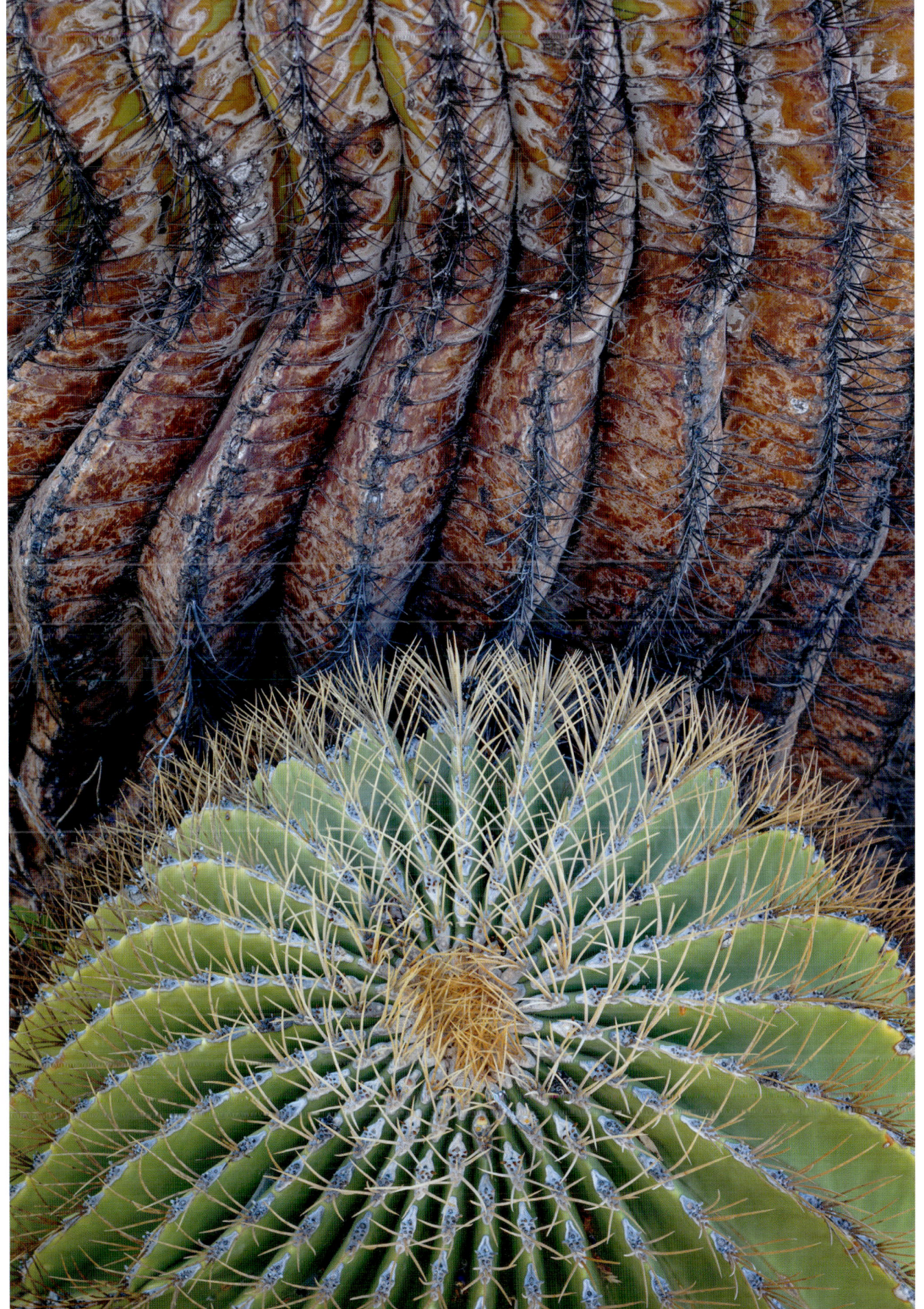

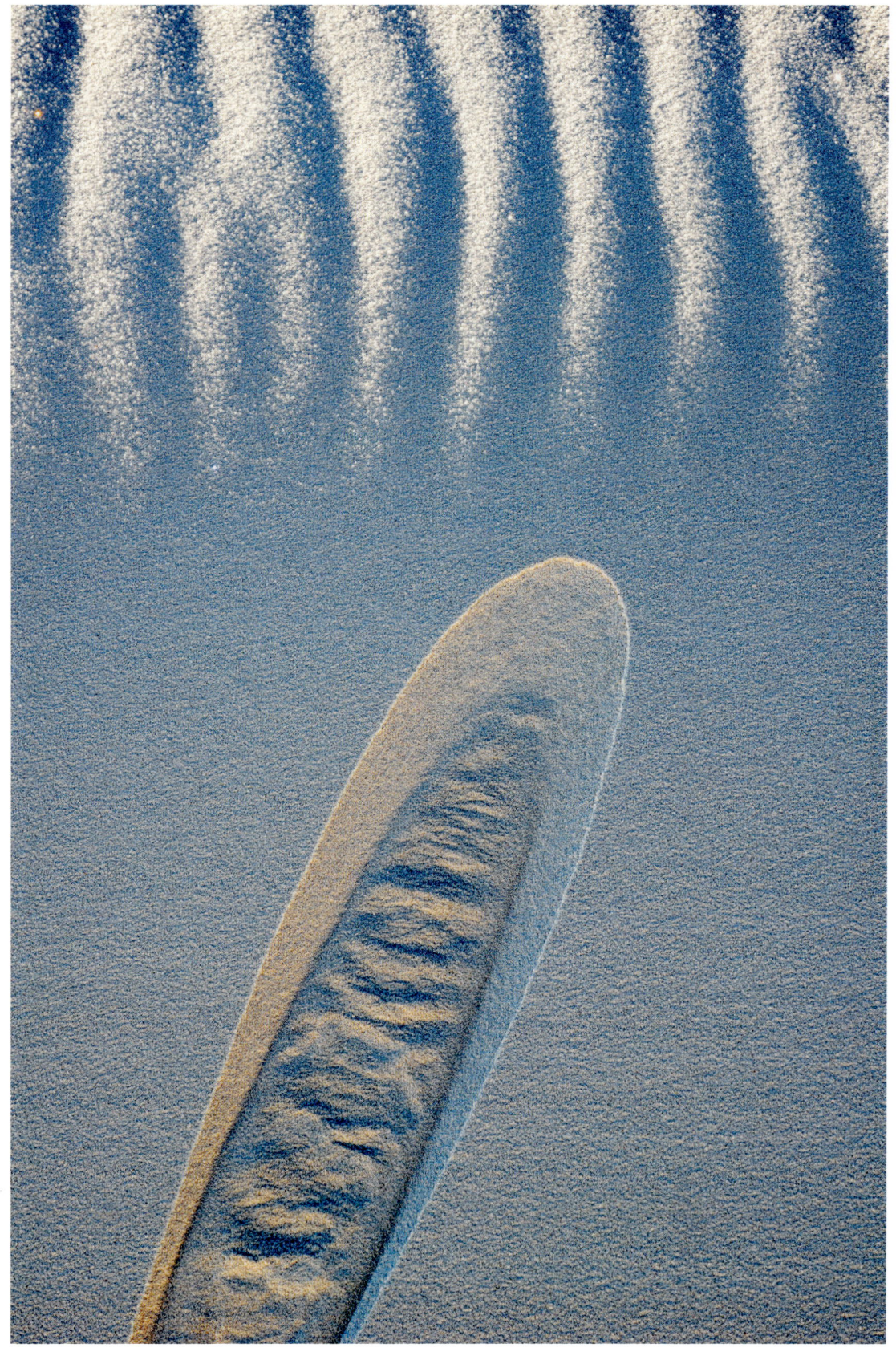

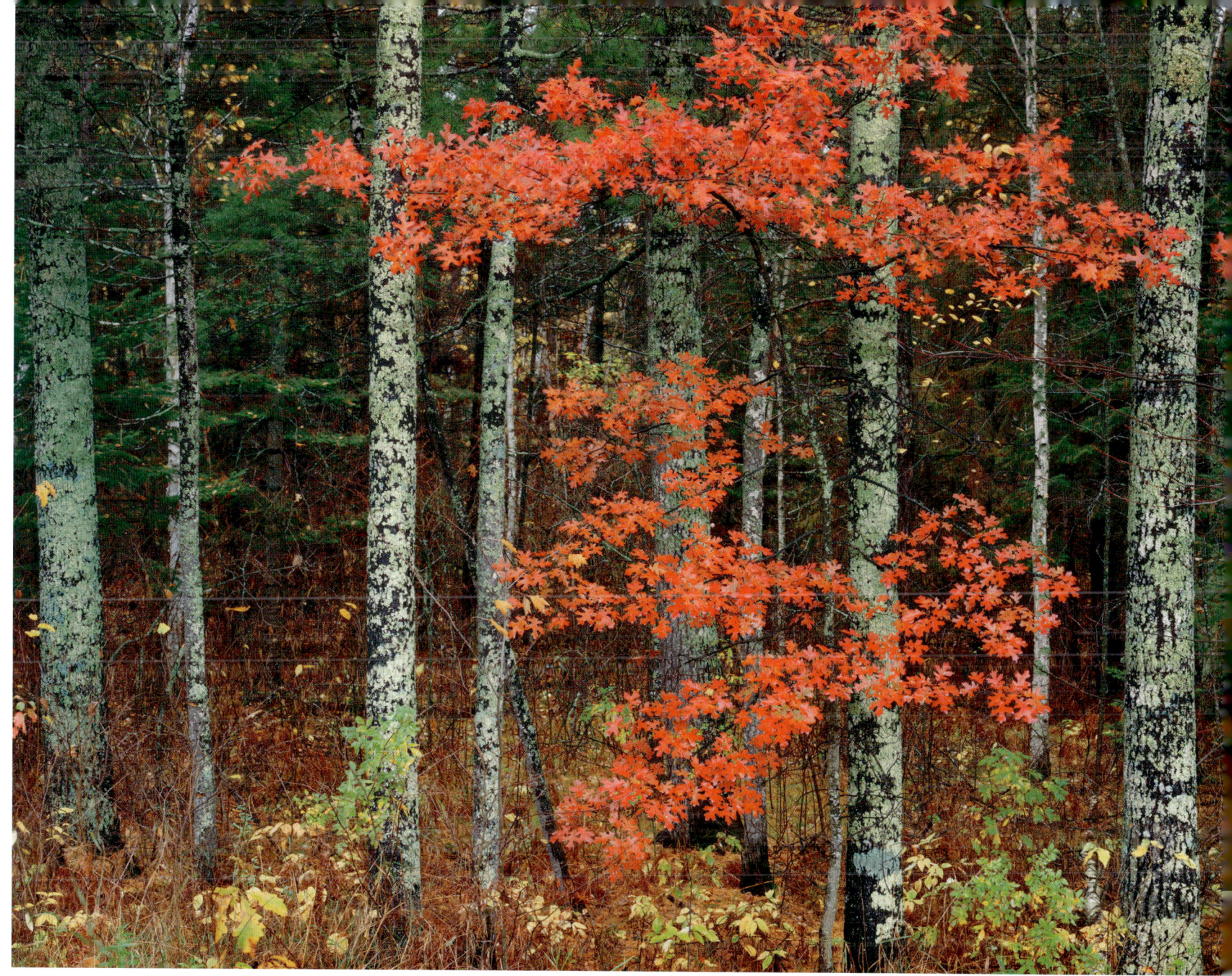

Unexpected designs in nature always attract my interest. At left, the subtle variations in the way these sand dunes slough away into an angle of repose became my subject. I crafted the image by making the key shape a diagonal, while setting it apart by allowing space around it. Typical dune patterns at the top of the image provide the context, and the top and both sides of the photograph work as a unit to frame the design.

With the image above, contrasts of fall-colored oak leaves against a tapestry of weathered, lichen-covered pines sets up a design conflict between complementary colors and basic shapes, stripes (tree trunks) and spots (red leaves). The trees form a repeating pattern of vertical lines while the amorphous splashes of red-colored leaves break the vertical lines, adding tension and creating interest.

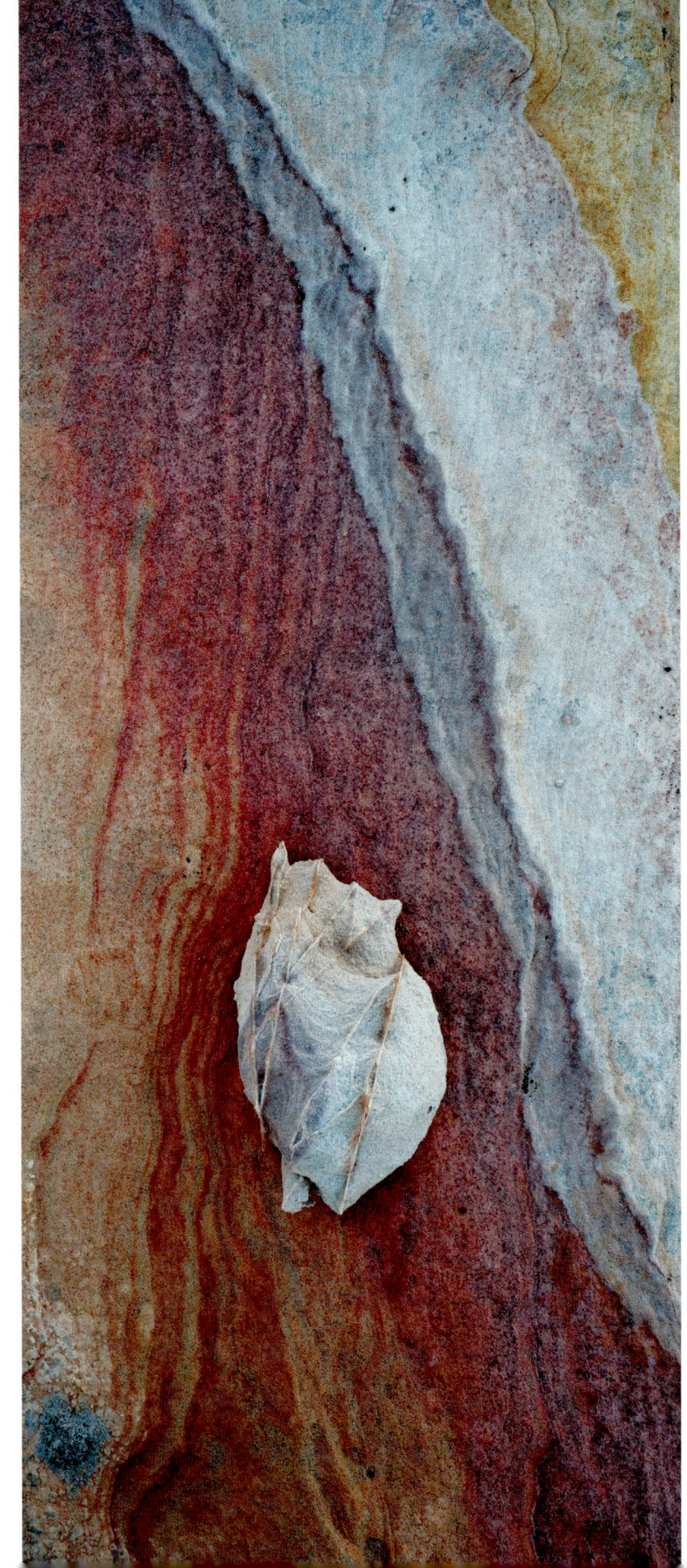

The simplicity of a solitary rock against the striated sand-stone works because the light stone stands out against the dark background. Subtle striations in both the background and the rock bring the composition together. The diagonal bands of color unite the frame into a vertical panorama.

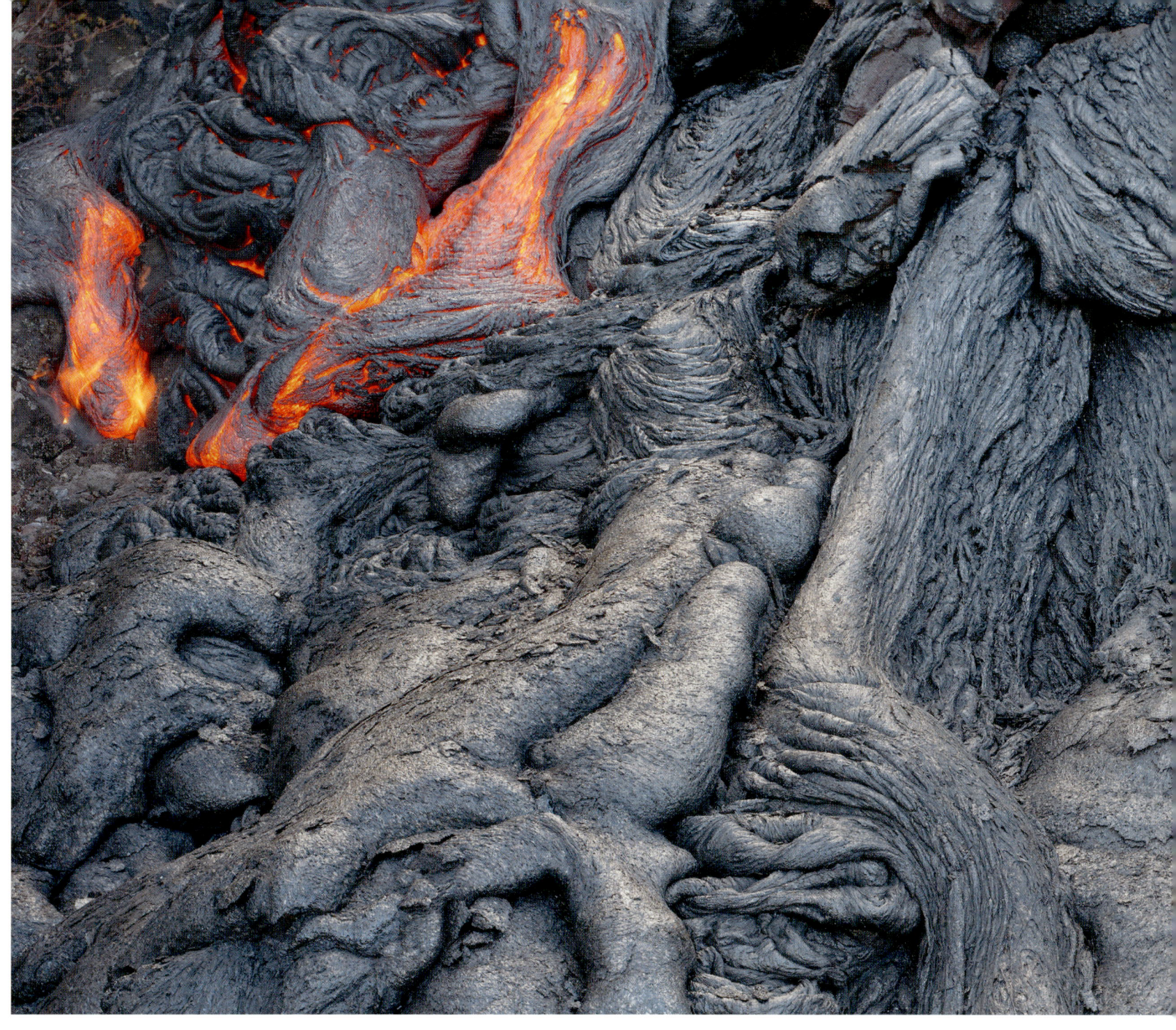

When I explored Hawaii's Big Island lava flows, I saw patterns everywhere. As the molten lava poured onto the land, it often resembled twisted tormented figures. For this image, I saw a horizontal panorama. I composed an image anchored by the red-hot lava in the upper left of the frame. The glowing lava supplies the information about an active lava flow, while the context is the panel of design.

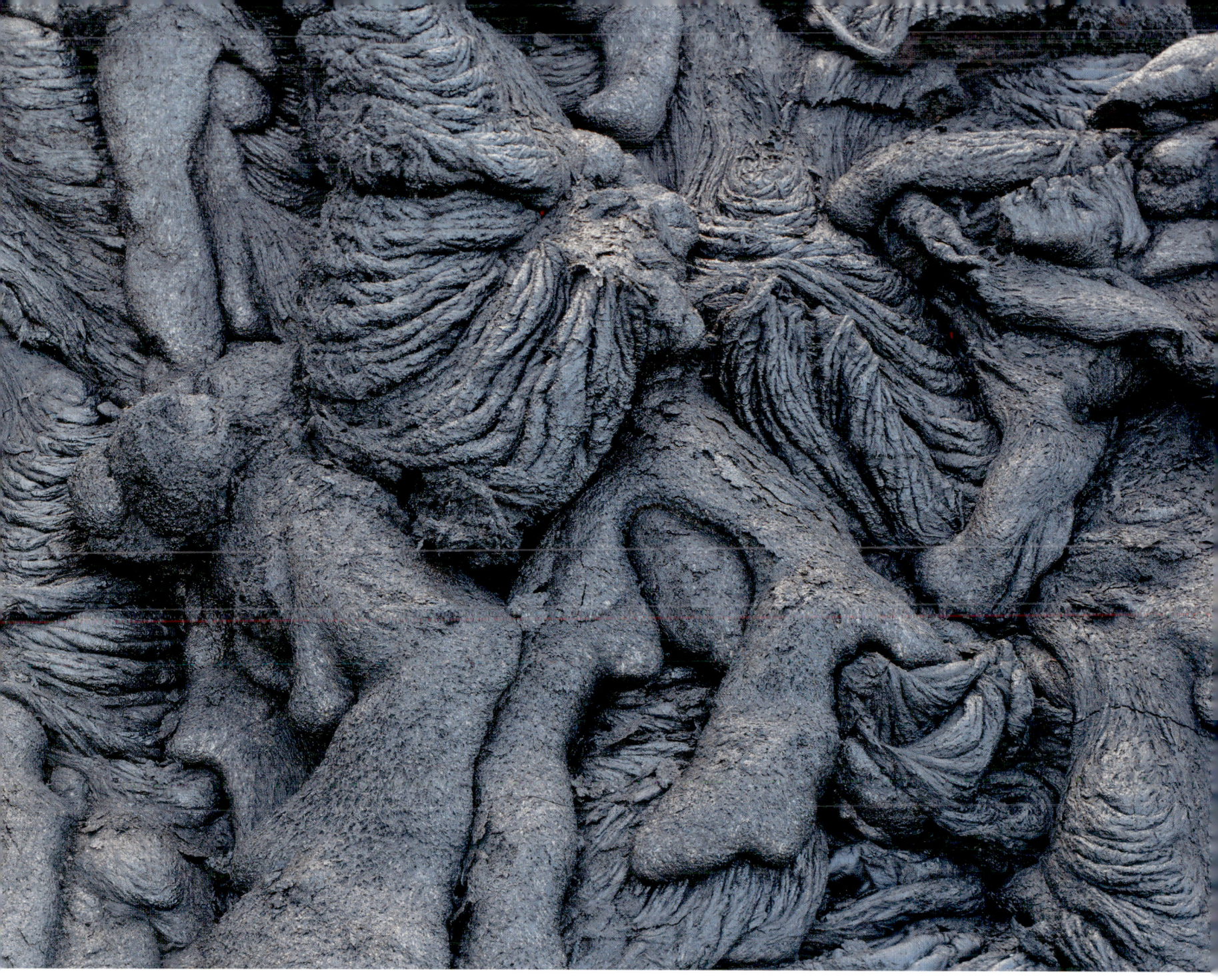

Images gain power through the relationship of colors. Some, such as the lava images, are nearly monochromatic, while the fall foliage image has bold contrasting colors. By cropping, either while shooting or later in Photoshop or Lightroom, I have removed all non-essential elements from my compositions.

This image of mountaintops covered with a monoculture of aspen trees sets up the viewer to expect a sea of vertical trees, blue-gray and naked. The eye-stopper occurs when the expected pattern is broken by a patch of blazing yellow-colored leaves that remain on a few of the trees.

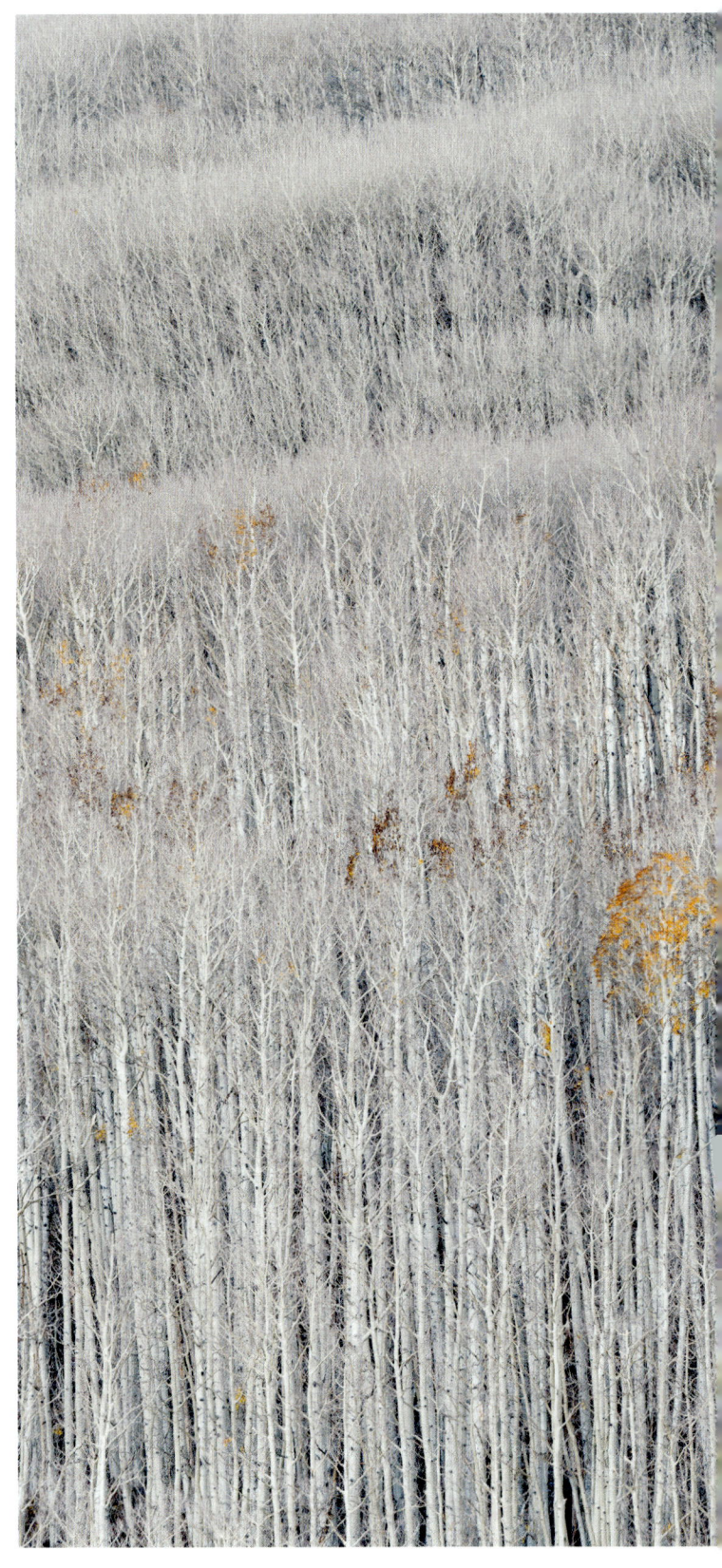

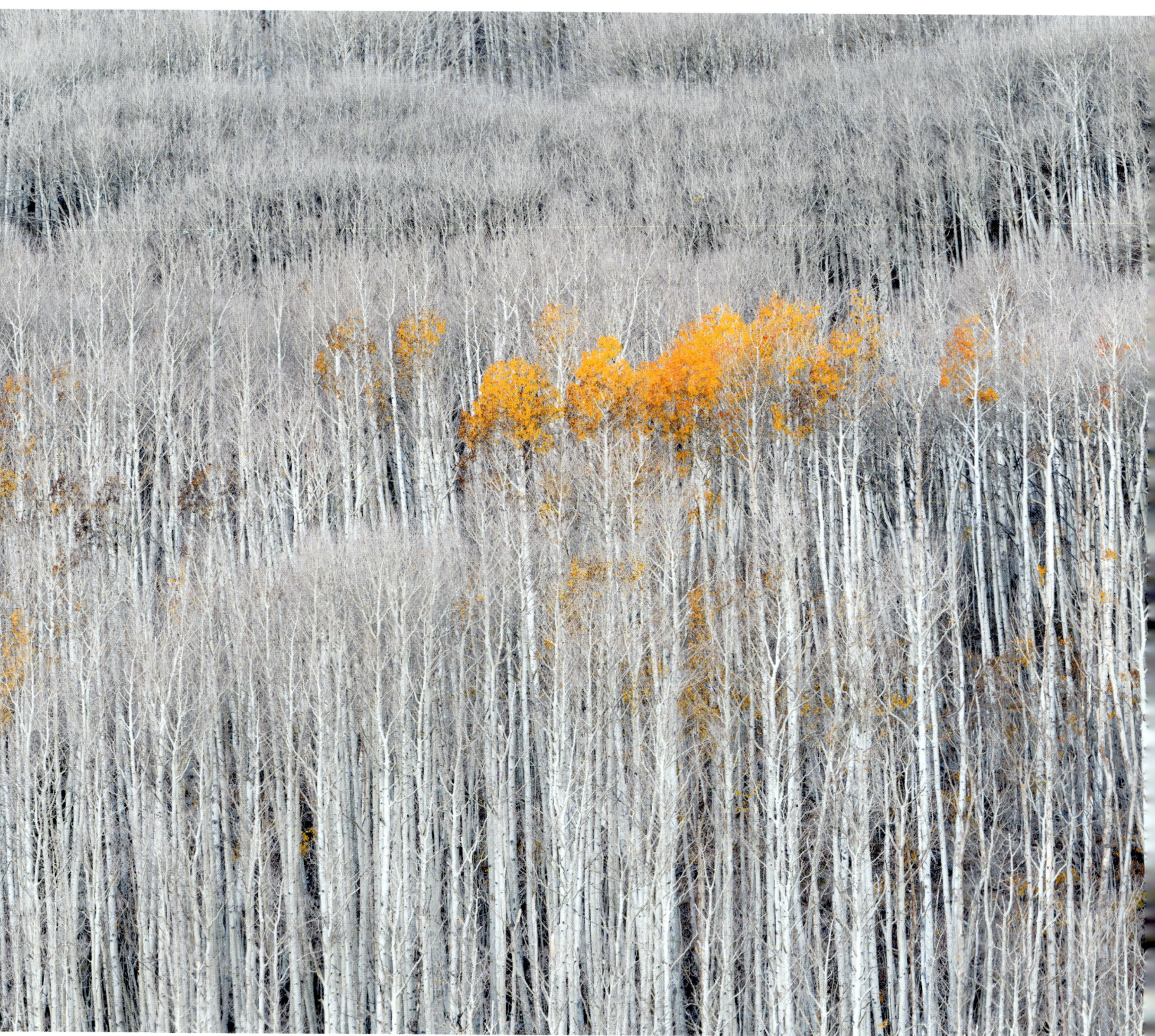

The contrasting textures of something as simple as the bark of two trees can create interest in a photograph. Here, stacking an aspen tree's smooth trunk against a ponderosa's vertically striated bark—overlapping the two with no background dividing the frame—emphasizes the contrast. While the ponderosa seems closer than the aspen, this is only an illusion. The eye responds to the color red, making it appear closer.

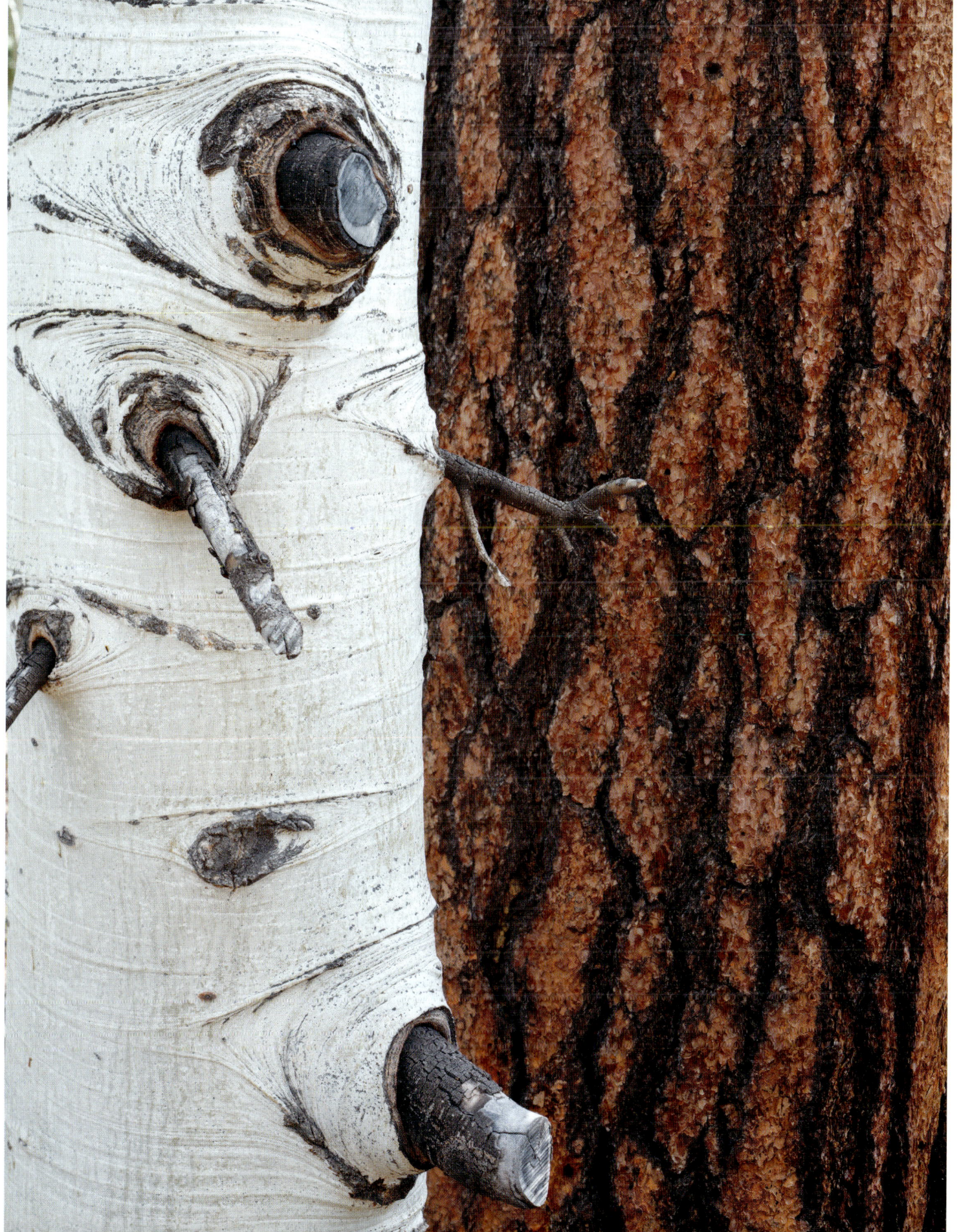

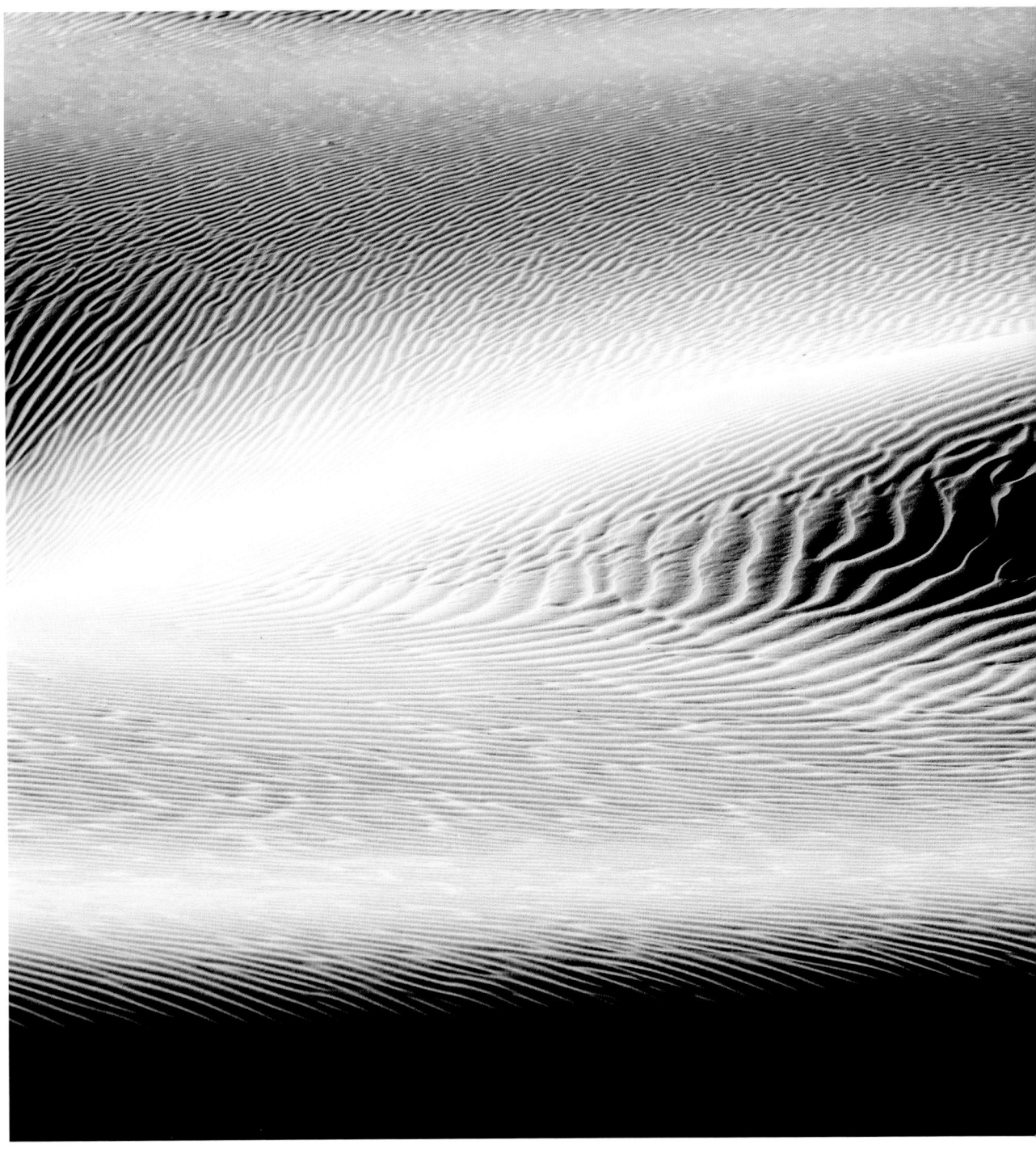

The contrasting lines on these sand dunes and the Z-shaped shadow become my subject. They cease to be sand dunes and instead become pure design shapes of light and dark.

While this image resulted from a stitched panorama technique, my approach to composition was the same. I bore my eyes into the viewfinder to see where the central element of the composition was located. Then, using the camea's live view function, I equalized the distances from side, top, and bottom, carefully adjusting the composition.

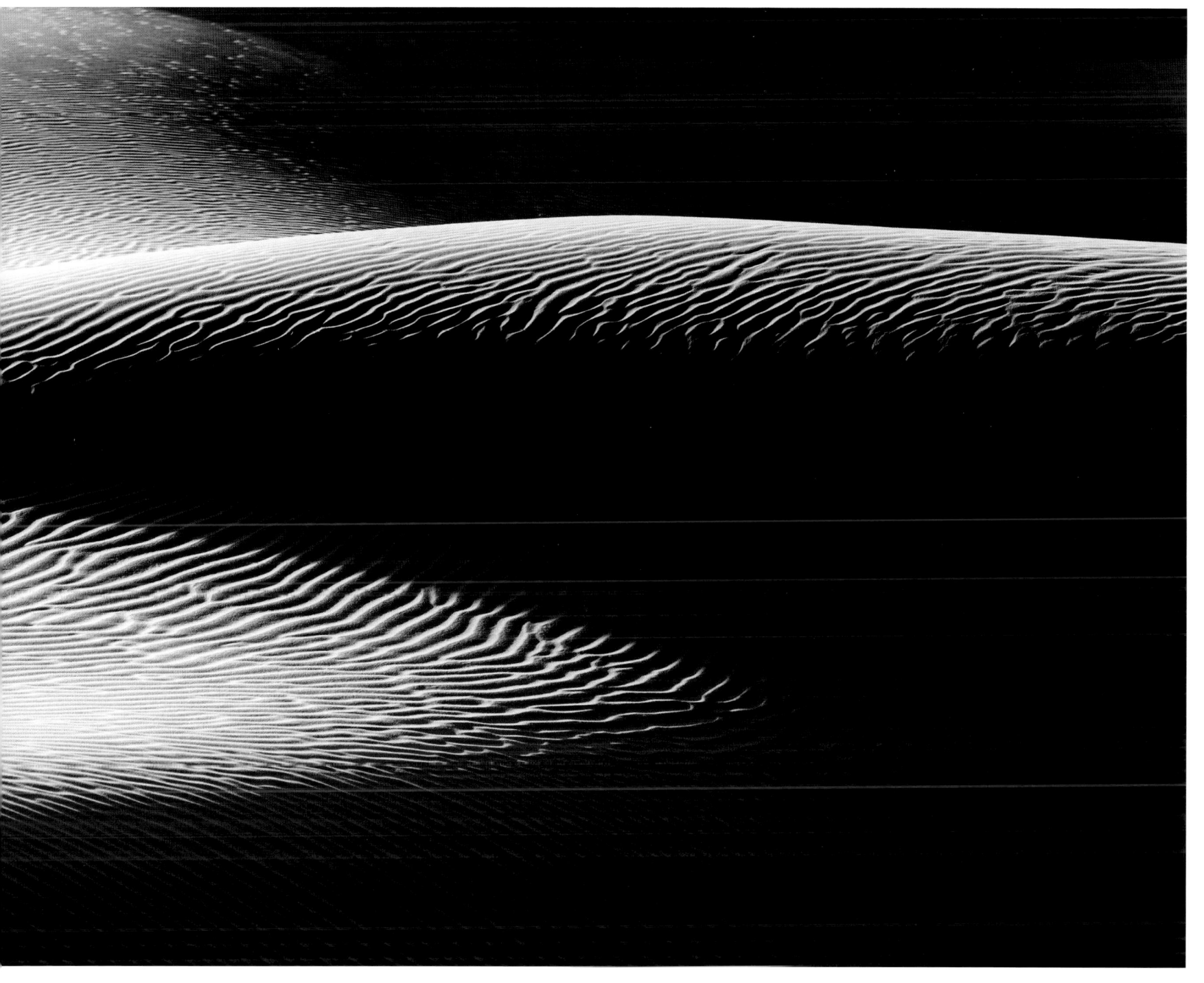

My first instinct was to make the image symmetrical, but then I changed the framing to give more space (weight) to the upper part of the image. By doing so, I was able to retain the subtle curve at the middle background.

One of digital photography's greatest assets is the ability to immediately review your images in the field and make adjustments during the shoot. In the past, pros loved using instant Polaroid prints to check lighting and composition. Now we think nothing about reviewing images only an instant after capture.

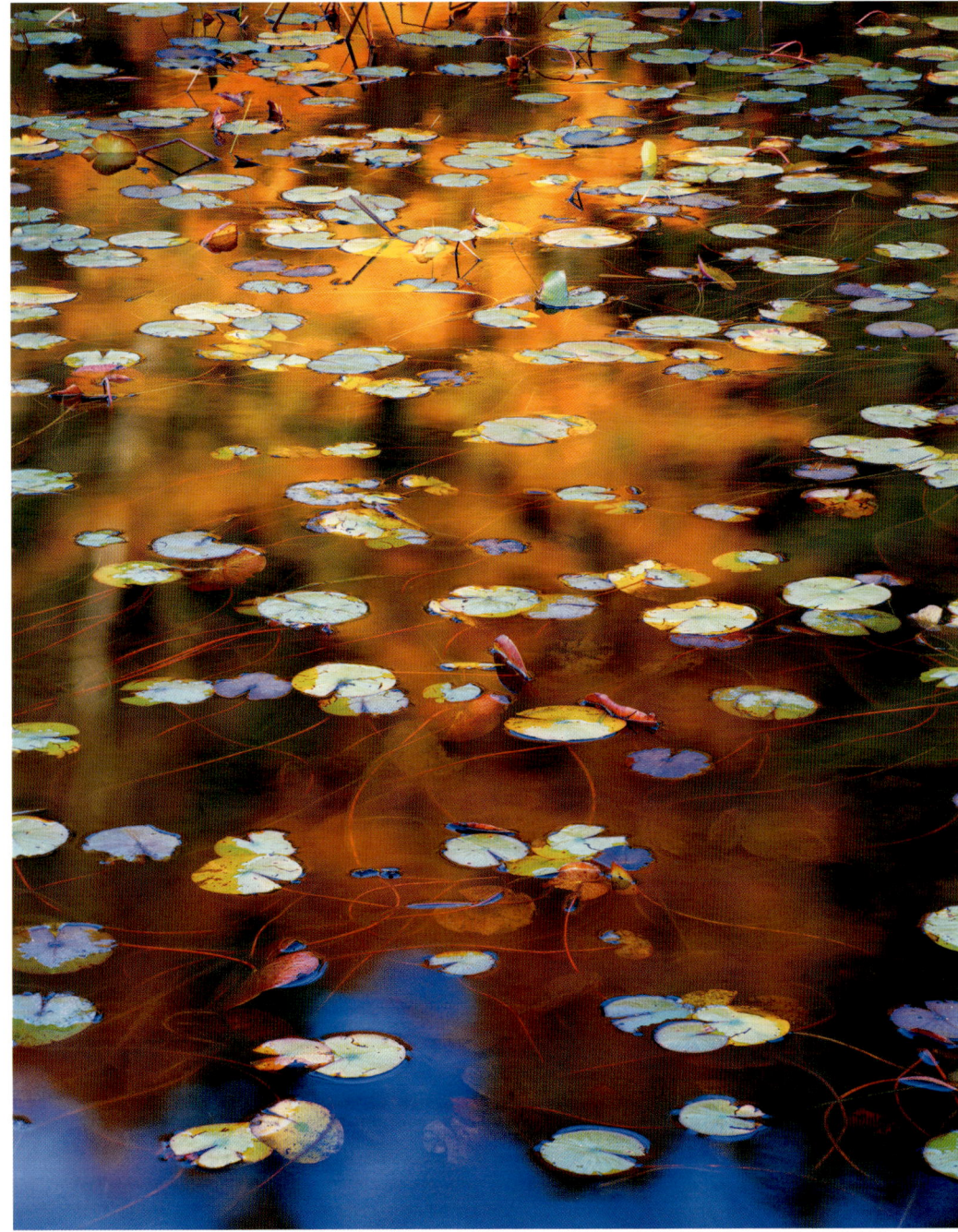

Bold designs make bold statements. They forcefully direct the eye to a subject. But what if your subject is an entire frame full of colors and forms? This was the challenge that was presented to me in the next two pond scenes. I solved the problem by using a shallow depth of field and maintaining sharp focus only on the water's surface, which allowed the background colors to become a mass of muted color, much like a watercolor wash. The lily pads are isolated due to the sharp focus, but they're components of a larger design that covers the frame, creating many points of interest. While this technique was previously only possible with a view camera, the tilt/shift lenses available on current DSLR cameras also allow the photographer to change the plane of focus to create this effect.

Similar to the first pond image, this image includes the floating water shamrocks in very sharp focus against the warmly lit (yet out of focus) background. The shallow depth of field acts to isolate each of the floating plants that are, in turn, part of a more de-centralized design.

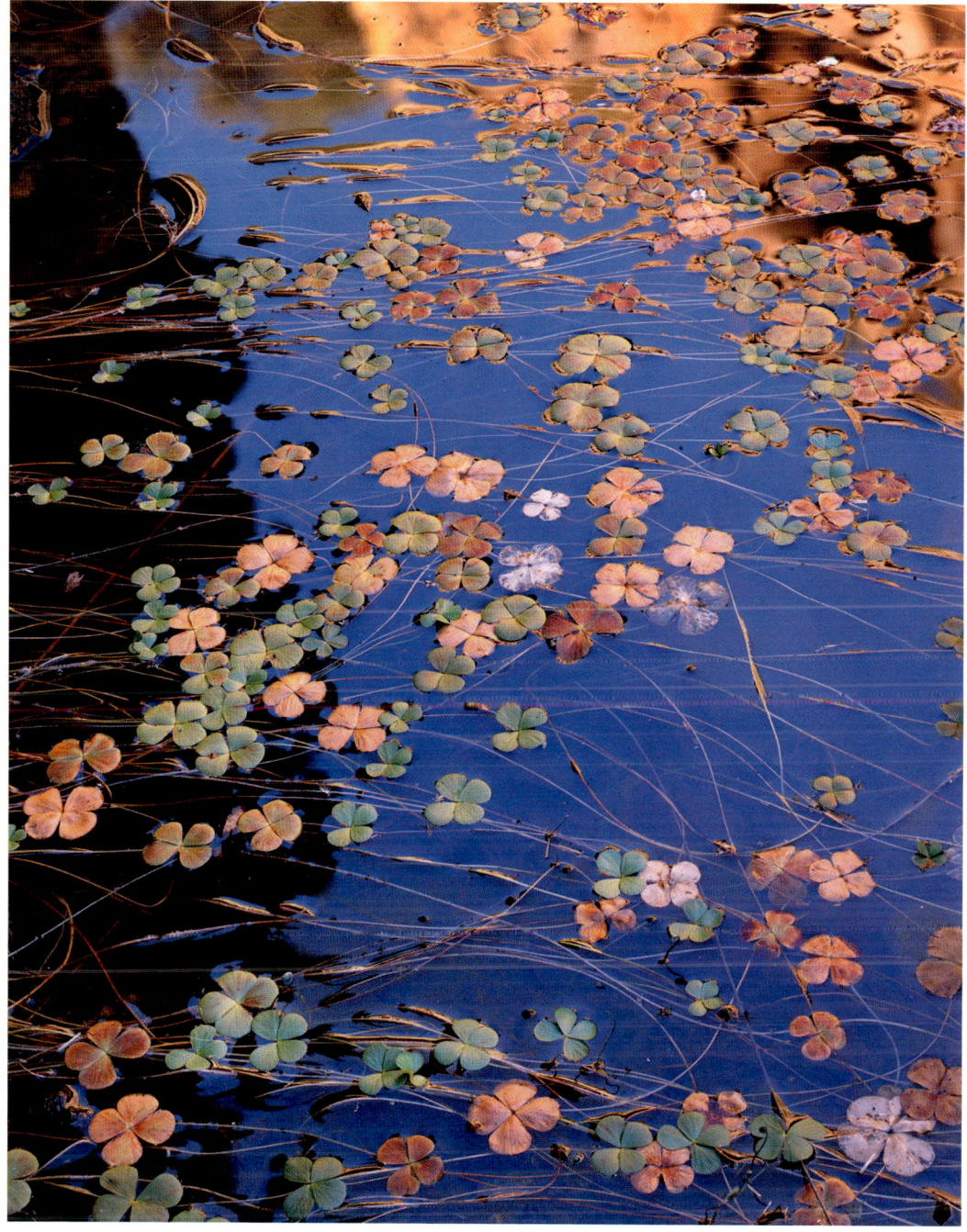

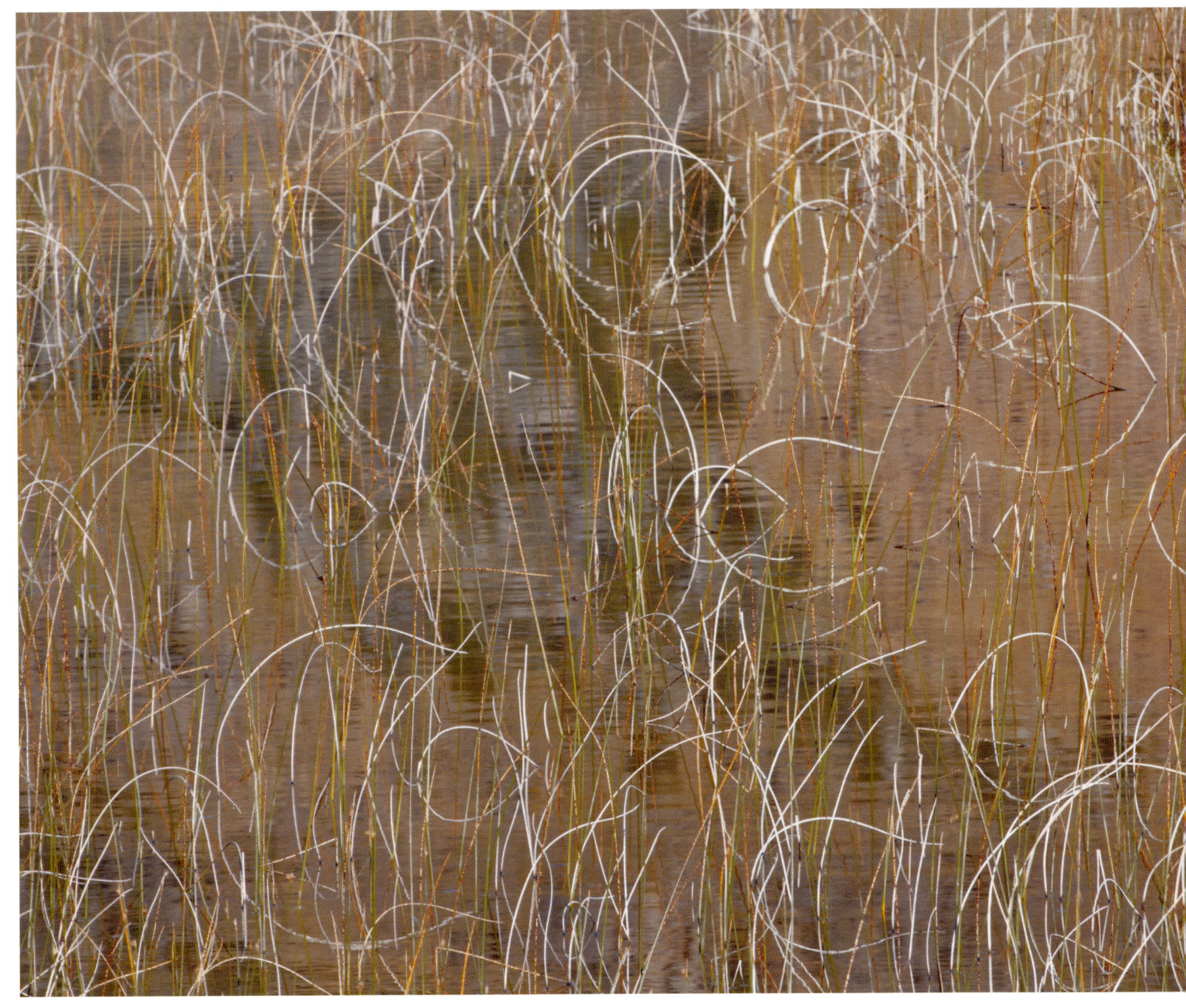

In this image, a simple pattern of curved shoreline sedges with their reflections completing a circular design is also spread across the entire frame. This sort of composition invites the viewer to spend more time exploring the entire image, edge-to-edge.

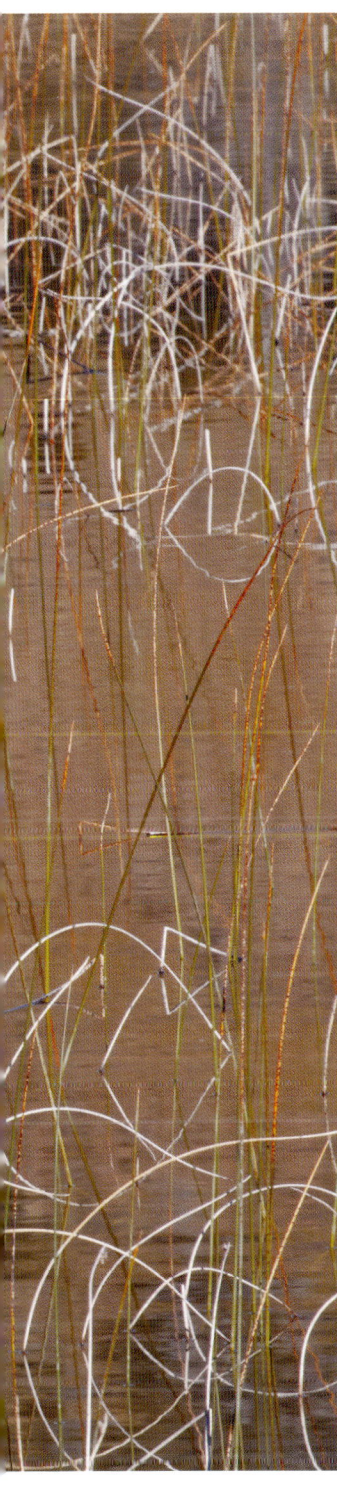

Tips for Creating Strong Compositions

I use the optional grid in the viewfinder to aid in establishing distances when crafting an image. But the truth is, after 50 years of serious photography, positioning of elements within a composition is baked into my muscle memory.

However, for those wishing to make better compositions, this checklist can get your thinking directed at solving problems within the composition.

1. Use the optical viewfinder to establish the framing and focus.
2. Use live view to carefully compose key elements of design.
3. Shield the light by using a Hoodman or simply shade your LCD screen with your jacket.
4. Walk your eyes around the frame, examining the corners and edges for distractions. Strongly highlighted areas at the corners and edges will draw attention away from the main subject area.
5. Make appropriate adjustments and take the photograph.
6. Then carefully pore over every detail, beginning with a histogram pushed as far to the right as possible without clipping the highlights.
7. Recheck focus, recheck composition, and shoot again. If you're the slightest bit unsure of focus or exposure, then bracket. In other words, after making the correct exposures with the correct focus point, take additional exposures setting the focus forward and behind the original point of focus. Expose properly and then make exposures over and under the metered reading. This will ensure the widest range of exposures to choose from.

Of course you're not done at this point; now you improvise by completely changing the composition from centered to off-center. Tilt: who says every scene calls for a leveled camera? The camera can be moved to accommodate the strongest composition, like playing the lines into the corners. In short, try anything that you feel helps to make a strong statement. You have the power.

Lines

By selecting a subject and framing it in a rectangle, we as photographers eliminate the extraneous, and emphasize the critical elements of our composition. Using lines that are present in the landscape is one of the strongest ways to accentuate the main elements of the composition. These lines can tie together the design elements by forming conduits for the eye to drive interest into the frame, from near to far. Further, lines that radiate from the corners also draw the eye into the composition.

For this image taken deep in the sinuous striations of the Grand Canyon's National Canyon, I used a wide, 14mm lens. This allowed me to work in a very small space, and to still convey the feeling of expansiveness. The lines reinforce the sense of the power and erosive nature that scoured these narrow slot canyons The lines push the attention to the central watercourse. The sensation of movement is what I was after and the lines point the way.

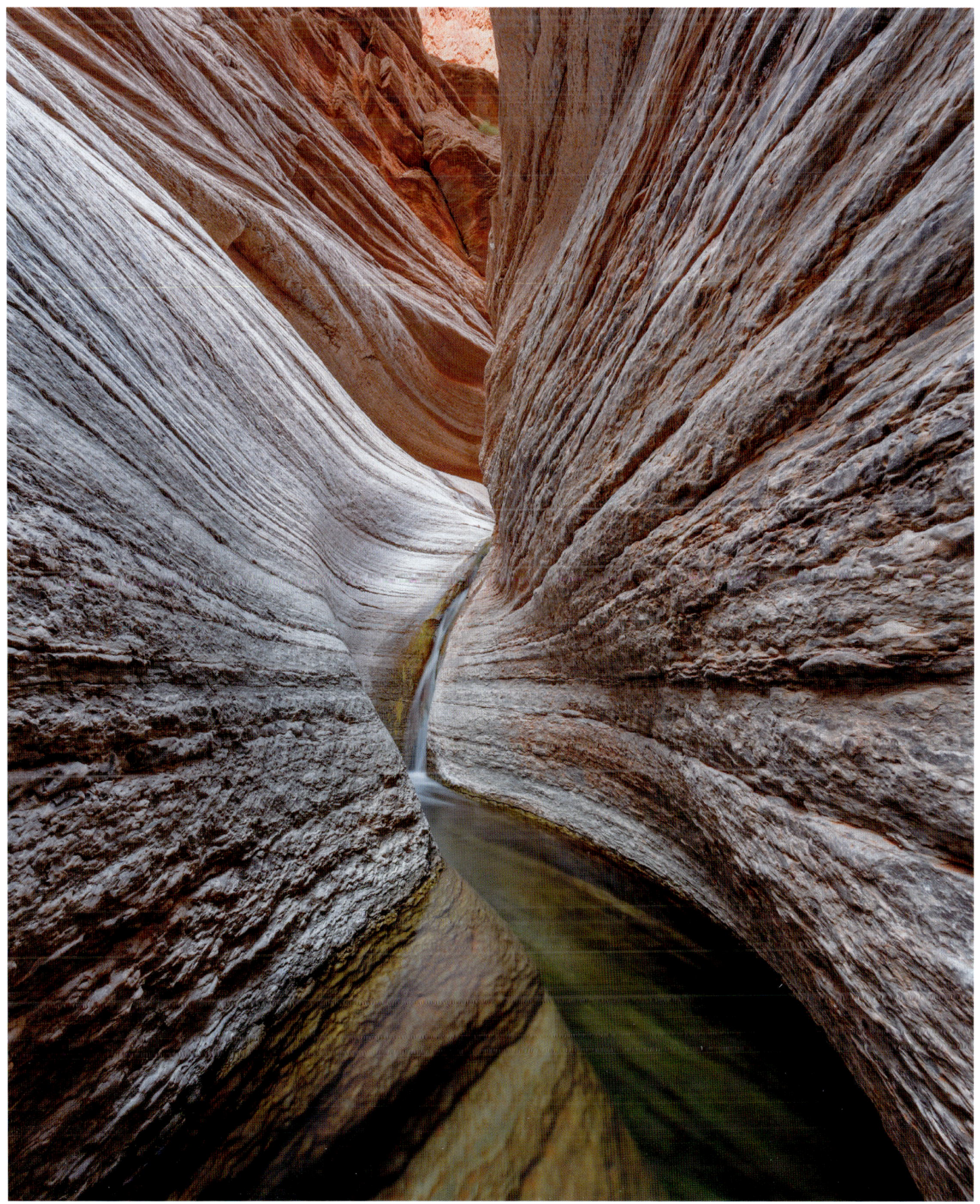

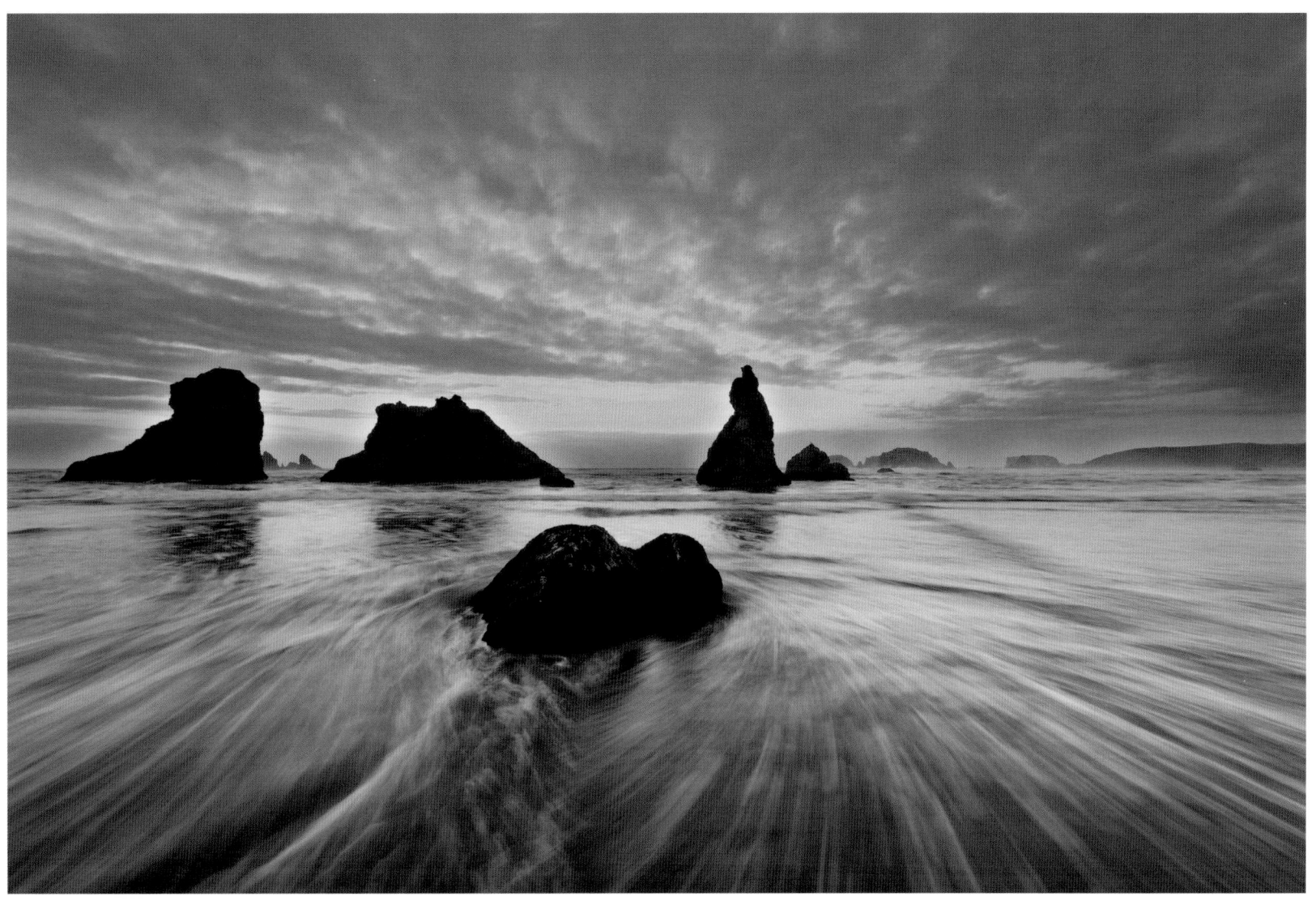

Lines need not be static elements in a design, however. The ebb and flow of the coastal surf off Bandon, Oregon creates lines that add immediacy and urgency to an image. With the black-and-white image, you feel the movement. To capture a similar image, simply spend time studying the recurring action of the waves. By carefully studying the swirling foam bubble lines, I was able to create a pathway radiating from the foreground corners toward the center of the frame. The space surrounding the foreground rock is critical. It establishes the rock as a central design element, prevents it from merging into the background of sea stacks, and anchors the composition.

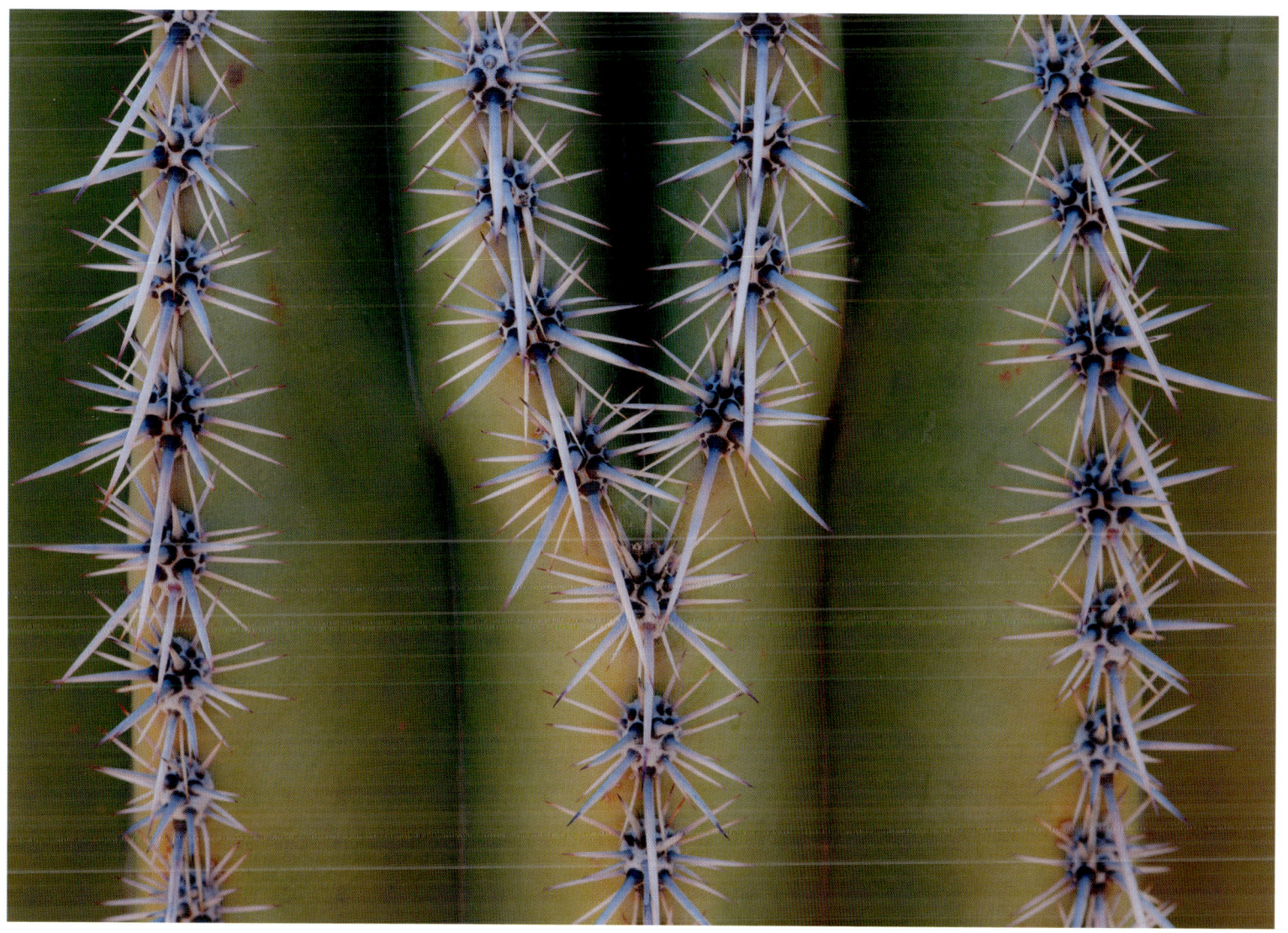

The arrangement of an image's lines requires careful planning to utilize the symmetry of the subject's elements and to fashion a composition that is balanced and compelling. This image involved careful camera positioning to produce equidistant spacing of the cactus columns and spines throughout the frame. The DSLR's live view feature is great for such situations. Each slight adjustment is easily seen on the LCD, so careful composing is possible. Some cameras can overlay a grid pattern on the LCD to further refine exact subject placement.

I had an assignment to document land stewardship on Native American tribal lands for *National Geographic* magazine. The Big Cypress Seminole Tribe's rehydration of swampland adjacent to the Big Cypress National Preserve in Florida was something I wanted to photograph, but after seeing many images of swamplands I knew I had to come up with a different concept. I was, after all, on assignment for *National Geographic*. The story was about water moving through cypress swamps. As I kneeled low in the swamp water, I carefully watched the water. (I had been briefed on the dry season concentration of alligators, cottonmouths, and mosquitos inhabiting this section of the swamp so, yes, I was carefully scanning the water!) At the same time, I noticed the slight movement of the water spangles floating on the surface, and these became the focus of my image.

I decided my exposure time should be exceptionally long to depict the water's subtle movement. I added both a polarizing filter and a neutral density filter, which allowed me to make two-minute exposures. When the film was processed, the paisley-like swirls on the water's surface created an entirely new subject. Although the lines were not straight, the patterns further visually isolated the cypress trunks and allowed the viewer to see the swamp over a period of time.

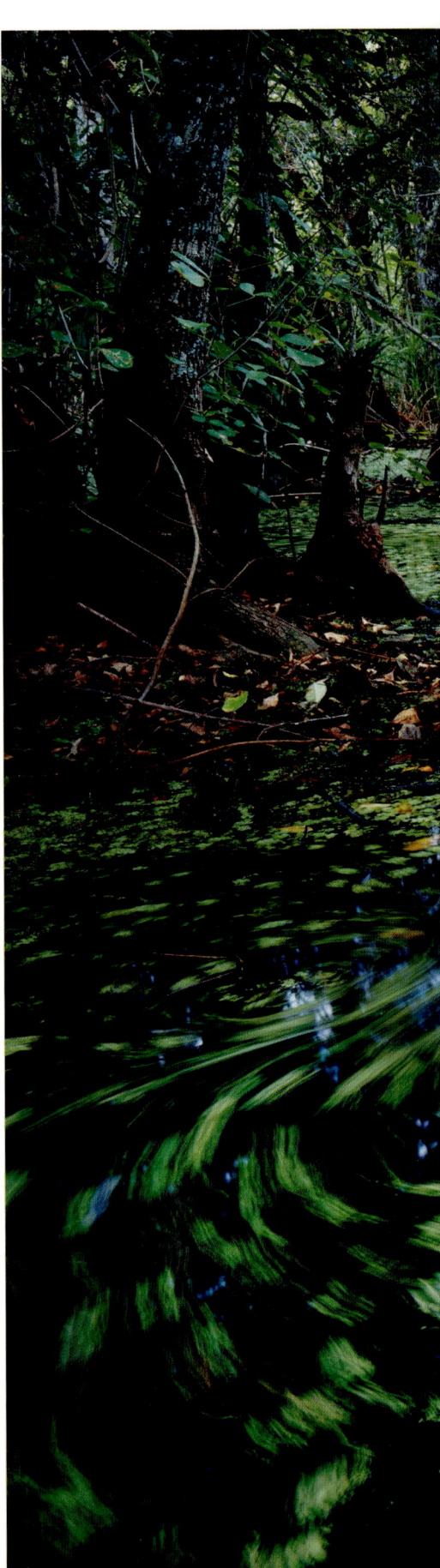

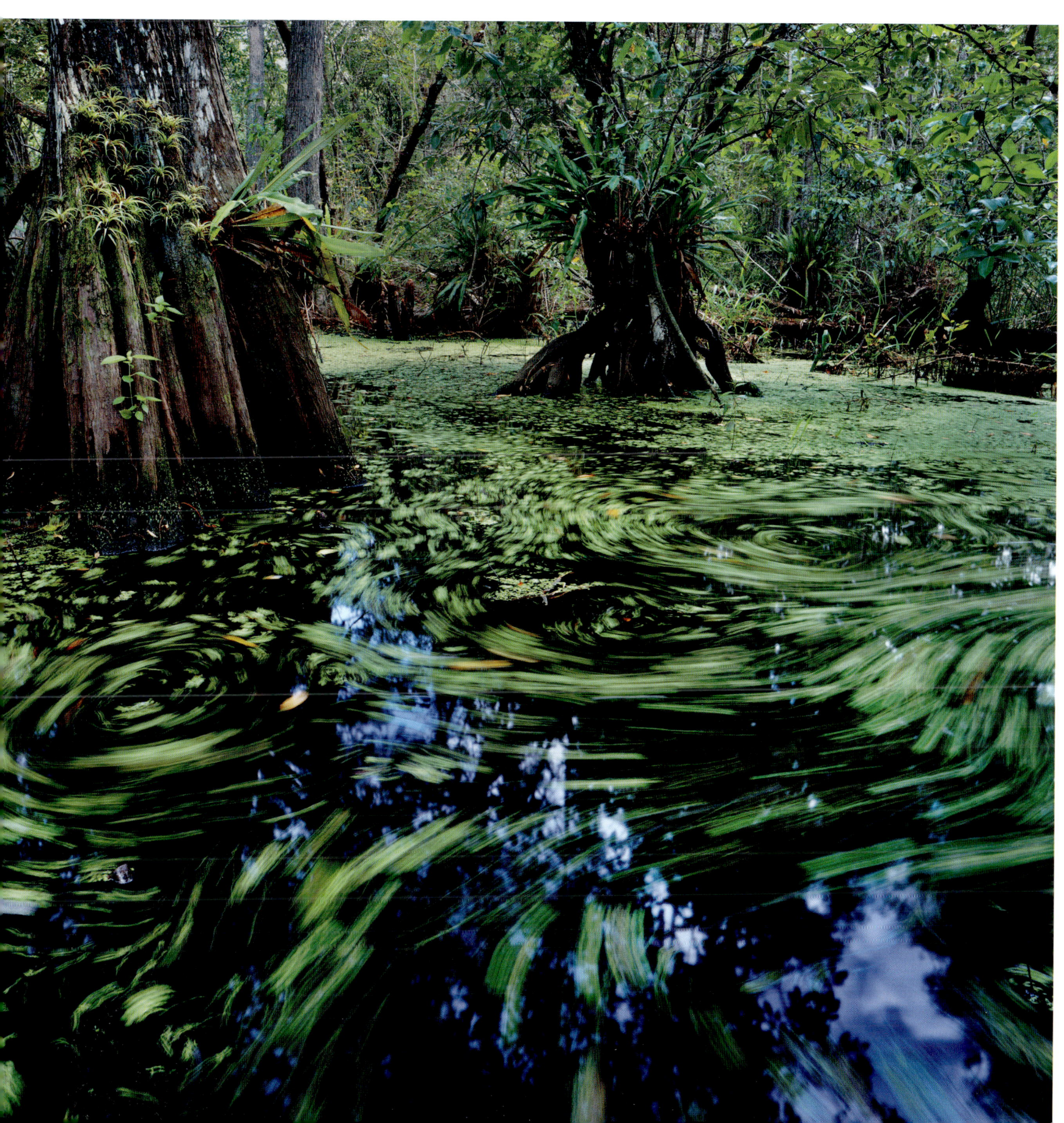

Sometimes nature intervenes when we least expect it, as it did when I created this image. I was in central Utah making long exposures of the Devil's Garden Metate Arch at night using my Nikon intervalometer. My intent was to create an image of star trails circling the North Star but an unexpected cloudbank came streaking across many of my exposures, ruining all chances of capturing the star trails. However, this four-minute exposure of the scene allowed the cloud movement to paint powerful lines through the central part of my composition. Serendipity had intervened to create magic.

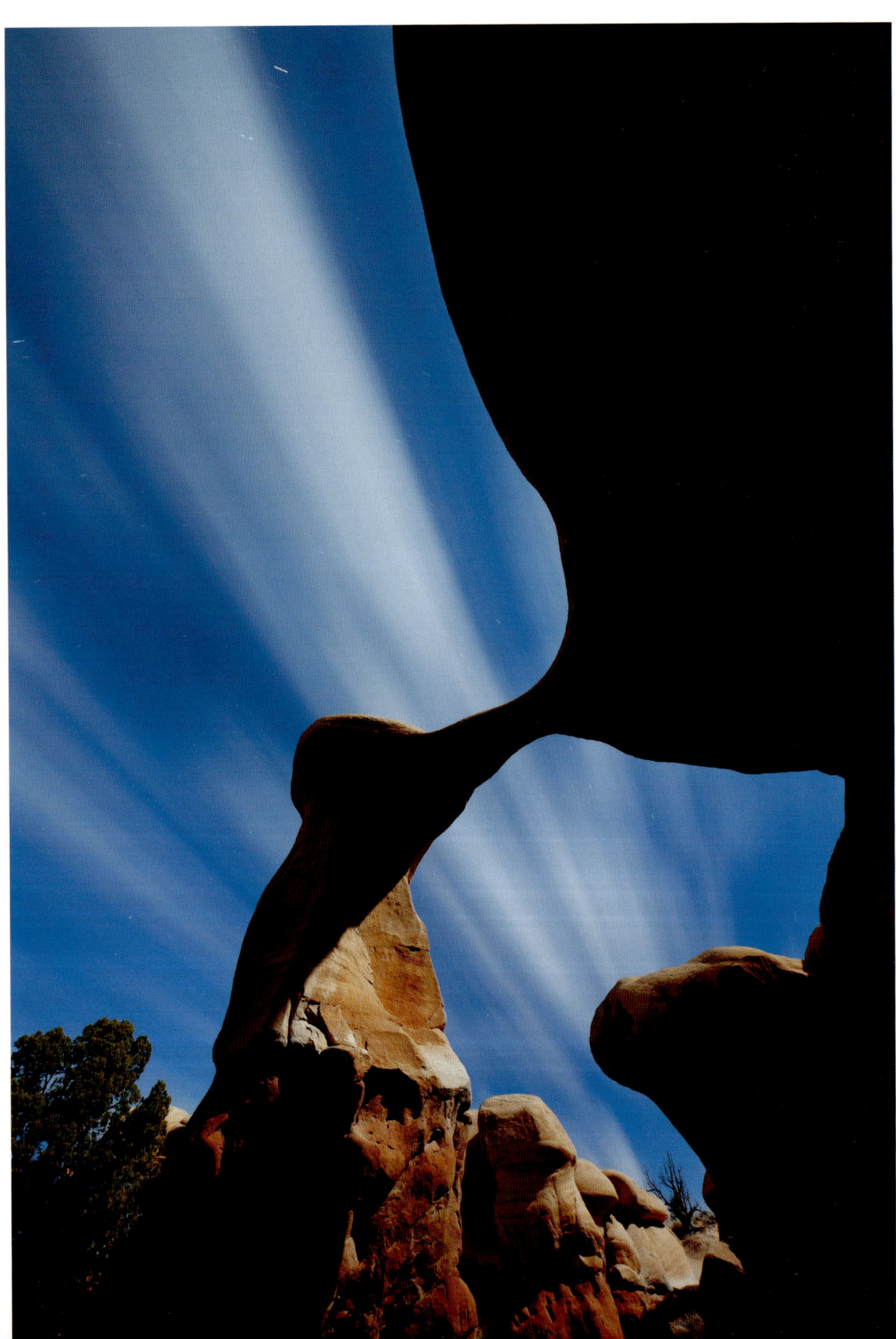

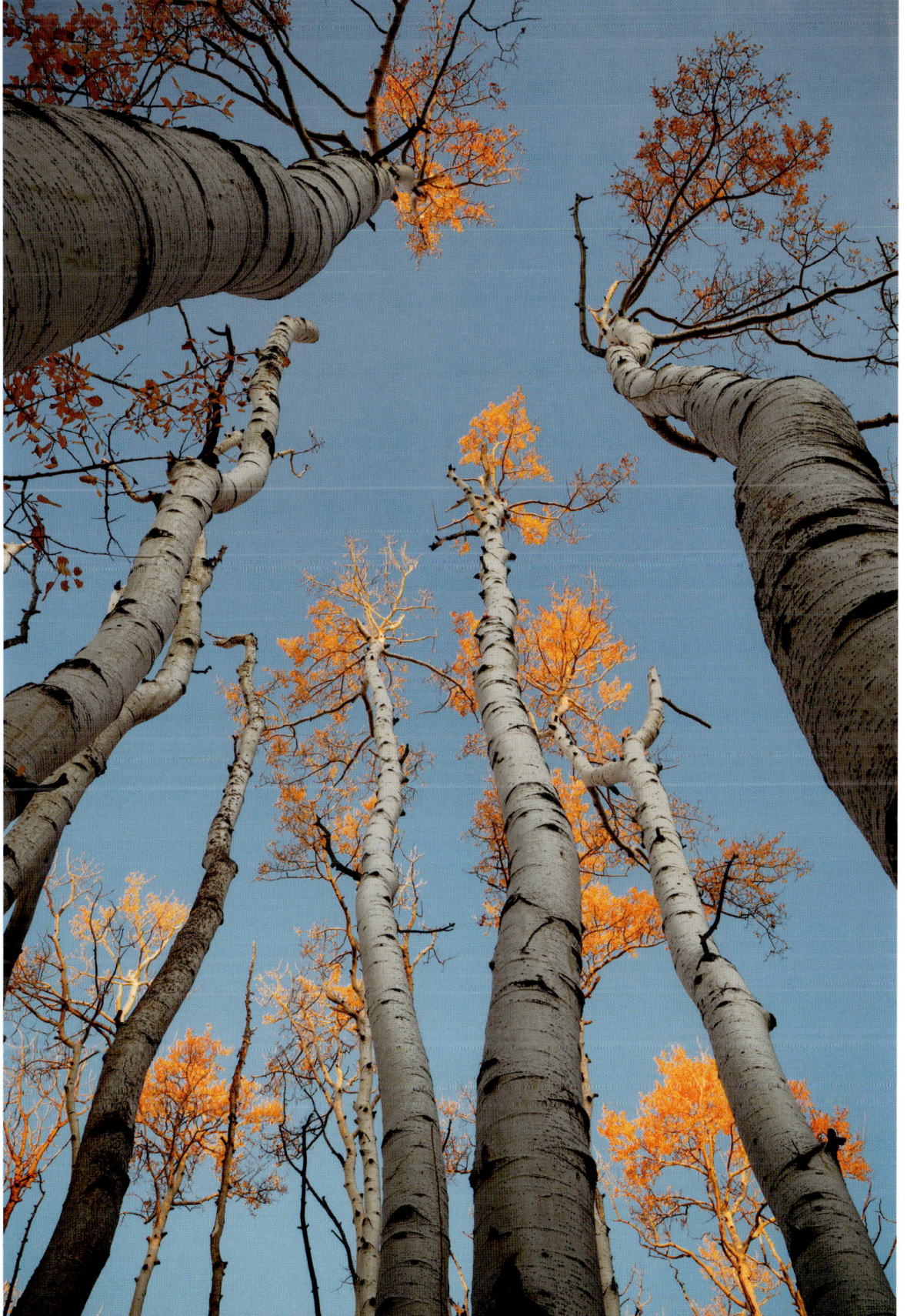

As lines guide the viewer's eyes, so do colors. Combine them as I did in this photo, with lines radiating inward and with the dawn-lit colorful leaves centered in the frame, and the impact is doubled. Aspen trees in fall color, against a blue sky, provide a strong destination for the eye after being directed from the corners into the main subject. The very first light of dawn further saturated the warm colors to increase the effect.

Near/Far

As you will see from the images in this chapter, lens choice controls how and what images communicate. A lens's effect can either work to reinforce your statement or to weaken it.

Wide-angle lenses have the virtue of providing a line of sharp focus from near to far. Many photographers, however, fail to realize the power of a wide-angle lens because they're too timid to place the lens right up against their subject. An image's strength is determined by the camera's placement in close proximity to the subject, which effectively increases the relative size and impact of the foreground against the background.

I was photographing an extensive growth of barrel cactus in the Mexican state of Tamaulipas and wanted to create an image that would lead the eye into an archetypical Chihuahuan Desert scene. Using a very wide-angle lens, I moved as close to the nearest cactus as safety would allow.

Although each cactus head is approximately the same size, the wide-angle lens distorts the size of the nearest cactus and intensifies the sense of perspective, leading the eye into the image. As you can see, the red spines and their delicate detail draw the eye into the frame and become a pathway to infinity. This approach allows an amazing amount of information to be imparted to the viewer. It's as if there's a macro image combined with a landscape image: the foreground provides details and the background provides context.

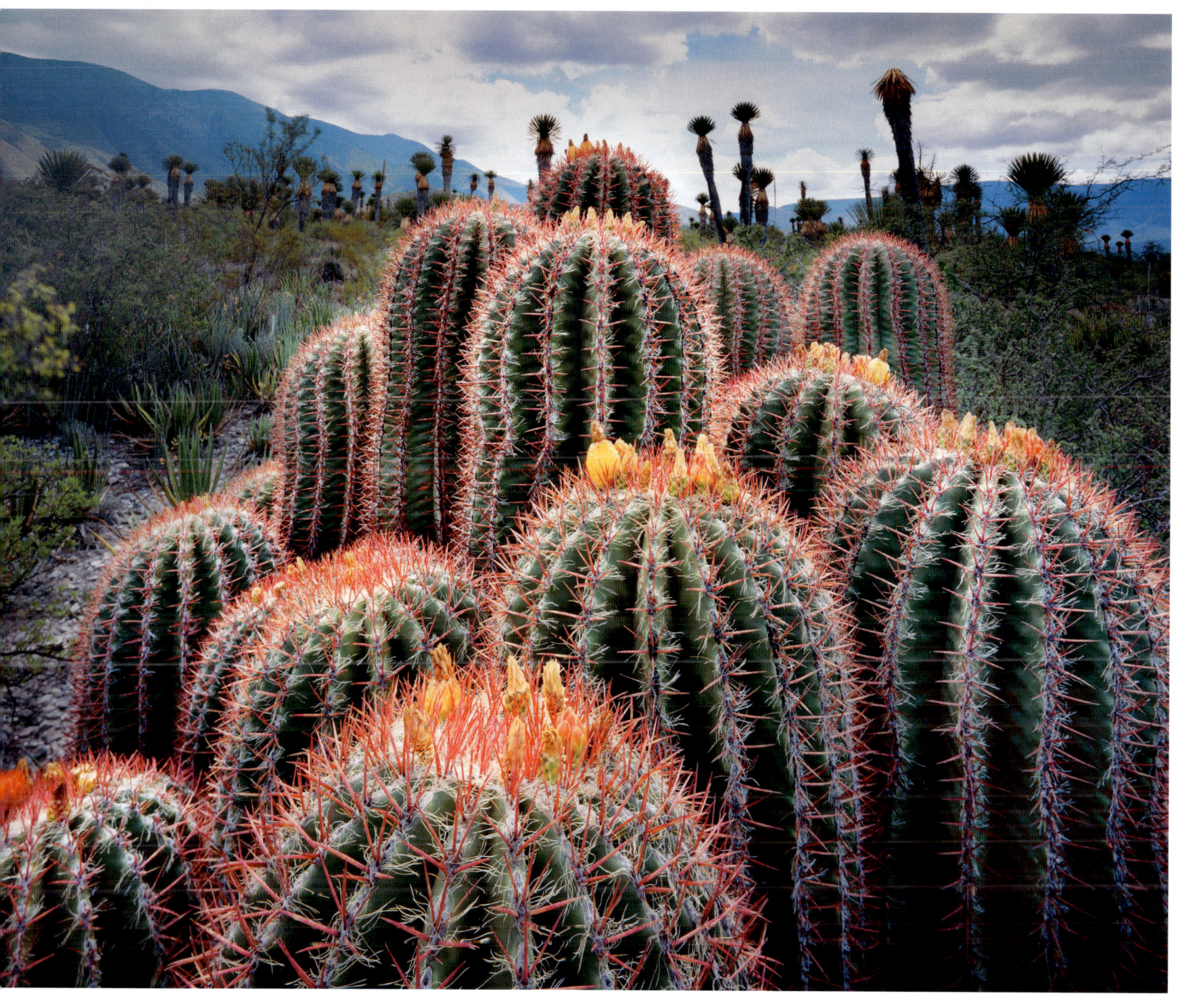

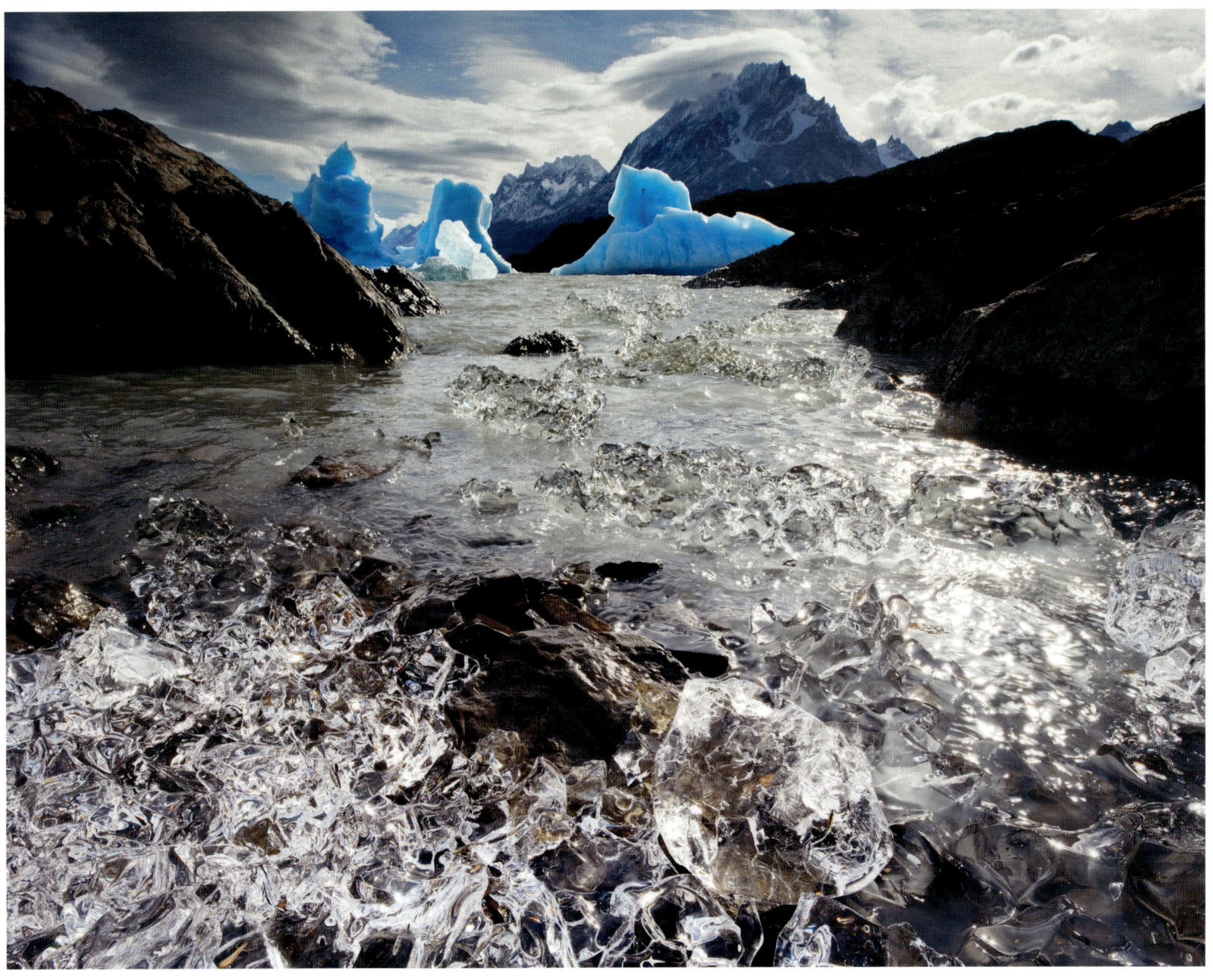

Similarly, ice fragments washed onshore in Chilean Patagonia's Lago Grey provide information about the blue icebergs and the storm-covered mountain environment and bring the viewer's eye into the frame.

In this image, layer upon layer of ice shards lead the viewer into the scene. Because it's all on a sharp plane of focus, all the elements read well and the image works. If the foreground was out of focus, it would break the pathway into the image and the viewer's eye would be pushed away. Whereas here

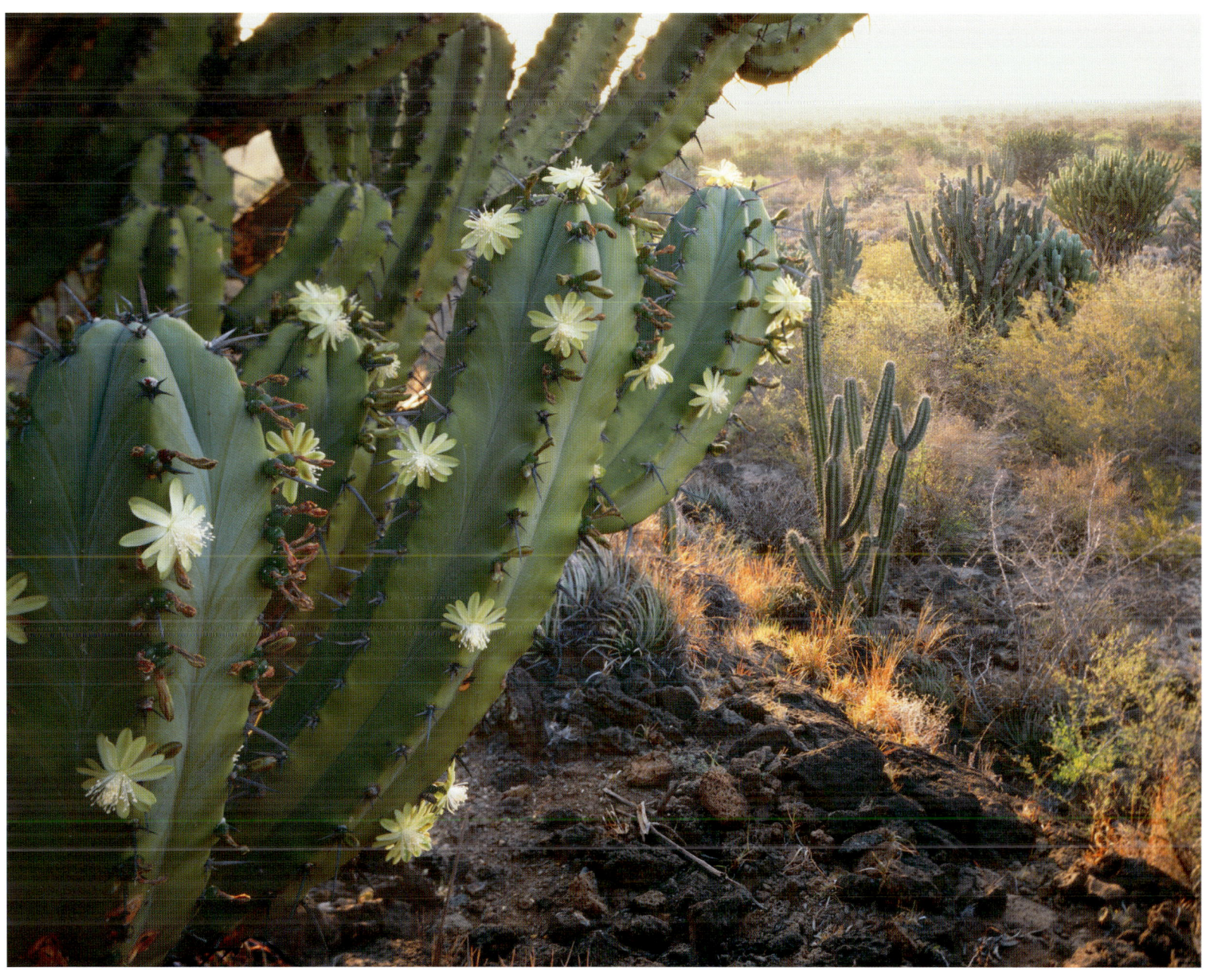

the near-to-far effect reaches from the bottom of the image to the top, other images can achieve the same effect by leading the eye from left to right or from right to left.

Tiny flowers in this garambullo cactus are inches away from my lens, and the plane of focus from left to right takes the eye into the frame along the powerful diagonal pathway. By using a wide-angle lens and a small f-stop, the depth of field encompasses the entire scene and the visual pathway is complete.

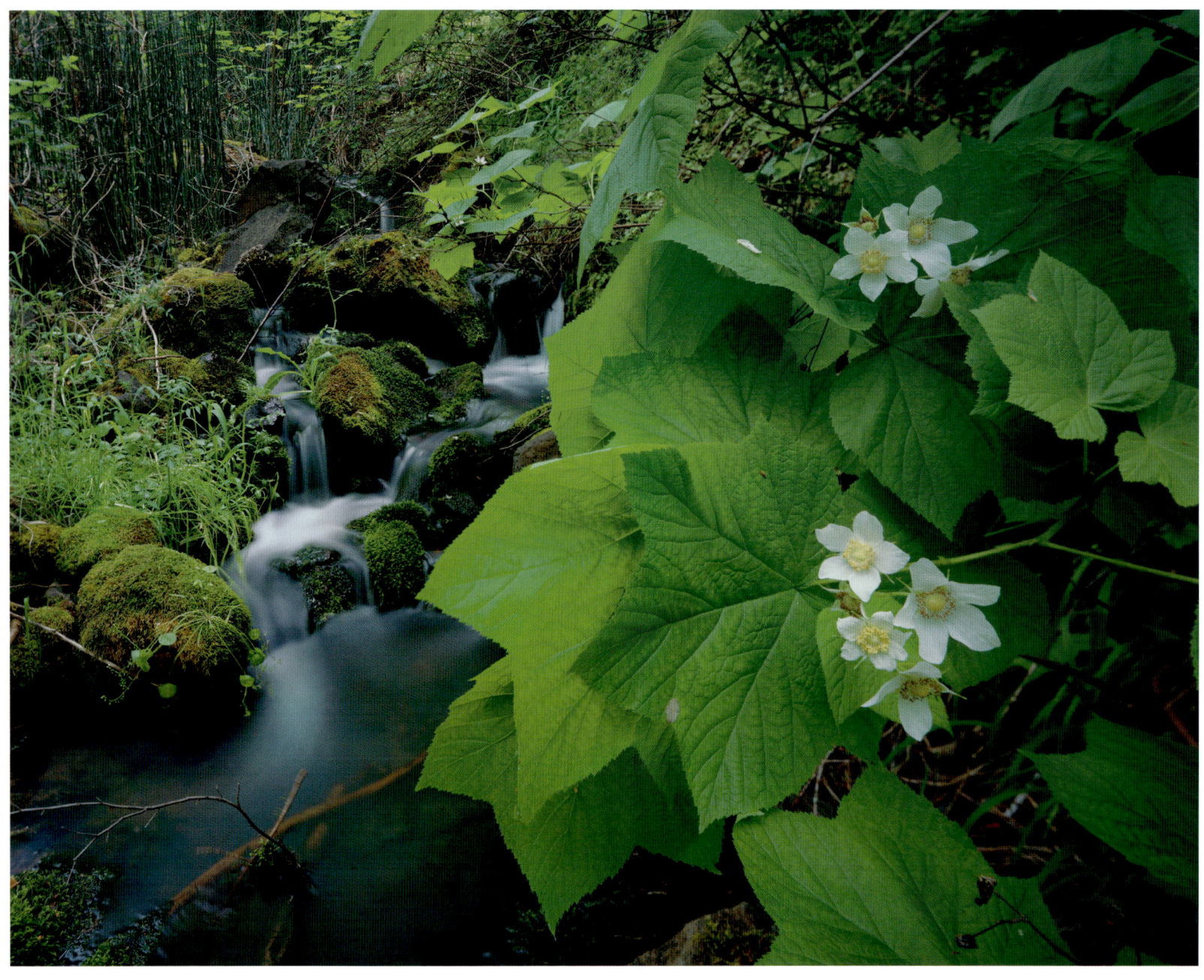

In this image, photographed at Joseph Creek in eastern Oregon, the flower on the right anchors the composition. At the same time, the flower also leads the eye into the frame and, ultimately, to the tiny waterfall. In these types of compositions, the foreground anchors the image, but it also requires a destination for the eye.

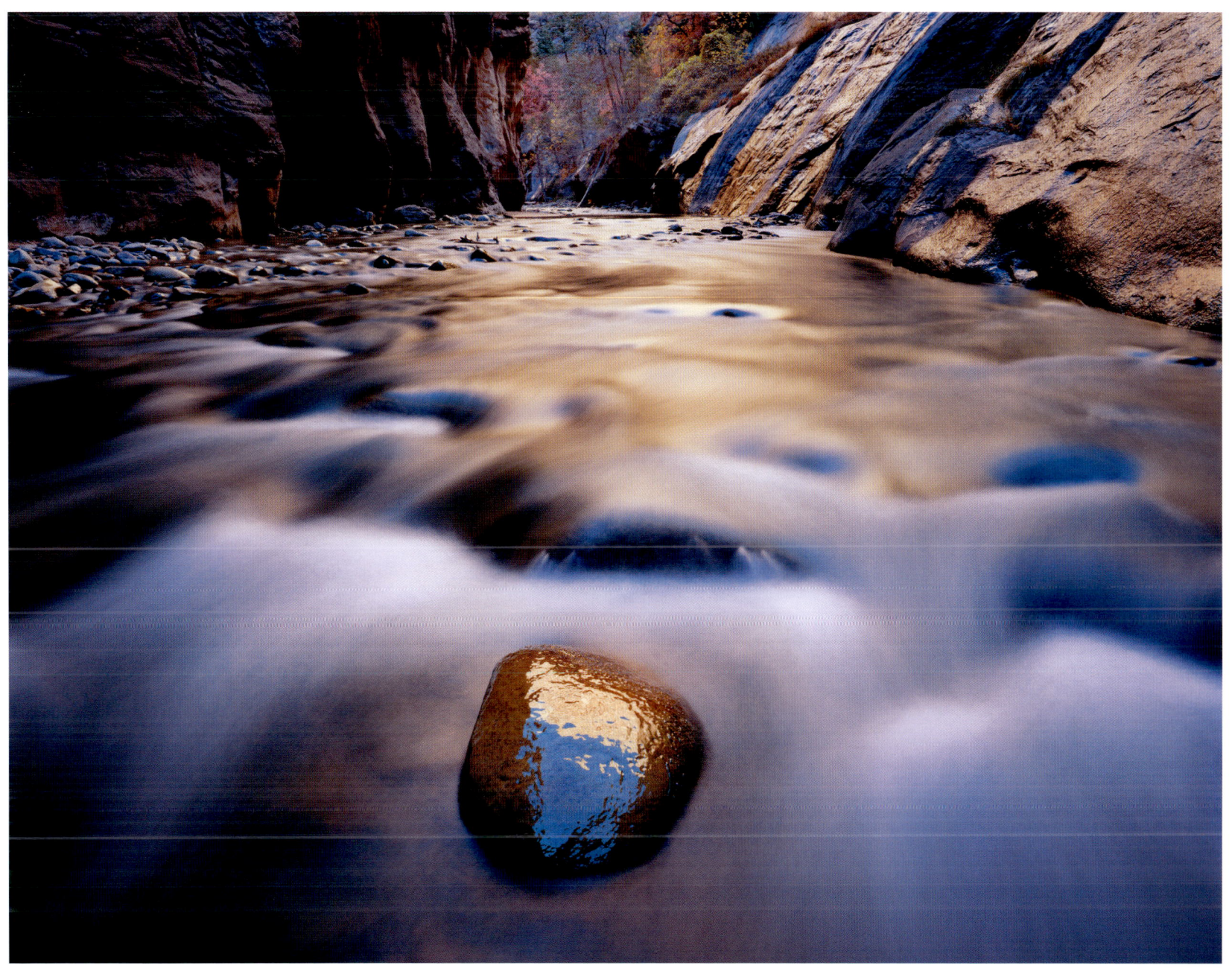

The foreground's central element can be further emphasized when it stands alone in sharp focus. In the fast-moving water of Utah's Virgin River, the wet stone becomes a mirror of the canyon and sky. The stone is a powerful foreground anchor while the moving water reinforces the pathway up into the canyon

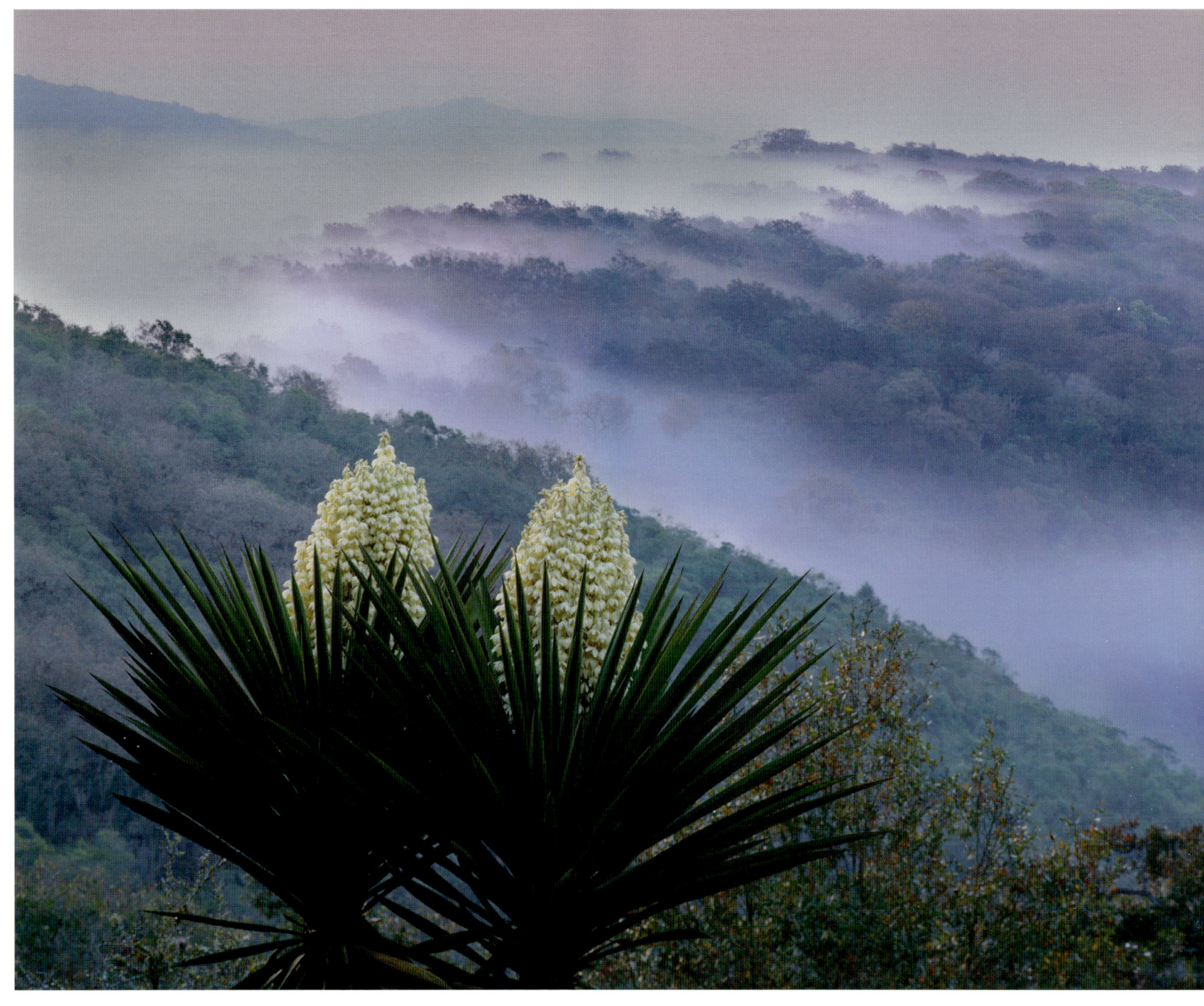

While much has been written about near to far as a technique, little seems to be discussed about the opposite effect: far to near. When the background is more important than the foreground, we can give it more power by using longer or telephoto lenses.

Here you see two views from Mexico's Sierra Tamaulipas, where I illustrated the collision of dry tropical forests with the desert. In the first image, I photographed the dawn light with fog streaming across the mountaintop forest using a normal focal length lens (a 180mm lens on a 4×5 camera) to provide a sense of place.

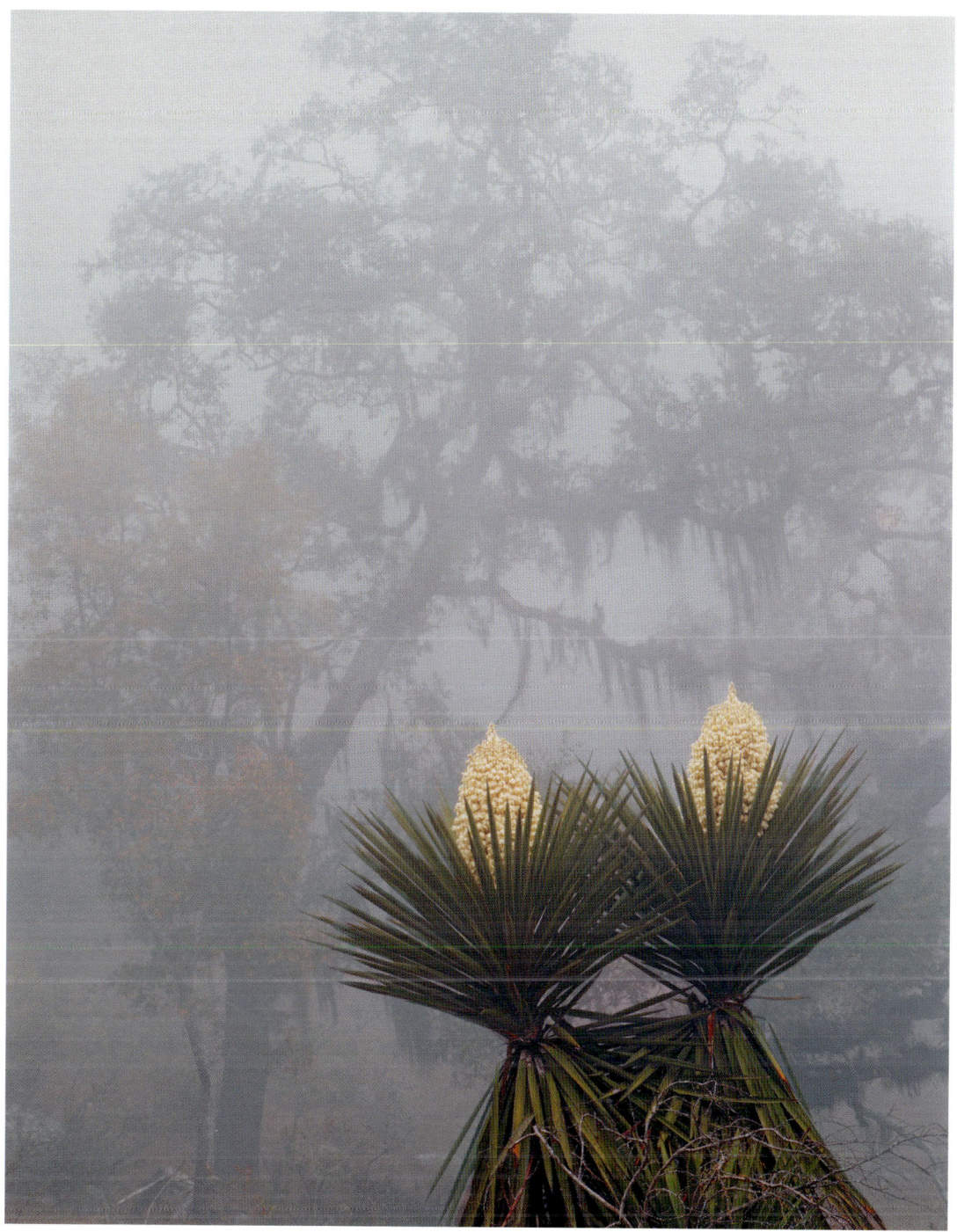

But I felt I needed to record the detail of the foreground set within the forest backdrop. The moss-covered trees in the background elicited a tropical feel, so in order to bring them forward, I photographed the scene with a telephoto lens (100mm on a 4×5 camera). The effect provided more information about the forest and the contrast in life zones. The telephoto perspective also provides a narrower view of a scene, which in this case helped eliminate the distraction of the sky.

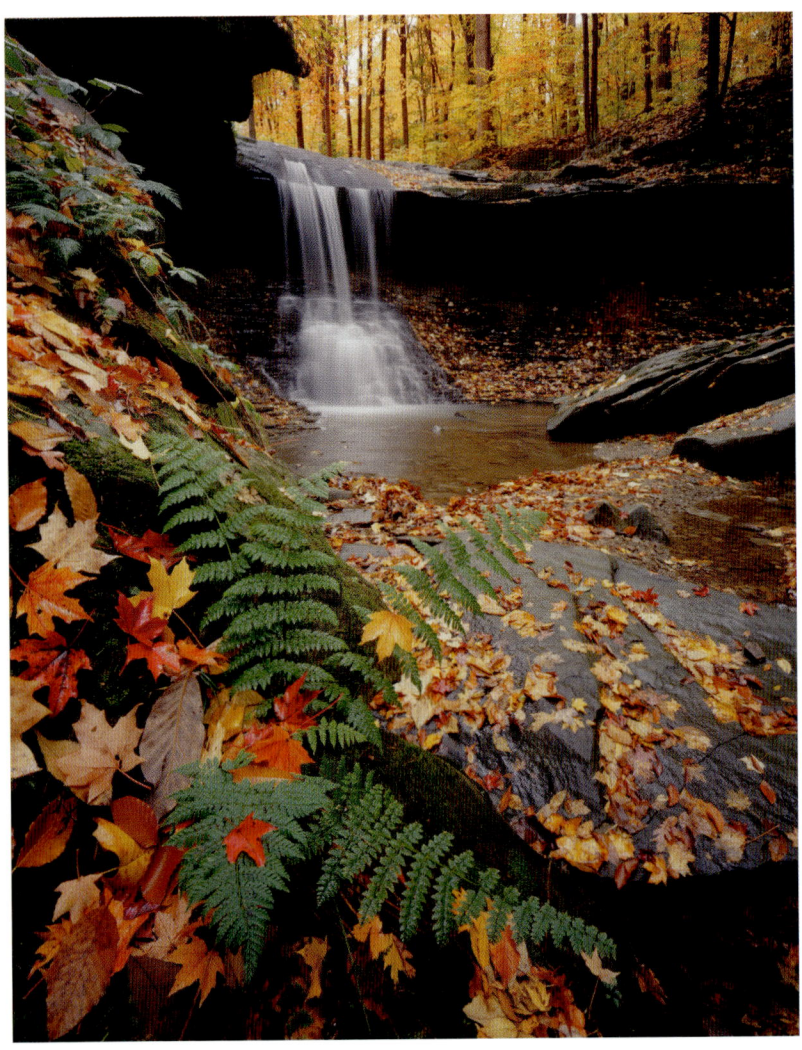

One of my favorite locations in Ohio is Blue Hen Falls. The fall-colored forest in these images provides a wonderful backdrop to the sinuous ribbon-like waterfall. With ferns covered with red maple leaves anchoring the foreground, I used a wide-angle lens to place the falls as the focal point for the eye. I wanted the viewer to see the brilliant foreground and follow the stream to the falls.

However, while this approach worked well to draw in the viewer, the emphasis on the foreground in the first image diminished the scale of the falls. By changing to a medium telephoto lens for the second photograph, I increased the relative size of the falls by emphasizing its scale beneath the forest. This perspective extends the view to the upper falls as well.

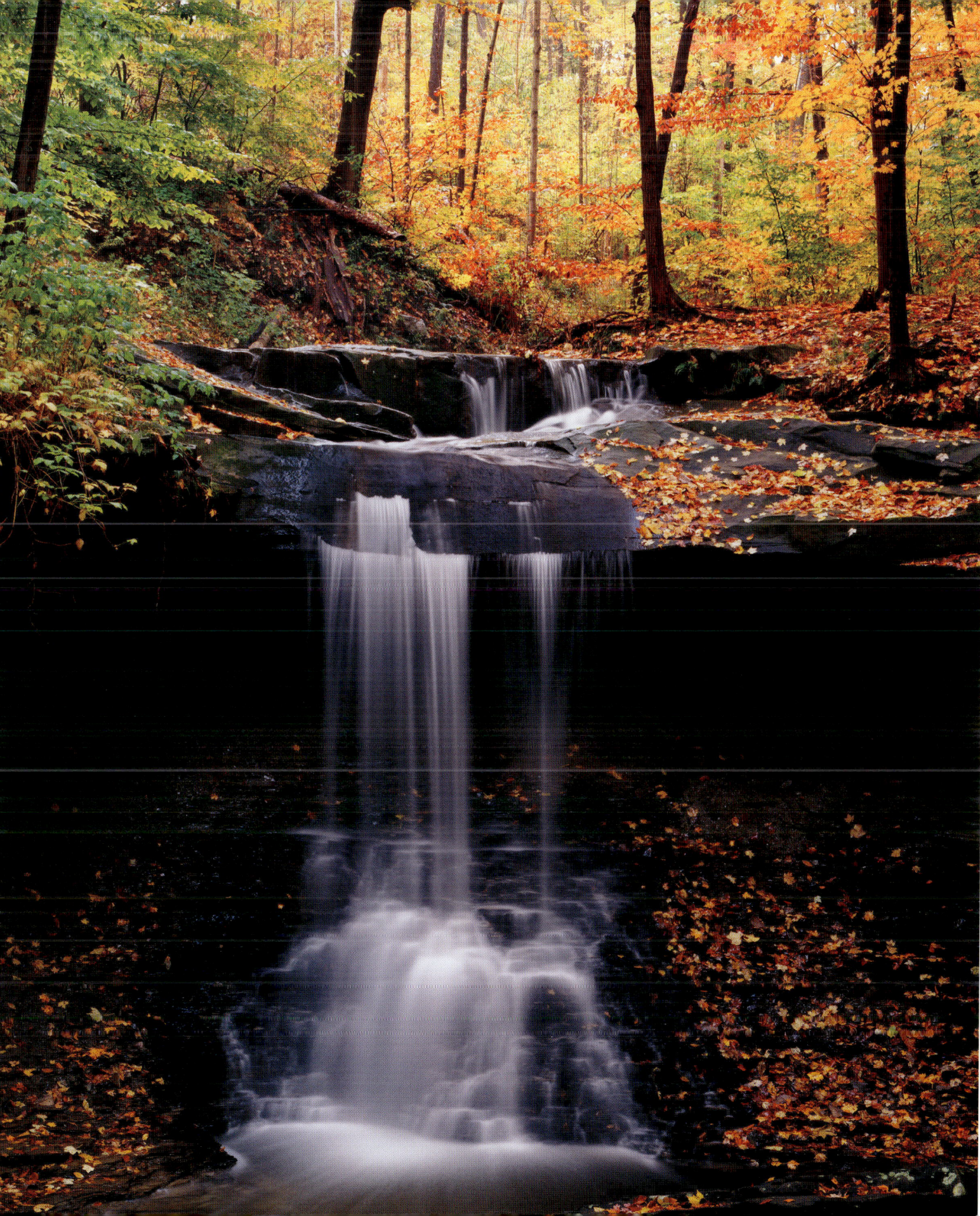

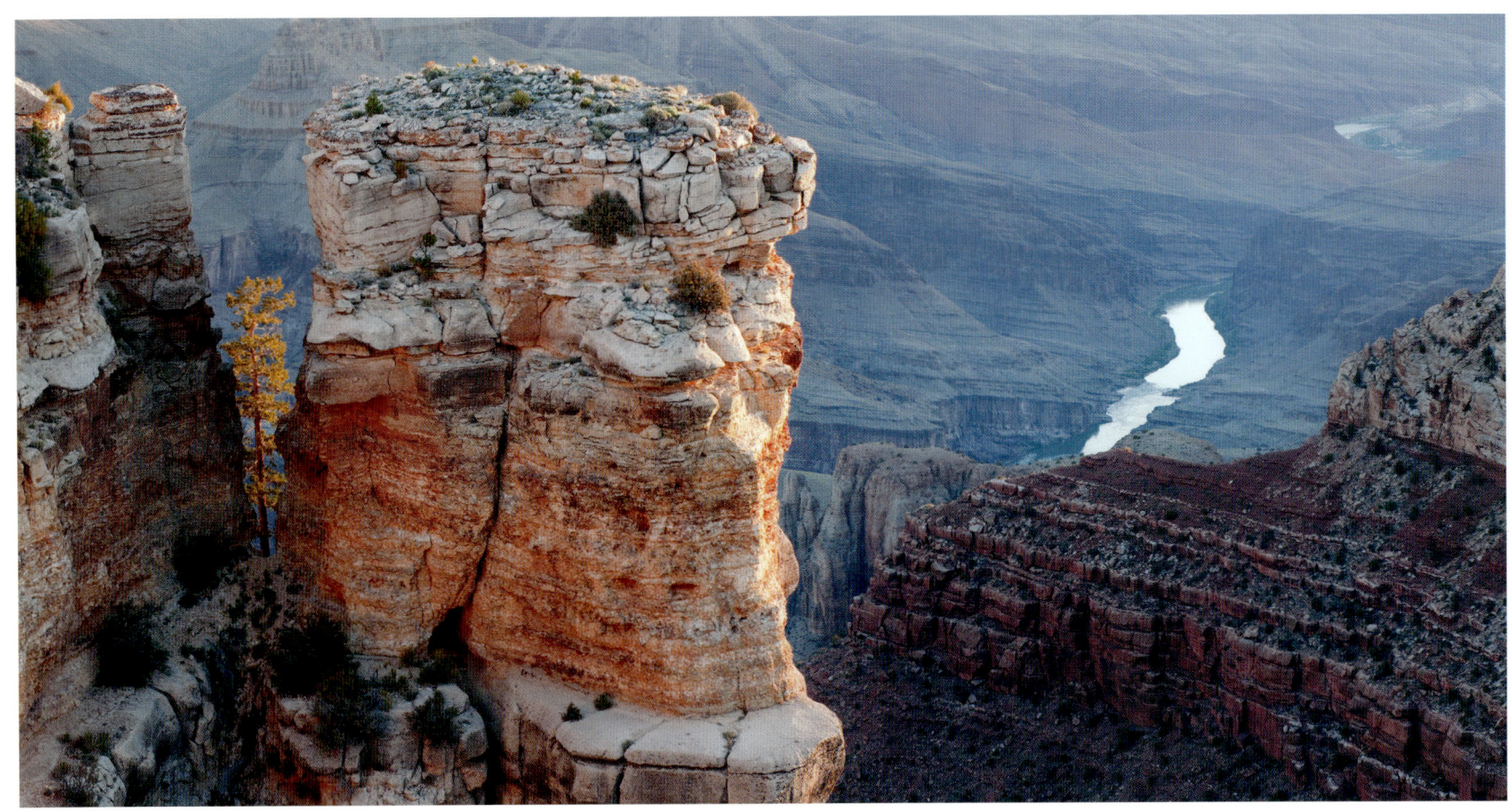

In this photograph, taken while standing at Moran Point on the Grand Canyon's South Rim, you can see the distant, tiny thread of the mighty Colorado River meandering through the canyon below. The river looks anything but mighty when photographed with a normal focal length lens. I chose this focal length to show both the foreground rim with a ponderosa pine in the notch to the left and the river below to the right.

In the next image, by switching to a very long telephoto lens (720mm on a 4×5 camera) I changed the emphasis from the tree and the canyon's rim to the river.

Have a good reason to use a certain focal length. It's one of a photographer's most powerful tools.

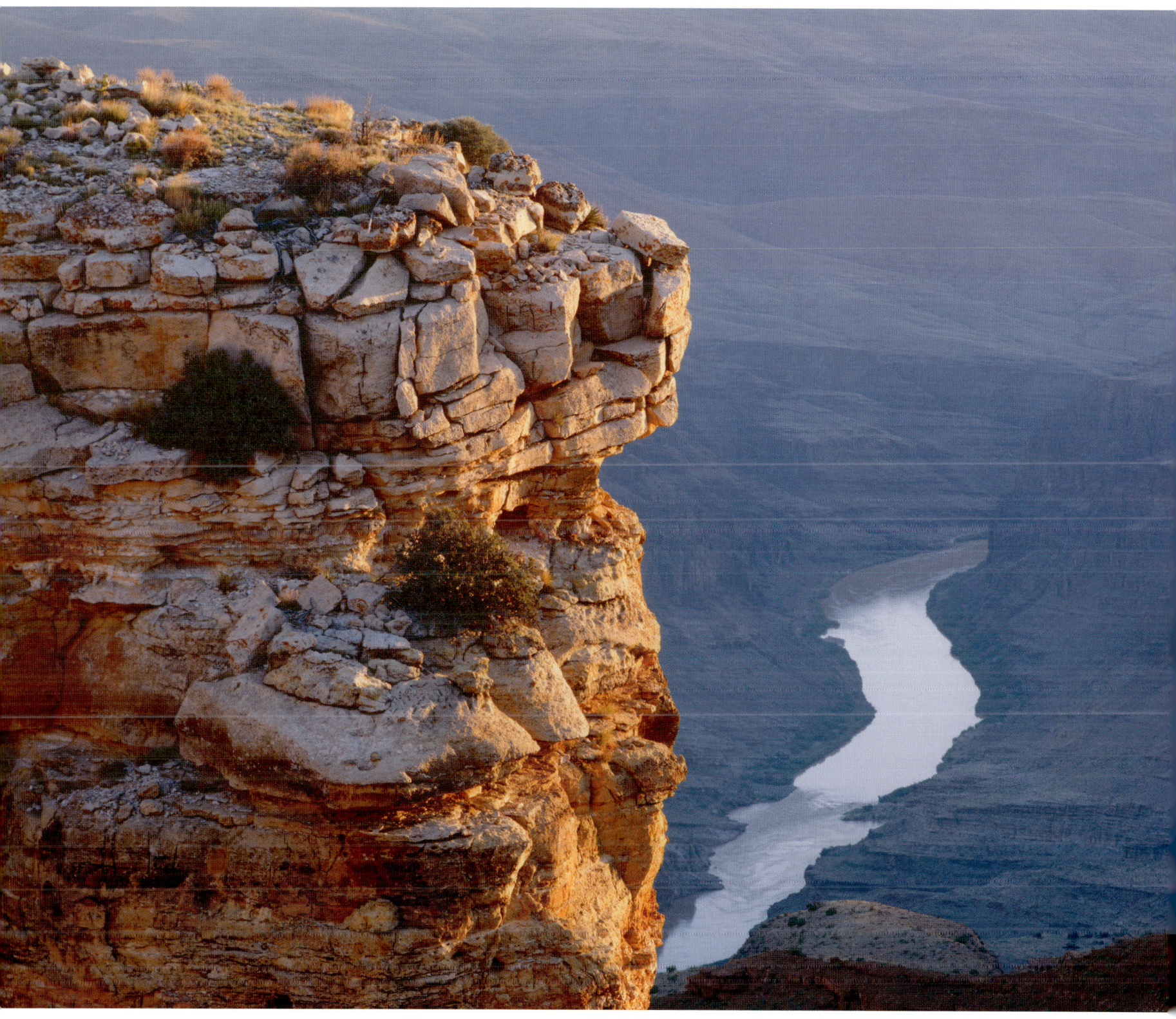

Illusion

Photographers who consistently and effectively reach vast audiences with their imagery are usually great illusionists. That's not to say they're inherently dishonest. Rather, they have mastered ways of tricking viewers' eyes into thinking two-dimensional objects are three-dimensional. By creating a sense of depth using shadow and light, texture, and the correct focal length, they can create pathways for viewers' eyes to walk into the photograph. That sense of depth is the mark of many successful images.

The trick is recognizing elements in the landscape that make this illusion of depth possible. I spend hours scouting locations searching for an interesting subject. I then visualize how it is going to look as the sun's angle changes. This is crucial, since cross-lit subjects anchor the composition as they emerge from the shadow and appear three-dimensional. As seen in this image, using shadows as a way to isolate the sunflowers of Colorado's Great Sand Dunes National Monument required moving the camera as the shadow moved. When the angle of the sun changes, so must the camera position, thereby creating a different composition. This is not easy and requires trial and error. I have had countless preconceived images fail in the end. At the same time, as the sun's position changed, I've also had compositions become apparent elsewhere and had to hurriedly change my camera position in an effort to capture the image. If I think a composition is really strong, I believe it's worth a couple days of my time to craft an image as best as I can.

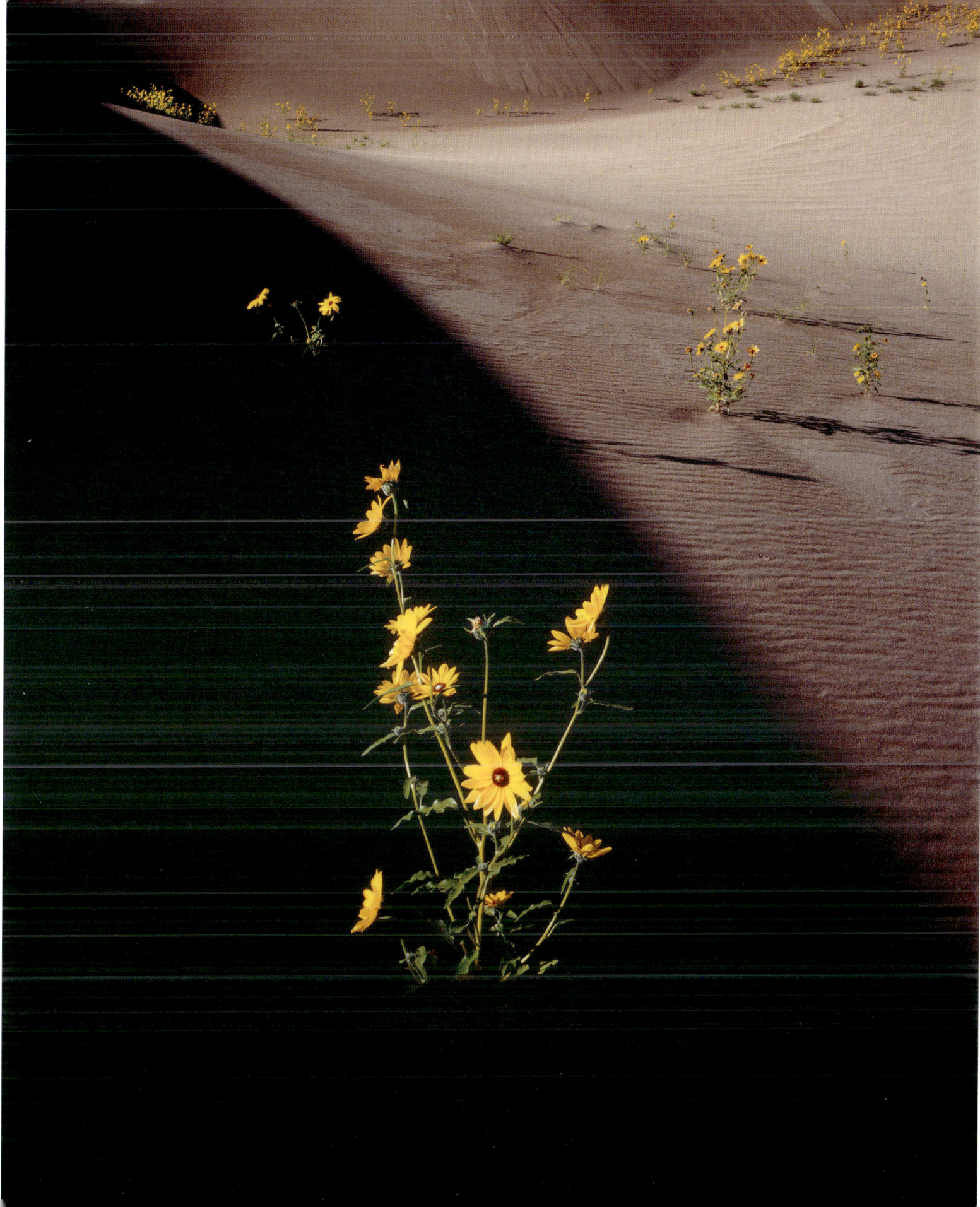

Sometimes even a couple of days are not enough time to create the best image of a particular scene. This image was the product of about two weeks of work. I spent days searching until I found several saguaro cacti with drooping arms. Then I watched how the morning light played upon each, until I decided to photograph this one. I liked the way the background cactus was framed by the foreground cactus limb. Each day I'd pack my stepladder and set off on a pre-dawn hike to visit my new friend. My assumption was that all the flowers would bloom together at some magical time. What happened was actually quite different: each night a few new buds would flower but those from the previous night would die. Over a period of a week, there would be one flower, and then two or three, until one day a crescendo of eight flowers dominated the foreground. And, as I had planned, the morning light's warmth illuminated the scene.

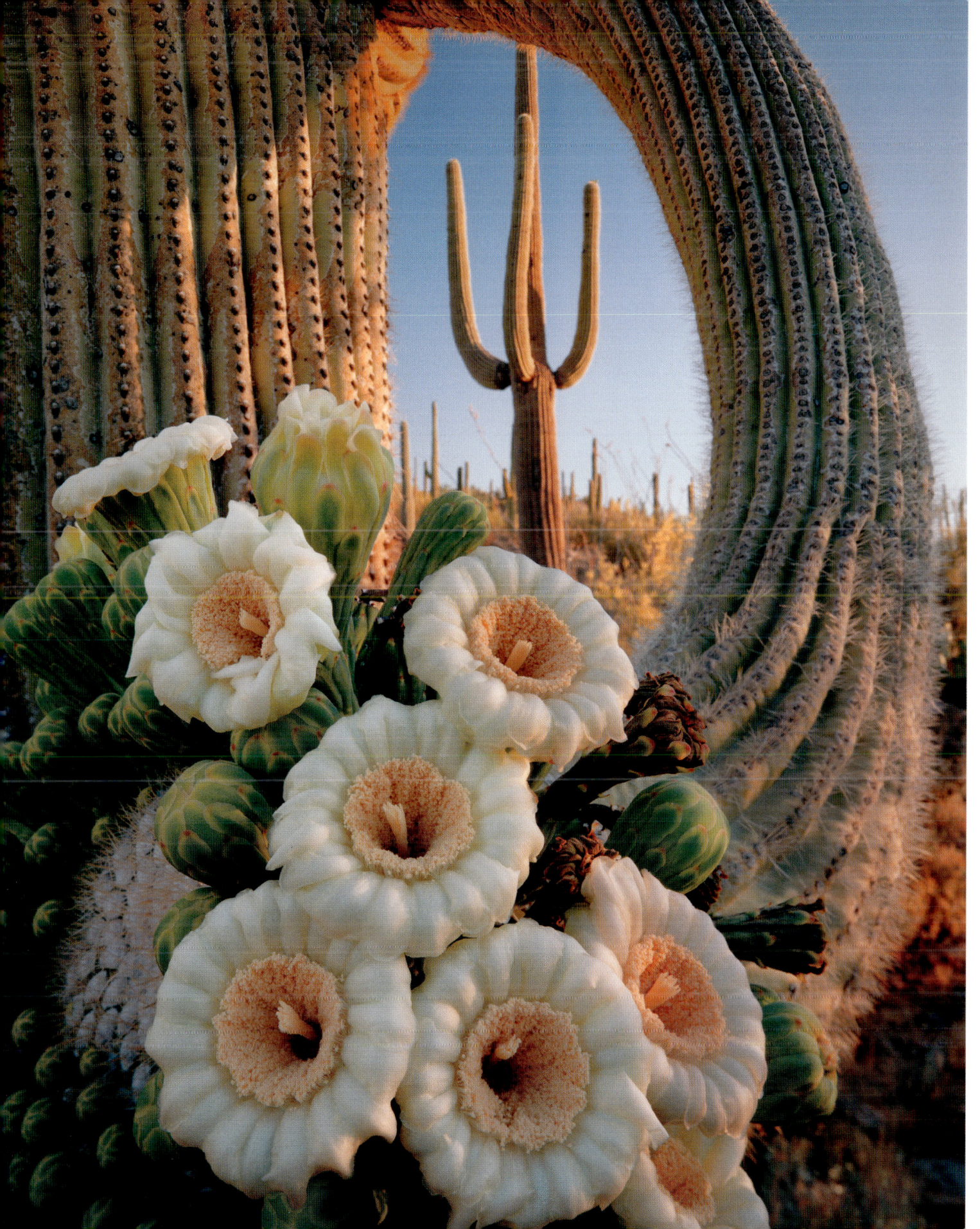

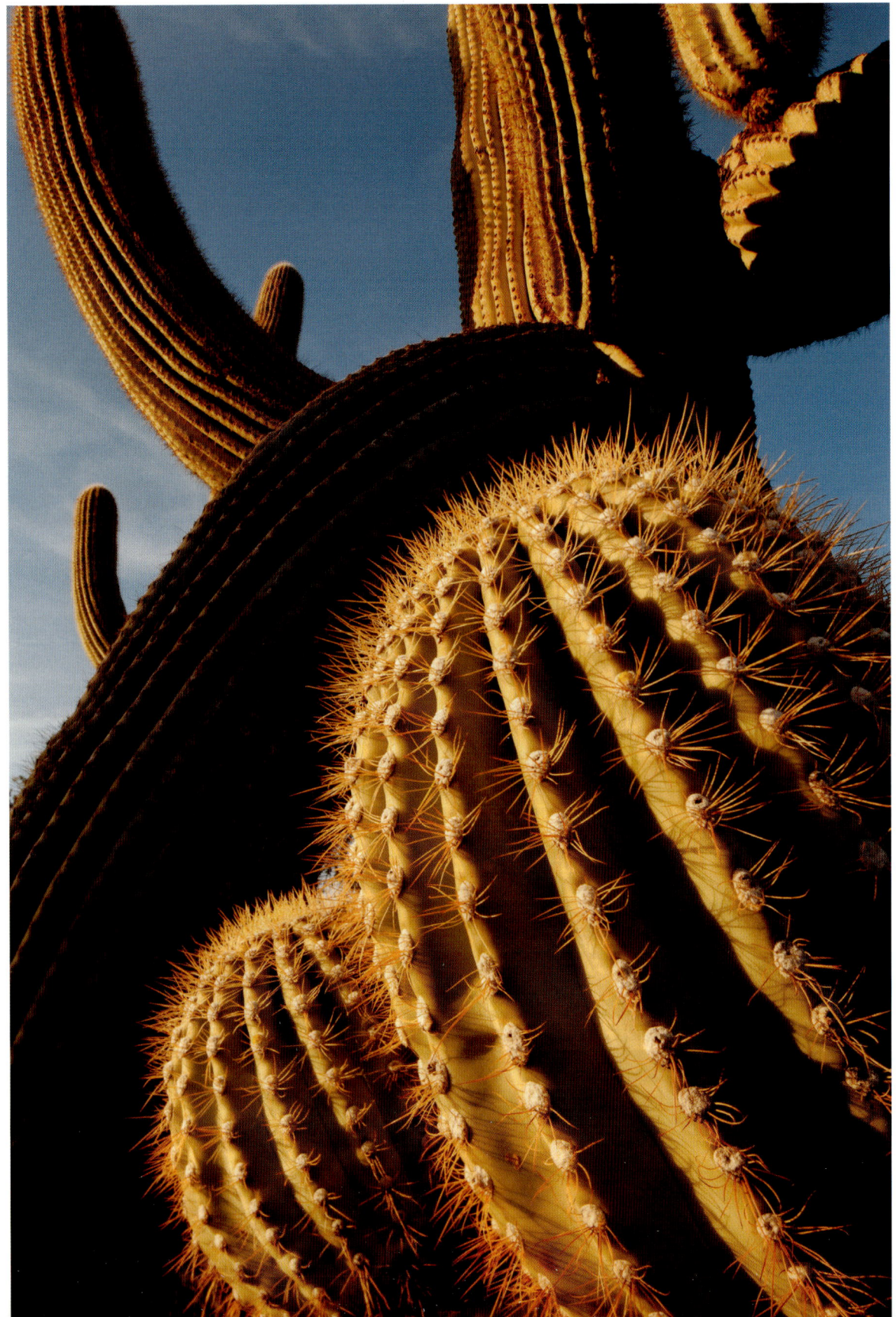

I wanted to emphasize the texture in the foreground arm of this saguaro, so I waited for the strong cross light of the setting sun. I created a compelling design that is surrounded by the curved background arm. To keep both foreground and background sharp, I used a 24mm, tilt/shift lens to change the plane of focus. This solved the problem of adequate depth of field by keeping all the design elements in very sharp focus.

In the image to the right, the foreground is secondary and becomes a frame through which we view the background. When making this decision early on, I selected a longer focal length to shift the emphasis to the background. The catch is, I wanted the image's depth of field to encompass the entire scene, so the focal length couldn't be too long. I chose a 240mm lens. My exposure time of more than one second allowed the slow, flowing motion of the waterfall to draw the eye, and the f/45 aperture brought everything into sharp focus. The stark contrast between the warm-colored tree bark and the cool-toned falls creates an interesting effect. The warm colors (red) seem to jump forward, strengthening the illusion of depth.

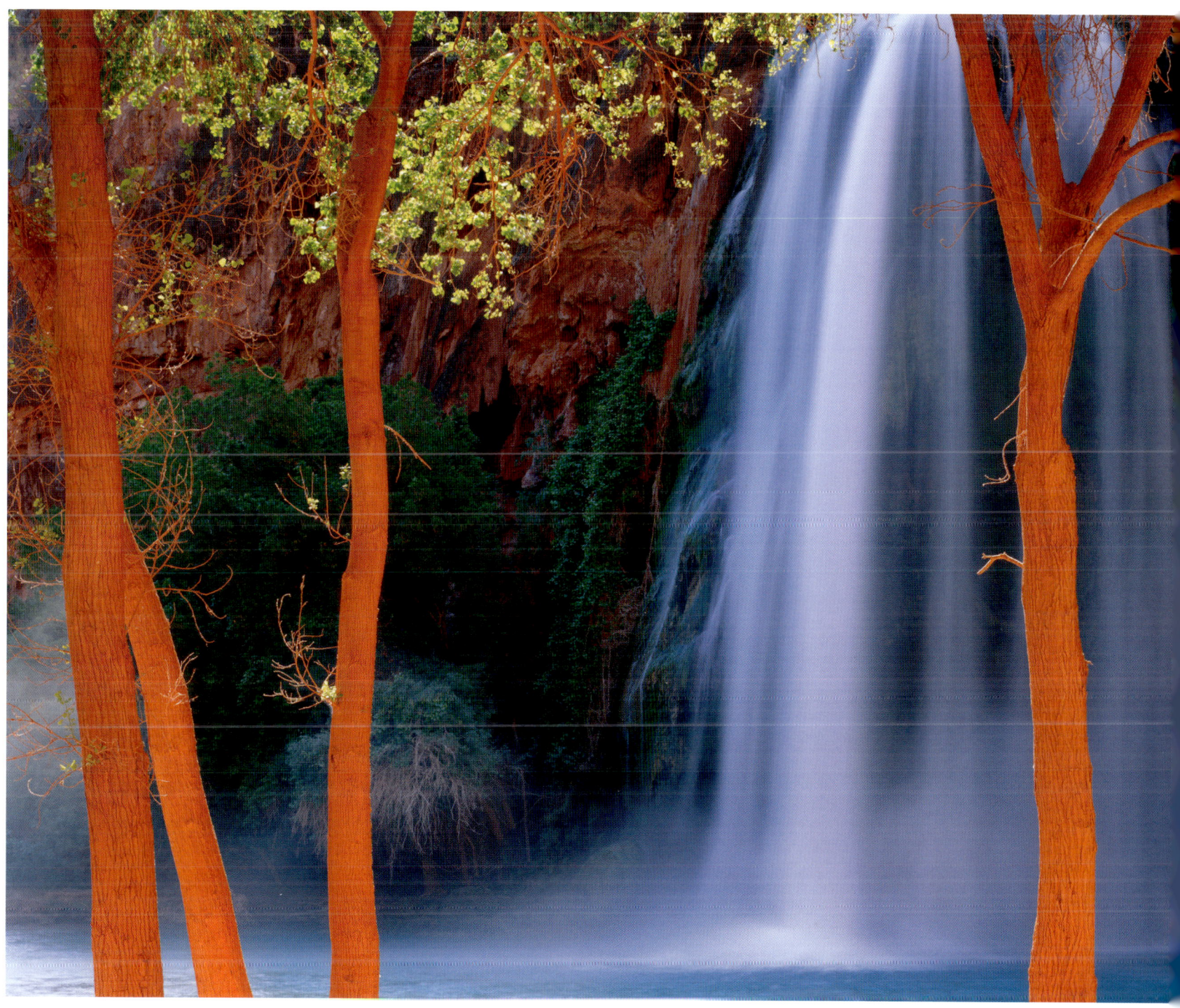

Framing can also solve other problems. For instance, in Arizona we have long periods of steel blue, stark, cloudless skies. My solution to this problem, exemplified in this image, is to frame the background with foreground subjects that extend upwards, covering the empty sky while enhancing a 3-D effect. The cross-lit, textured foreground saguaro cactus frames a natural pathway for the eye to travel into the scene. Much of the sky is covered by the sheer size of the foreground.

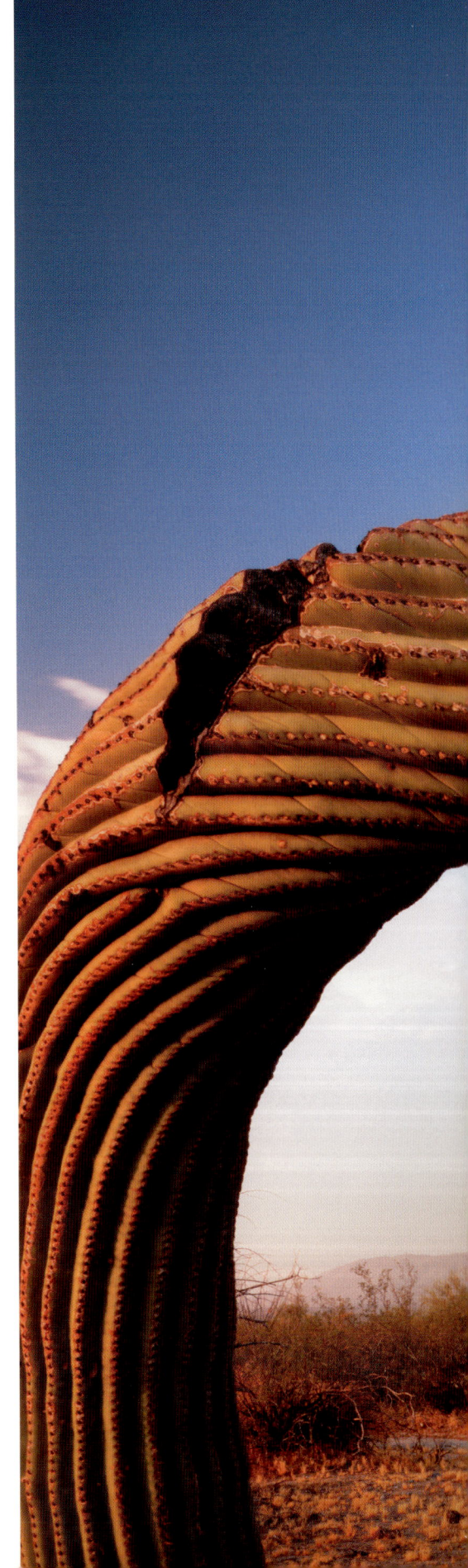

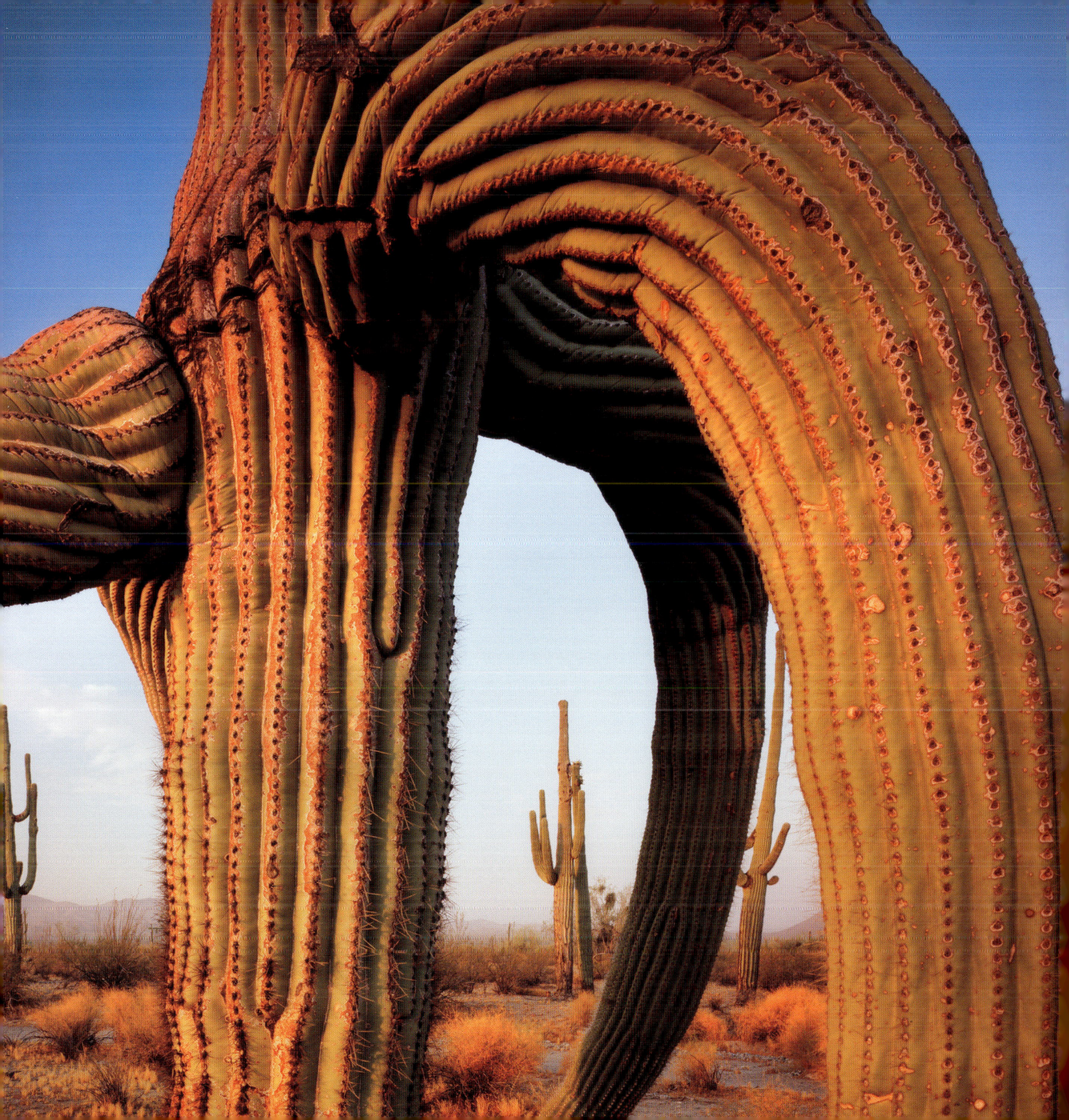

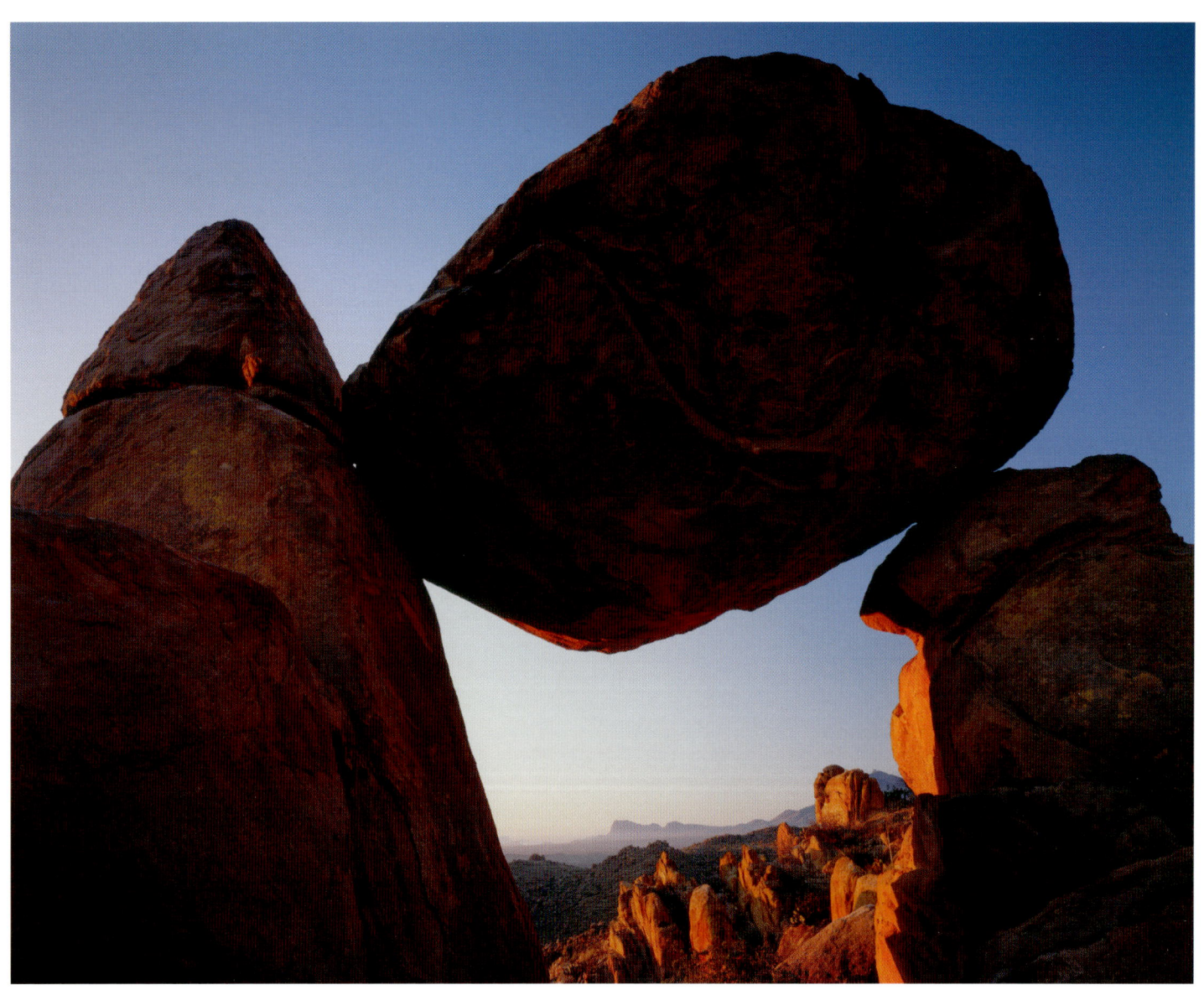

This image is all about impact and solving the problem of an empty sky. Heavy shadows emphasize the massive scale, attracting the eye. Yet the eye falls into the portal and is drawn toward the background boulders.

Slow Down

I find that while working with the incredible new DSLR cameras and their ability to capture quickly changing situations, I need to fight the impulse to go fast and, instead, need to consciously slow down. Of course, the first impediment to racing along is being bolted to the ground with a tripod. Why a tripod? Tripods place the camera in a fixed position, which in turn allows the photographer to make incremental, slight, and subtle changes in the composition without starting over again. Furthermore, by using a digital camera's live view function, we can now see the entire framed composition.

Placing the camera on a tripod also gives the photographer more options for smaller f-stops and greater depth of field, as well as longer exposure times to record movement. No doubt, it is a hassle to carry a tripod, but the shooting options it offers and the benefits outweigh the inconvenience

Once I have decided the best time to photograph and the best position for the camera, I'm free to think about what I'm trying to say. Do I want the foreground to jump into the viewer's eye, maximizing impact with a wide-angle lens? Or do I want to bring the background forward using the telephoto lens? Often, while teaching workshops, I find that when I tell students to tighten up a composition, they simply zoom their lens. By doing so, they negate the effect of the focal length they originally selected. It's far better to keep the focal length (for its desired effect) and move the entire camera—and the photographer—either forward or back.

Framing

We habitually view the world through frames. From televisions to computers to smart phones, we see the world framed by some kind of window. So it should come as no surprise when photographing that we create a virtual window to isolate our chosen subject from the grand landscape. The key is to seek out elements within the landscape to frame our vision.

Massive lenticular clouds form the symmetrical frame in this image. The grandeur and scale of Chile's Torre Grande is monumental but its scale becomes even more impressive when viewed under the vast Patagonian sky above Lago Grey. The clouds in this photograph effectively frame the peak and focus the viewer's attention while also adding drama and excitement to the composition.

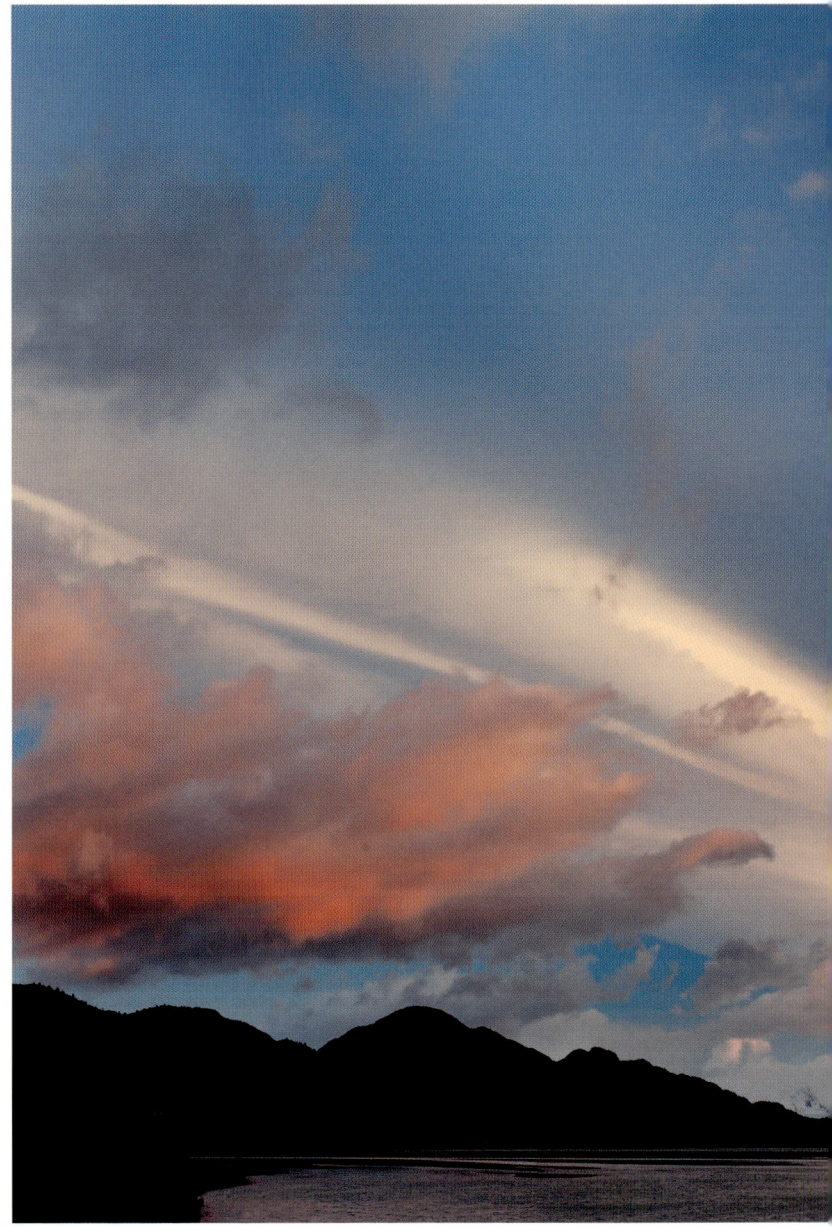

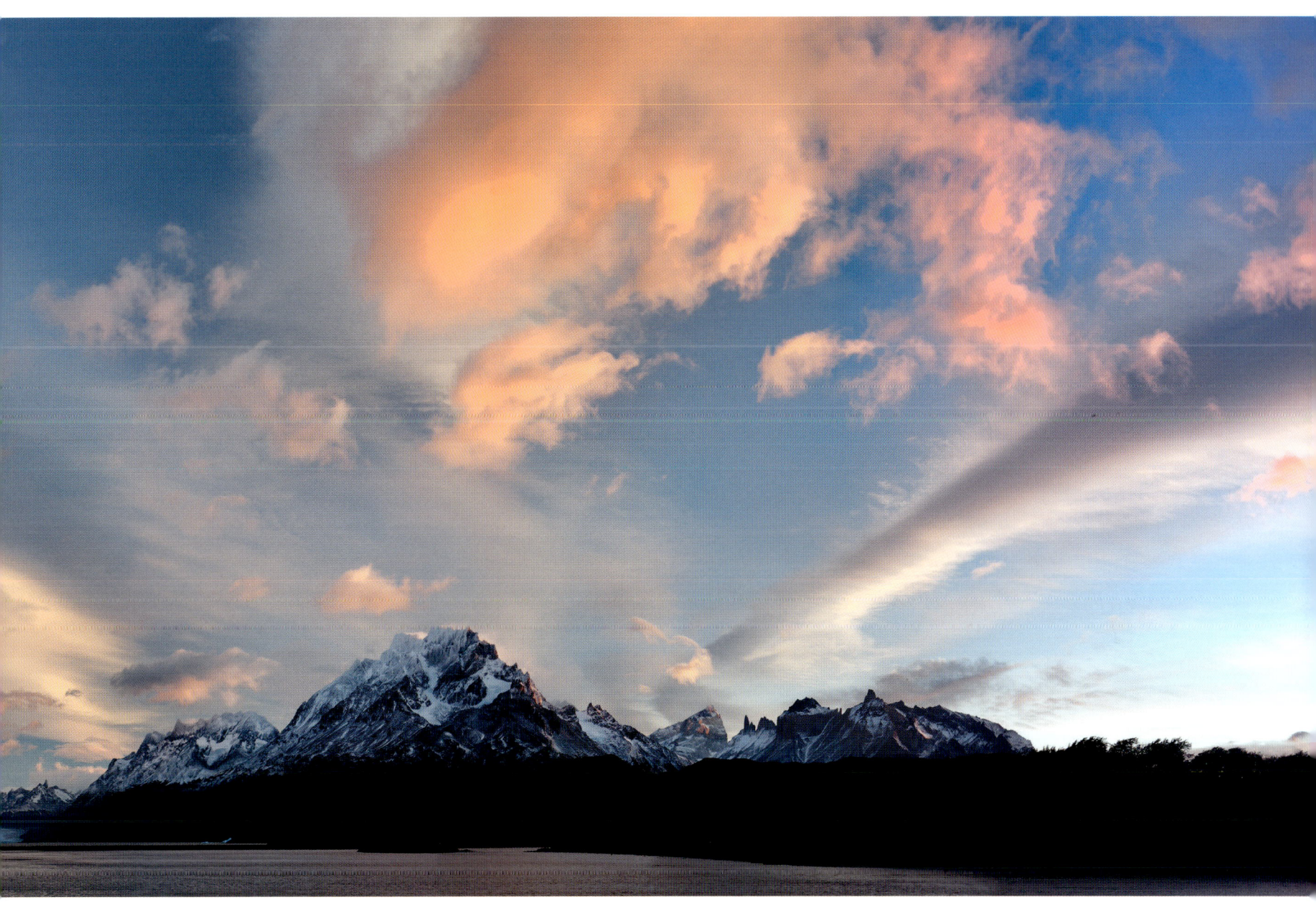

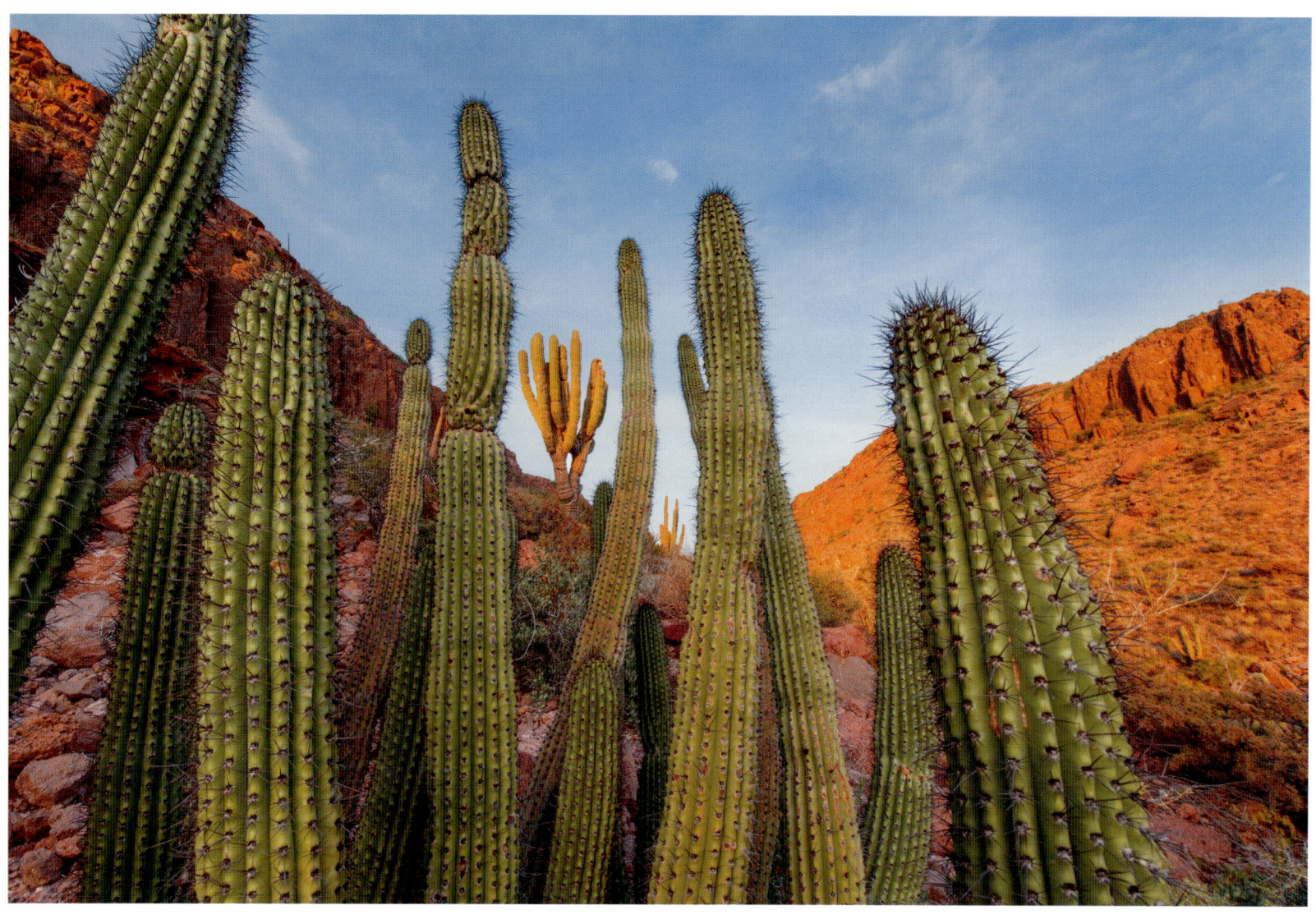

Rising columns of an organ pipe cactus form a natural window around the giant cardon cactus on the background ridgeline. The warm sunset light reinforces the sense of peering through a window. By looking through the darker frame of the cactus into the background, the eye is led toward the light and into the composition.

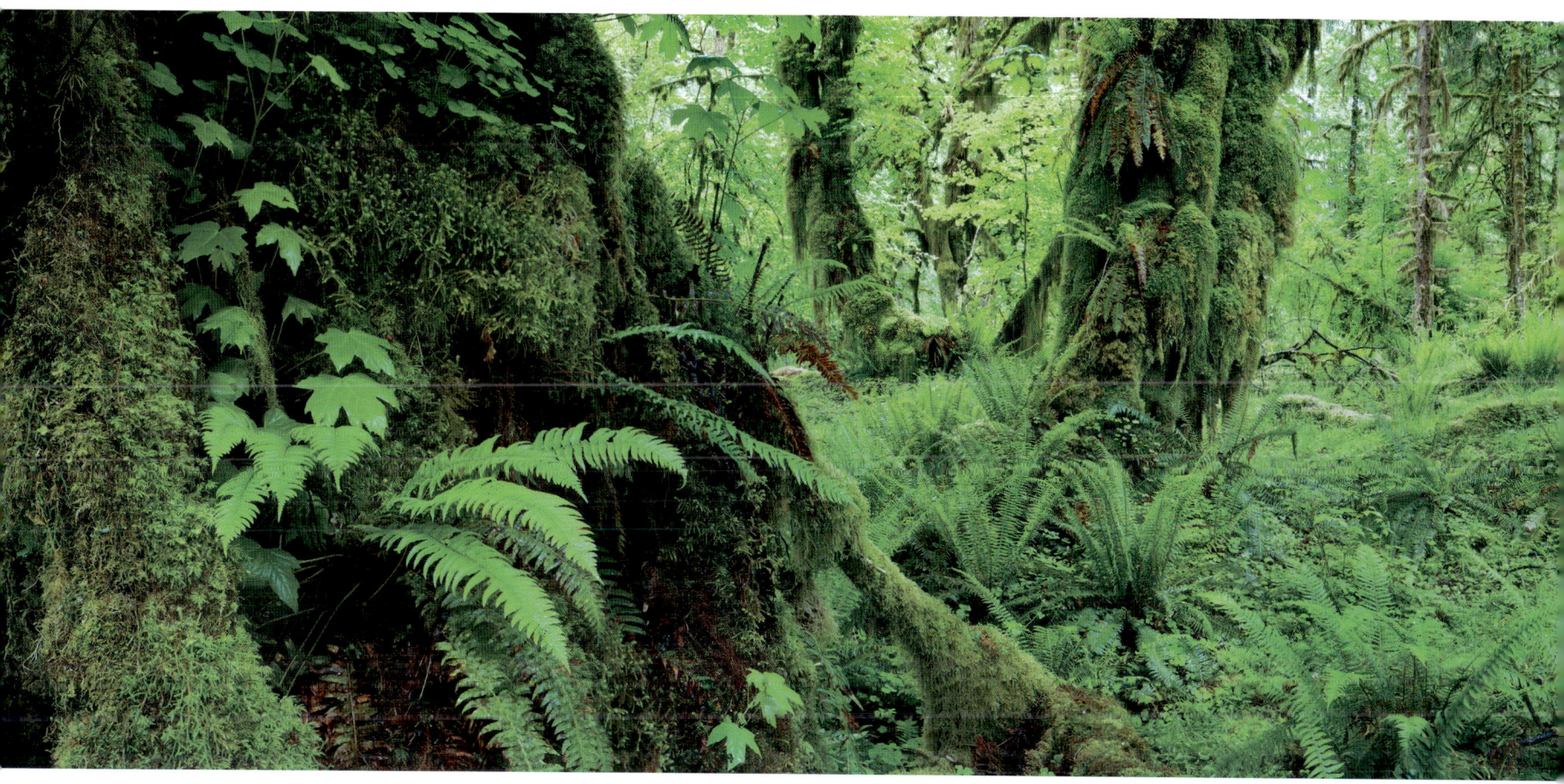

Frames can also be reference points that break a complex scene into pieces that a viewer can more easily understand. They can turn a dense Olympic National Park temperate rain forest, as seen here, into a logical design that is framed by progressively smaller tree trunks. The trees' decreasing sizes from left to right add perspective and they anchor the composition on the left portion of the frame. Delicate ferns are also framed by the dark maple trunk at the left, and the trunk's mass is balanced against the open forest on the right.

In yet another temperate rain forest, this one in California's Prairie Creek Redwood State Park, the twisted, moss-covered trunks form a natural window that encircles the forest scene.

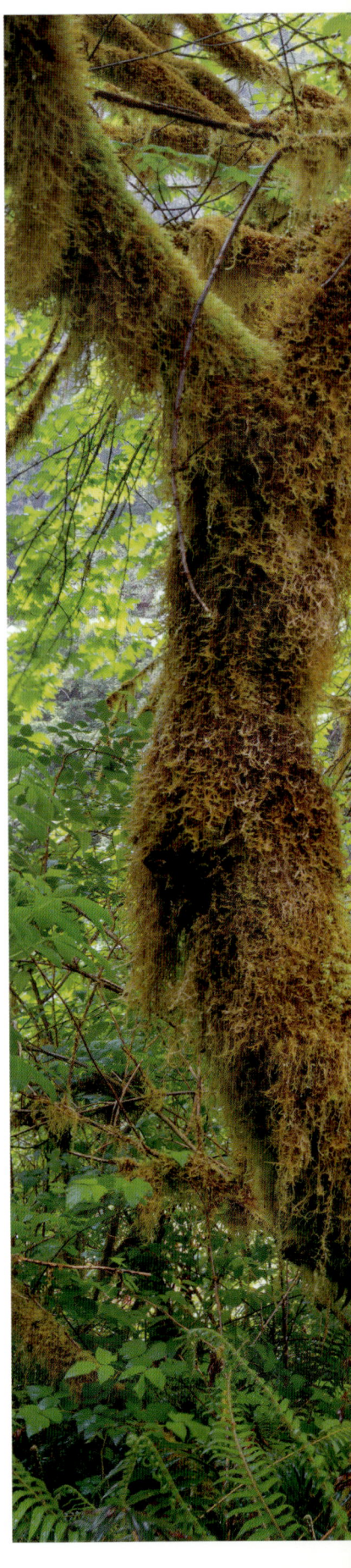

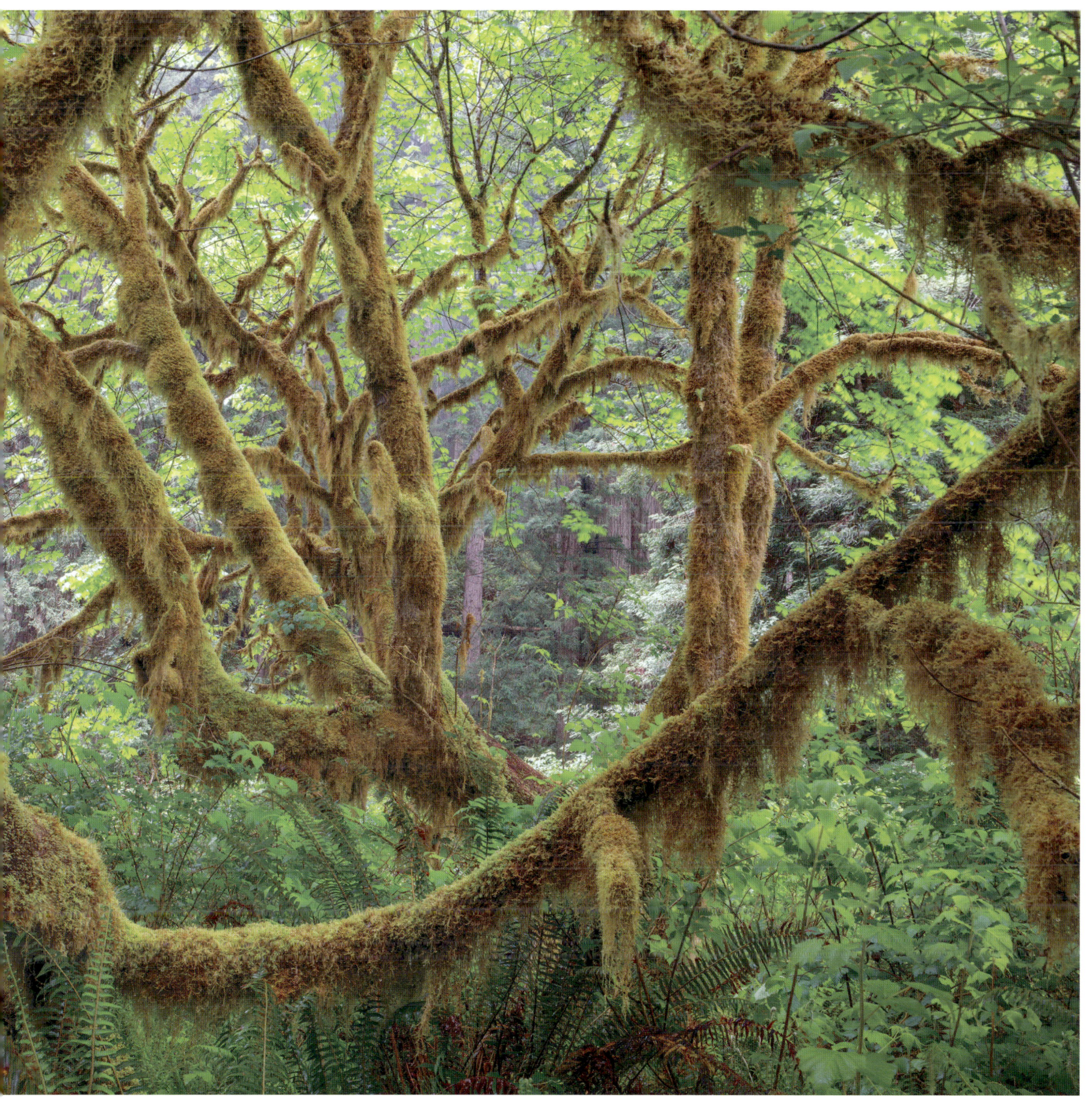

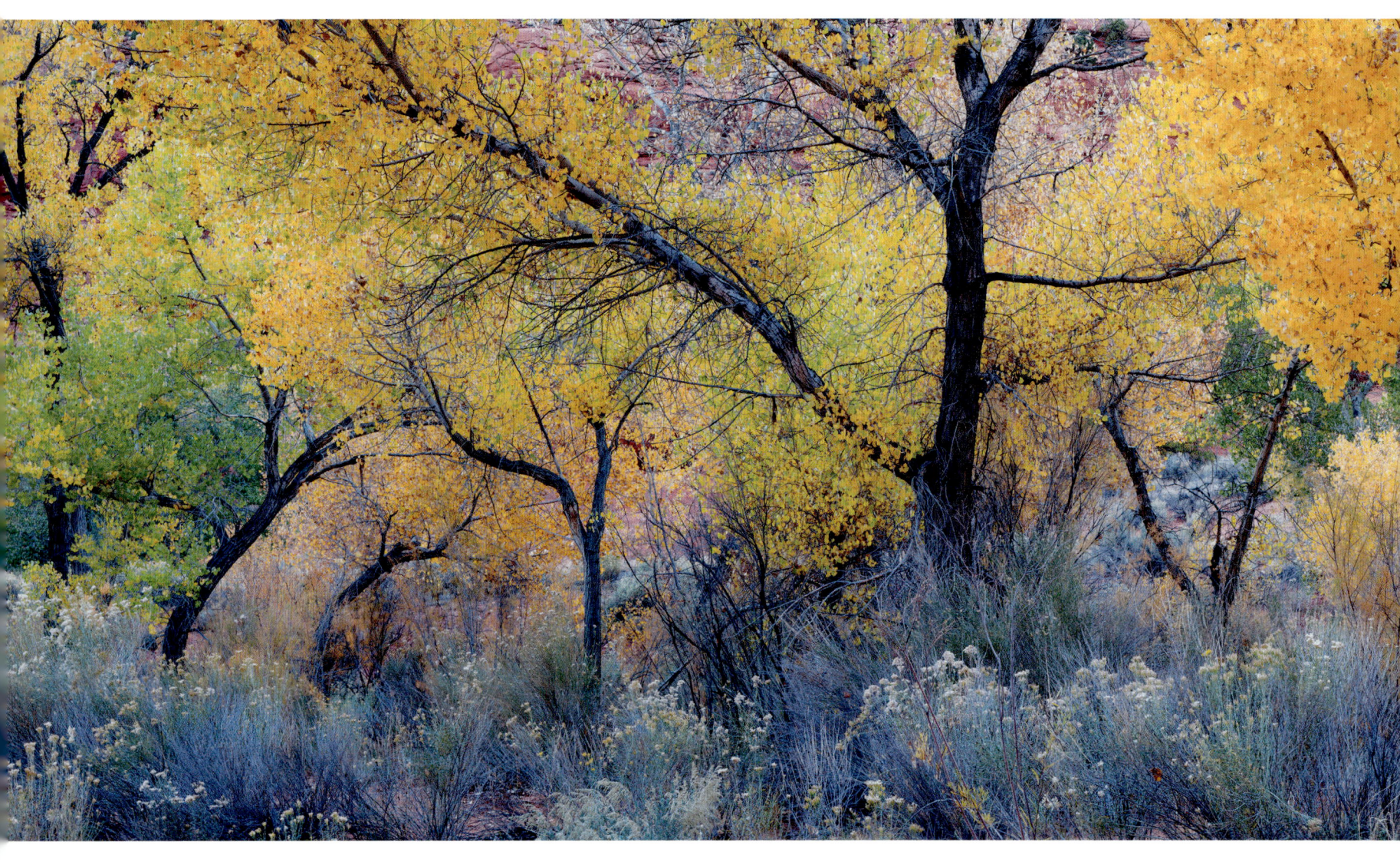

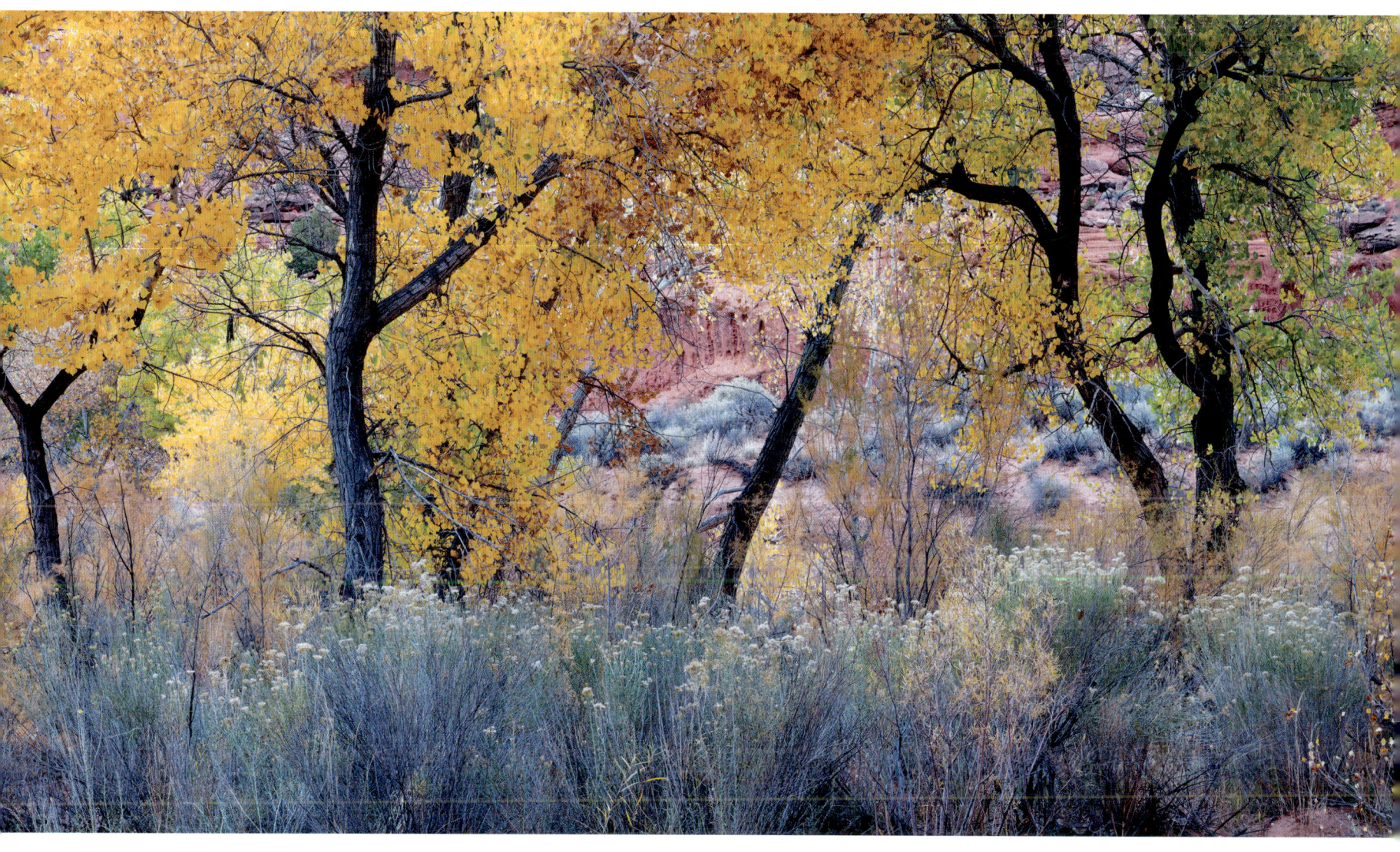

Framing in this panorama is more complex. The colors of Escalante's cotton-woods are framed, yet are also part of the canyon forest scene. The dark shapes of the foreground trees become a frame in the composition. In order to be effective, both near and far elements need to read cleanly without overlapping. The tree trunks collectively form a web of repeating design elements that tie the composition together. The frame pulls the elements together.

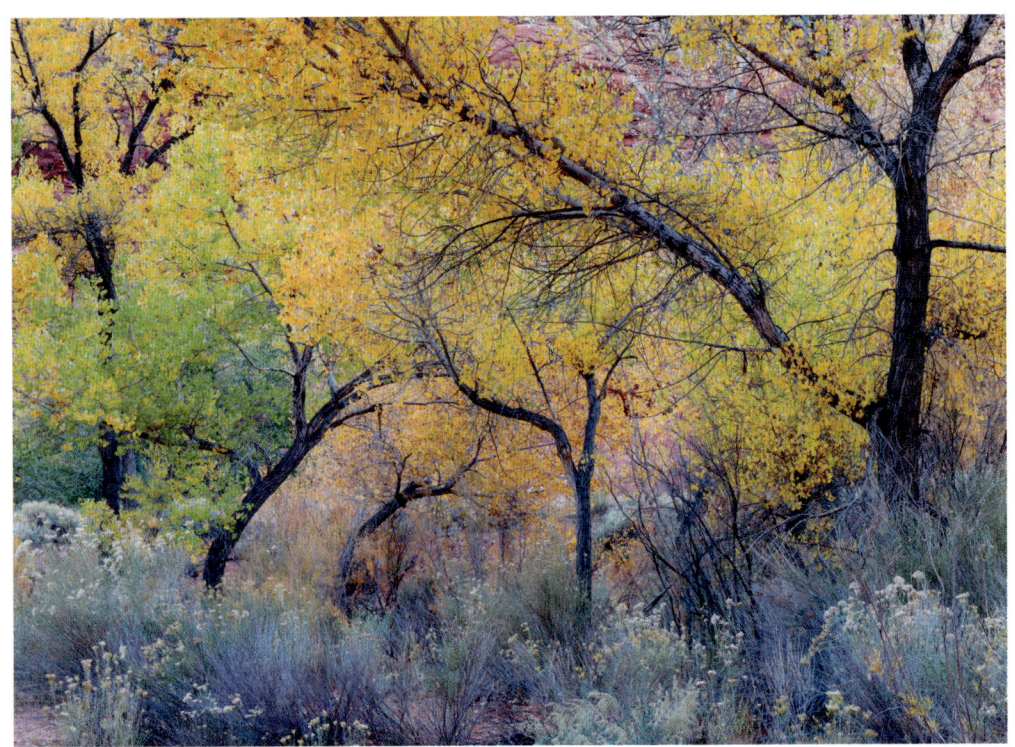

As an exercise, let's dissect the image to find other compositions within the large panorama. Train your eye to find elements in the grand landscape that can function as a logical point to frame an image. We can craft a balanced image by placing trees to form different frames in the same scene.

The left side has a perfectly arched frame encompassing the fall foliage. By balancing right and left distances of the trees to the frame's edge, we can create another compelling composition, as seen above.

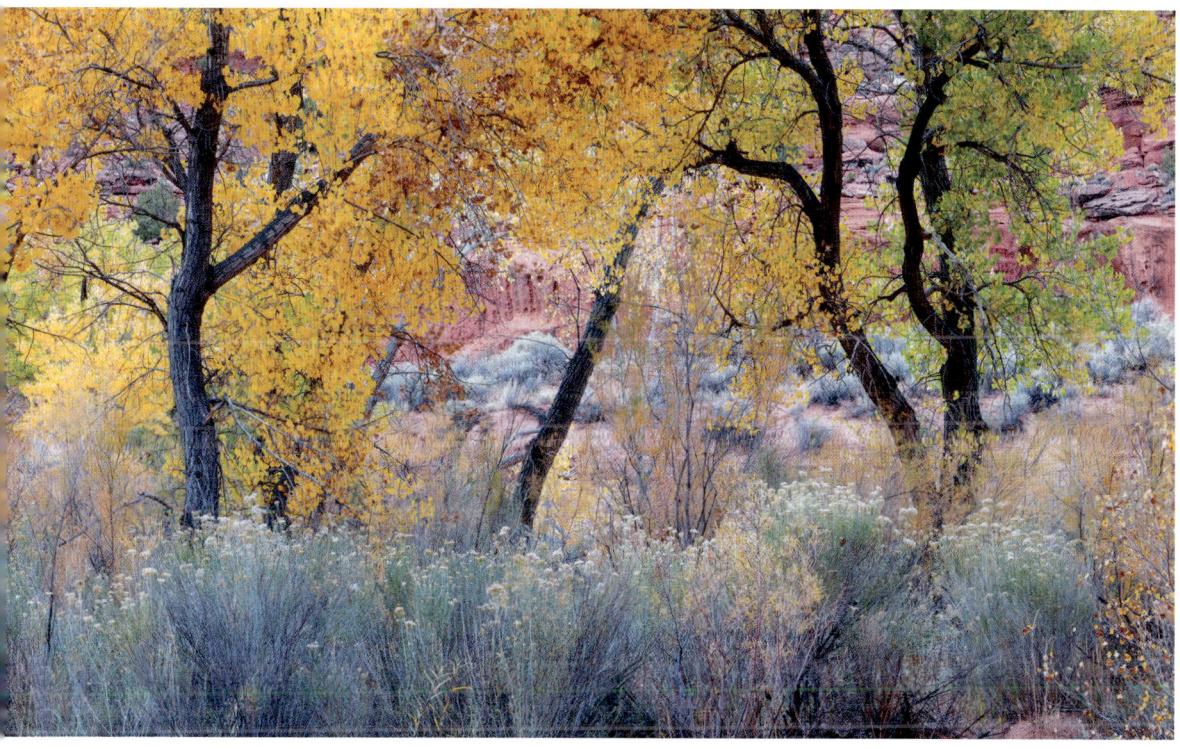

Similarly, the equidistant dark tree trunks of this third image balance the composition while the blue-green rabbit brush in the foreground forms a horizontal line anchoring the scene.

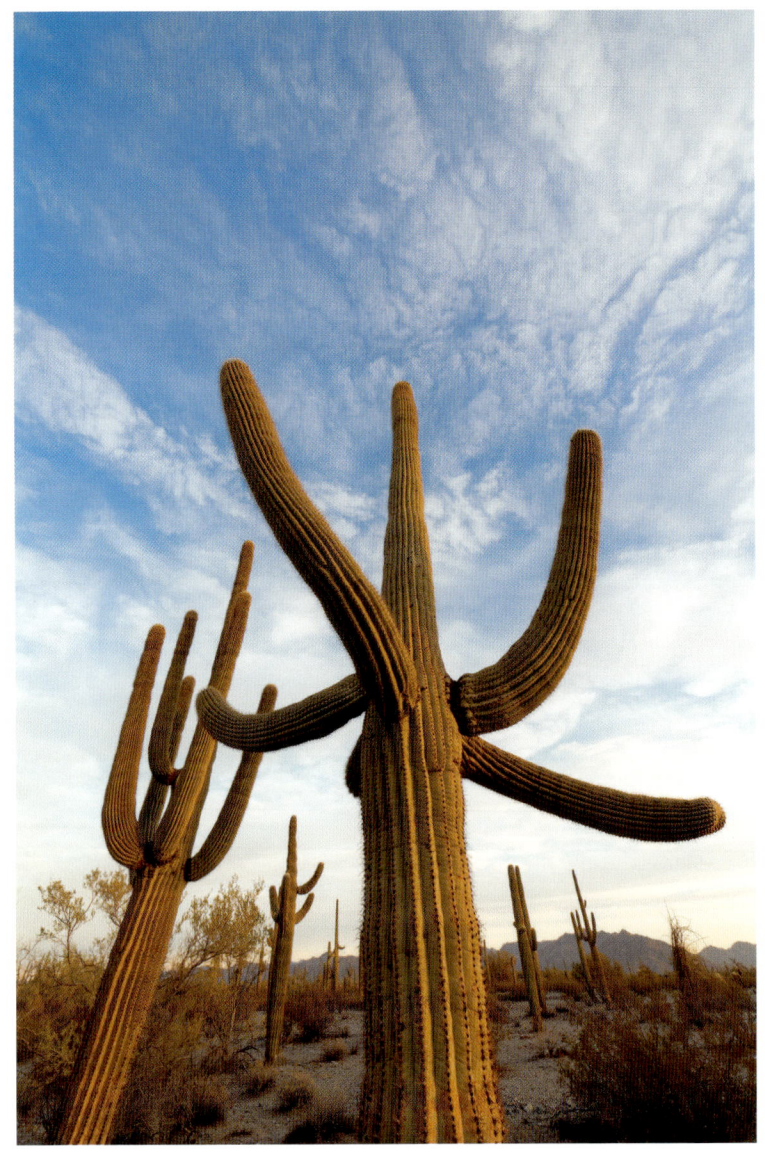

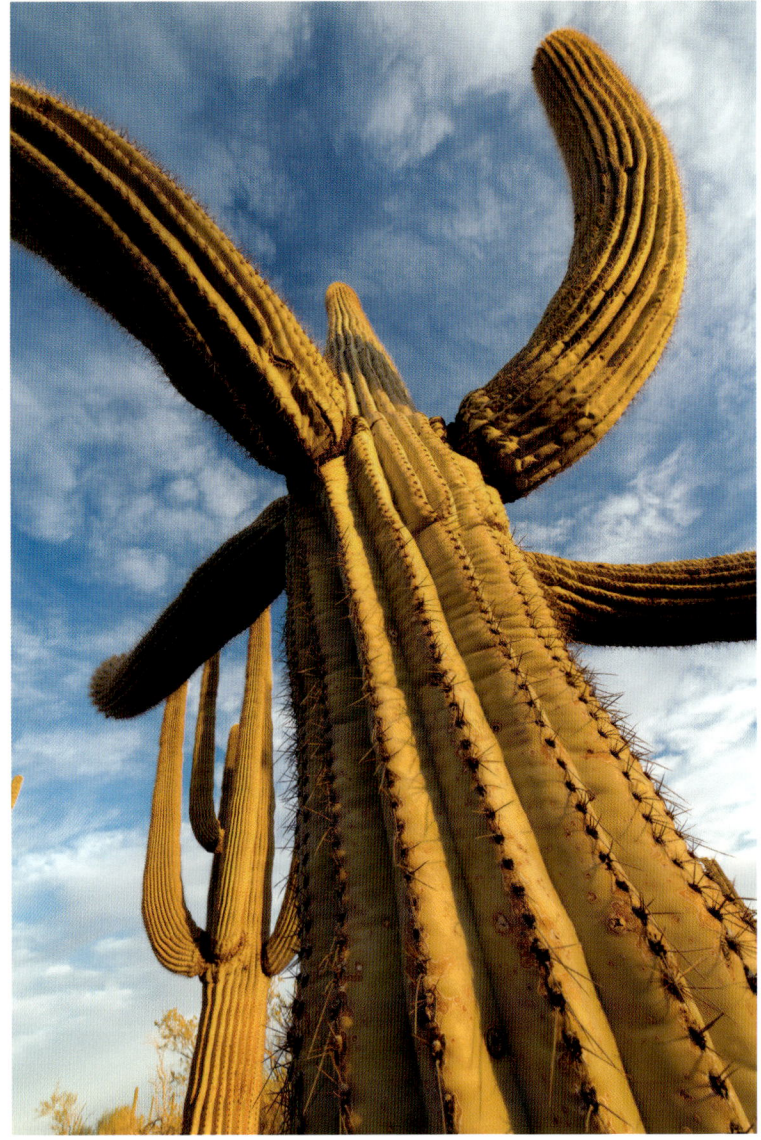

In the first of three different compositions of the same scene, I decided to frame the cactus in the background with the arms of the near cactus. My initial attempt shows the relative positions of both cacti. I used a very wide-angle lens (14mm) but, as you can see, the lens distorts the image when aimed up at the saguaros.

In this second image, I tried to eliminate distortion by moving closer to the foreground subject. This emphasized the size differences between the two cacti, but they merge and the image really does not read well. The image is poorly crafted and looks confusing.

My solution was to get closer still and lower the camera position. I further simplified the scene by including only two cacti, which eliminated the distorted background caused by the extreme wide-angle lens. By framing the image in this way, I simplified the composition, covered the sky, framed the background, and created a window using elements within the landscape. The other problem to overcome was choosing which cactus would appear to be leaning. To resolve this issue, I positioned the camera so that the foreground cactus was leaning into the frame and the background cactus was roughly parallel to the edge of the image. This gives the illusion that the background cactus is vertical (but we know from the first image that it was actually leaning toward the right).

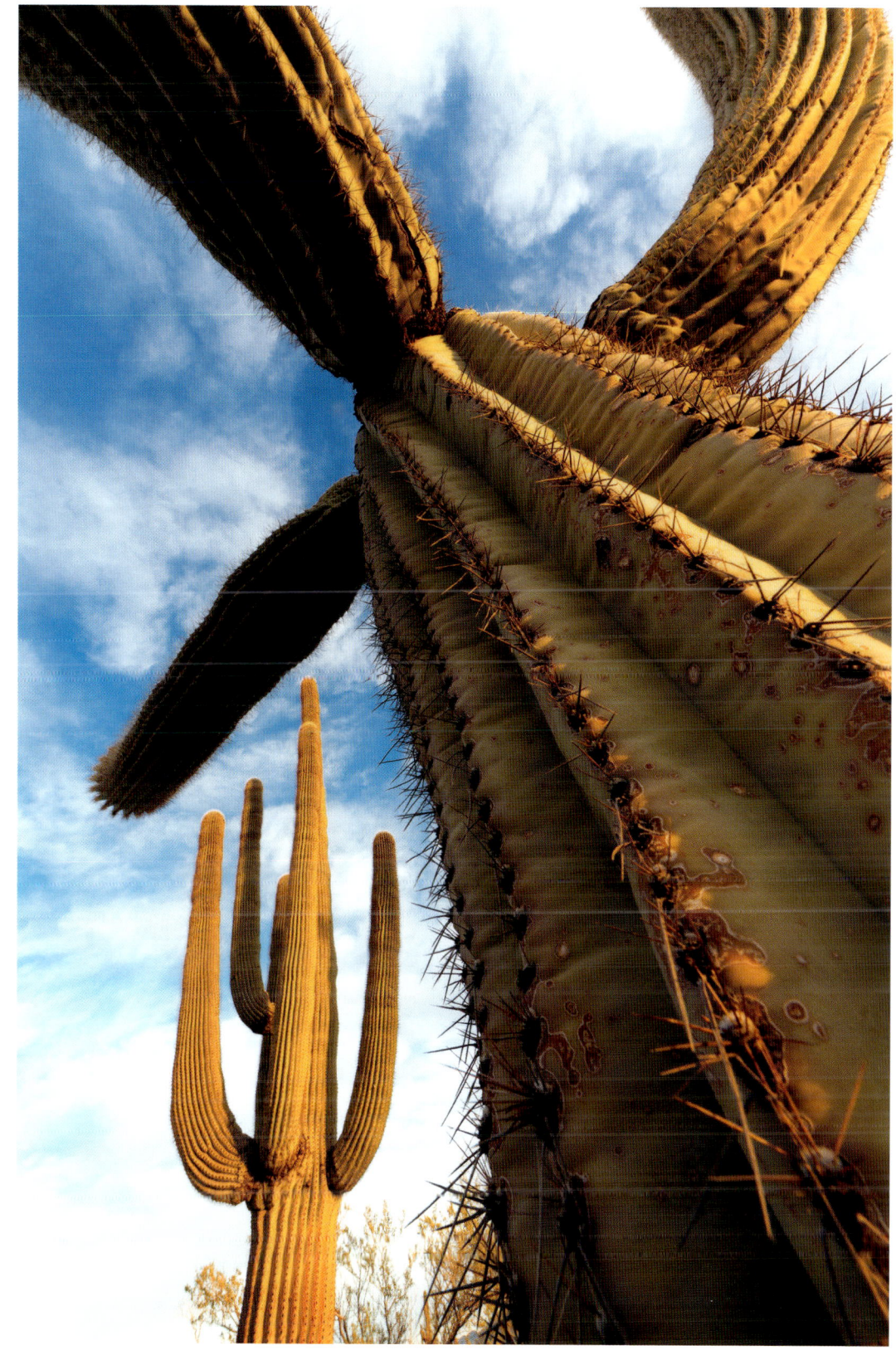

By surrounding the principal foreground design element with a frame of light-colored sandstone, the honeycombed sandstone concretion stands alone and does not merge into surrounding dark-toned formations.

Each time we visualize potential images, we're also envisioning isolating the subject by framing it. Spend time searching out elements in the landscape to form logical windows into the image.

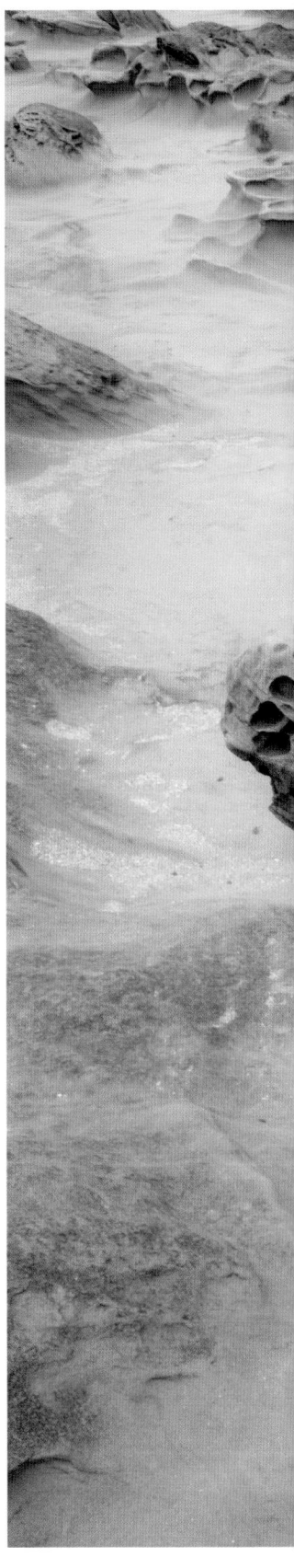

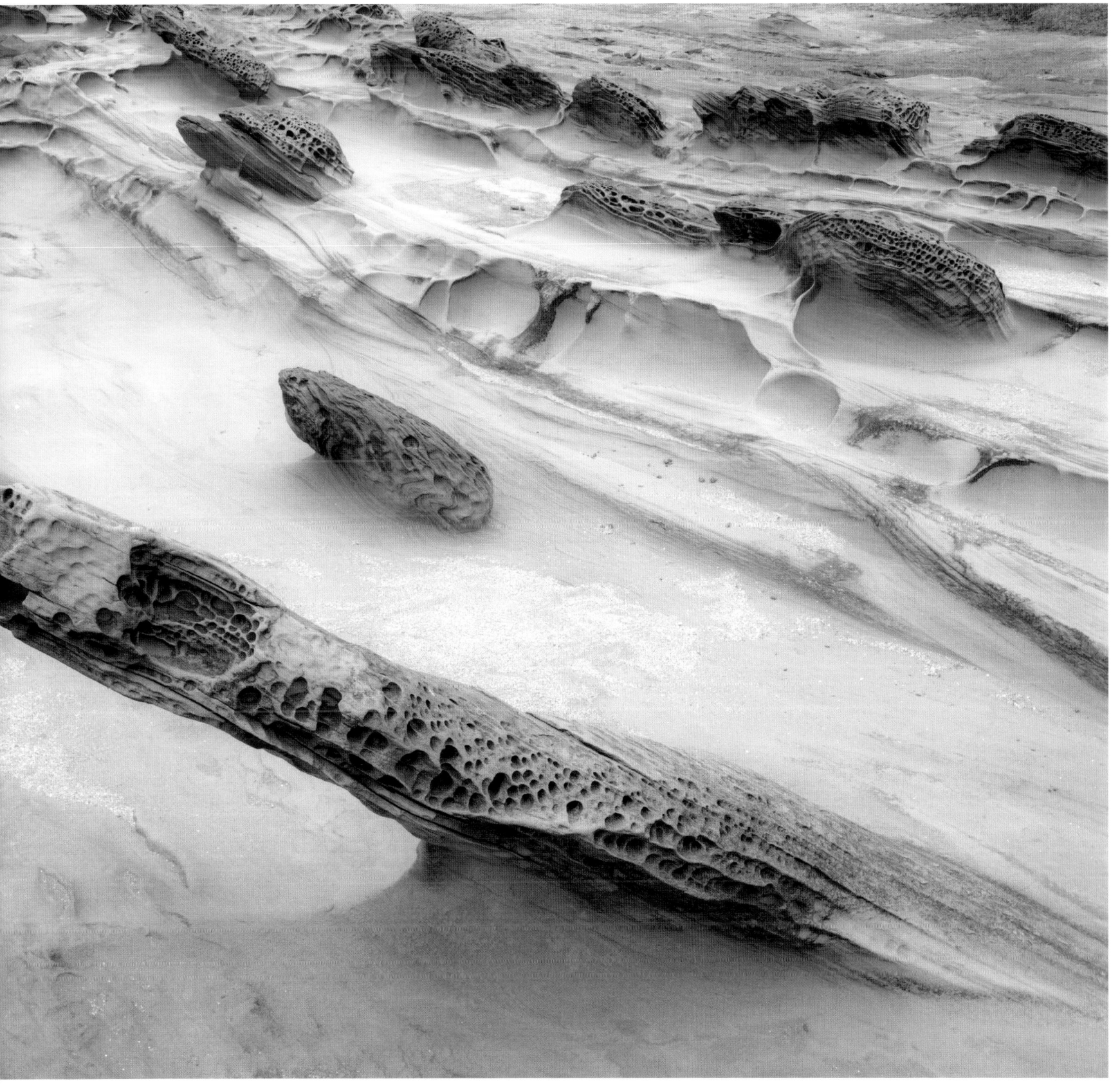

Light

Many landscape photographers say that light is everything. It illuminates and colors our world and it transforms the mundane to magical. Light can add a spiritual dimension to a scene and engender a deep sense of love of place. Its transformative power is undeniable, yet when magic is in the air, I sometimes fumble to record its sublime wonder. I'm often faced with the opposing feelings of just wanting to watch, and those of capturing the scene. When the confluence of solitude and light combine with inspired compositions, I feel privileged and delighted. It's when I feel most creative.

Standing in pre-dawn hours, enduring freezing temperatures is what photographers do. The payoff is that fleeting moment, such as in this image, when the rising New Mexico sun imparts the sense of the divine to a small icy pond and signals the primal beginning of an ancient migration ritual as the Bosque Del Apache's sandhill cranes rise with the sun. With such scenes, it's the backlight that makes the most memorable images. By illuminating the rising vapor, the light also cleanly silhouettes the birds as they emerge from the golden mist.

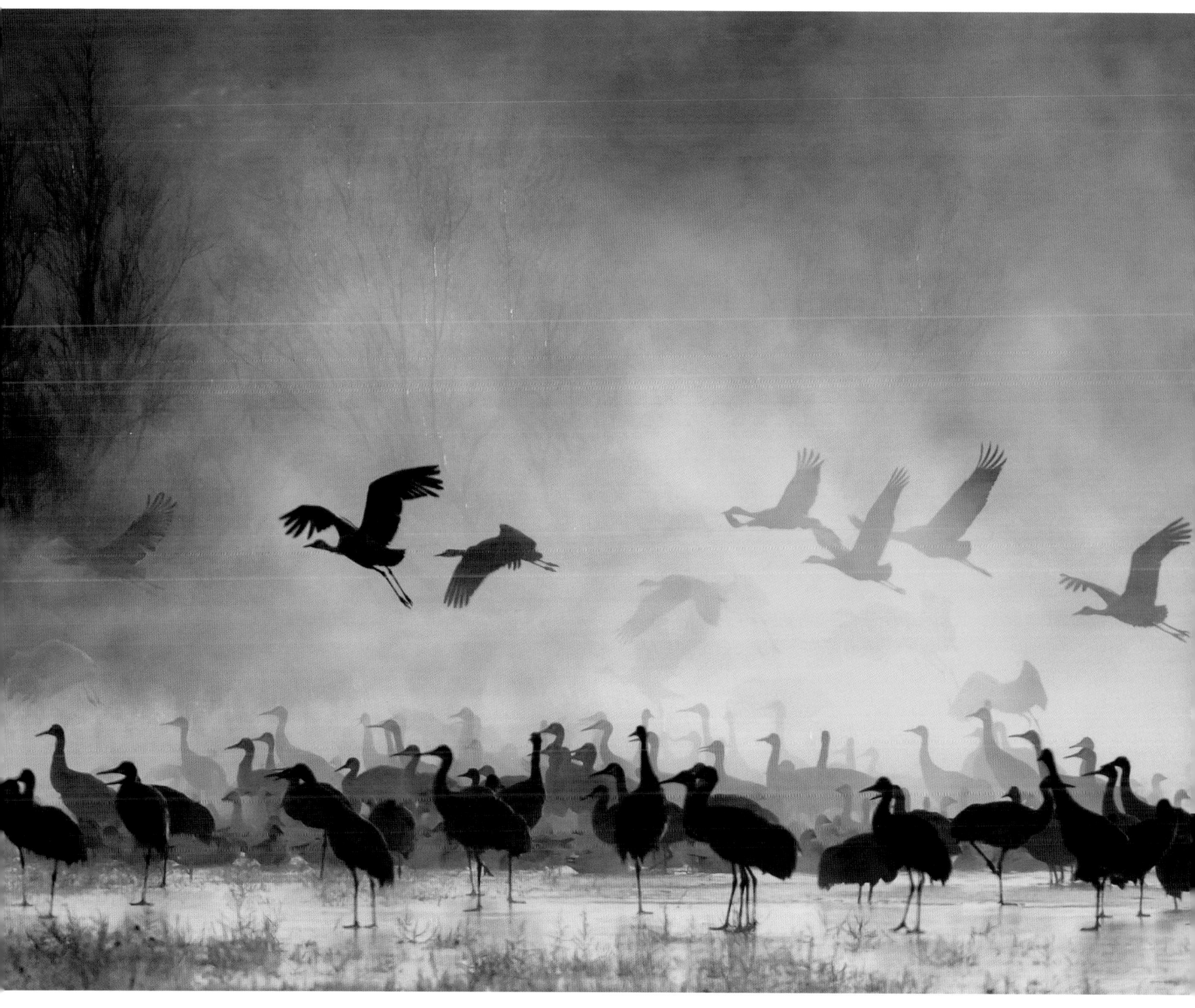

I often talk to my subjects and urge even inanimate objects to perform visual acts. I vividly remember waiting for another sunrise in the foothills beneath one of the world's great mountain escarpments, Chile's Torres del Paine. The sun began to illuminate the Torres, when, almost on cue, a giant lenticular cloud slid into place behind the mountain's reddened stone face. As I carefully spoke to myself, "Don't screw up, Jack," I walked a tightrope between making a photograph and being overwhelmed by a magical experience that I wanted to embrace. It's that sense of awe that gives images power. As Ansel Adams said, he was recording his feelings as much as documenting the place.

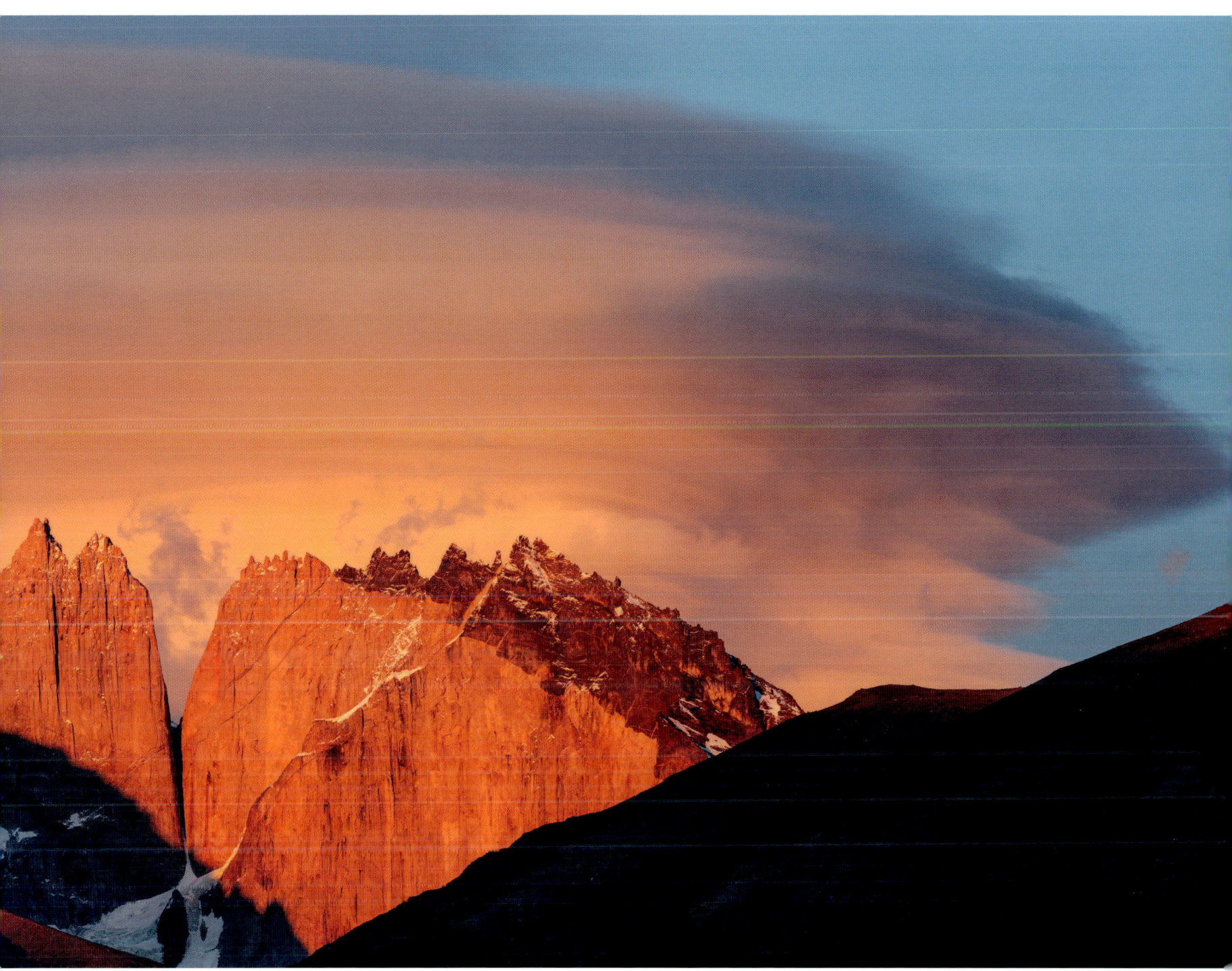

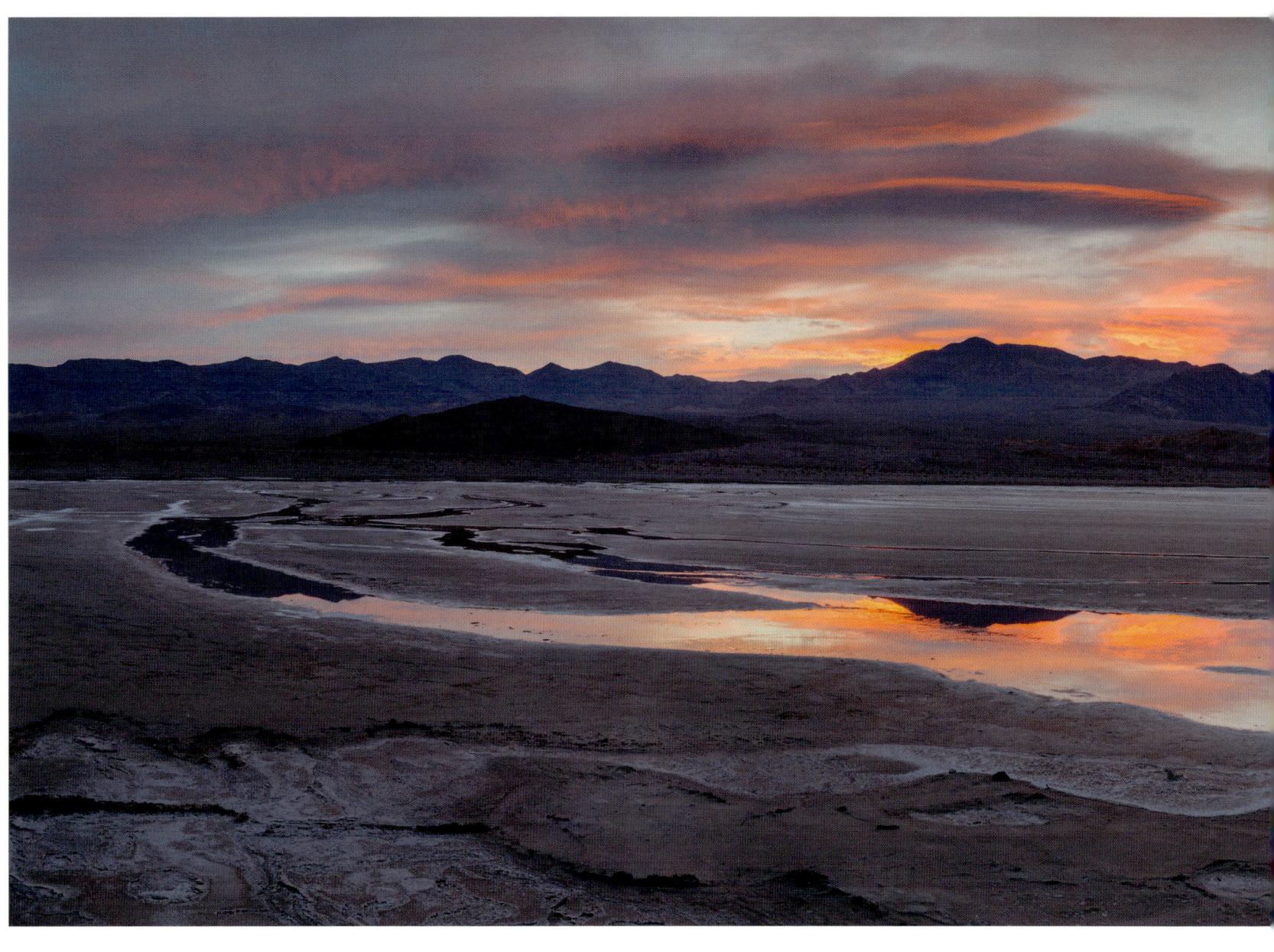

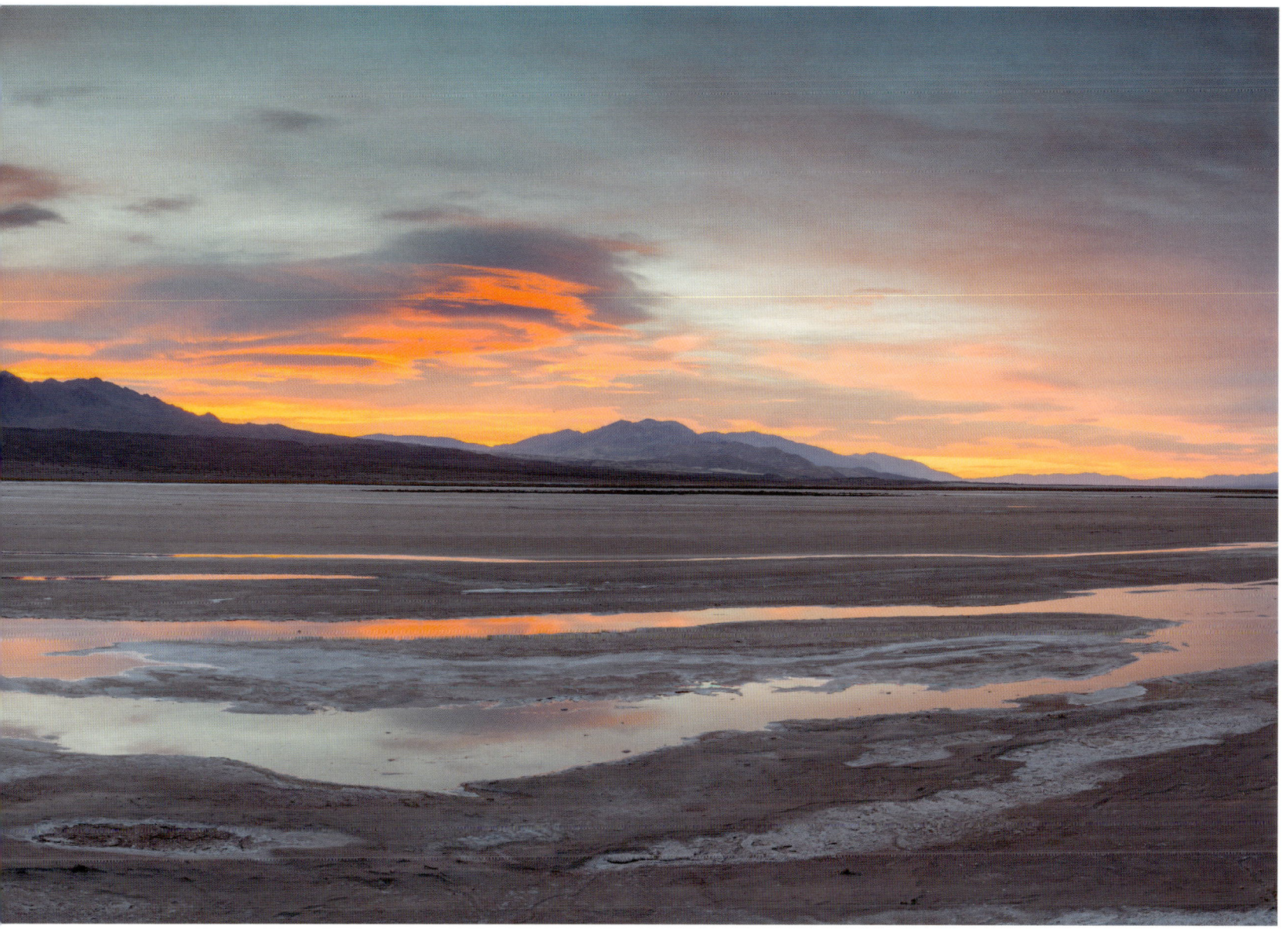

Quiet solitude deepens the connection to the land, and with our senses free from distraction we are open to the design and light. Crunching along the salt flats of Death Valley, where I photographed the image, I feel anything but death. The cloudy sky is fulfilling its promised beauty as color begins the march from the east. I move quickly, watching as the rapidly transitioning light works magic on the rivulets, turning them gold.

In rapid fire, I made several decisions: to create a panorama and to capture the image from a direction that would maximize the reflection of color from the sky. And, after much scrambling, I decided on a foreground that I felt was most compelling. This, of course, is a proximate solution in a very fluid situation. As I begin the tedious process of creating a stitched image panorama I make small mistakes. I curse myself. I worry. Then, I simply stare and rejoice.

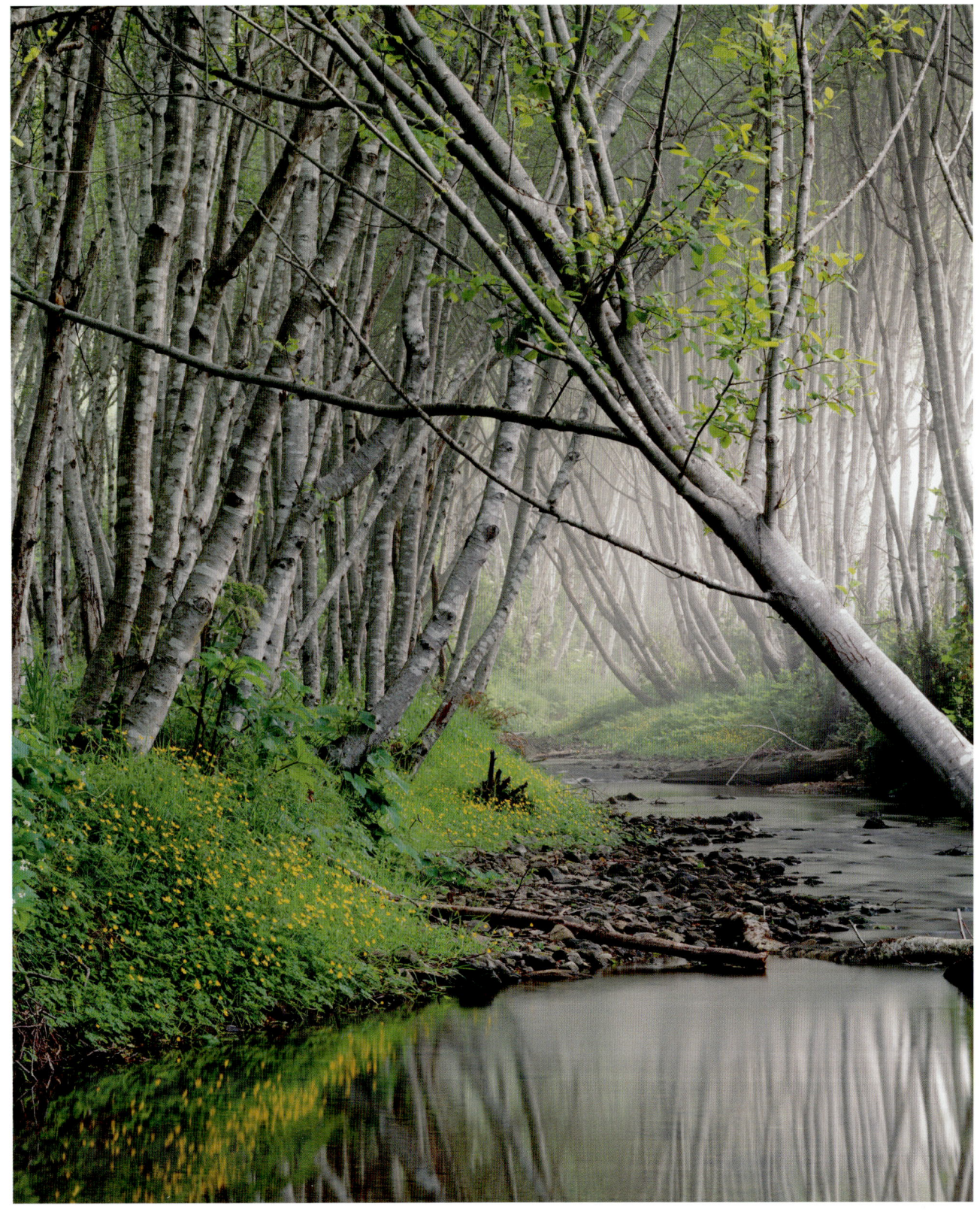

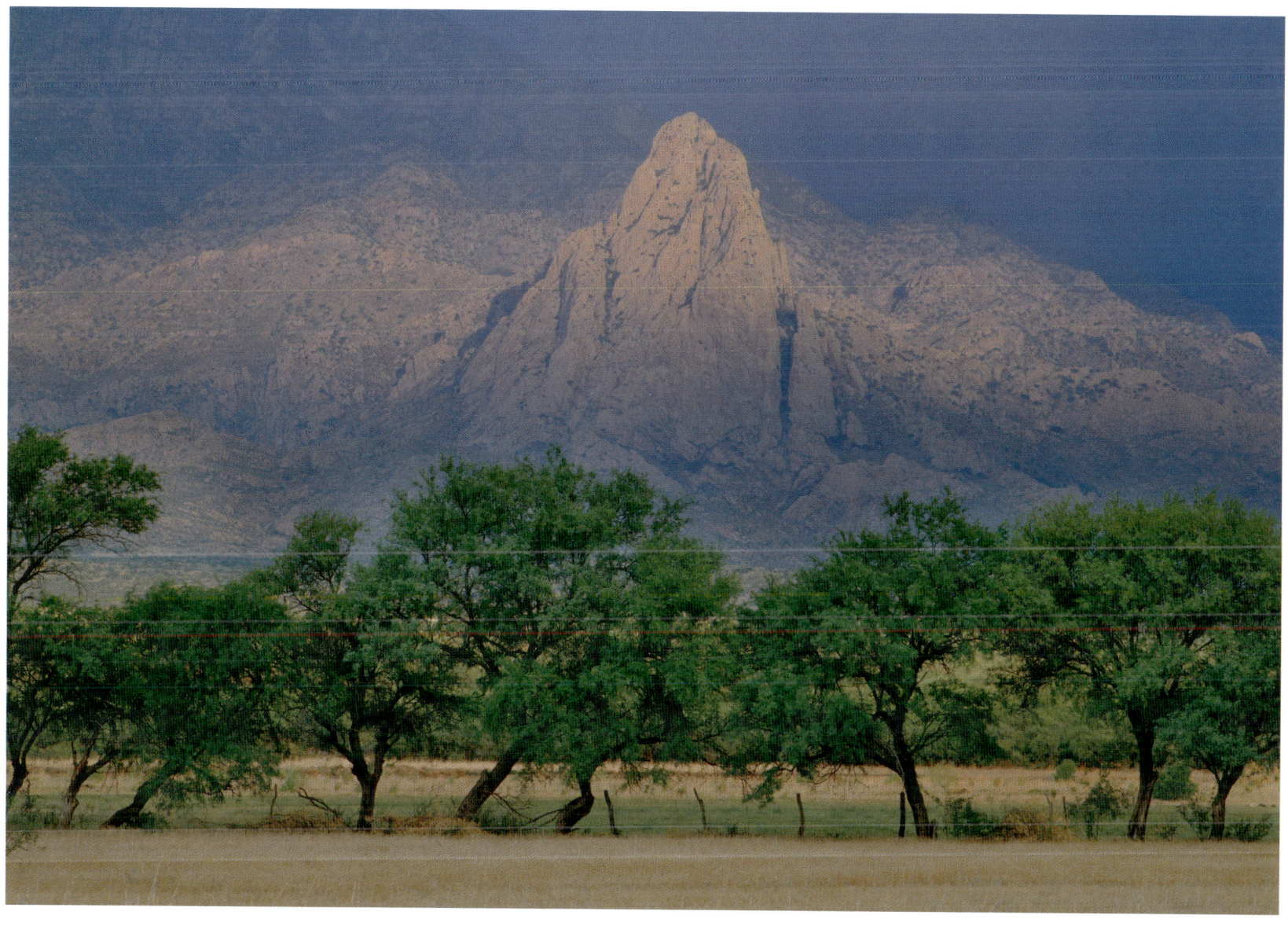

Not all magical light is the warm illumination that results from working at sunset or sunrise. Softly lit alder forests, as seen on the left, can enchant in a far different way. The very lack of color and soft tonal range can evoke a feeling of tranquility. When I created this photograph, I was illustrating how the Sinkyone Intertribal Wilderness Council was preserving and rewilding creeks by creating a series of ponds to promote fish migration. The light was eerie and soft. As I set up to make a photograph, the fog wafted into the scene, creating a world of muted white bark, yellow flowers, verdant banks, and a stream reflecting it all.

A point of light can draw the eye and hold it. The Santa Rita Mountains rising from Arizona's Sonoran Desert uplands have a feature known as Elephant Head (above). I had always been attracted to this rocky outcropping. With the sun sporadically poking through holes in the cloud cover, I noticed a spotlight effect as light transitioned across the land. I chose a telephoto lens to eliminate the distraction of the sky, and I waited.

This image is grounded by a line of mesquite trees and amber grasses, while layer upon layer leads the eye upward to the stone face with its softly lit illumination. The color, the light, and the layers make the composition work.

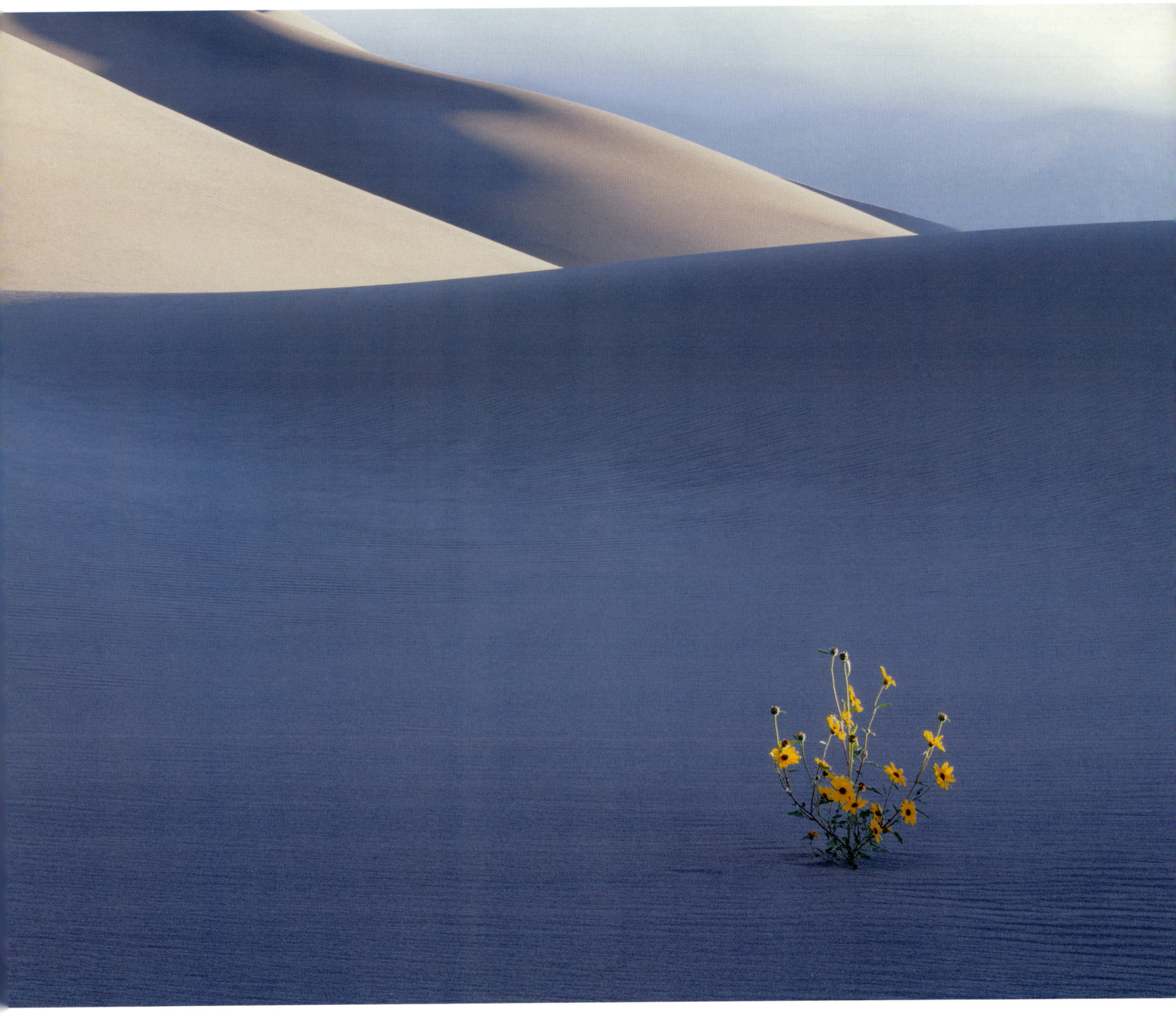

Light colors an image. Its cool blue spectrum inhabits the shadows and warm tones fill areas that are directly lit by the sun. While setting up for this image, by watching and anticipating the light's pathway, I was able to highlight the warm-toned yellow sunflowers against the blue shadow of the Great Sand Dunes National Monument in Colorado. The decisive moment was when only the flowers were illuminated. The image came to life in the early morning light, while the background's shaded ridgelines completed the design.

An image can have a totally different feel depending on whether we choose to emphasize the light's cool or warm color range. We can bolster our image's message by the feeling of coolness or warmth. Sometimes we can play one color against another, creating interest in the juxtaposition.

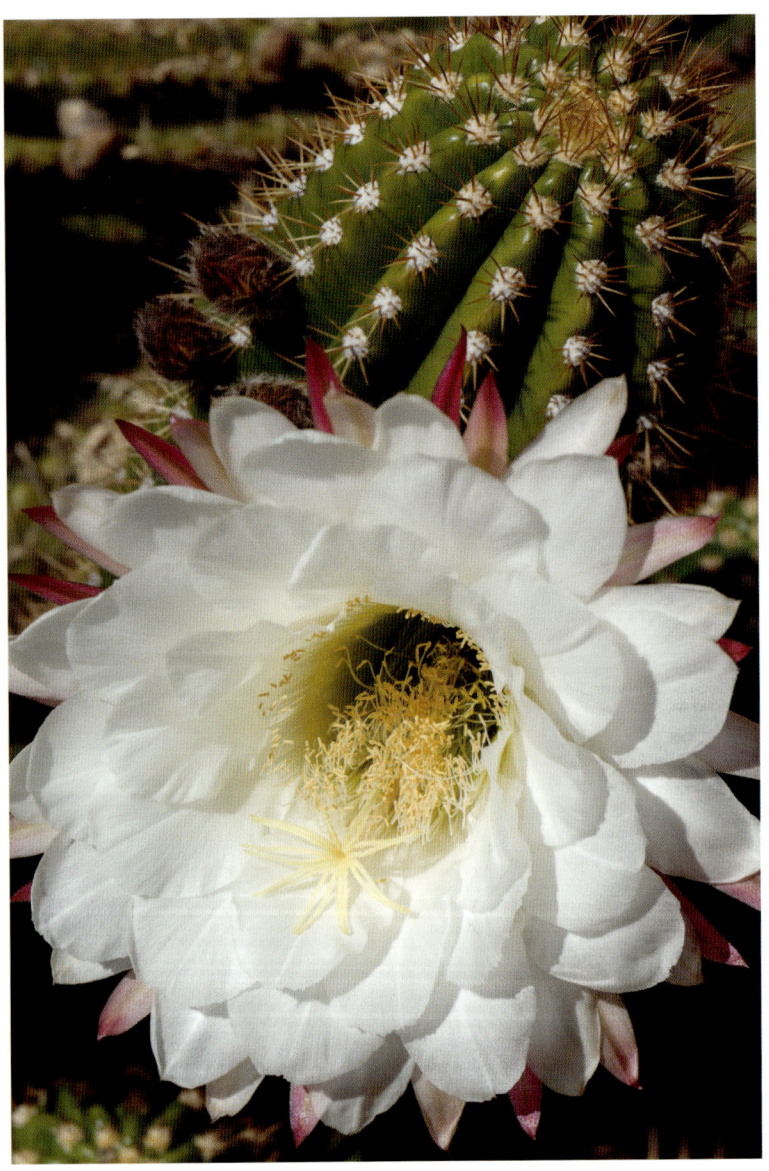

Light can make or break a photographer's best intentions. It's no great surprise that landscape photographers gravitate toward early morning or late-in-the-day photography. The intensity of the light is diminished and, as the light sweeps across the land at a low angle, it highlights the land's texture. The high contrast in midday light can ruin an image. When the difference between the whitest whites and the blackest blacks is extreme, the mid-tones are minimized, and the nuanced and pastel colors vanish.

My midday images of a beautiful showy Trichocereus cactus flower present a stark contrast. In the first image, the flower appears harsh white with little detail in the shadows. There simply is no elegance in this photograph.

By shading the entire scene, I was able to show the subtle colors in both the whites (highlights) and blacks (shadows). The shadows are more open and wonderful pastels are now visible. It became an elegant image with a totally different feel.

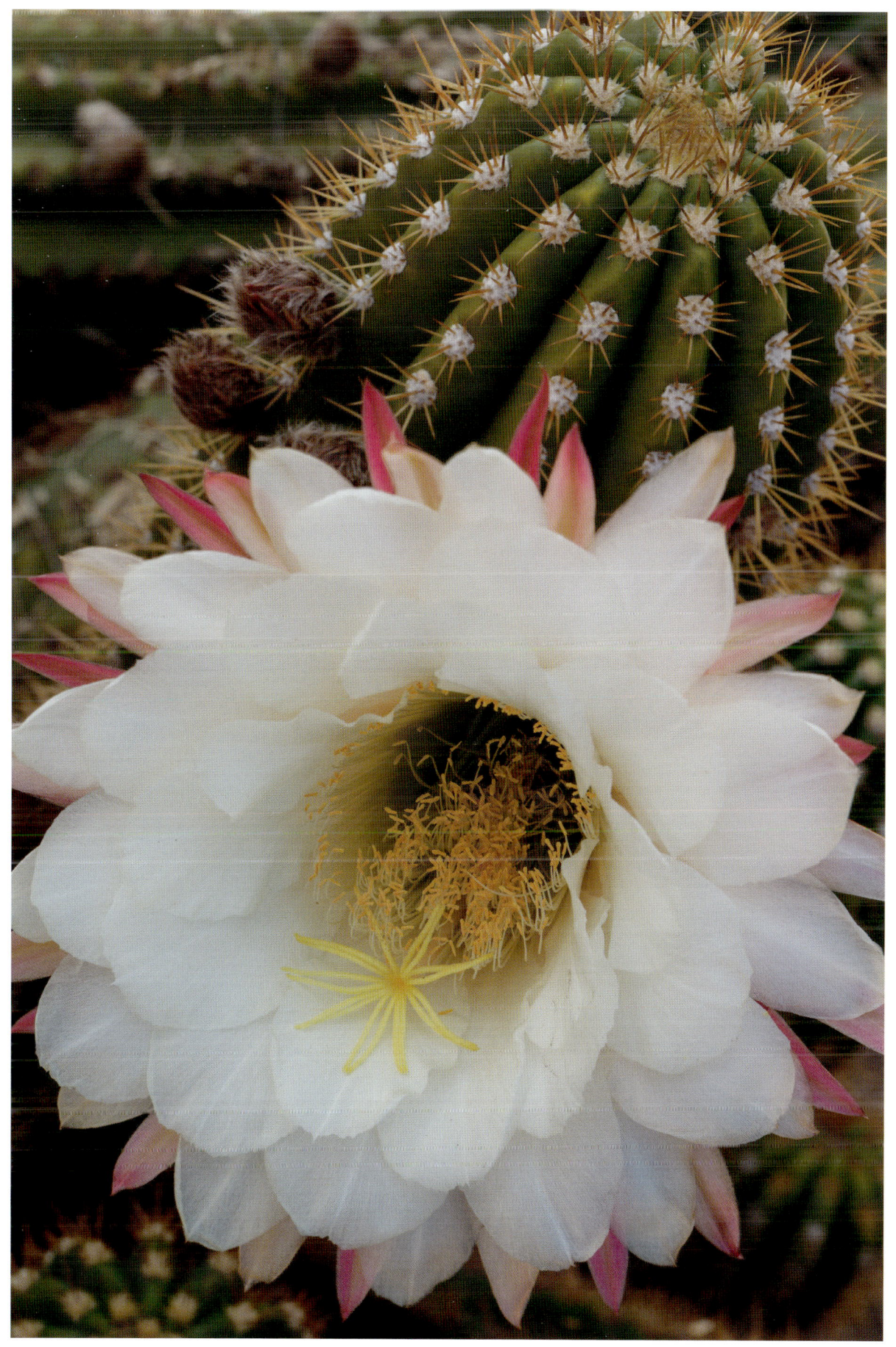

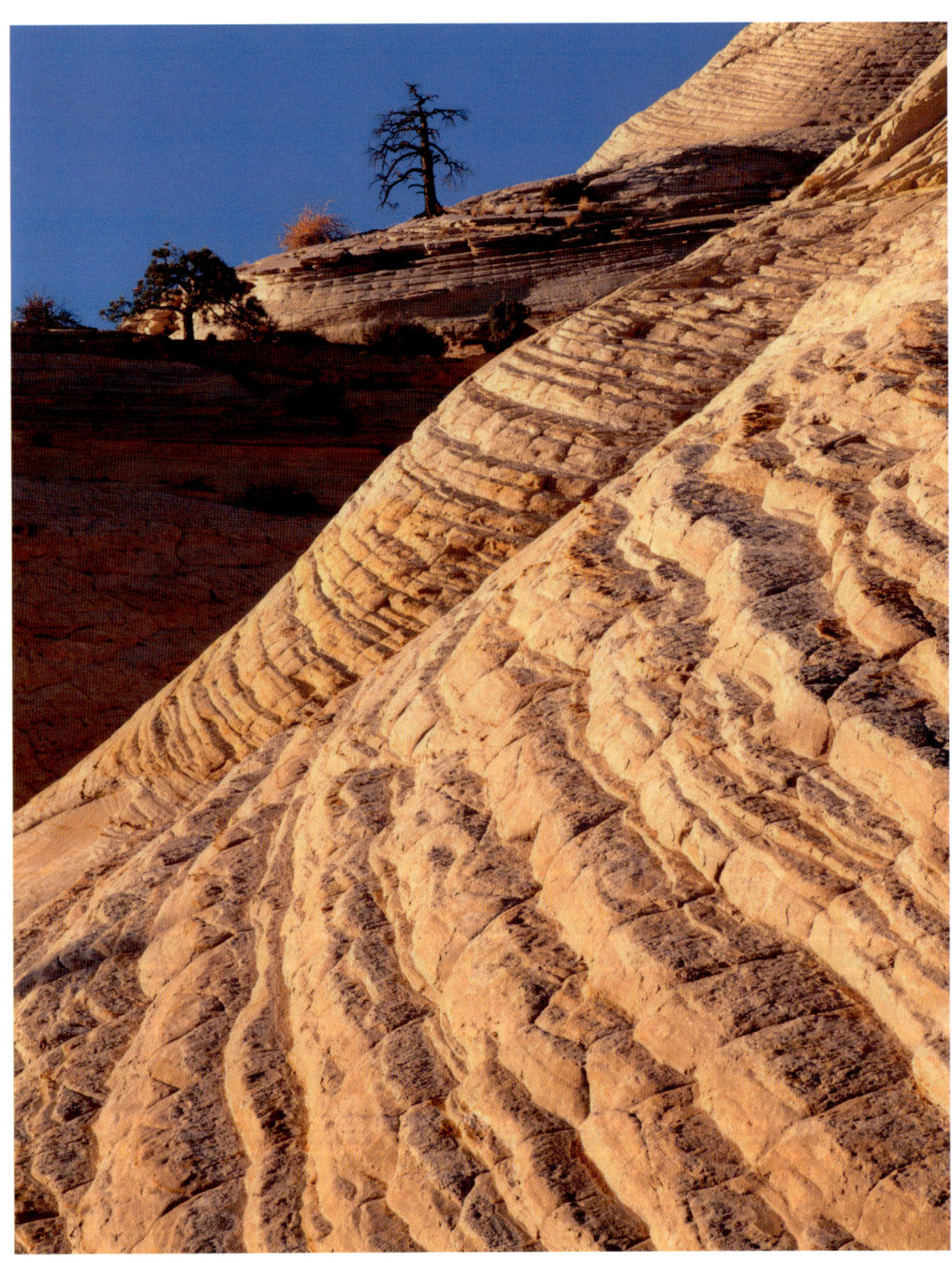

As light traverses the landscape, the color of the light shifts. Sunlit highlights are bathed in warm color, while shadow areas become cool in color. Photographers benefit from "riding the light." (In other words, by continuing to photograph as the light makes its transition across the landscape.) Then they can carefully examine the results to find that magical interplay of warm and cool colors.

Notice the color shift between these two images; the first having been captured only a few minutes before the second. When the sun is closer to the horizon the shadows are longer and bluer, as demonstrated in the image to the right. Becoming a student of light quality is key to creating great images.

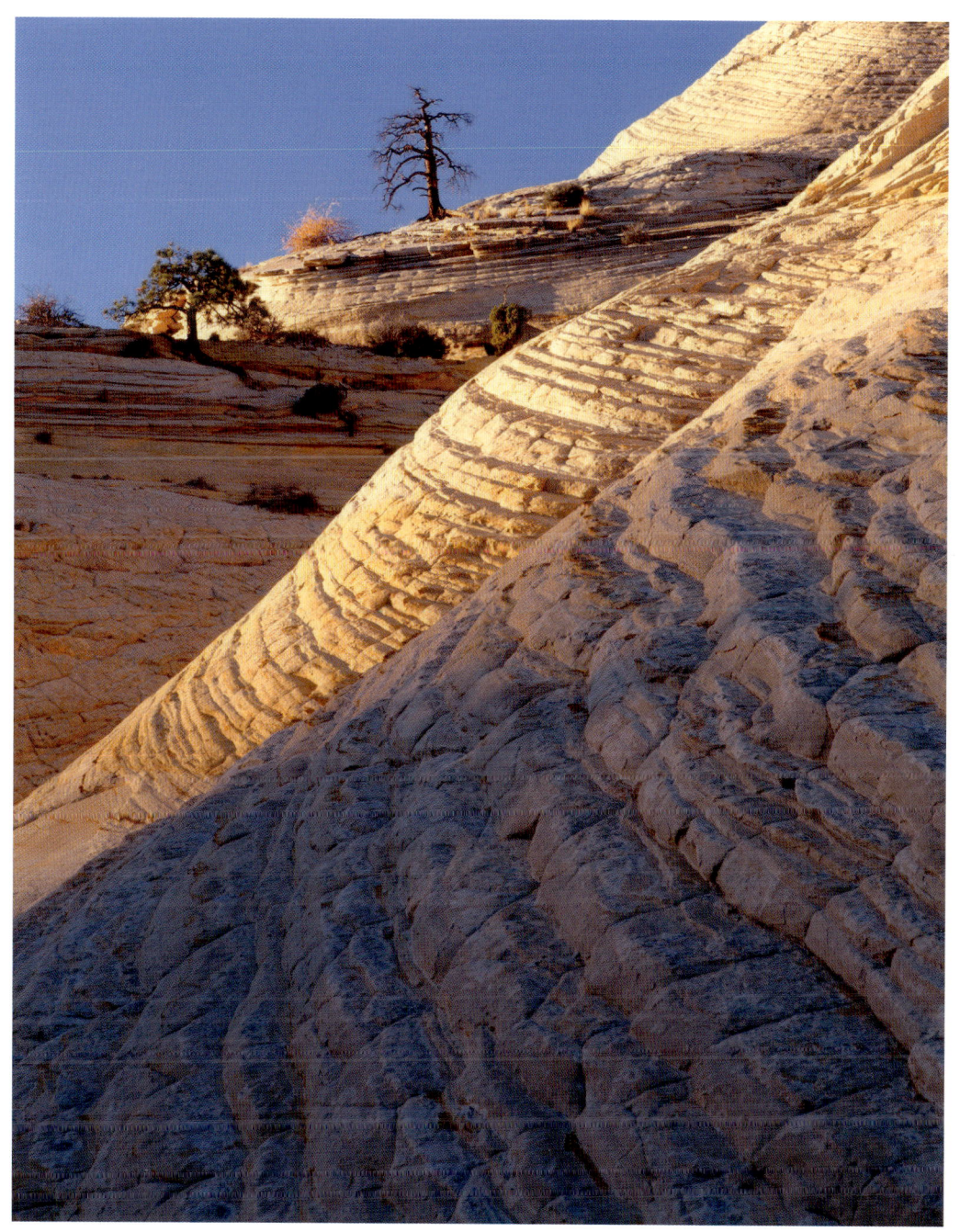

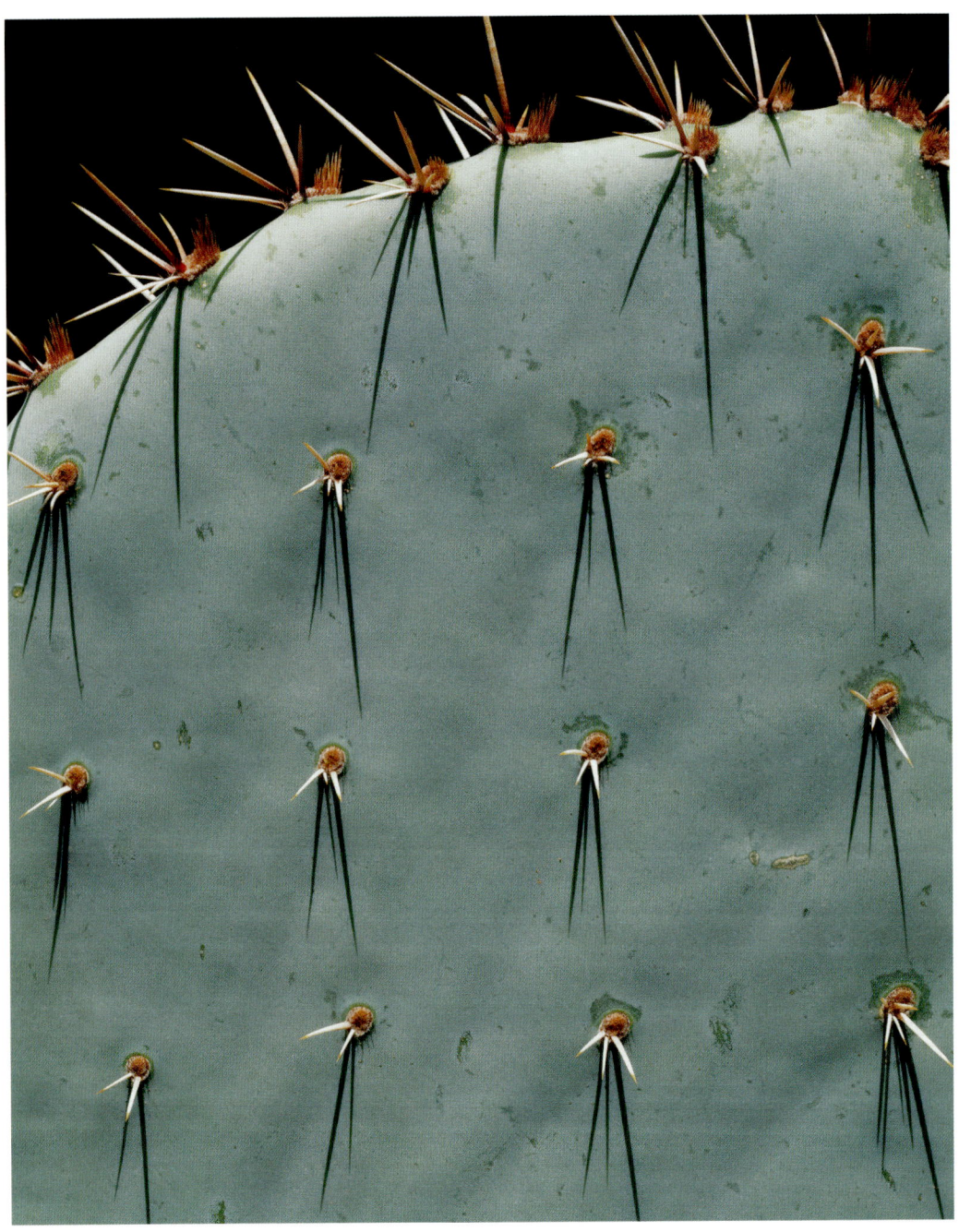

Light creates form and it's a wonderful, and useful, exercise to simply watch the light's transition and transformation of a subject. As the sun makes its way across the sky, it changes the basic design of a subject.

The simple play of light and shadow on this prickly pear cactus has a completely different look and feel between these two images. In the first image we see the effect of the harsh, overhead, midday light and the second image shows how the sunlight transitioned slightly to backlight the subject.

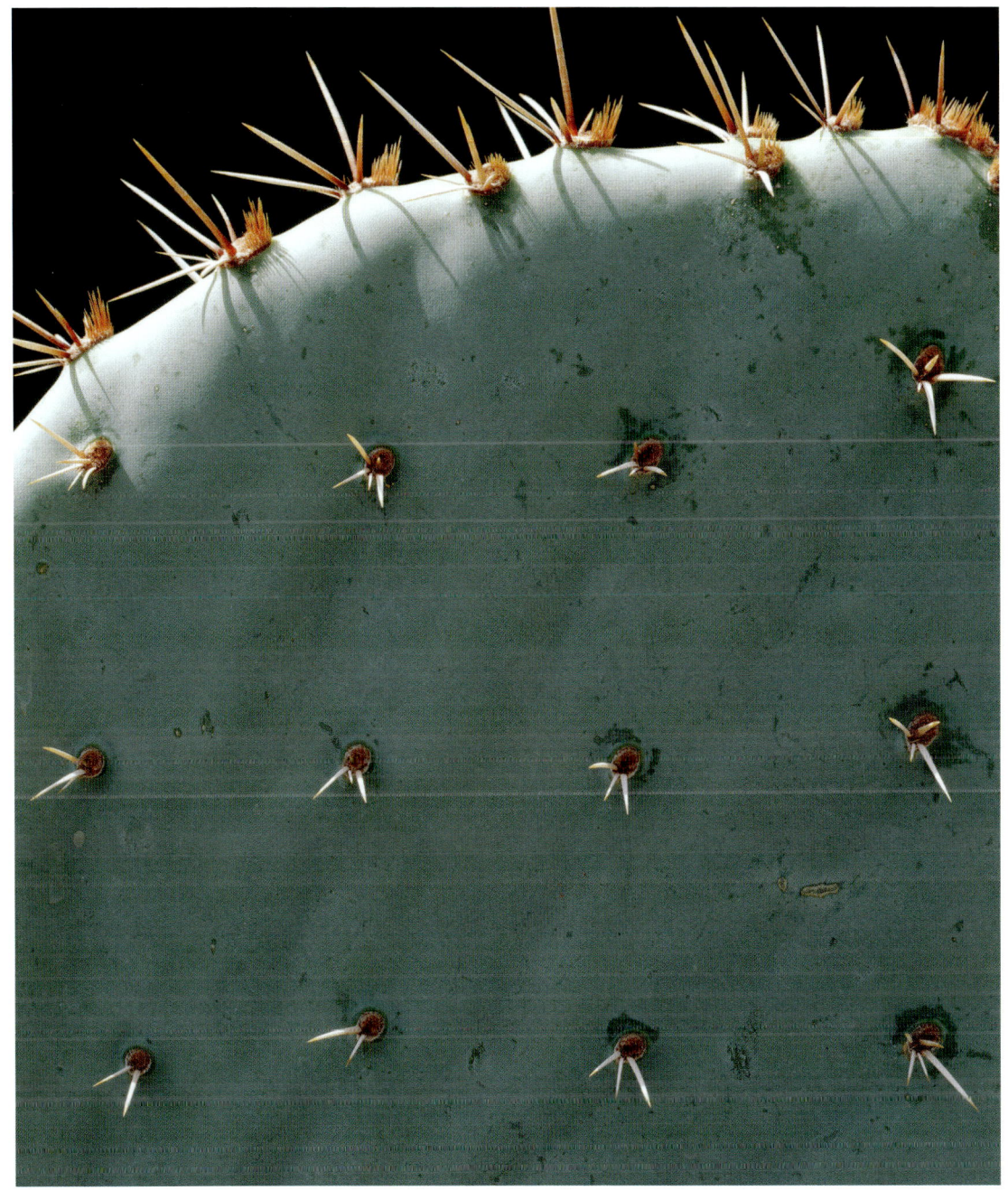

Juxtaposition

We all react to contrasting elements in images. They can be warm-toned colors like red and yellow against cool-toned colors like blue and cyan. Contrasts can be softness against hardness, life against death, large against small, or different shapes juxtaposed against each other. Contrasts add to the power of an image.

Primal themes are very powerful. The charred lodge pole pines that died in the Yellowstone National Park fire poured nitrogen into the ground. In amazing juxtaposition, yellow arnica flowers burst out of the carnage. The classic and powerful visual play on death and rebirth adds strength to the image. From a design perspective, contrast is added by the different colors as well as the divergent shapes of straight lines and circles. The resulting image gains visual intensity from its many juxtapositions.

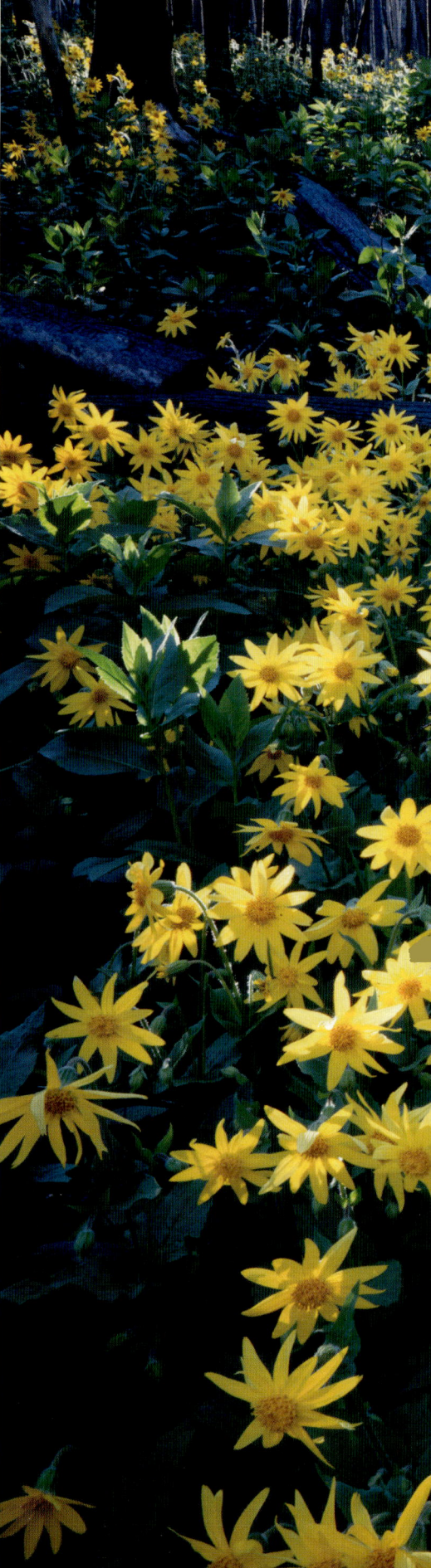

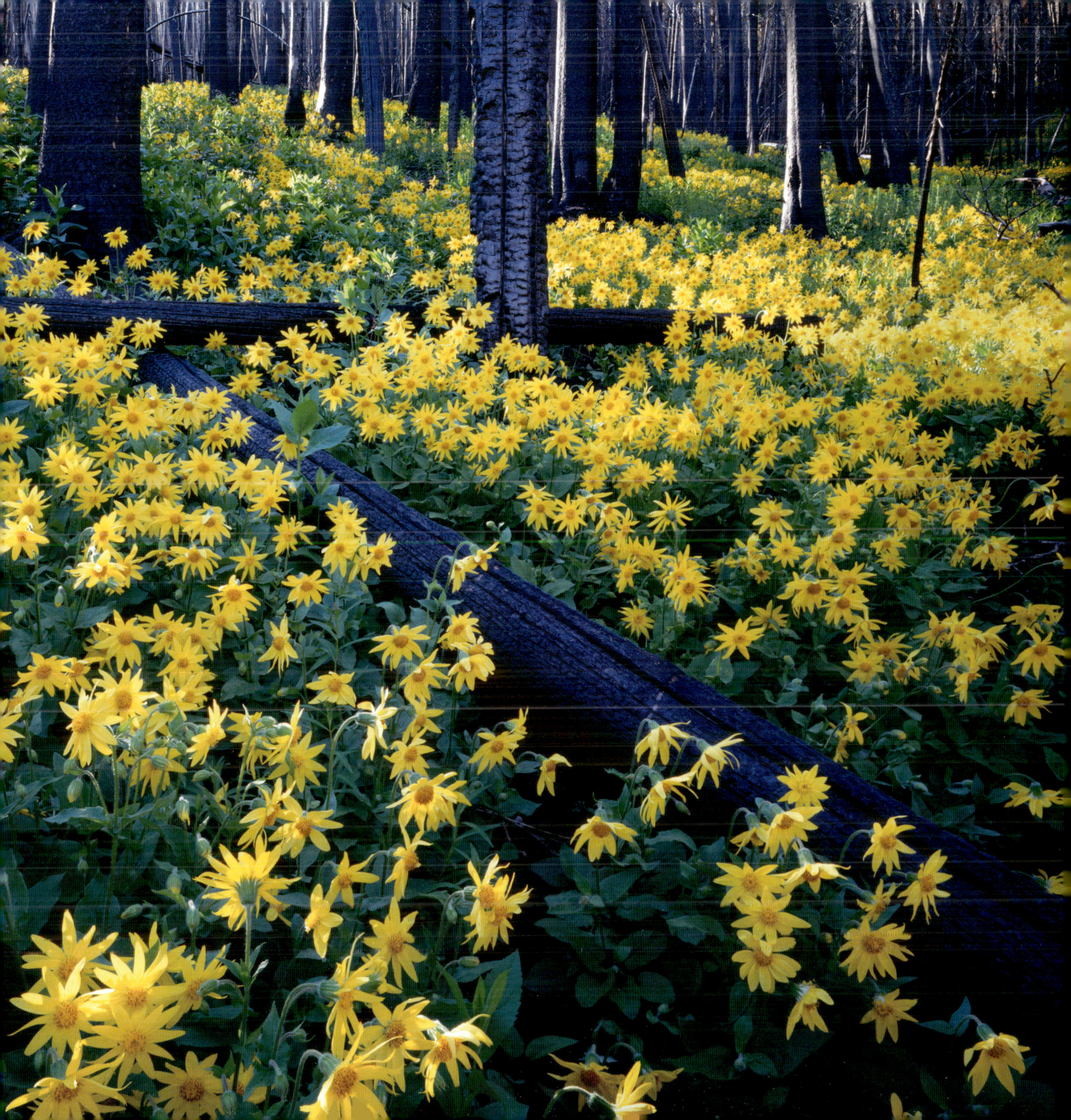

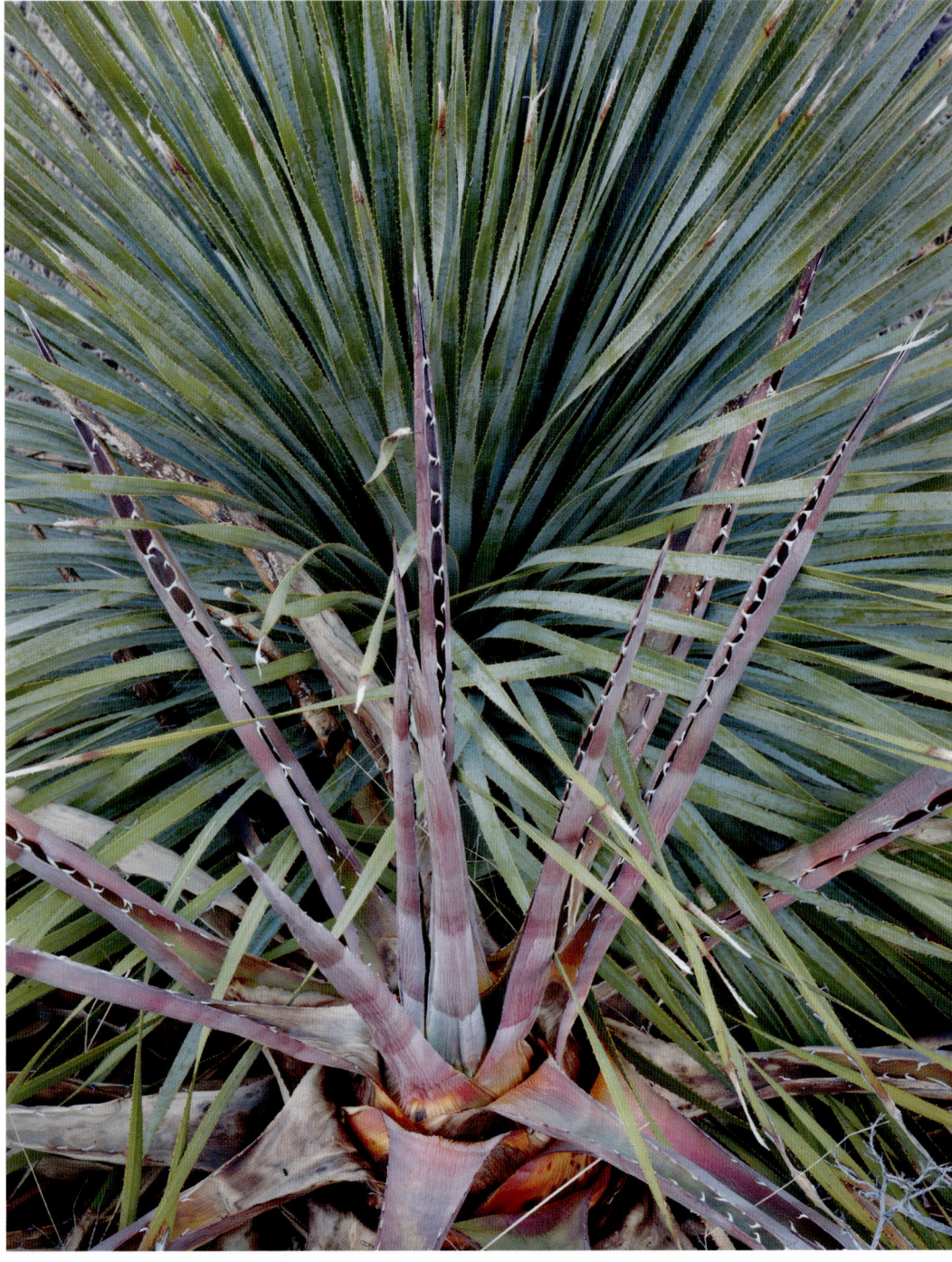

Contrasting colors are also visually compelling when similar subjects have related shapes. Here we see two desert plants, an agave and a sotol, growing next to each other with intertwined blades. While the shapes of the two plants attracted my eye, the juxtaposed complementary colors stopped me in my tracks. The realization that one plant is dying while the other lives adds yet another layer of interest.

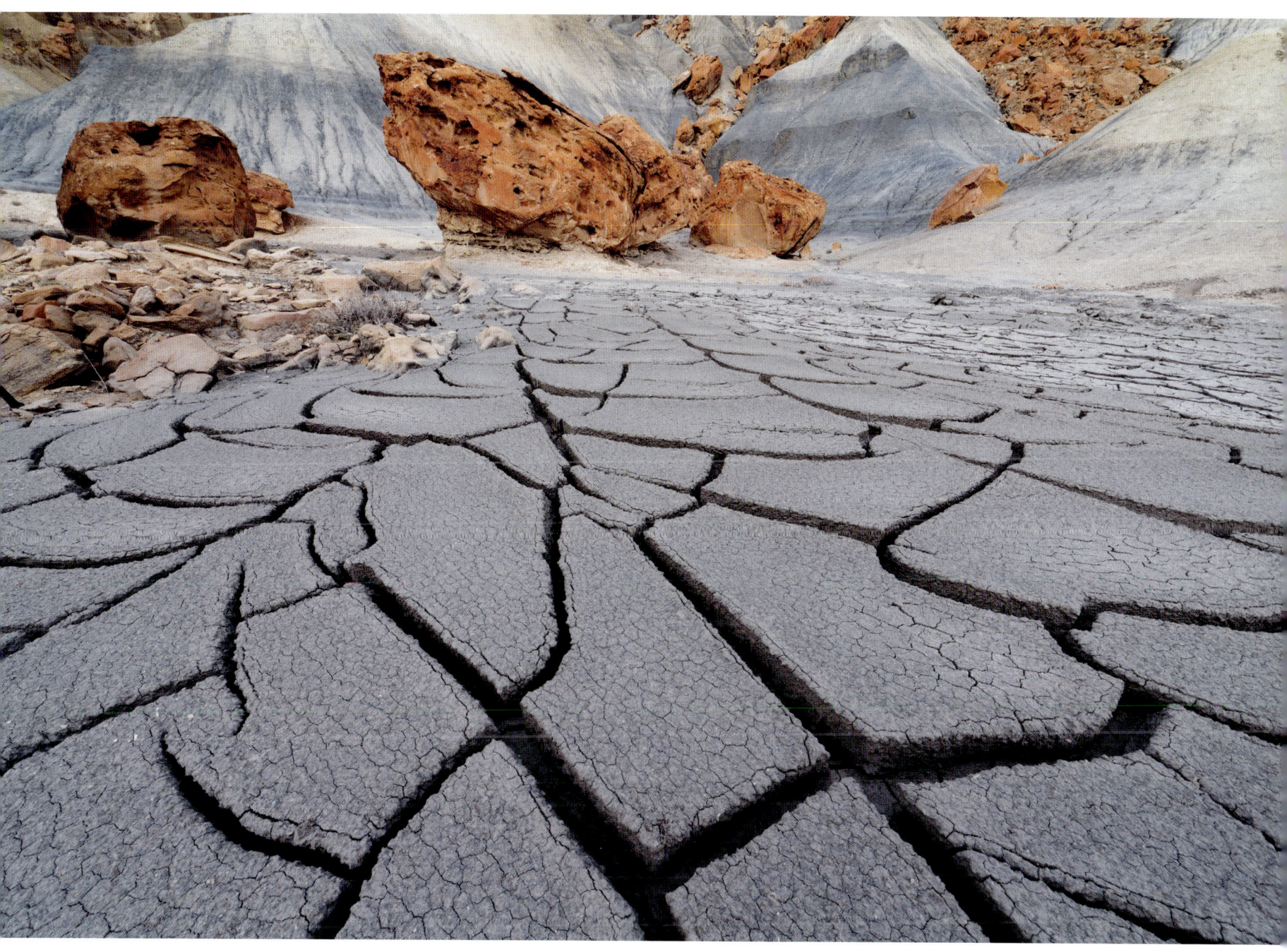

In this image, stark cracked lines in blue/gray clay set up a bold composition. The lines push the eye toward contrasting-colored boulders, playing cool colors against warm colors, while the straight lines of the cracked clay are contrasted against the rounded boulders.

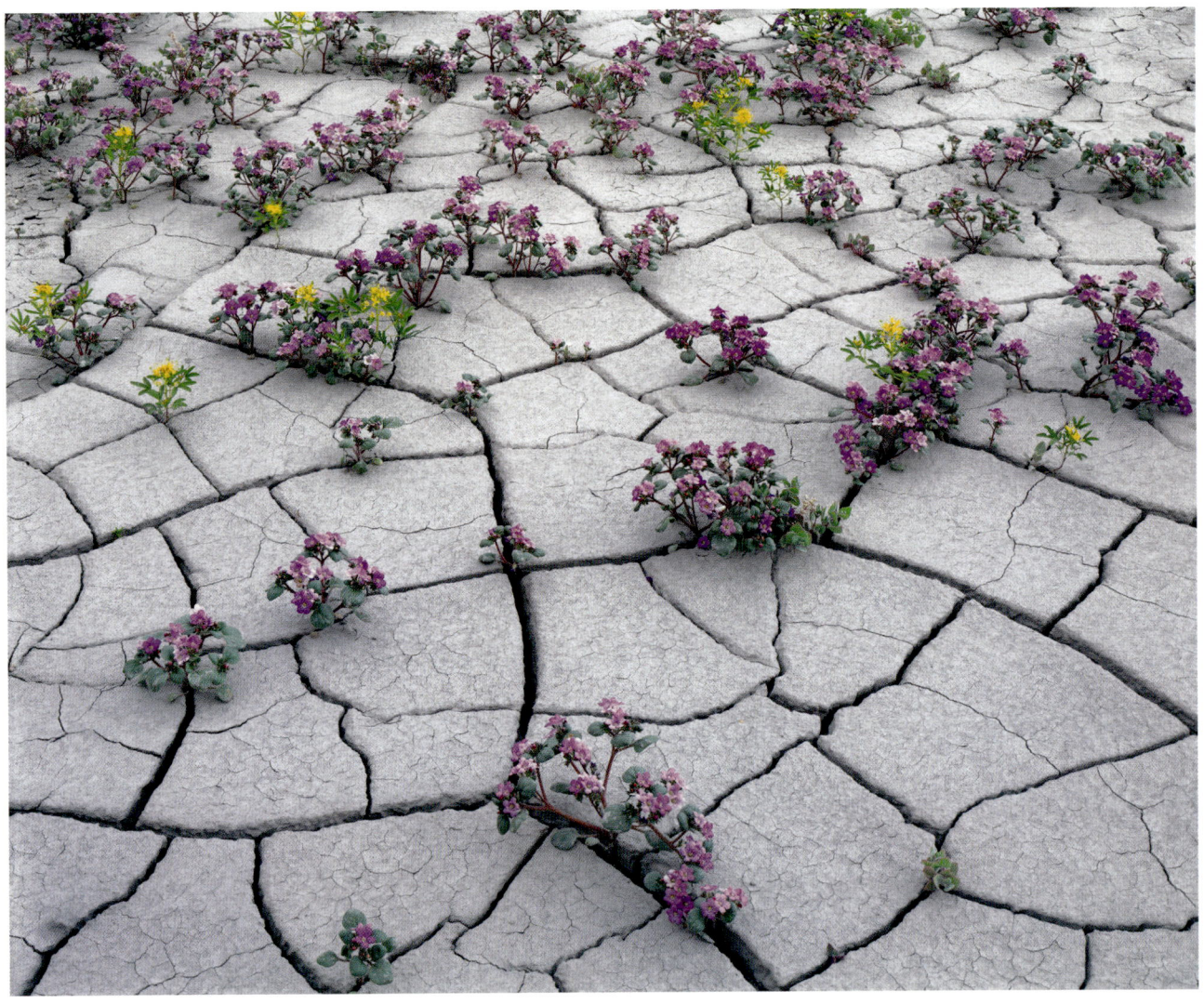

Life pouring forth from a desiccated valley in Utah's San Rafael Swell provides another example of an image that draws us in. Survival and flourishing amid adversity is something we all relate to. Viewing this image as a metaphor increases its impact.

To the right, the curvaceous sinuous lines of a Manzanita juxtaposed against striated red sandstone combines as many juxtapositions as I can cram into a single image.

- Straight lines and curved lines
- Warm colors and cool colors
- Organic plant against hard stone
- Round leaves against striped stone

As the number of juxtapositions in an image increases, so does its power.

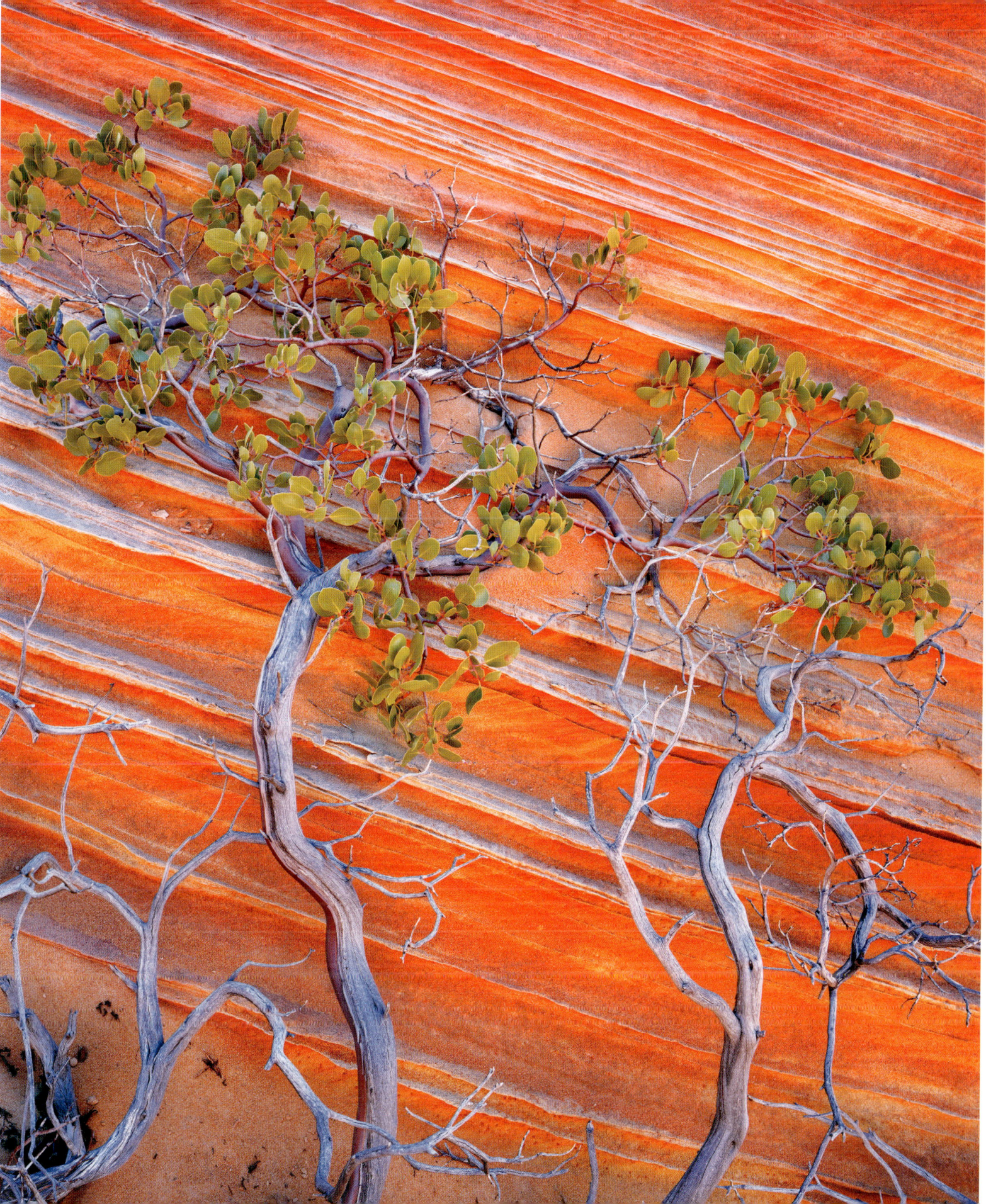

Working the Situation

Occasionally, strong images appear to suddenly jump into my camera, but that's not the norm. I usually spend a lot of time fussing about compositions. I circle the principal elements to imagine compositions, I change the camera angle, I shoot into the light or with the light, and I change lens focal lengths. I call this working the situation.

Of course, there's always something about a subject or scene that draws my initial attention. The challenge is to create an image that shows the viewer the aspect I found so interesting. After hiking all over the White Sands National Monument in New Mexico, I found a curved yucca emerging from a partially buried base in a pristine section of dunes. I loved the simplicity of the scene. The series of six images shown here demonstrates how I worked the situation.

My first image [1] was made as the pre-dawn Earth-shadow light began to illuminate the sky. I wanted to show the transition of color in the sky and composed accordingly. I left plenty of room at the top of the frame to illustrate the light known as the Belt of Venus and photographed the progression of the light's intensity and color until I felt I had what I was after. Ultimately, this occurred when the first light of dawn kissed the mountainous background.

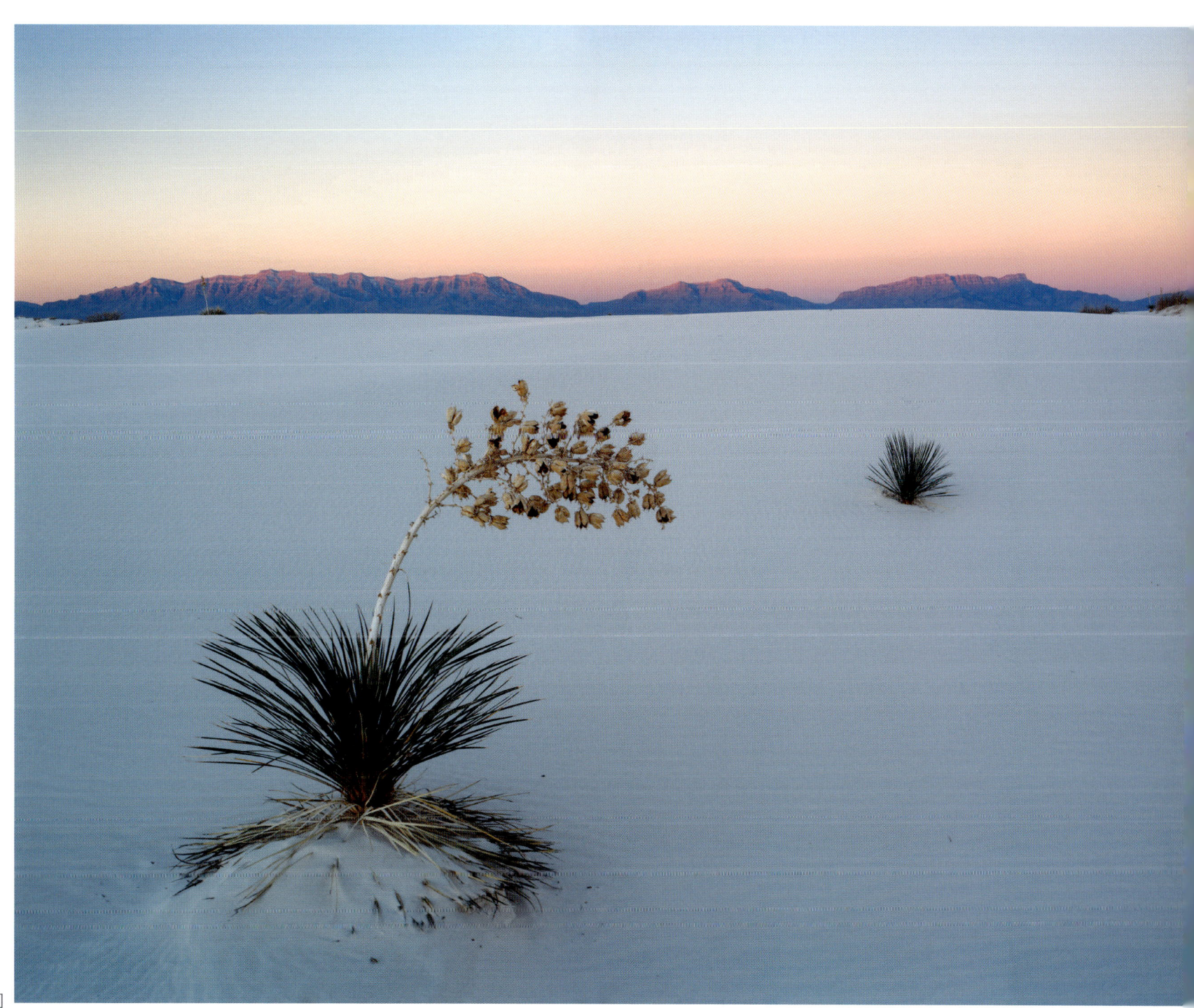

[1]

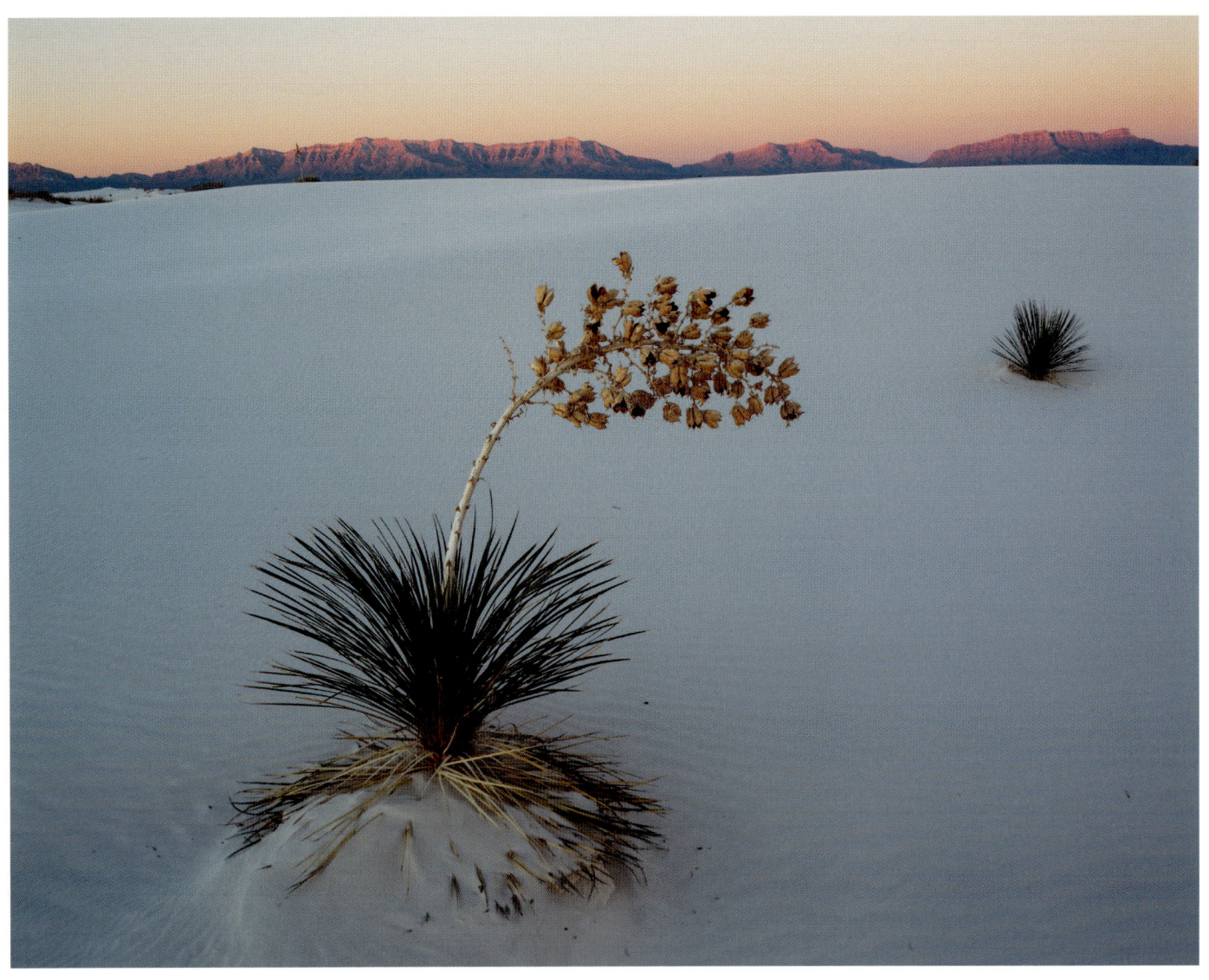

[2]

Then my attention shifted to the mountains, which were becoming more important as they became illuminated. I had lost the gradation in the sky, so I deemphasized the sky by tilting the camera downward. The result is seen in the second image [2].

While I felt the composition worked in the second image, it was not as strong as my initial image. I took a few remaining sips of coffee and watched and waited.

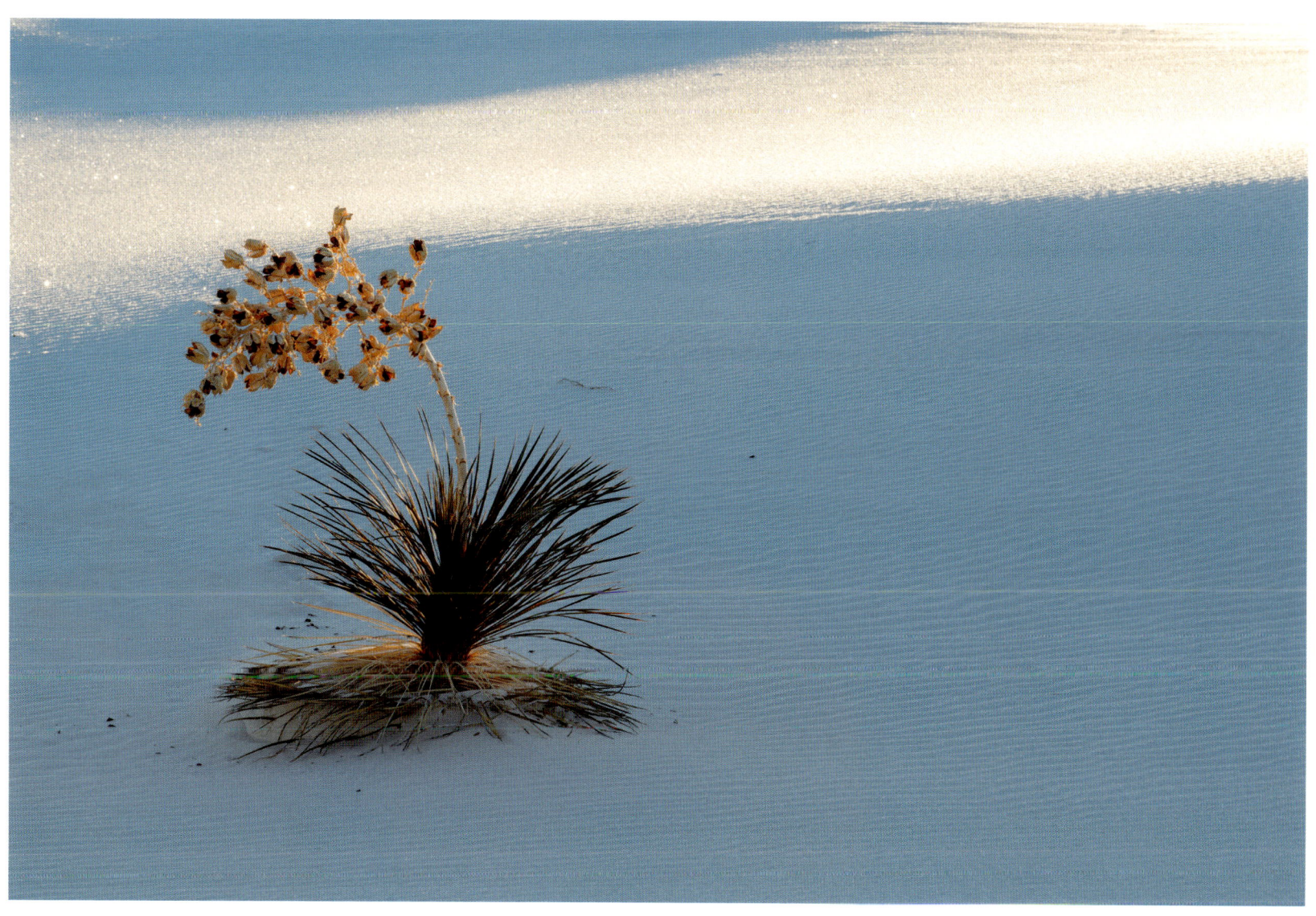

[3]

As the sun rose higher, new elements of design became apparent. Strong shadows extended across the dune field, creating new but quickly changing opportunities. Where once I enjoyed the luxury of slow, deliberate, and careful composing of photographs, I was now hurriedly reacting to shadows on the move to capture the third image [3].

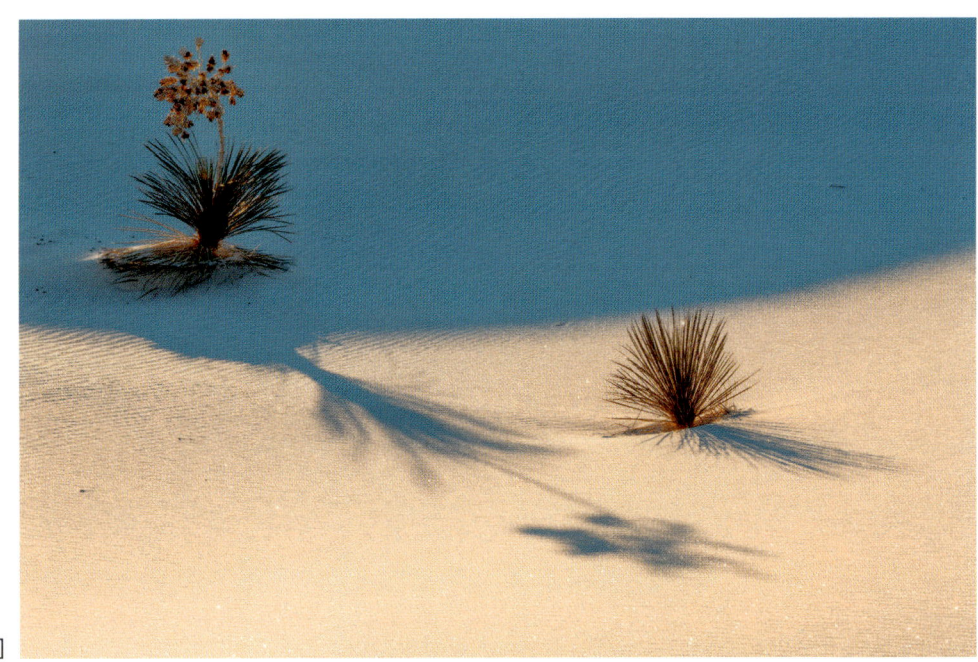

[4]

I watched the yucca fairly glow in the dawn light as shadows created form and design. In this next photo, I shifted position to emphasize the shadows of the yucca itself [4]. But my own footprints were mucking up the composition so I carefully repositioned to avoid showing my missteps.

One of the things I learned from the publishing world is to make images in both vertical and horizontal orientations, so I oriented the camera to portrait position to photograph the fifth image [5].

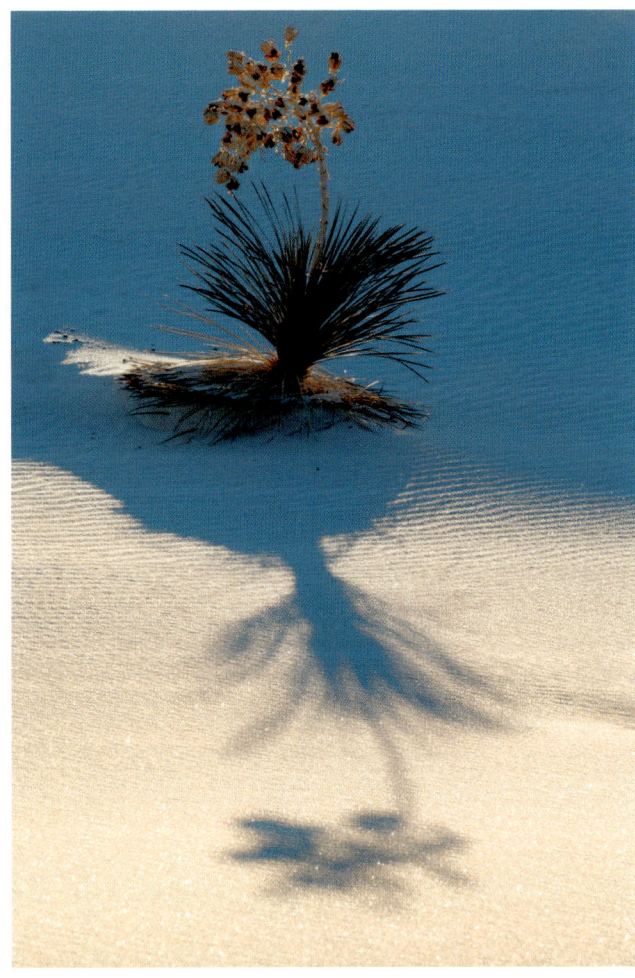

[5]

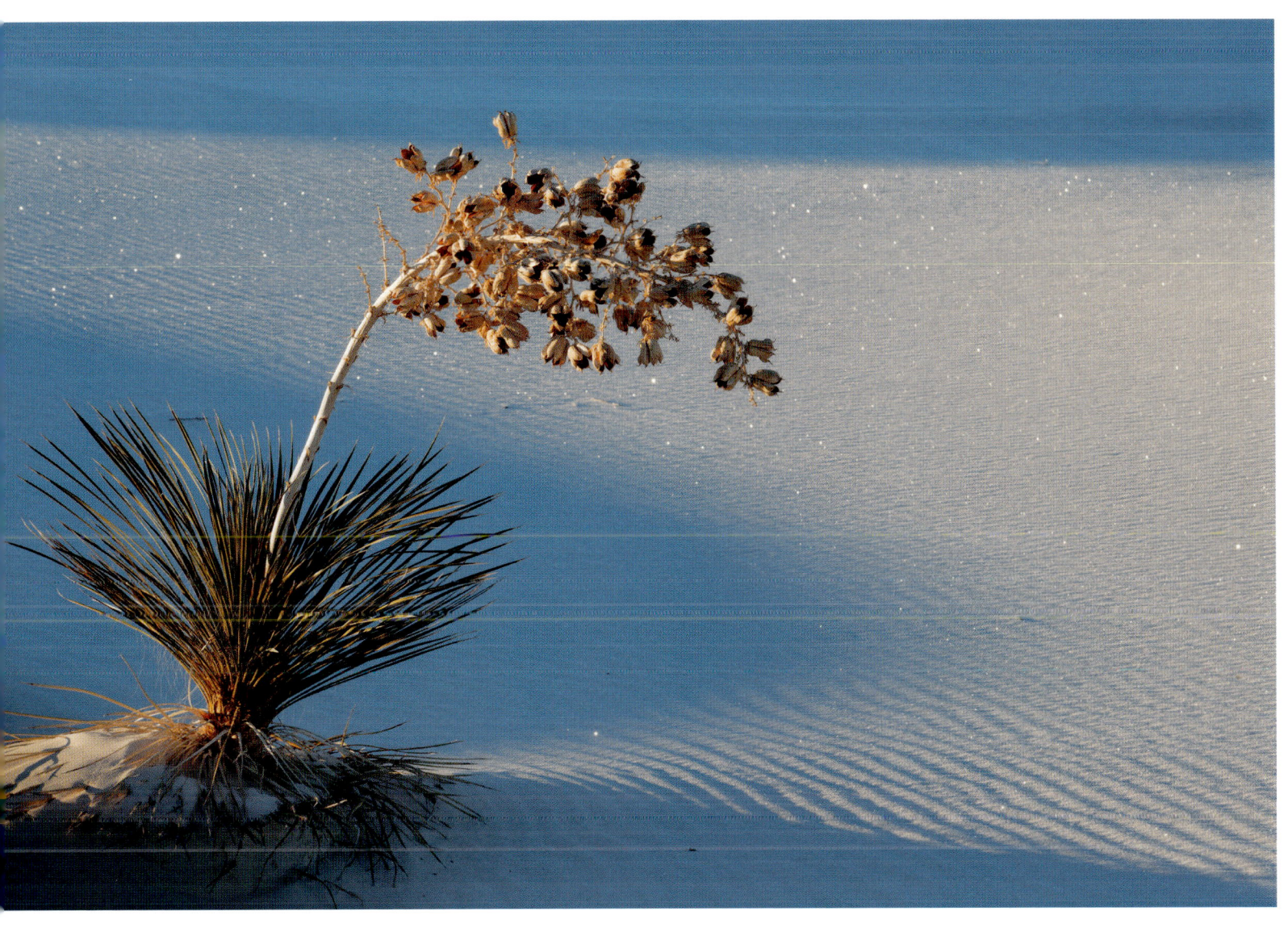

The placement of the yucca stalk against a dune-shadowed background afforded me a new way to frame. In the sixth image, using dark shadow bands at the top and bottom of the frame, I was taking advantage of natural landscape elements to concentrate interest on the curved yucca [6]. But let's look at the distances around the frame. The base of the yucca nearly mirrors the distance of the top shadow line. The yucca blades at the left are set off, and are illuminated and framed against the background shadow. Finally, the direction that the yucca is leaning leads the eye into the frame.

Although I captured multiple images of the same scene, each photograph was still a product of careful composition. Nevertheless, they were created quickly with the rapidly changing light.

Working the situation is another way of thinking outside the box. My goal for these two photographs was to create an image for my German calendar, which celebrates the designs in stone that are particularly visible here in the American Southwest.

I wanted to show the slippage that occurred eons ago in these petrified sand dune formations. The misalignment of rock layers along the fracture line was what piqued my interest and the contrasting subtle colors added to the composition. I felt satisfied with the design in the first image, but I wanted to try something different.

To create the second image, I shifted the principal subject from the fracture line to the striations of blue. These are two approaches to the same scene, but with a subtle shift in the center of interest.

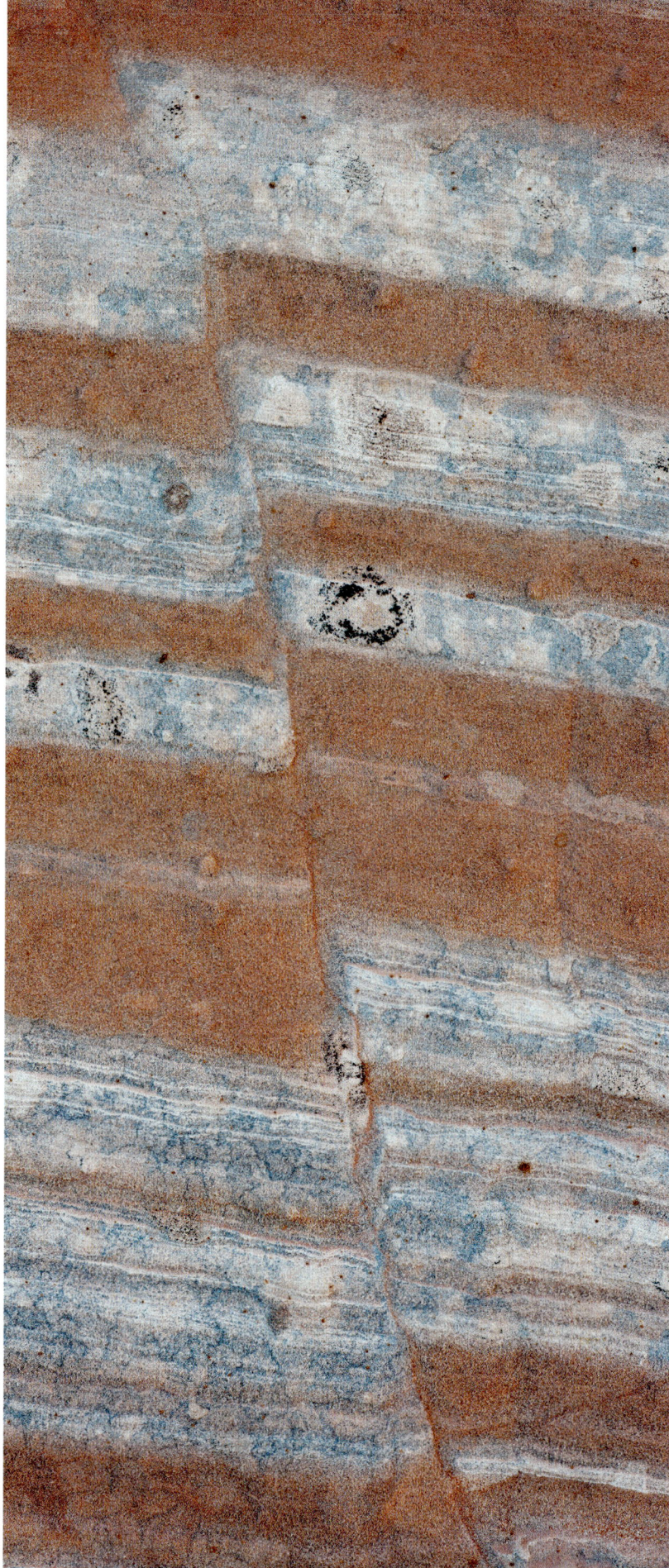

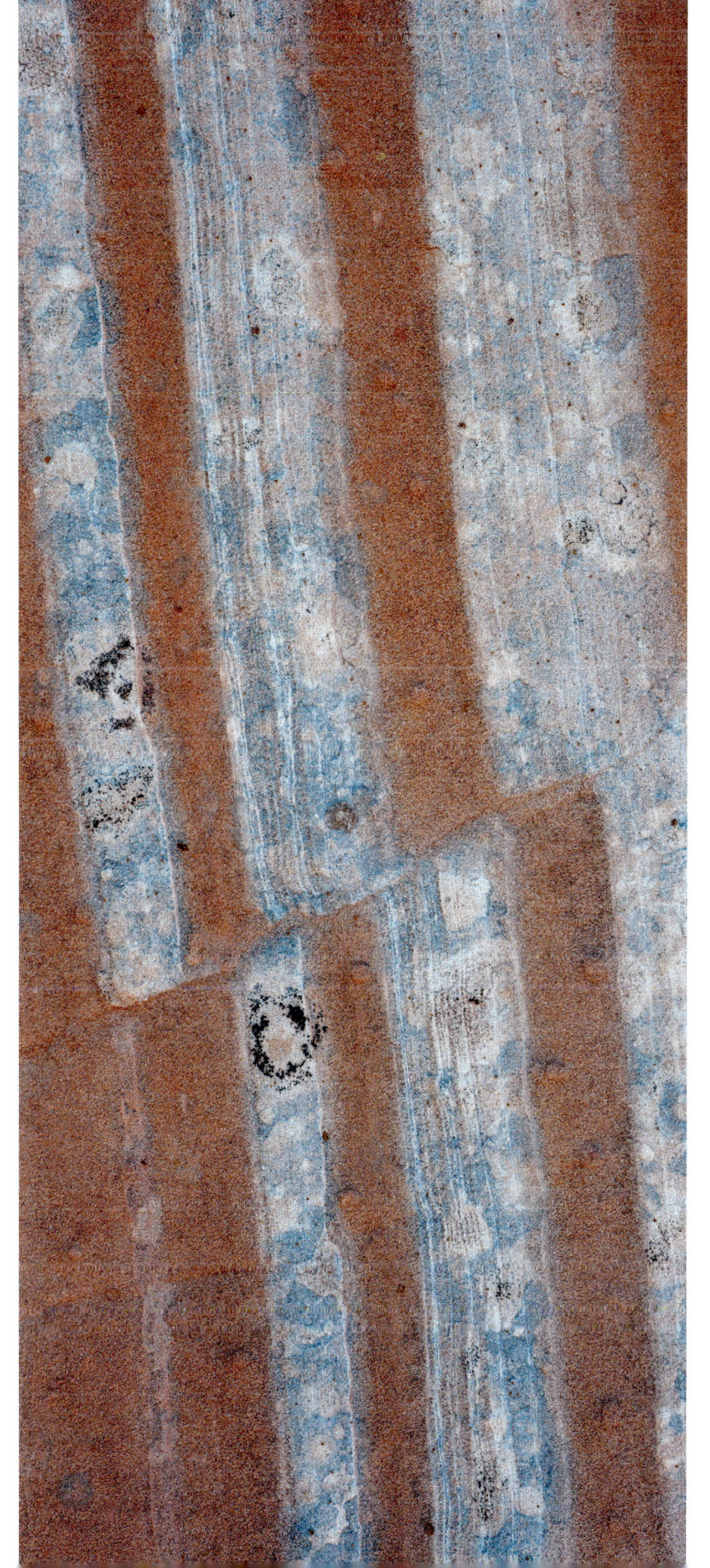

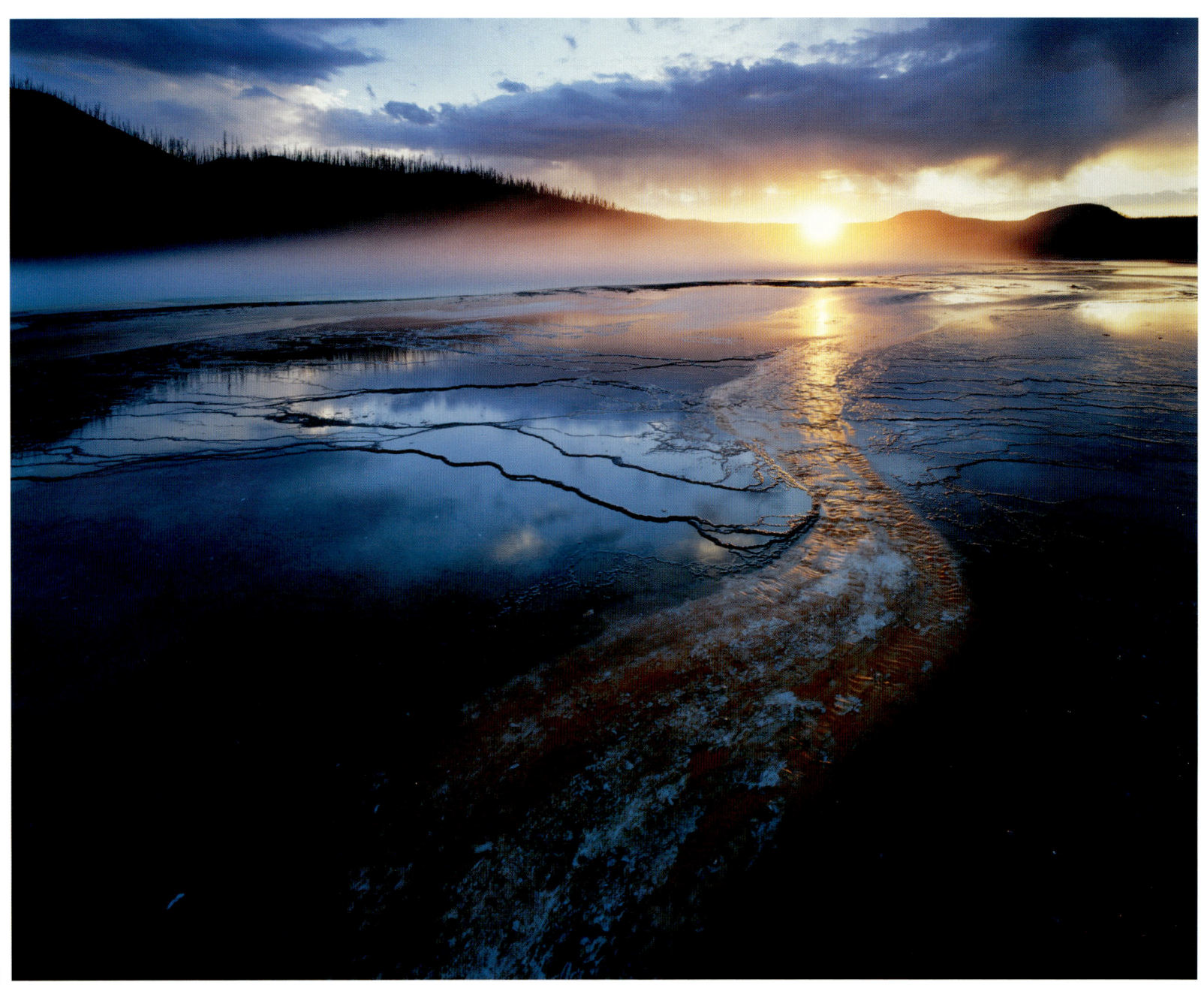

[1]

Many years ago I photographed the Grand Prismatic geyser pool in Yellowstone National Park. More recently, I was teaching nearby and wanted to revisit the pool and photograph it again, this time using my new Nikon D800E digital camera.

I remember being instantly in love with this geyser, especially at sunset. The sinuous rivers of red algae seemingly run right into the setting sun. But as the saying goes, "you can't put your foot into the same river twice." Time and weather conspired to show me something different and I captured this first dark, moody image [1].

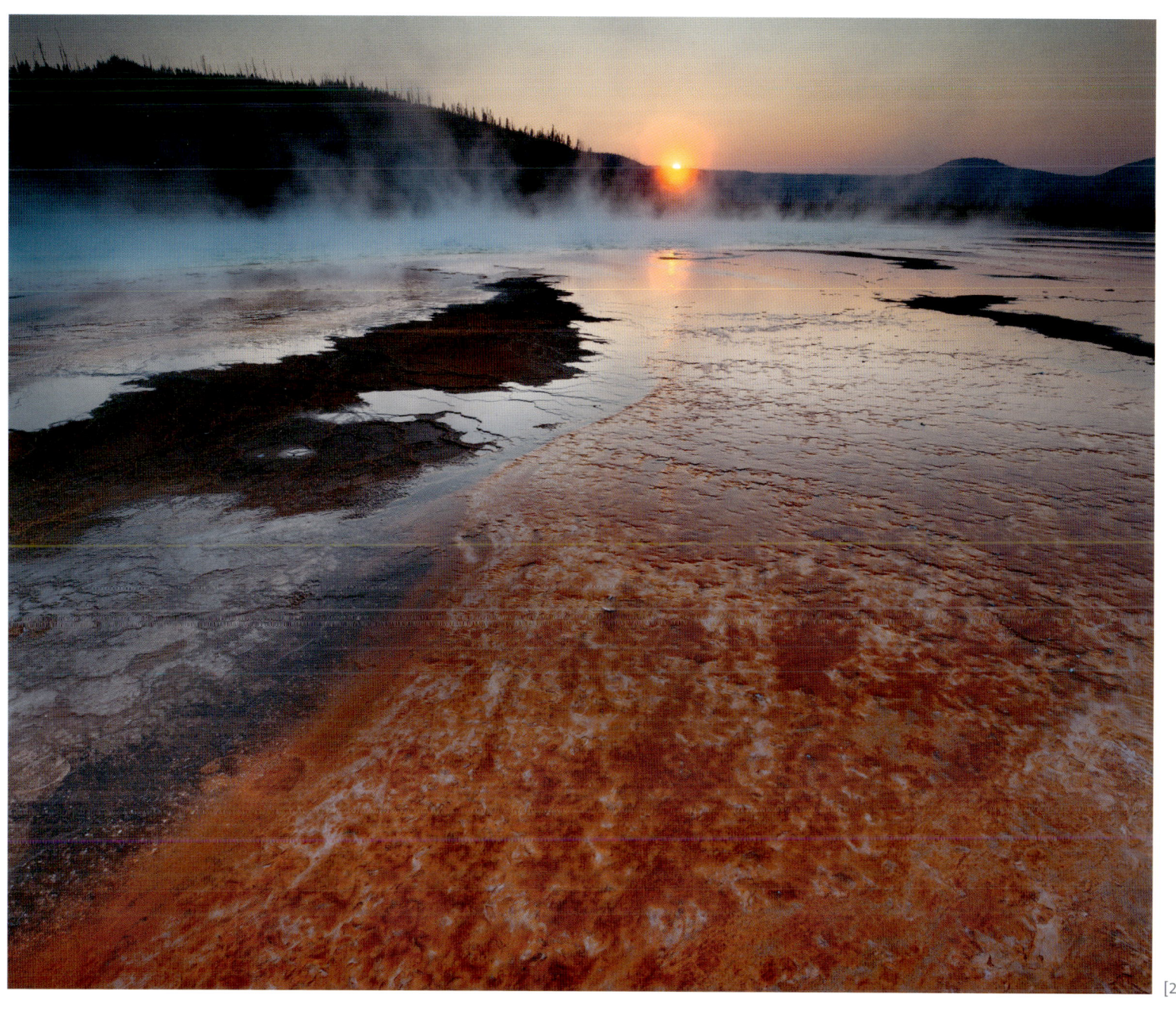

[2]

Before taking the second image, I concentrated on the details within the rivers of red. I worked the situation and achieved this very different result [2].

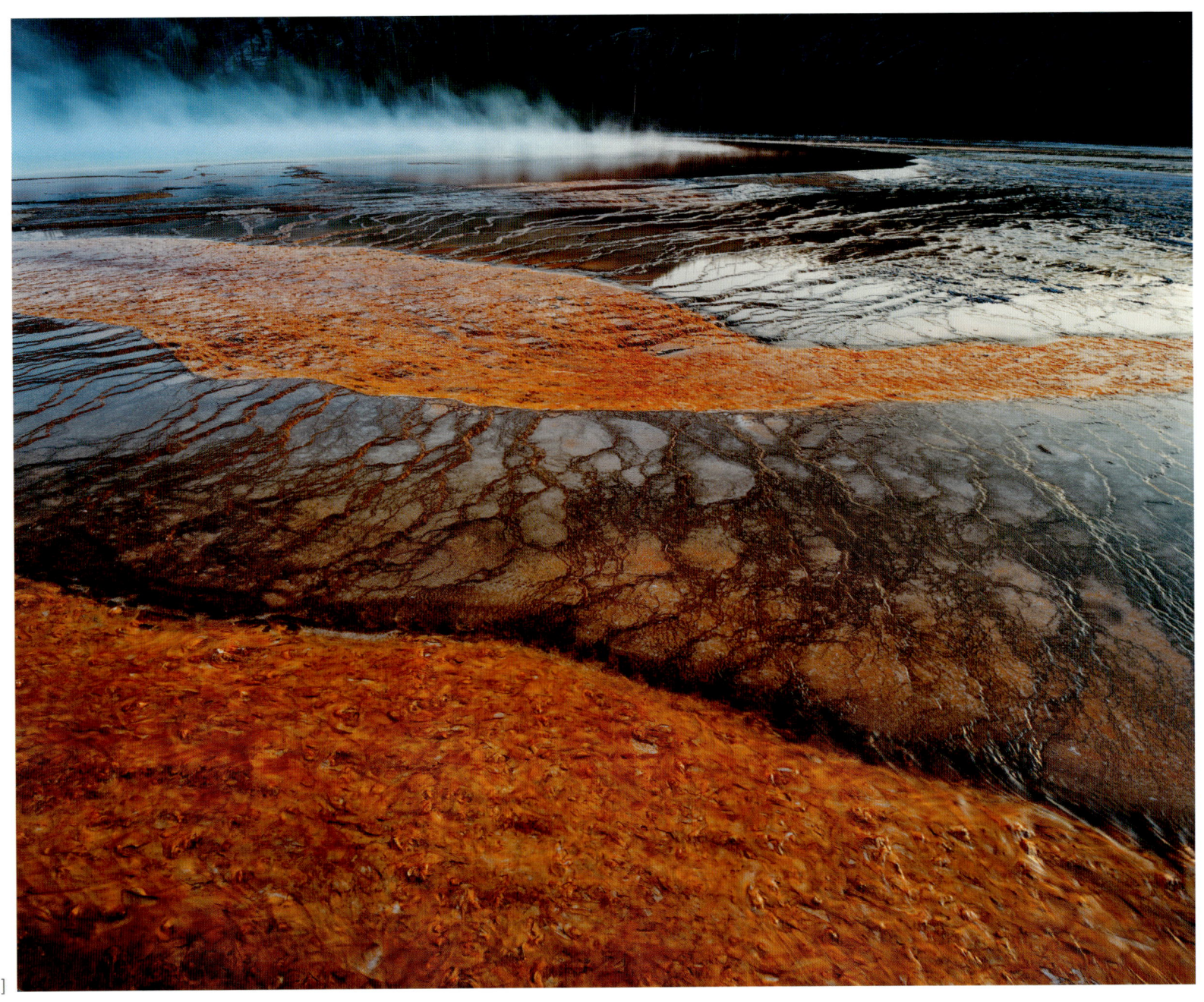

[3]

As the algae painted the surface of the bacterial mats, they were juxtaposed against the turquoise geyser water. As the angle of the setting sun became pronounced, it highlighted the edges of the bacterial mats, creating bold diagonal lines that I was able to capture in the third image [3].

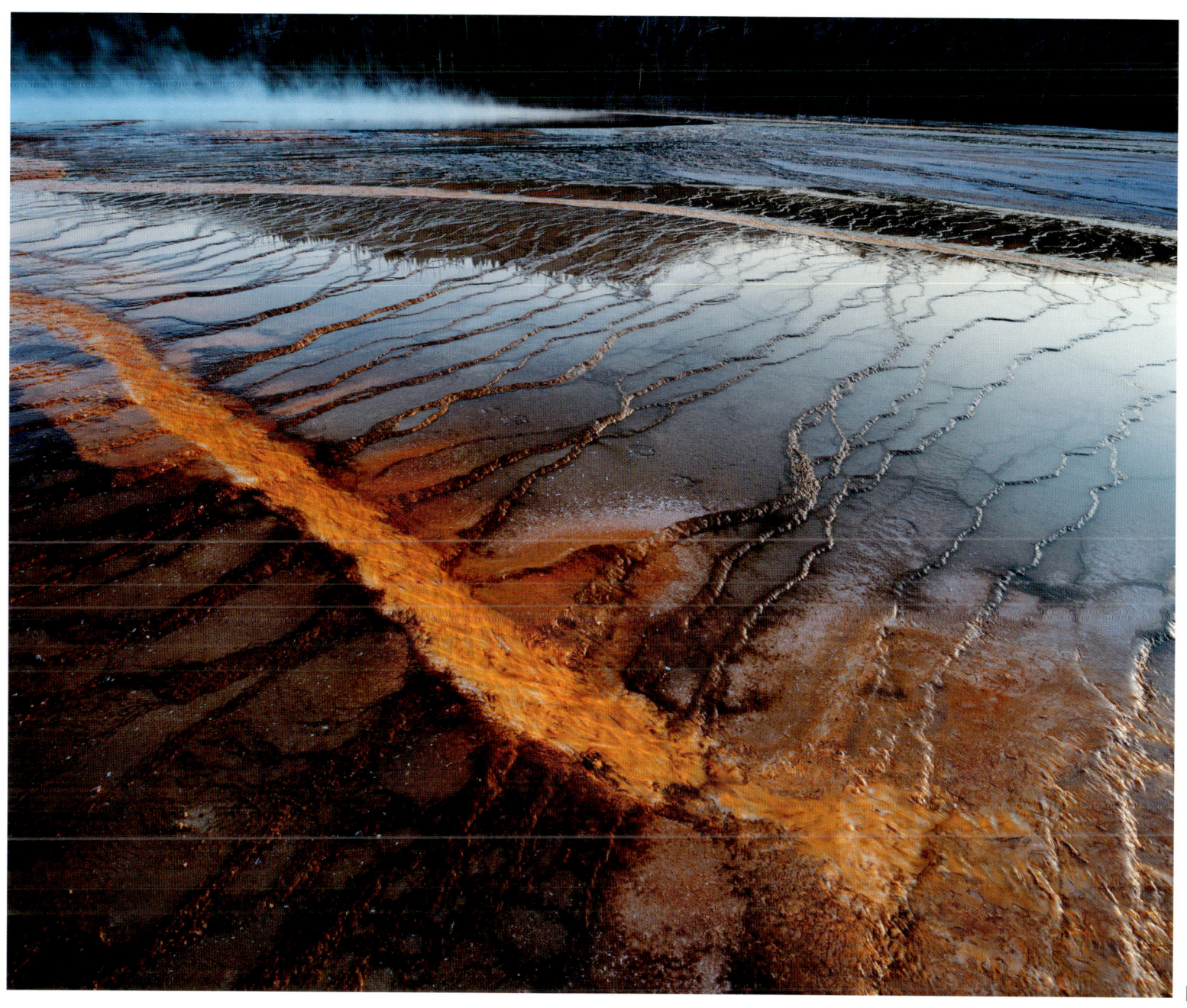

The changing light shifted the emphasis, creating yet another design [4]. So light creates shapes and forms, which, in turn, change compositions and design.

Direction

Strong images take the viewer on a journey. By directing the viewer's eye into and through the frame, photographers can strengthen their composition. Strong angles, movement, and flow can direct the viewer's eye to where the photographer wants it to go.

While photographing flamingos in Mexico's Yucatan Peninsula, I saw the pandemonium associated with takeoffs as a lesson in fast action. The giant birds lean into their flight pathway as they run across the surface of the water. I wanted to lead the birds to give more space ahead of their trajectory. So as I photographed, I built the composition from the lower right corner, driving the interest to the upper left of the frame, which can be seen here.

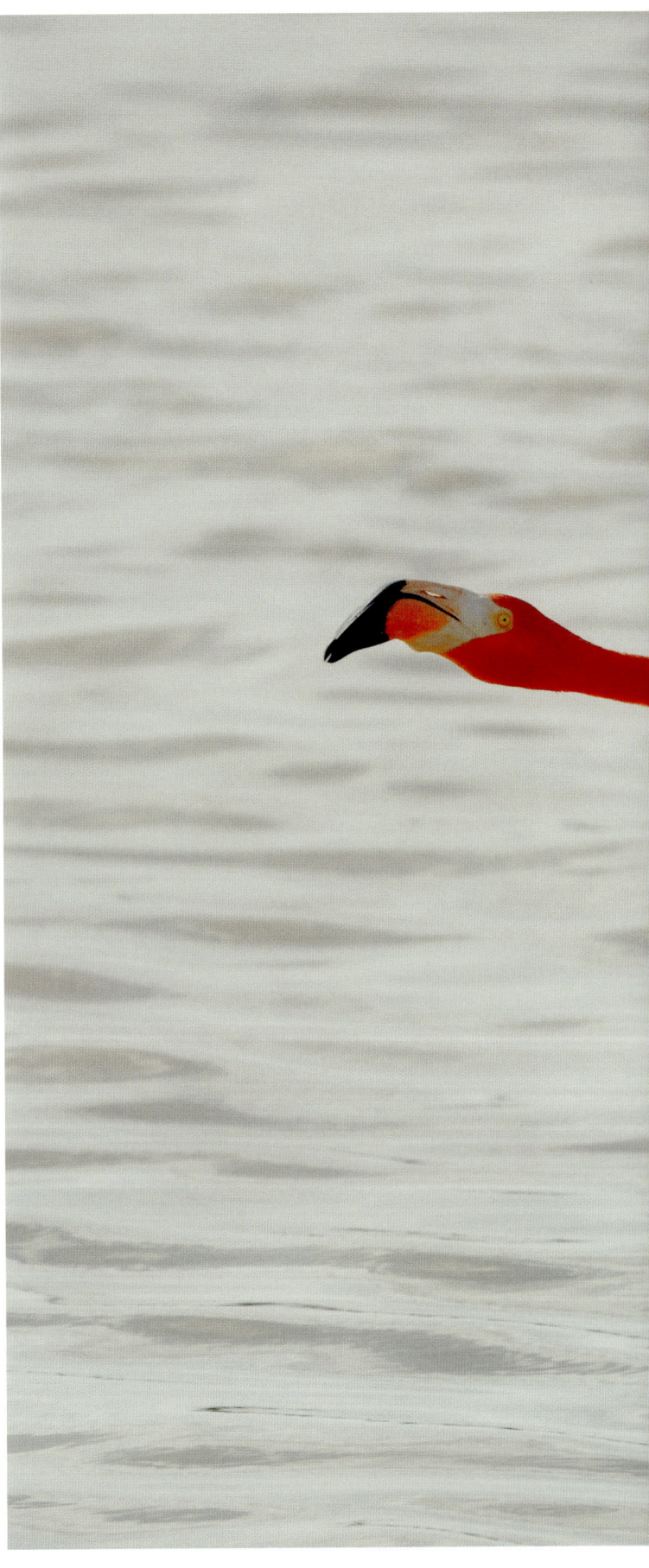

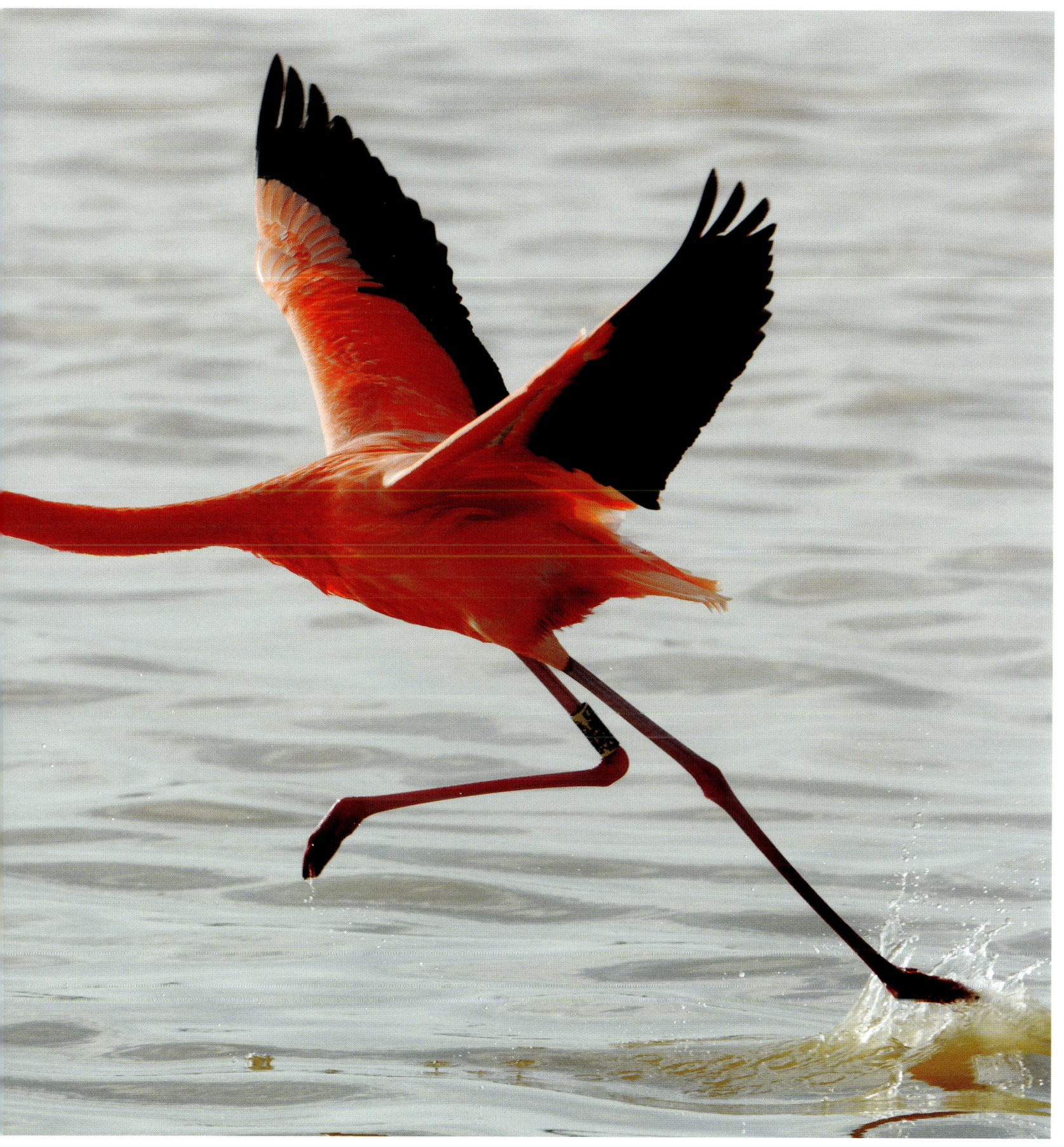

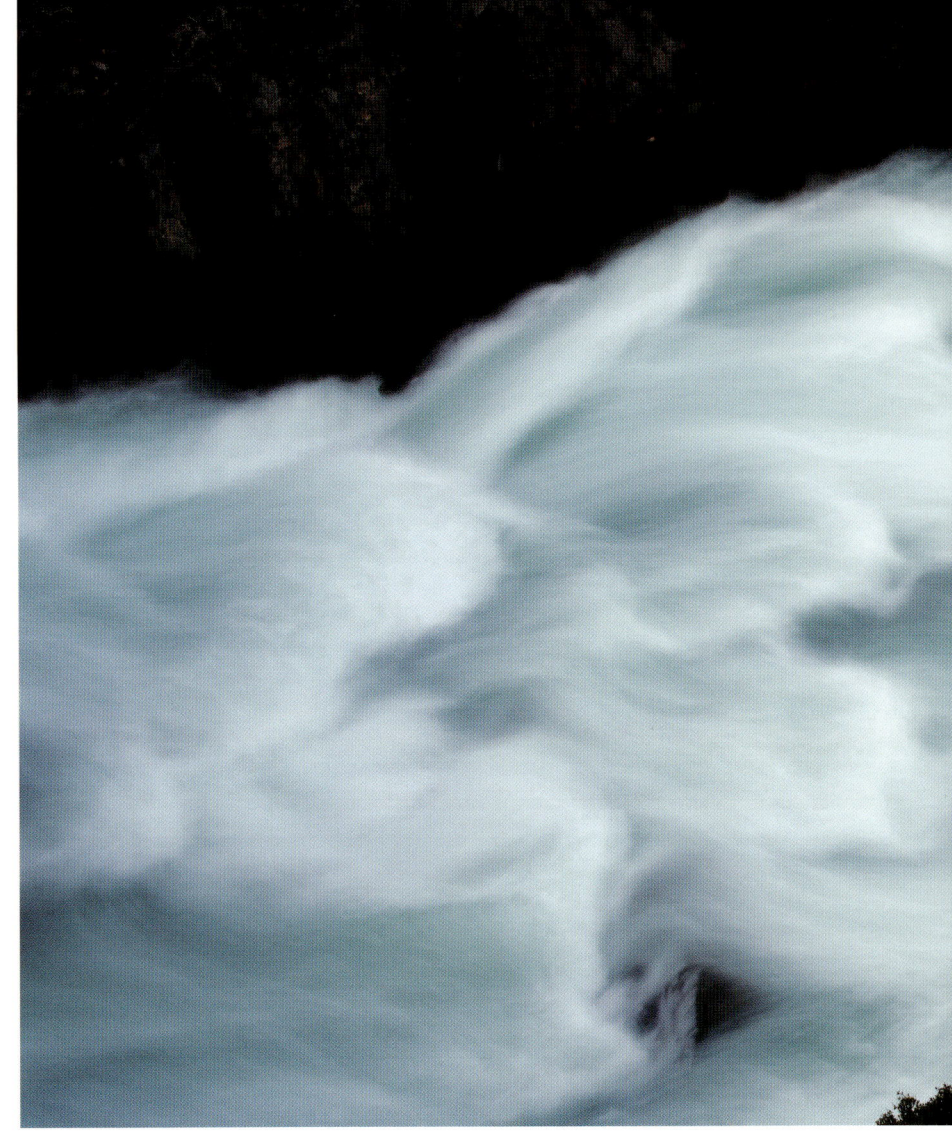

The raging El Salto Grande in Chile churns through a narrow gorge, compressing the glacial-colored water into a mass of turbulence. I watched the river's direction and noticed a lenga tree perched precariously at the rim of the abyss, its wind-sculpted shape mirroring the direction of the waters below. By placing the tree to the right in my frame, I effectively reinforced the river's direction. Creating a composition, such as this, with additional space to the left, provides a destination for the eye. To further test my composition, I sometimes convert a color image to black-and-white, as I did in the monochrome photograph. Conversion to black-and-white simplifies the image, removing the distraction of colors and allowing us to focus solely on the strength of the design.

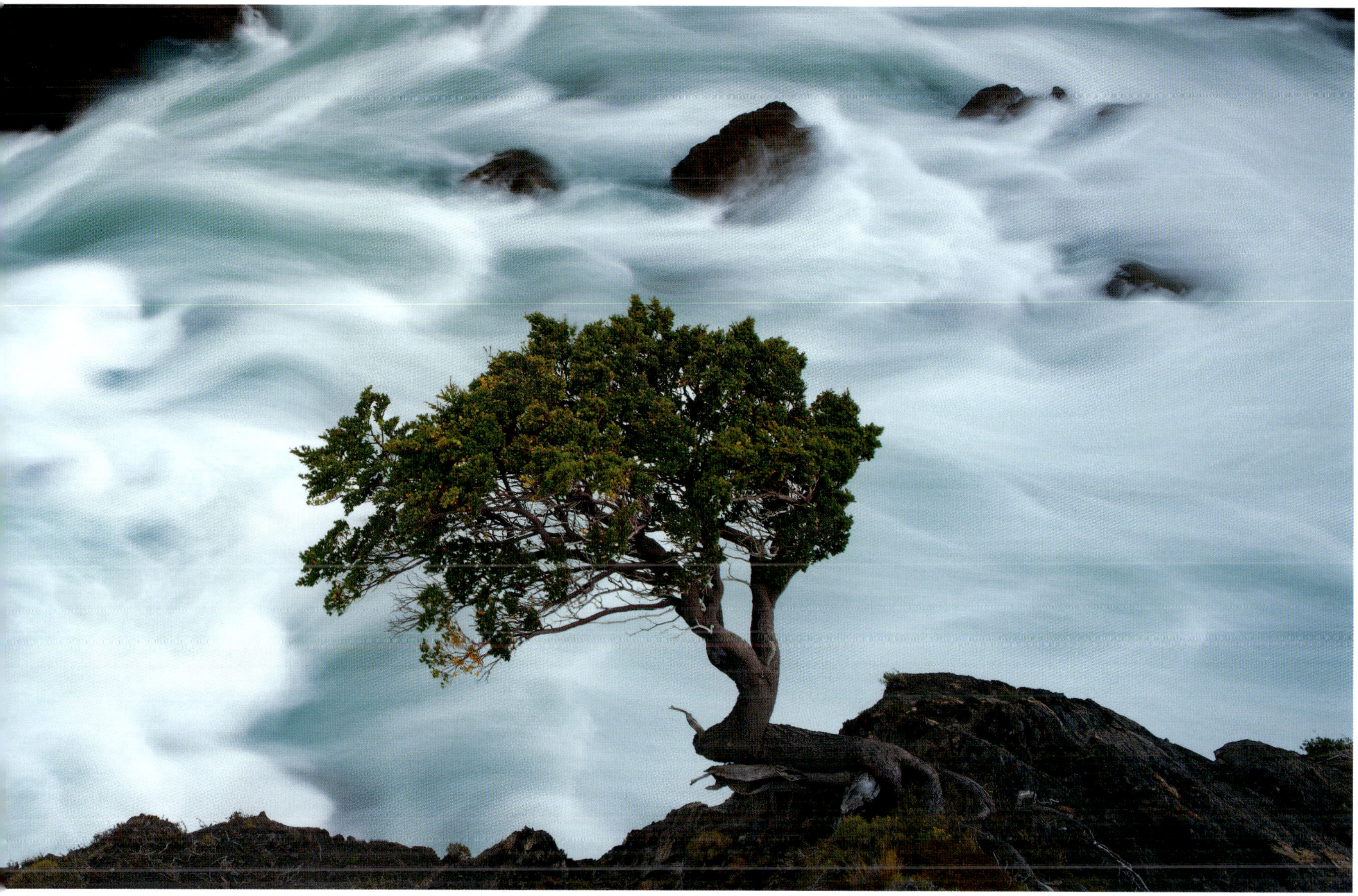

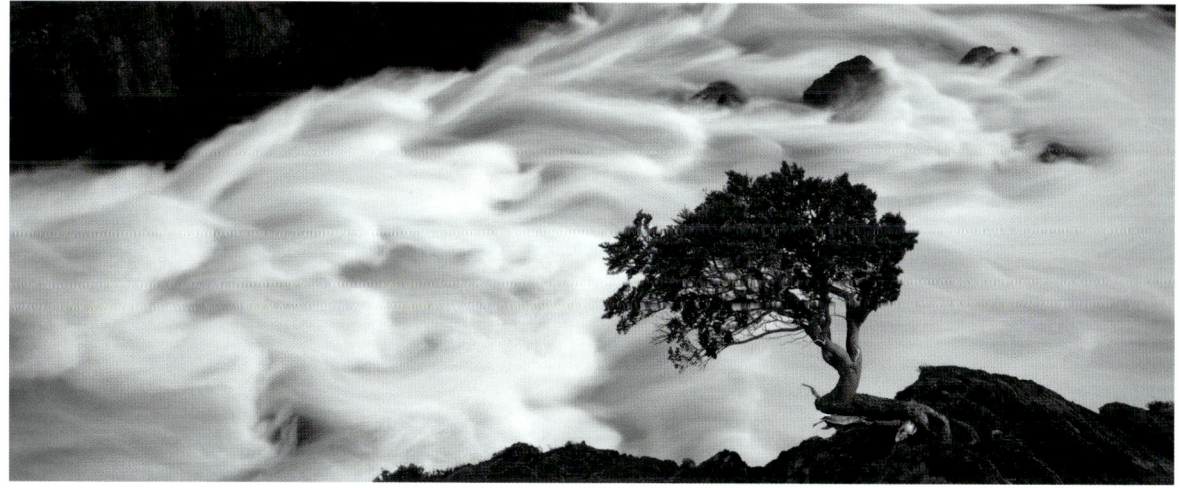

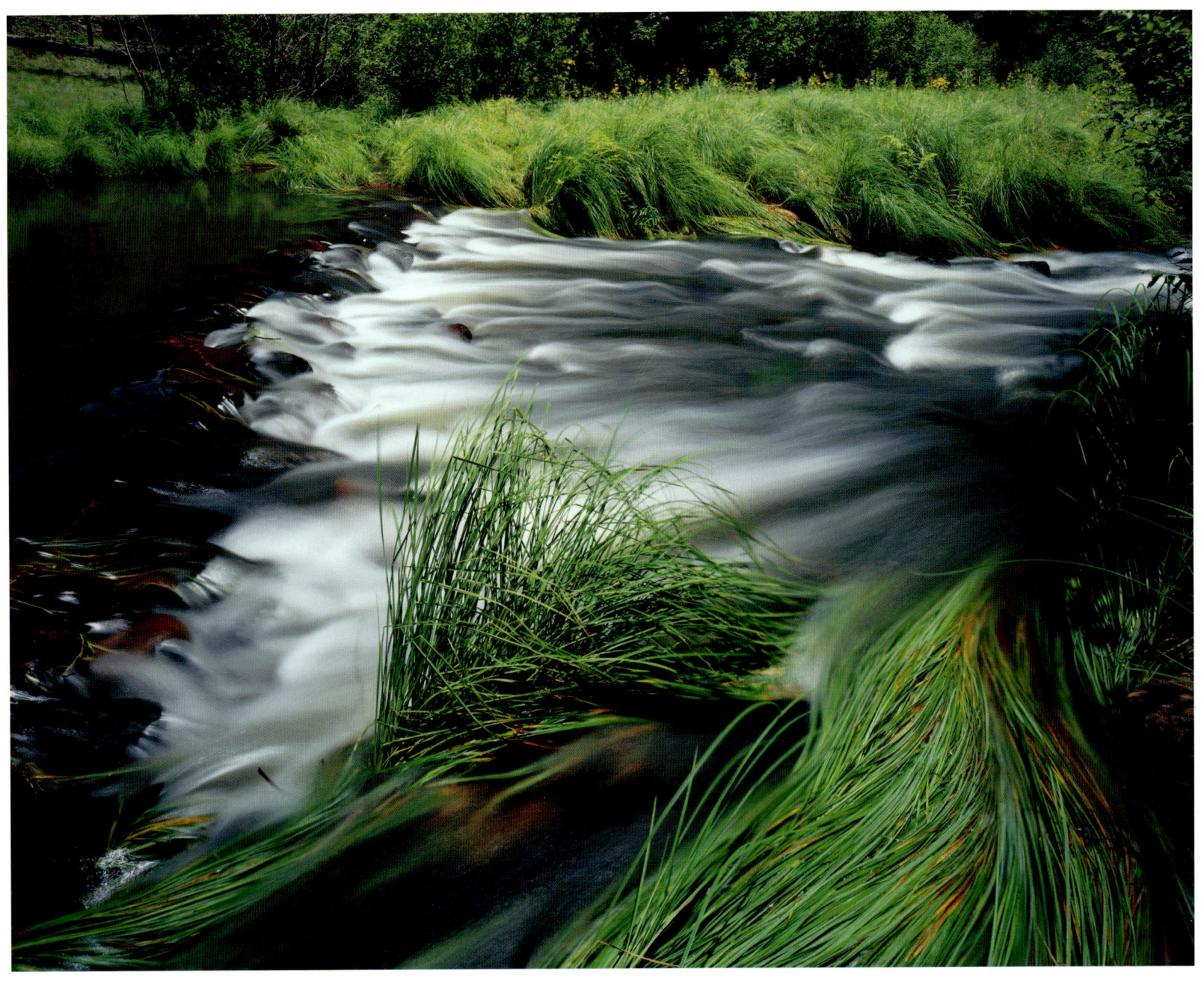

Water is one of those primal elements we all seem to react to. By using longer shutter speeds, we can increase the impact and emphasize the direction of moving water.

Here, the streamside sedges reinforce the sense of direction. The lines radiating from the corners give even more power to the composition by pushing the eye from the lower left and toward the center-right side of the image. I used a polarizing filter to emphasize the white water highlights and darken the streambed. The net effect emphasizes the contrasting bands of light and dark in the flowing water.

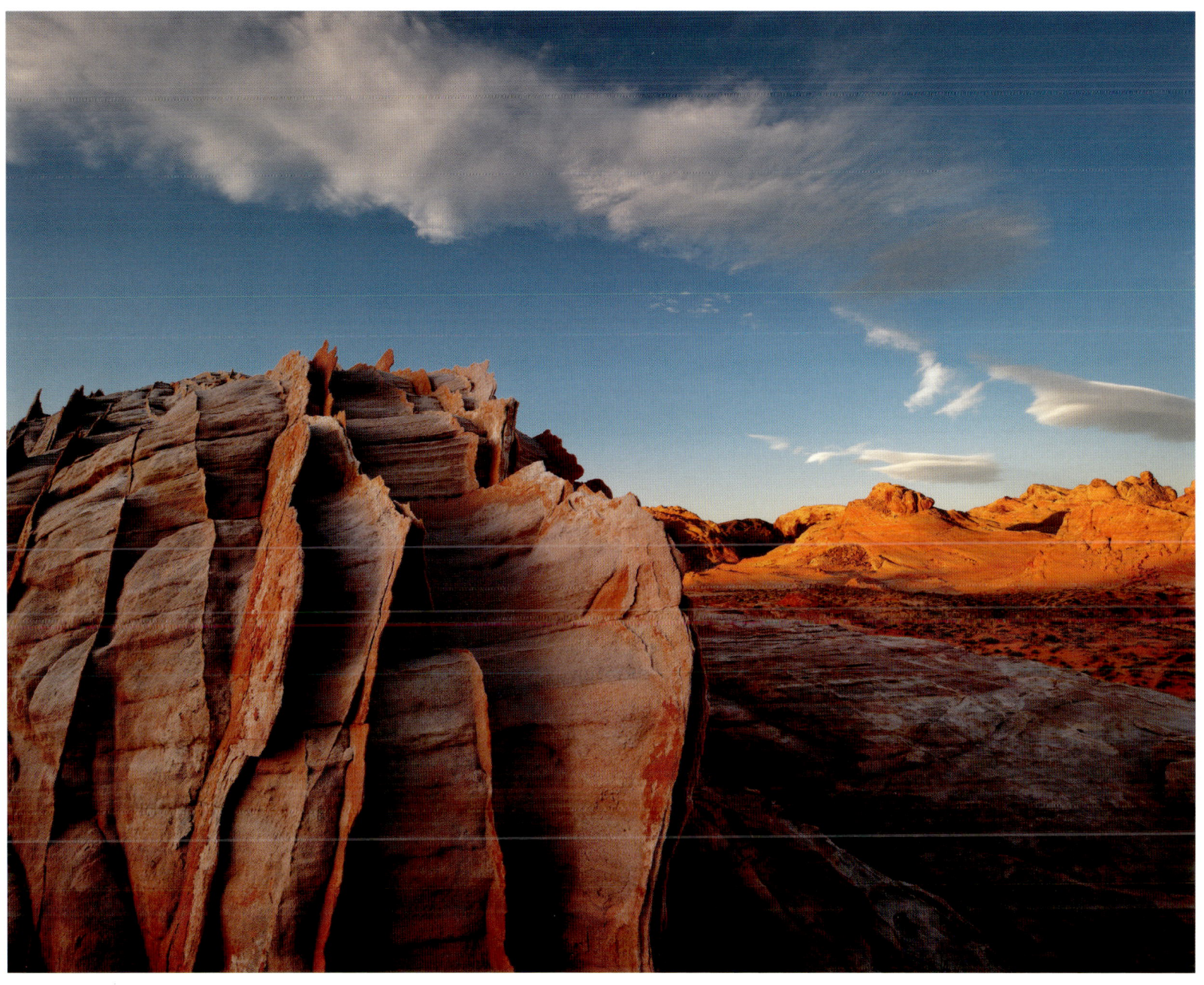

Just spending a little time watching and anticipating the movement and flow within a scene is time well spent. The simple act of noticing the direction of moving clouds and planning an image can make the difference between success and failure.

On a visit to Valley of Fire State Park in Nevada, I wanted to illustrate the delicate geology and sandstone fins along the ridgeline. I picked a spot that I thought might get early light. As I watched the pre-dawn light appear, I noticed clouds building to the left. I quickly changed my camera position to accommodate the cloud line entering the frame from the upper left. The resulting image captured the clouds, directing the eye into the frame from the upper left. The lines of sunrise light across the sandstone reinforce the design and direction in which the viewer's eye is drawn.

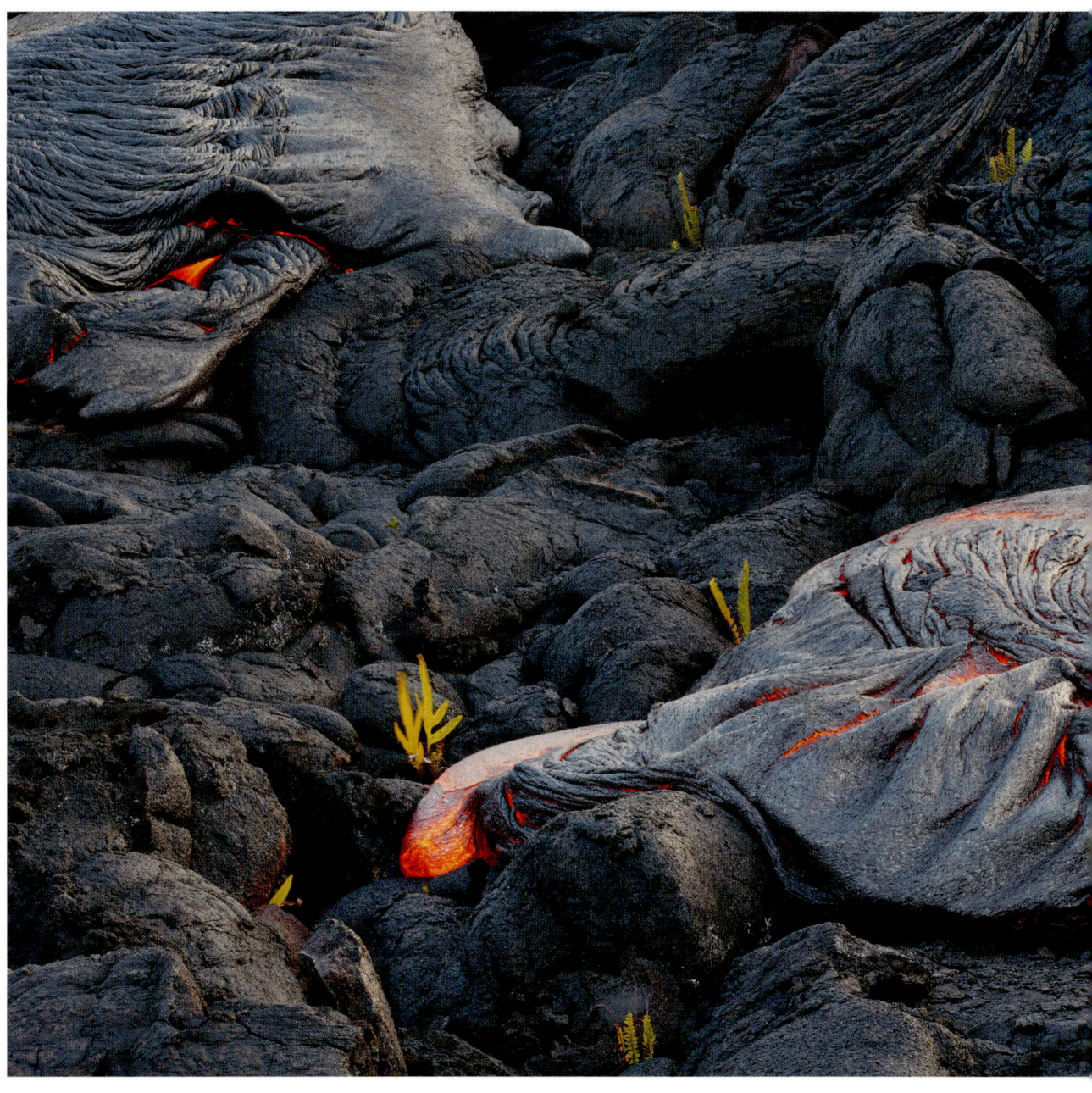

Direction into a frame can heighten interest by creating a collision. Here, the sense of impending doom creates concern. As the molten lava flowing on Hawaii's Big Island oozes along, threatening delicate plants, there's a sense of tension. The direction of the flowing lava creates impact; the power radiates from both right corners and leads the eye into the frame.

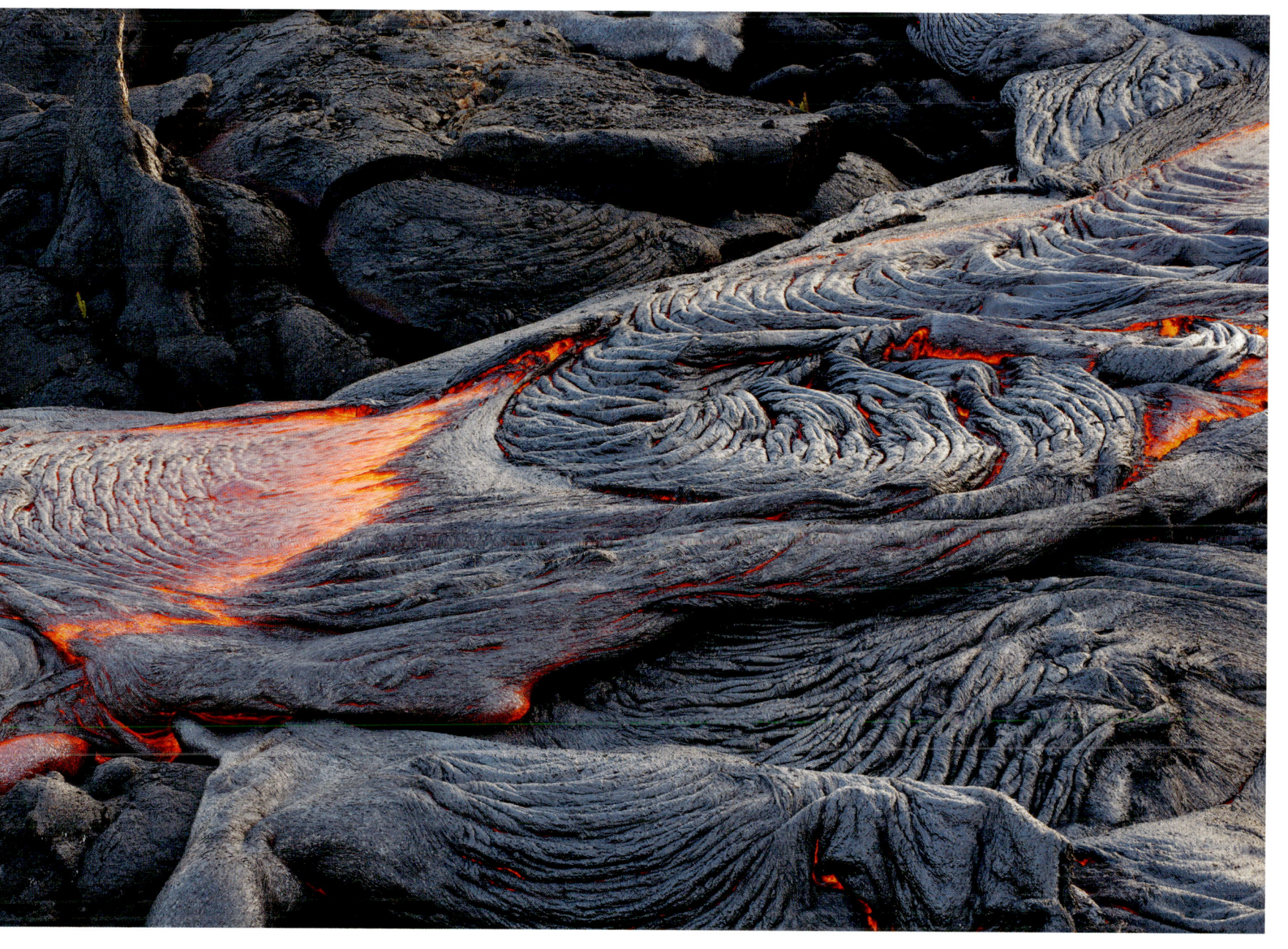

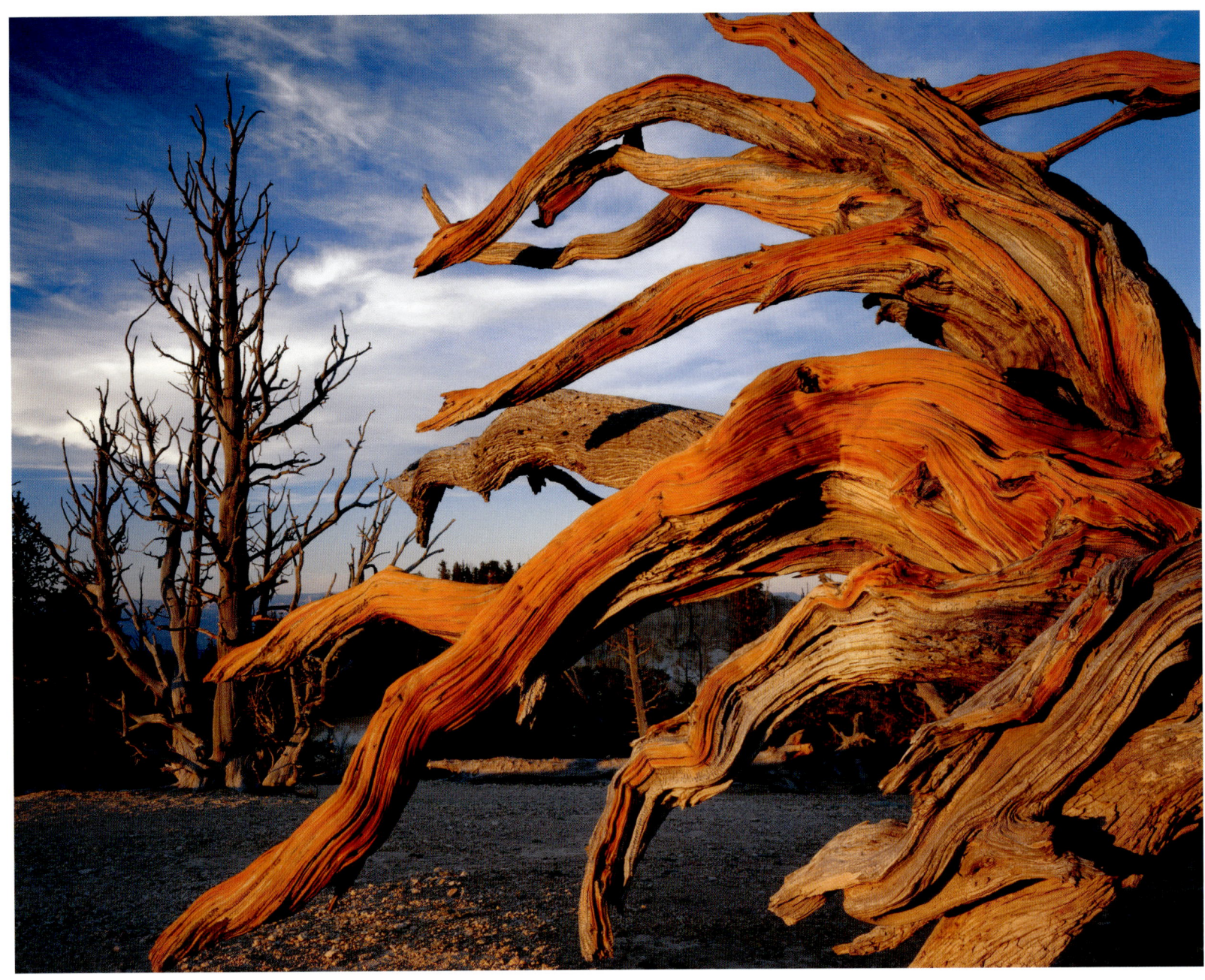

Direction into the frame fulfills a purpose. Besides pushing the eye into the frame, it also creates interest while at the same time providing information. By illustrating the texture and detail of the foreground roots in this image, the felled bristlecone pine's roots direct the eye into the forest on Bryce Canyon's rim. The roots direct the eye with lines while emphasizing the weathered texture of the ancient trees.

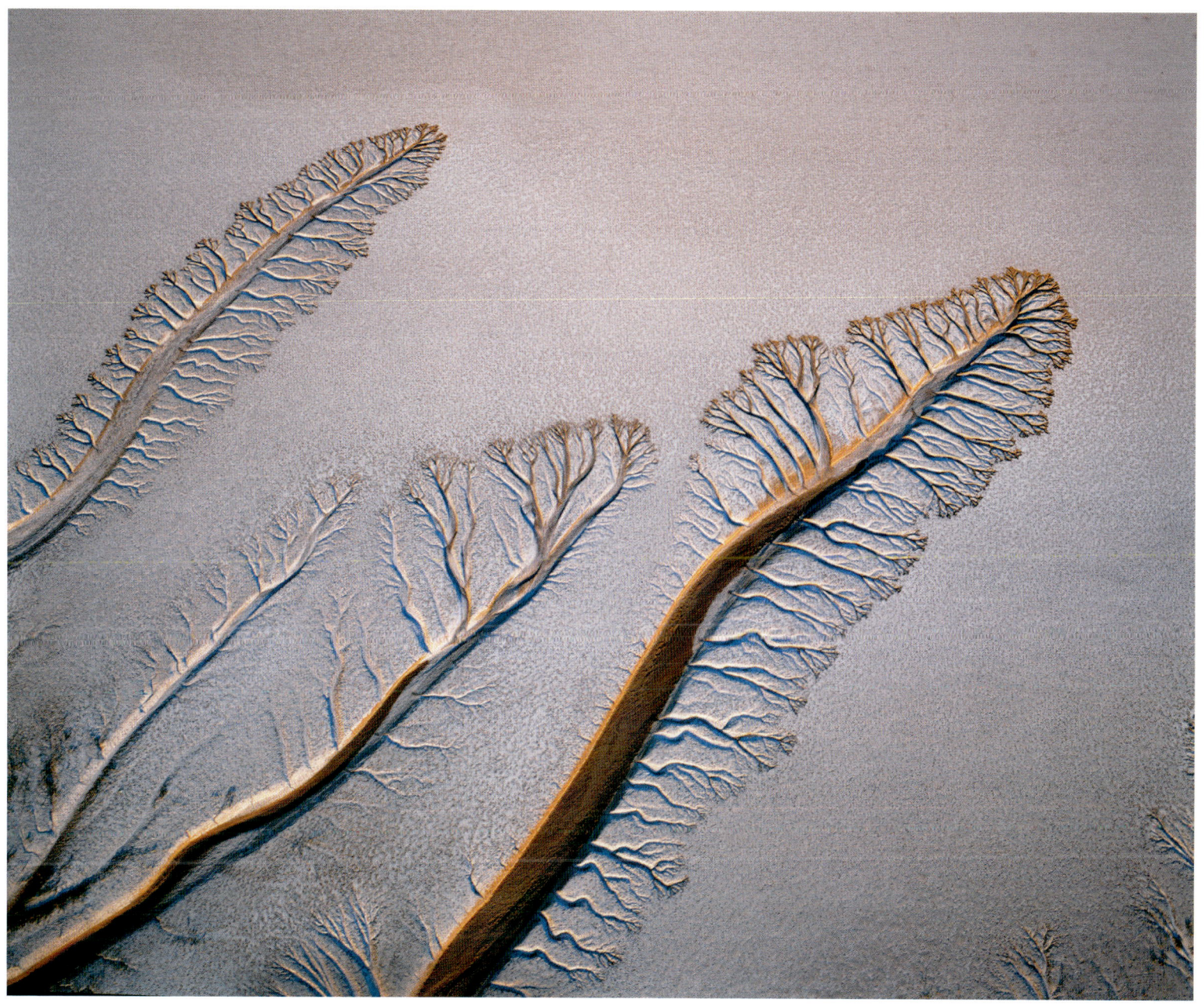

The strong lines created by eroded drainages in the Colorado River Delta drive the eye upward into the frame. They resemble trees, as each delicate river course split appears to be the branching of a tree. By leaving space at the top of the frame, I emphasized the upward direction, further reinforcing the illusion of trees growing. The more passive lines at the lower right provide balance to the photograph.

Feeling/Voice

Images can evoke feelings. They can whisper or shout. By determining the contrast, color, action, or perspective, we can refine our message. For instance, coastal tidal pools can be tranquil reflection mirrors with an empty beach, like the first image on the right, reinforcing the vastness of the scene.

Alternatively, by concentrating on the action of onrushing surf, we can achieve a totally different feeling, as shown in the second image.

In both cases, I made a conscious decision of what I wanted the viewer to react to and focus on. I want people to share my feelings when they view my images.

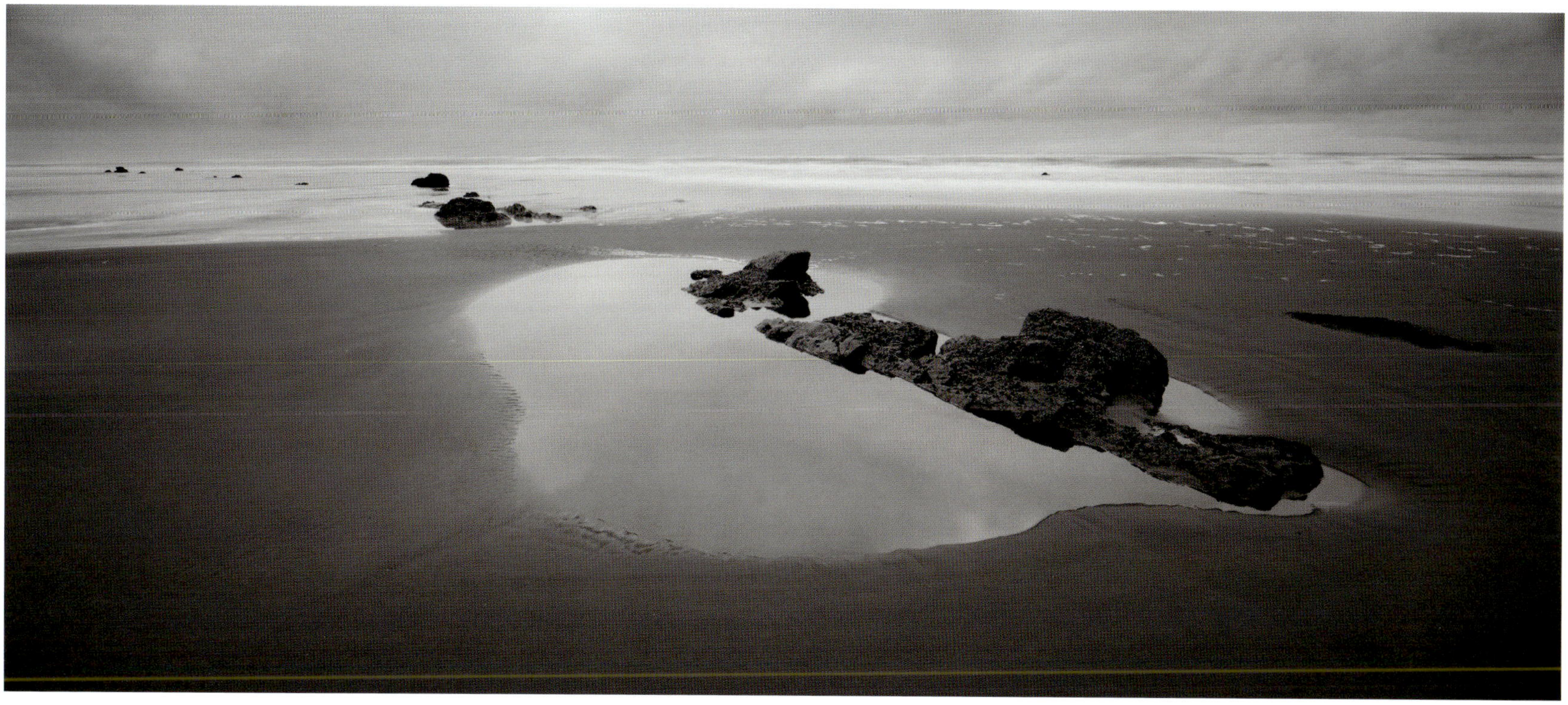

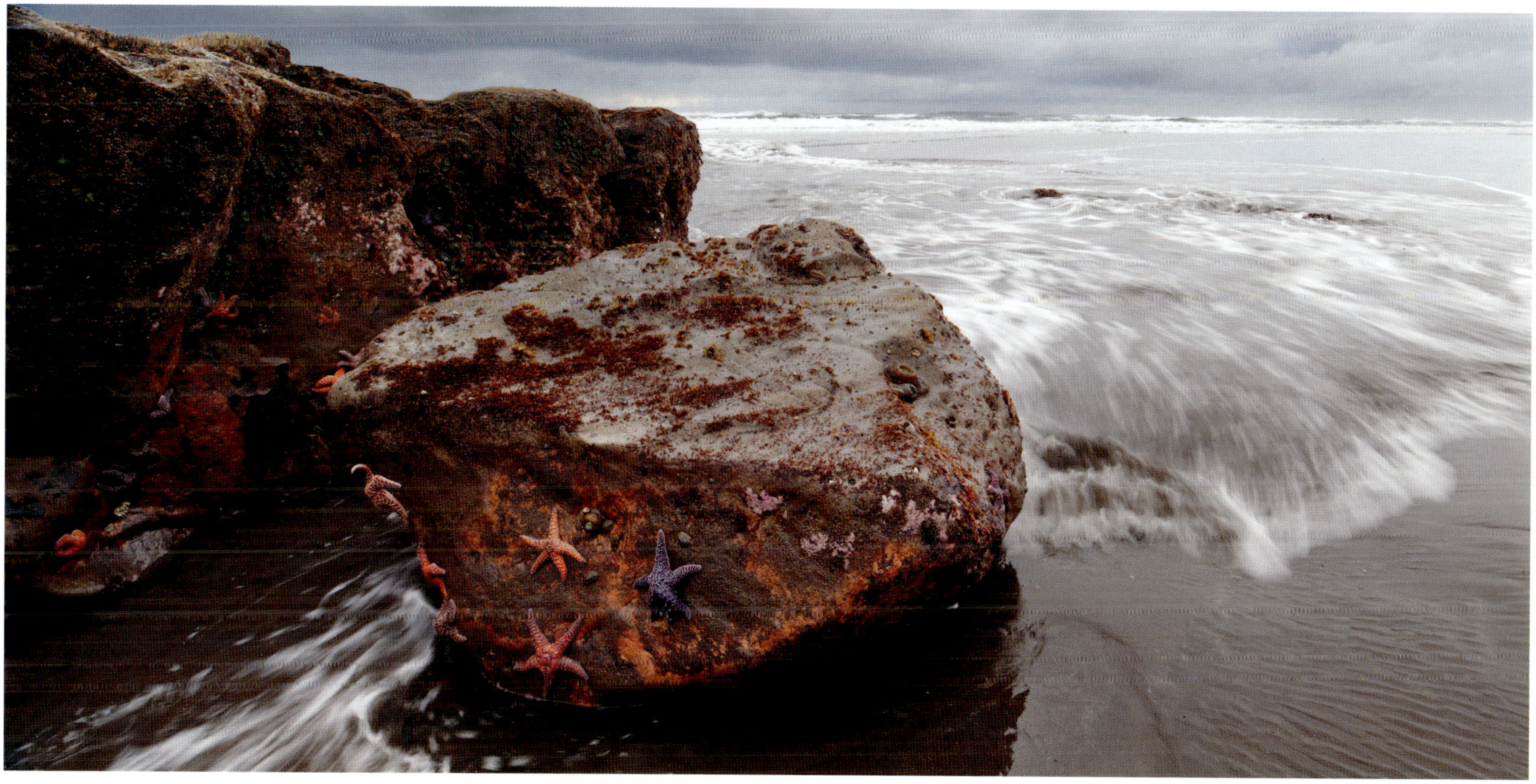

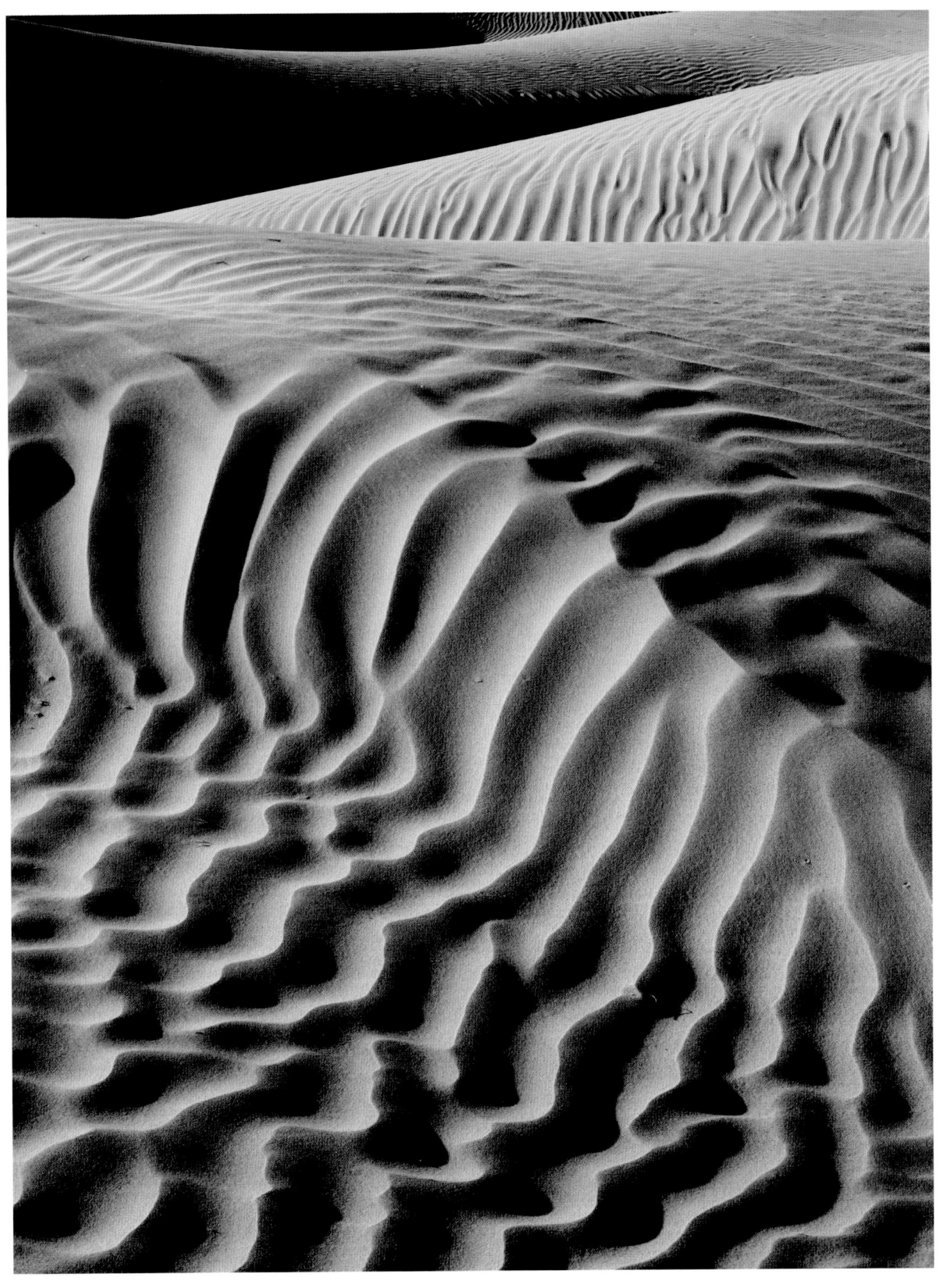

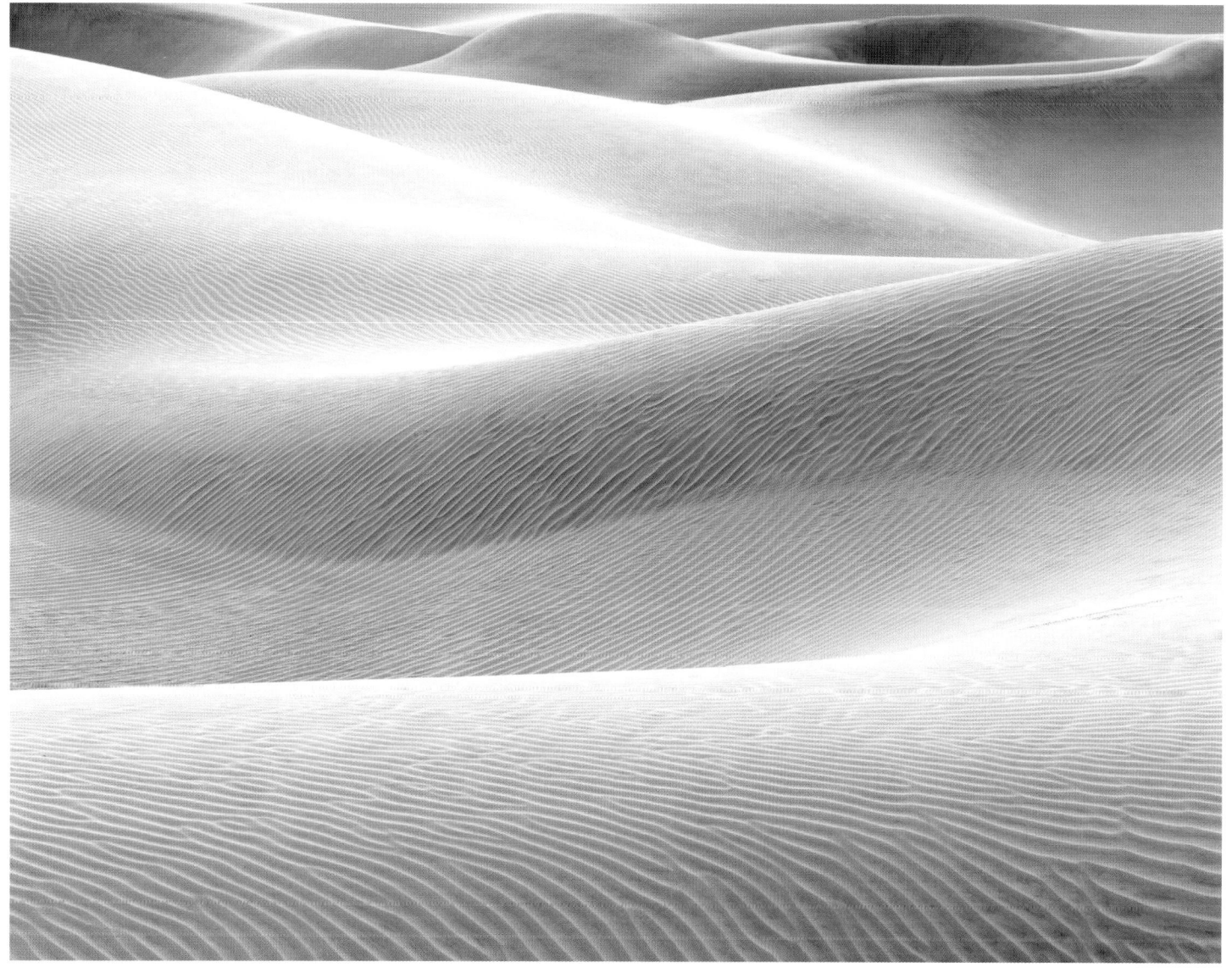

Sand dune patterns vary in the way in which they are sculpted. Some can shout with bold, high-contrast statements of designs emphasized by strong cross light, as with the dunes seen on the left.

Or dunes—even those in the same area—can whisper a totally different message if axial light is used to present a shimmering softness. In the photograph above, the shadows are more open and contrast is minimized, giving the interpretation of a sensual feeling.

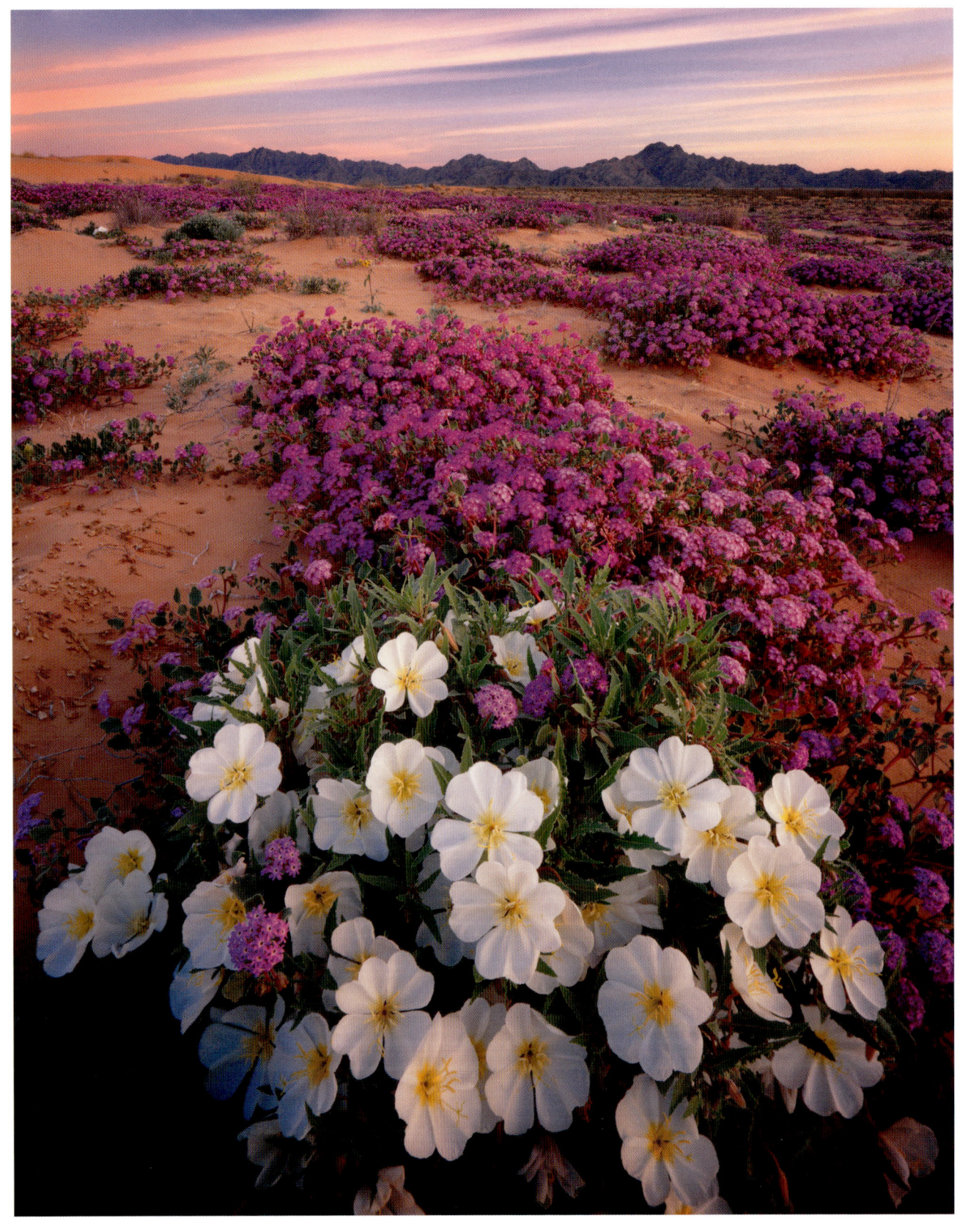

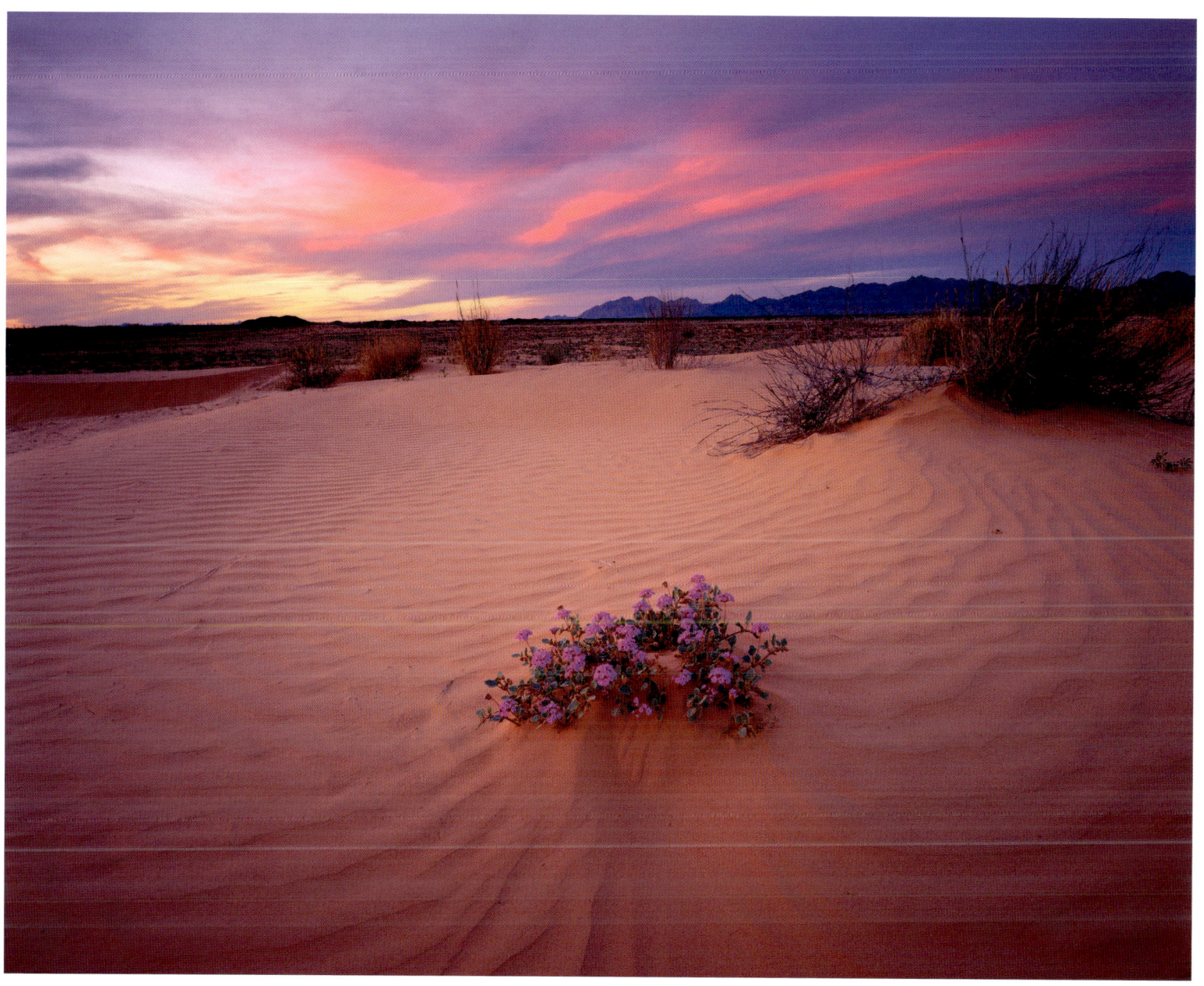

My book on Arizona gave me the excuse to spend a couple of weeks camped along the Mexico-Arizona border. I was surrounded by a sandy wilderness perfumed and colored by a floral explosion. Intoxicating doesn't begin to describe the feeling; it was as though the desert was pumping as much life into a short period of time as possible. My heart sang as sheer joy directed my camera to capture the image seen at the left.

I had other feelings as well. Hiking alone in this otherworldly setting, apart from my city home, I was a solitary figure in the vast Sonoran Desert. That was my mood when my eyes locked on to a solitary sand verbena under a sky crimson with sunset afterglow and I captured my mood on film.

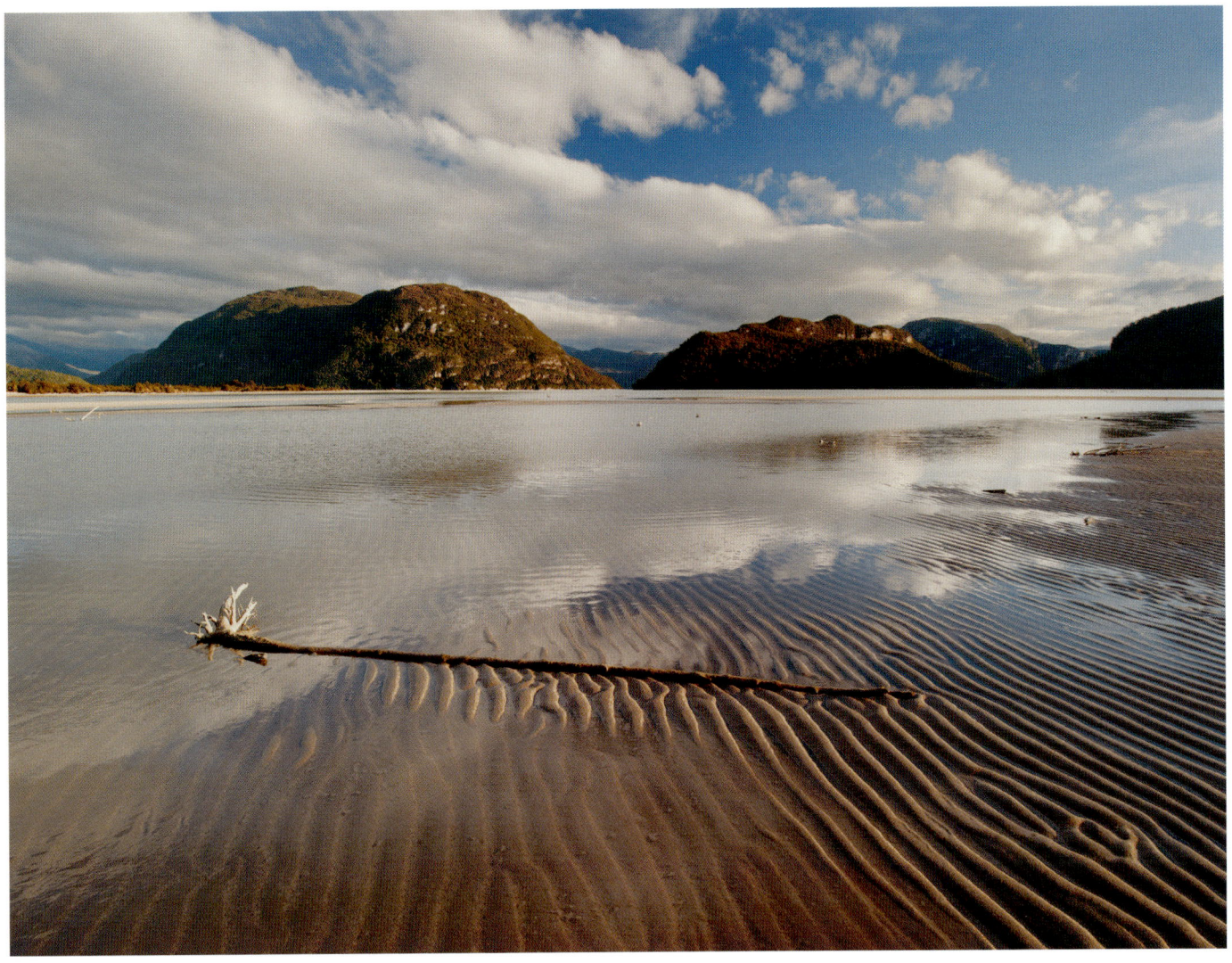

I was at the terminus of Chile's Rio Baker, where it emptied into the fjords through a series of estuaries. The vastness overwhelmed me. It was indeed the big empty, the wild end of the Earth. Everything was on a grand scale and I felt tiny.

Those feelings controlled my vision. Surrounded by big mountains, big river, big sky was little Jack. As I stood on the shifting tidal flats, my feeling of smallness and inadequacy directed my composition like an unseen hand. In front of me, deposited by the immense river was a felled skeleton of a sun-bleached tree.

The scene didn't need any fancy treatment. I chose a straightaway approach that simply honored the scene before me. The grandeur trumped anything I could attempt and the voice of the image was not mine.

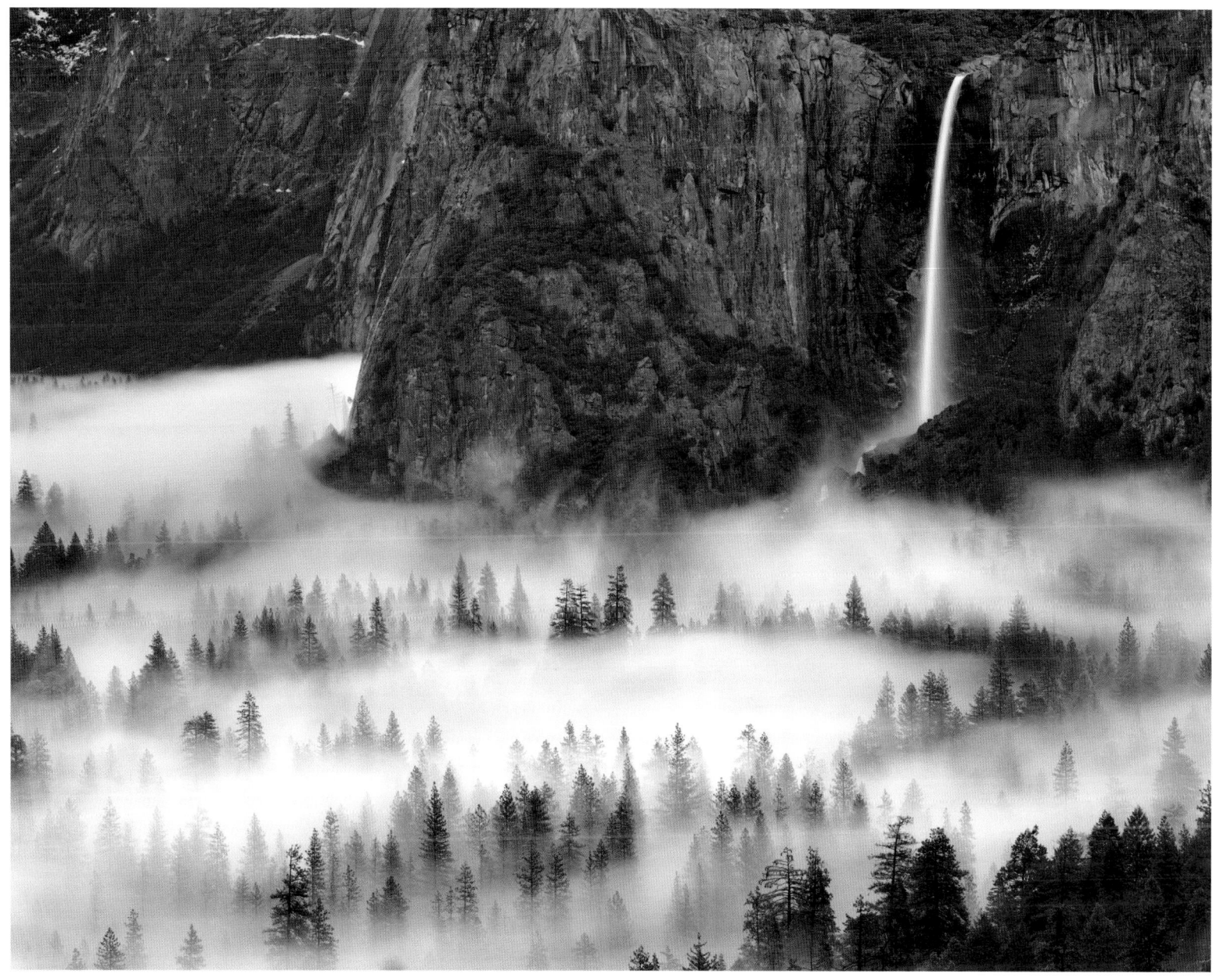

Yosemite National Park's tunnel view overlook is one of those visual icons that Ansel Adams gave the world. He pointed the way and his work has invited battalions of photographers to view the American West. I remember smiling after seeing a photograph of a young and vital Adams, cooking on the tailgate of his station wagon. His hair was matted and he looked as though he had been camping awhile. I felt a kinship. I knew he loved the land, and each time I visit Yosemite I can't help but think about Ansel.

During one such visit, a storm was clearing and the fog hung low in the valley. From where I was camped, there was no visibility. I decided to drive higher out of the valley to gain a better viewpoint. As I watched, the fog began to boil and sink through the conifers below. I felt the joy Adams must have felt in this sublime setting and I preserved it in this image.

When I lived in Chicago I would have scoffed at the idea of possessing strong feelings for a piece of real estate, and yet I do. Wild rivers, empty deserts, and dense rain forests have become my friends. Images become invitations calling us back for a visit. And so I continue to return to these very special places.

Negative Space

There's a time when the subject matter shifts from what you have originally planned. This occurs when the negative space, or the background space, or a vacant shadow area forms an interesting design element in itself. I can recall photographing hoodoo rock formations in the Grand Staircase-Escalante National Monument in southern Utah. I was carefully crafting an image that featured two giant boulders, with a narrow sliver of daylight in between. As I was photographing the boulders, I soon recognized that my subject was no longer the rock formations, but had become the sky in the triangular space between the massive black shapes. I wanted to further emphasize the triangular section of sky and the solution came with patience and a passing cloud. Thanks to the unexpected appearance of the cloud, the eye would now lock on to my selected area of interest.

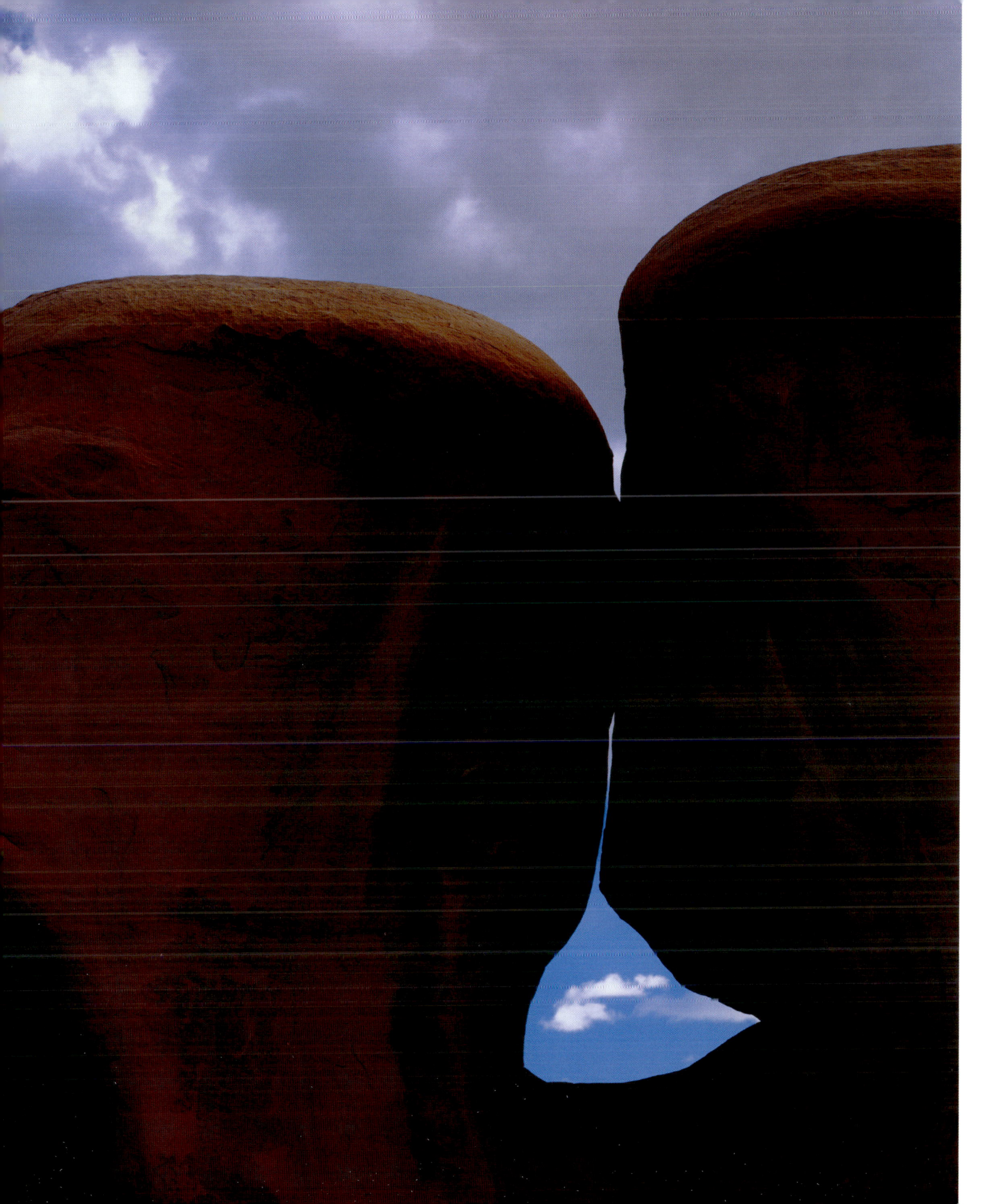

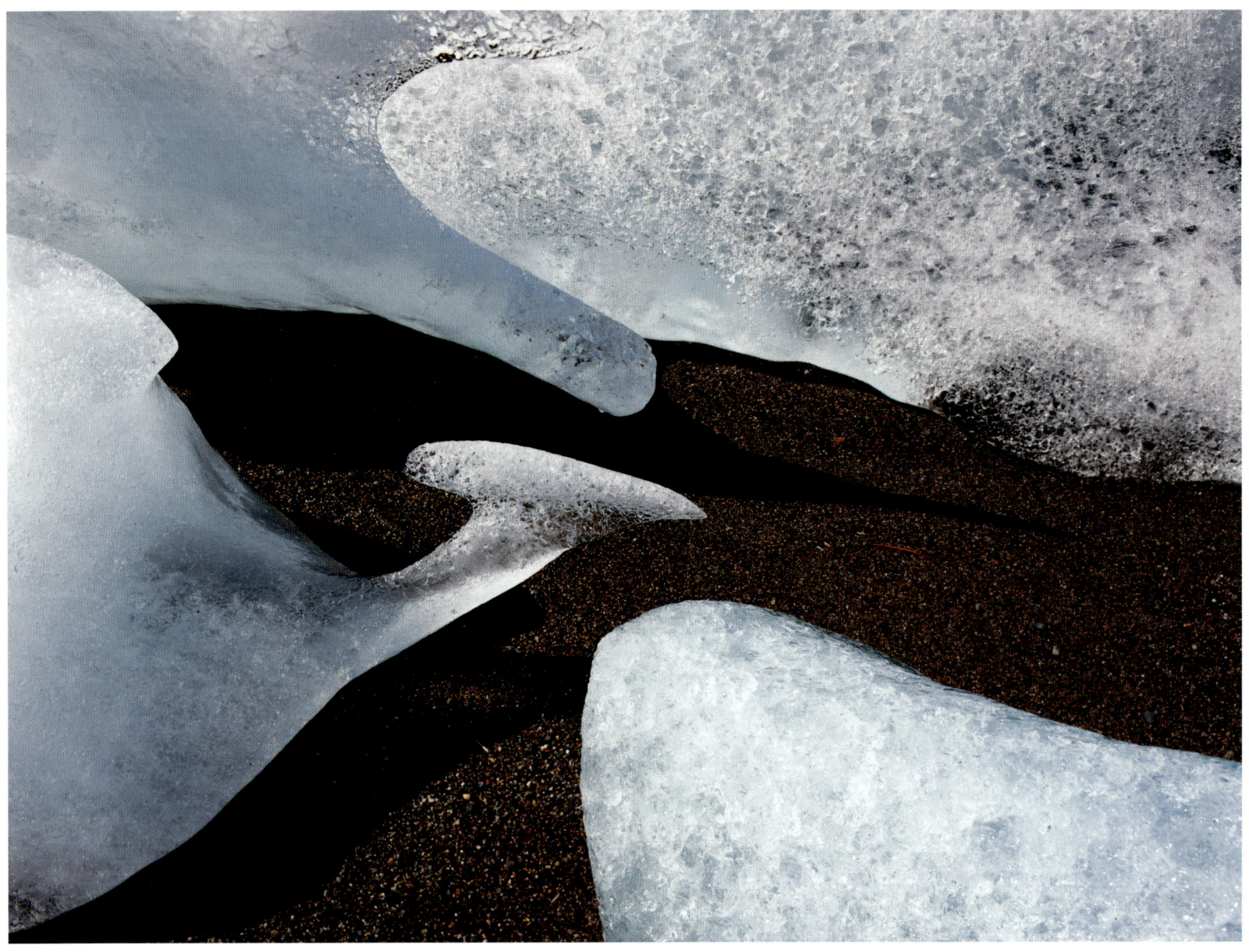

Predictability is the enemy of great photography. Being open to the surprises and visual gifts along the way can redirect our vision to the unexpected magic. While walking along the iceberg-strewn shoreline in Chile's Patagonian region, I found myself at a loss for what to photograph. I had made the grand overview images, but I felt I needed something different and more interesting. I became increasingly drawn to the smooth shapes of ice juxtaposed against the black sand beach. I focused my lens on a delicate shape that stood out boldly against the dark background. The image I was after showed the blue ice patterns, but as I studied it, another design shape emerged in the form of the dark area between the ice chards. That design, shown here, was reinforced by the needle-like shadow on the sand. The negative space represented another design.

For a long time I had wanted to photograph the full moon rising in Joshua Tree National Park, which is located in southern California. When I finally got my chance, I used a telephoto lens to capture a detailed view of the moon against the eroded boulders that help define the park. Before I set up to photograph, the key was to back farther away from the subject in order to gauge exactly where the moon would appear. I have many friends who swear they can predict the moon's position with various smart-phone apps, but I like actually seeing the moon. Once I spotted the orb, I moved my camera into close proximity to align the lunar path with a crevice between the granite boulders.

As I photographed, I began to see the distinct shape of a bird's head in the notch between the boulders. The design elements then shifted into simple shapes of blue, black, and white. One of the things I emphasize to students is to squint while looking at images. This reduces photographs to shades of dark and light. An image viewed thusly is reduced to design elements and no longer represents a particular subject ... it's just a design. It's a good way to test a composition.

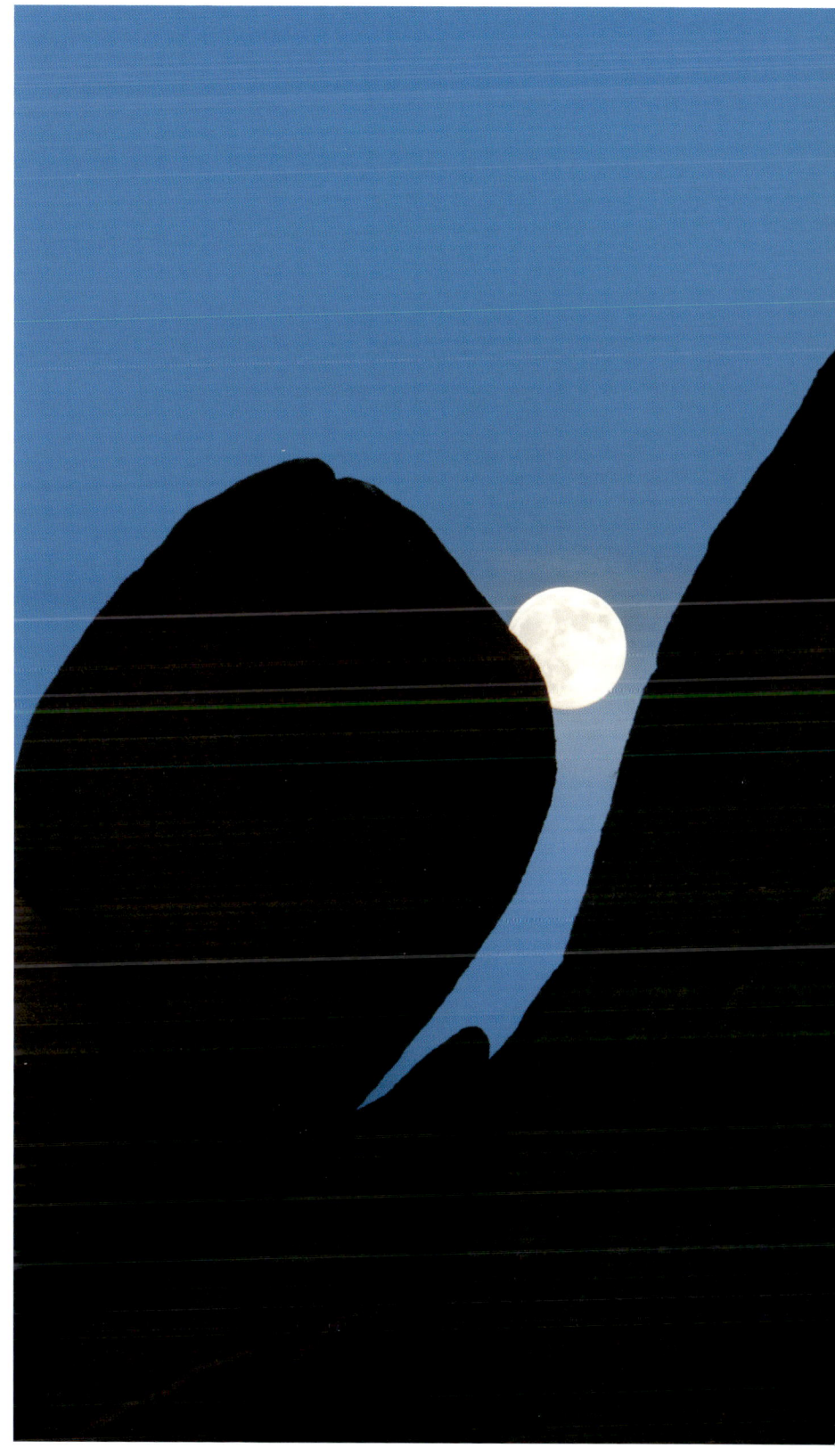

Dark shadows are powerful design elements that create shapes and subjects in tandem with the documentary aspects of an image. An image that carefully utilizes the strength of negative space has extra power. In this photograph, the curved shadow line against the bright blue sky forms a bold black shape that occupies almost half the image area. Its power is undeniable. The scale of the Sossusvlei's red dunes of Namibia is dramatically presented with the shadow creating a black exclamation point.

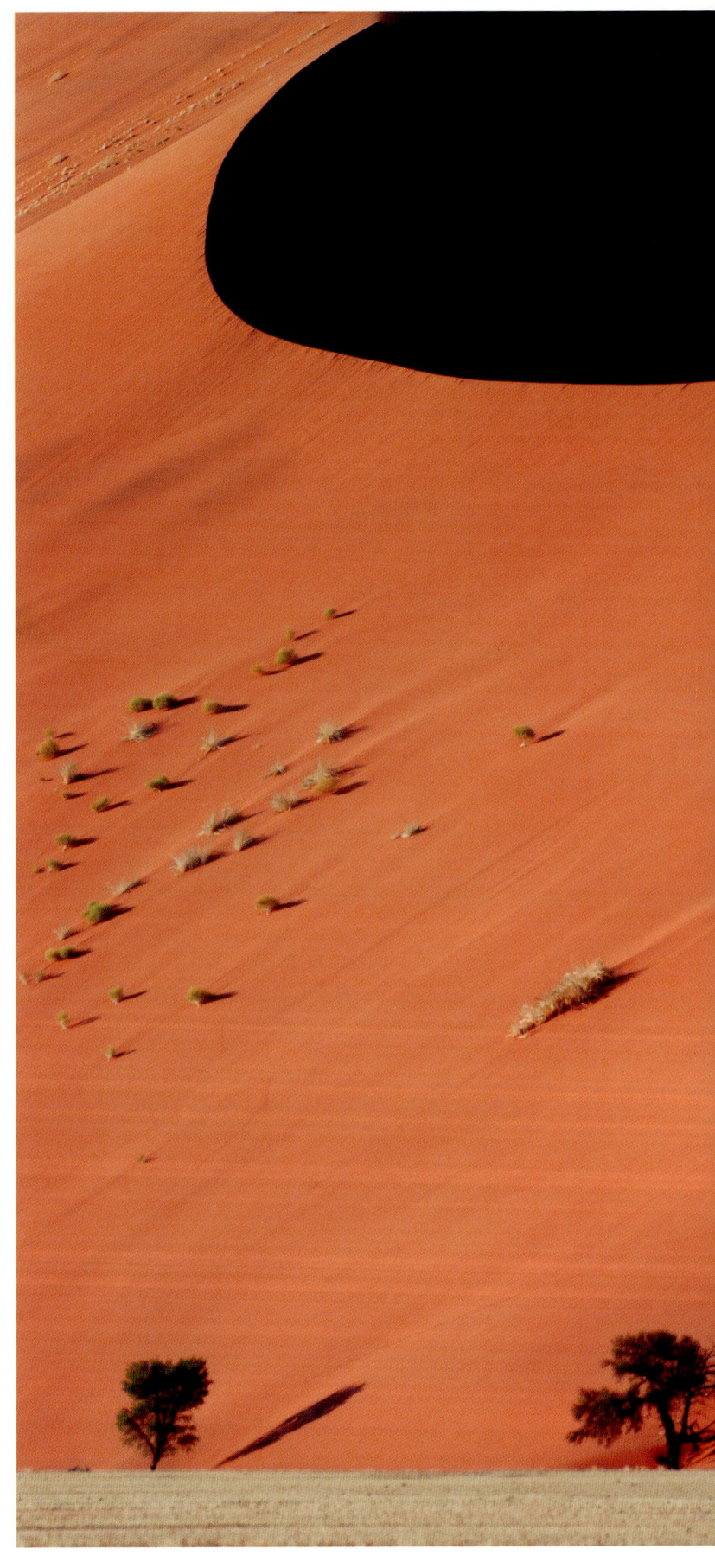

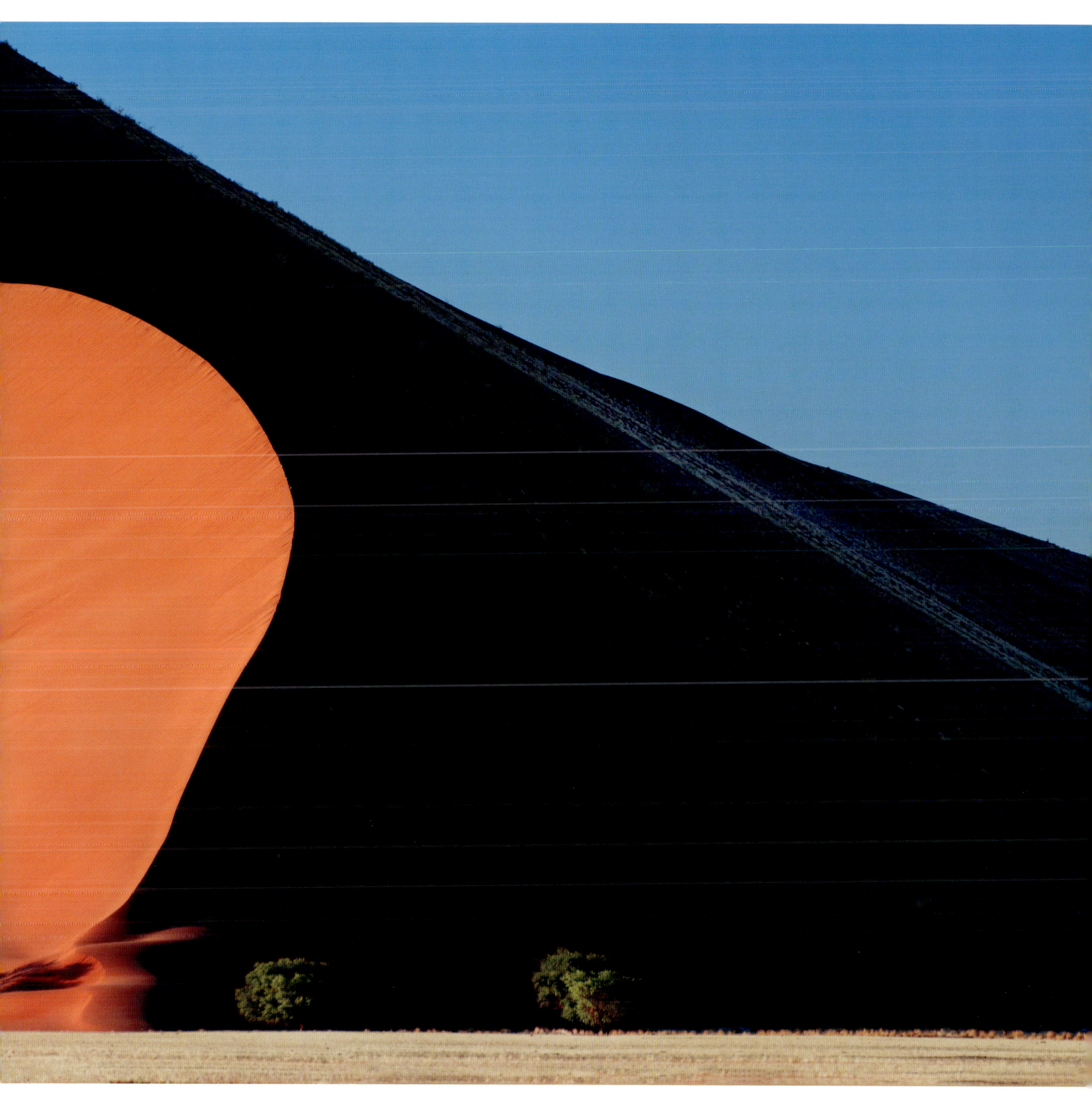

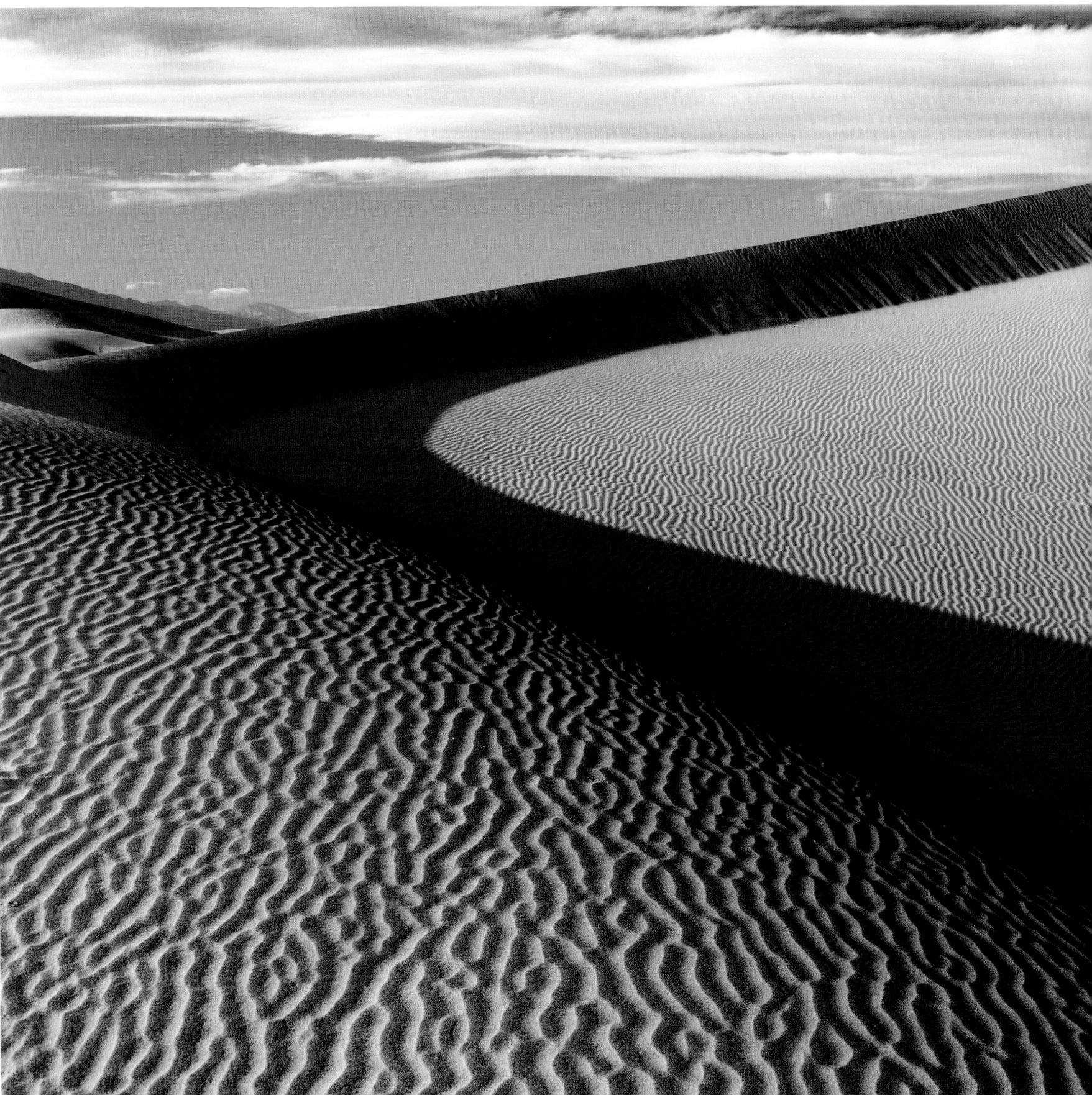

Converting an image to black-and-white can emphasize shadow shapes even further. The contrast can be increased without the associated color shifts that affect color images.

In this image of Death Valley's Mesquite Flats Sand Dunes, I increased the contrast in the patterns to strengthen the triangular shadows bordering the wind-sculpted dunes. As a result, the Y-shaped shadow line turns into a key design element. When I squint at this image, it becomes purely a design of blacks, whites, and greys. Exactly what I was after.

Experimenting

Walking the fine line between absolute failure and creating something never seen before is called experimentation. I hear people say, "You can't stop down beyond f/16 or f/11 because diffraction will doom your effort to failure." I hear warnings about the need for High Dynamic Range (HDR) in order to capture full shadows to highlights. People also tell me that panoramas aren't possible without first making sure the camera's nodal point has been set. And, some say that an image must be composed using the rule of thirds, that it can't be centered, or that midday light must be avoided.

However, in order to create something really innovative you have to break the rules. I break all these rules and more. They're merely starting points. But why not push the edge of the envelope? And since digital cameras supply us with a virtually unlimited number of images, the old adage "just one more" has never been truer. Now, like never before, we can experiment without paying for film and processing while getting instant feedback.

Deep in the Prairie Creek Redwoods State Park in northern California, I became enamored with a scene of a fallen redwood covered with sorrel and sword ferns. I loved the design of a horizontal tree trunk with stately mature redwoods rising in the background and created the image shown here.

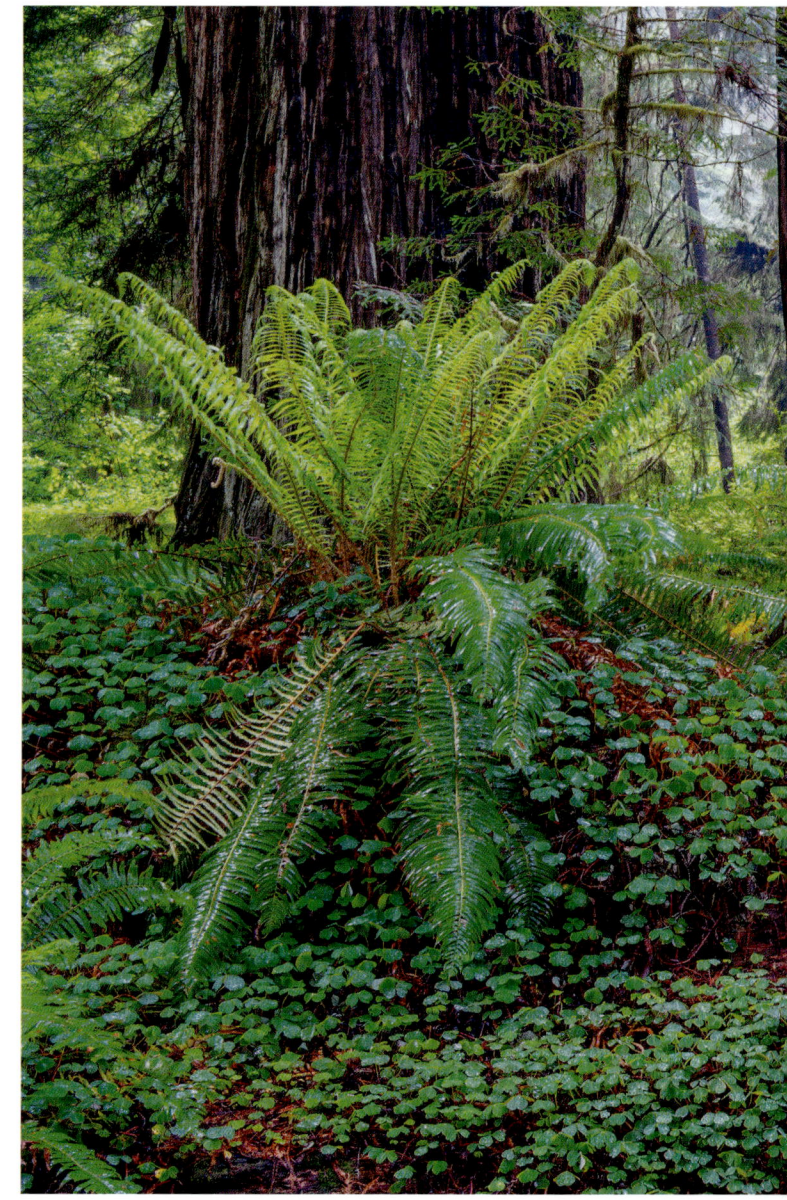

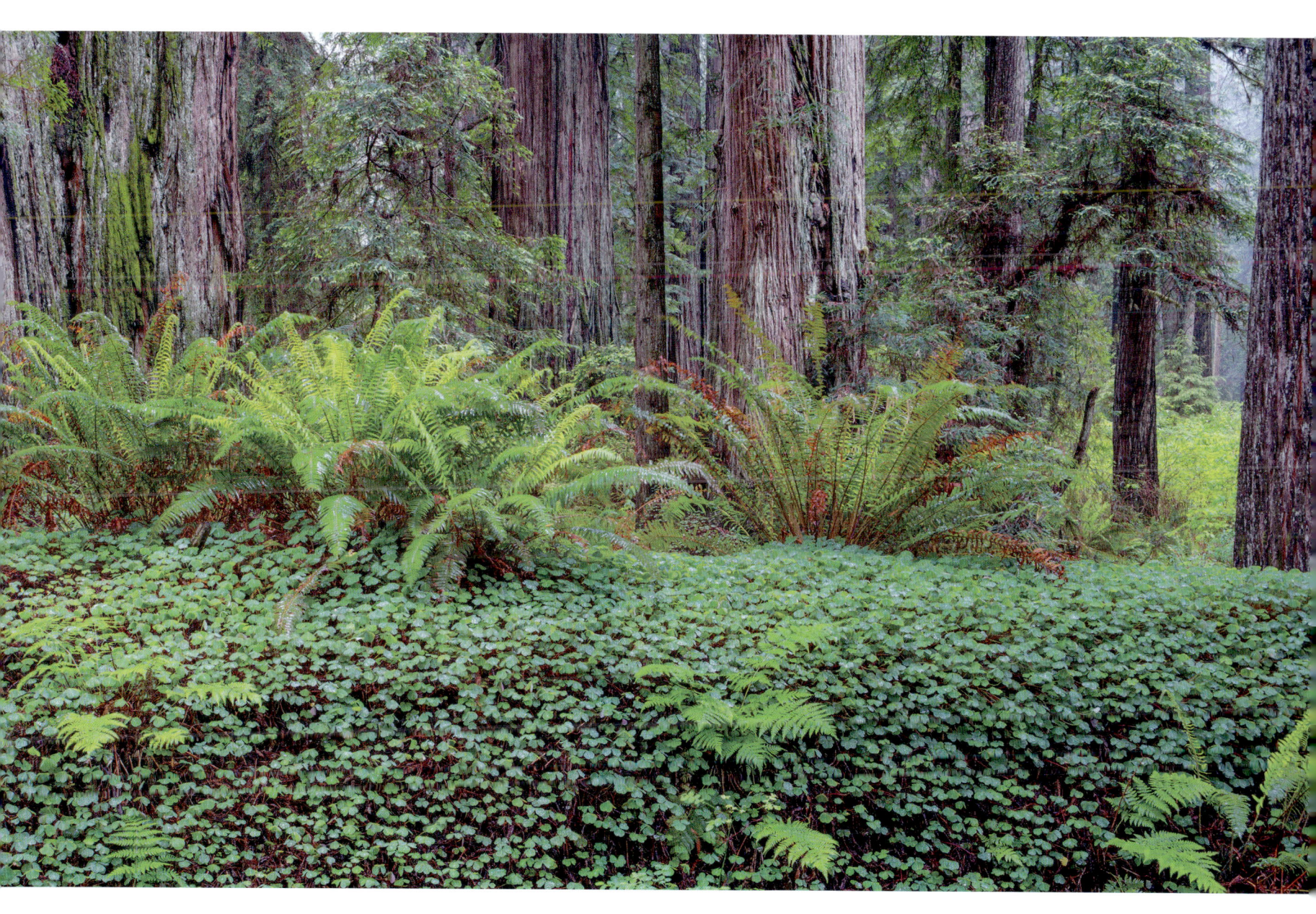

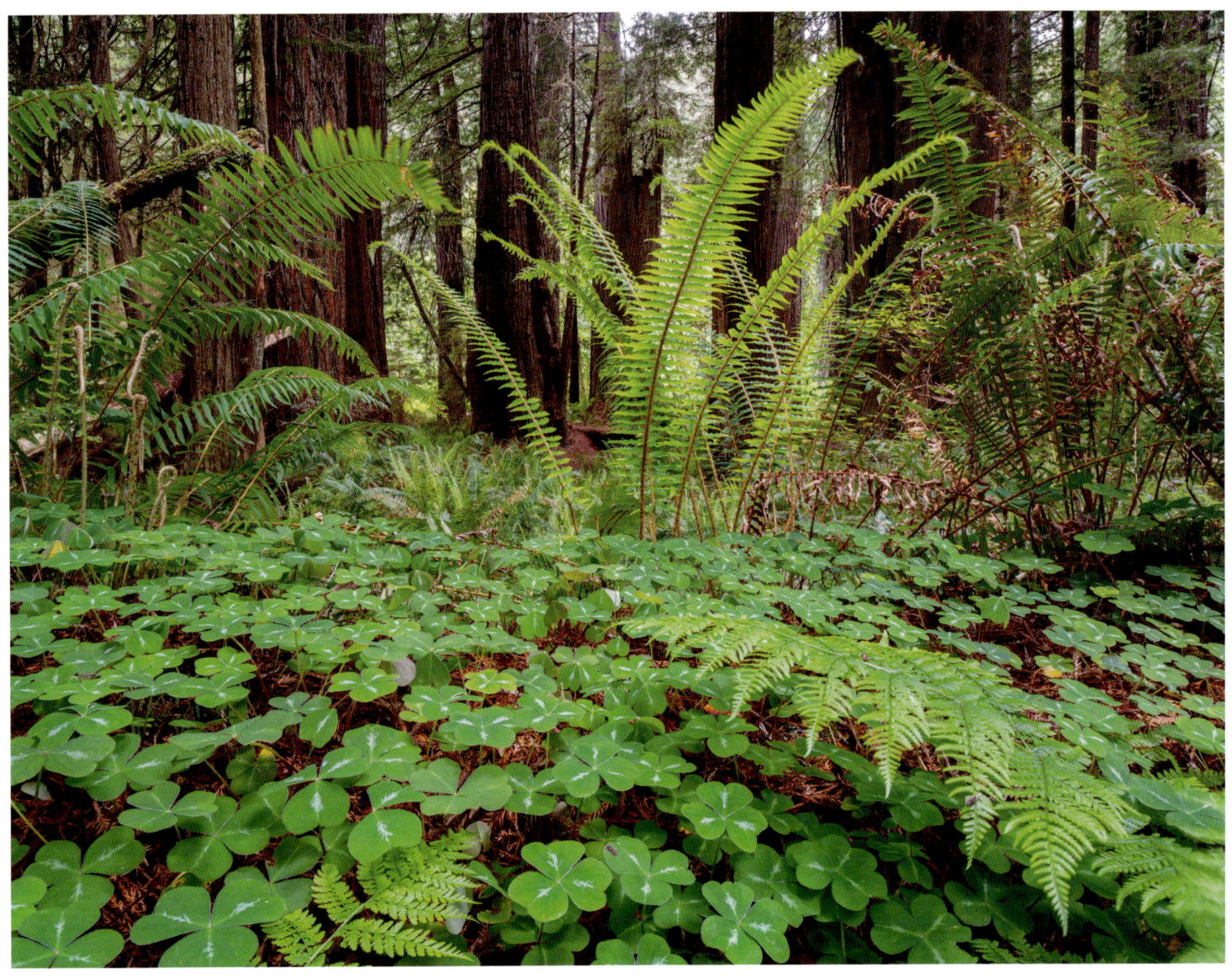

The Prairie Creek Redwoods scene was so good it composed itself. But I felt the sorrel and ferns were getting lost in the scene, so I got closer until the details and design of the sorrel became apparent, as seen in the image above.

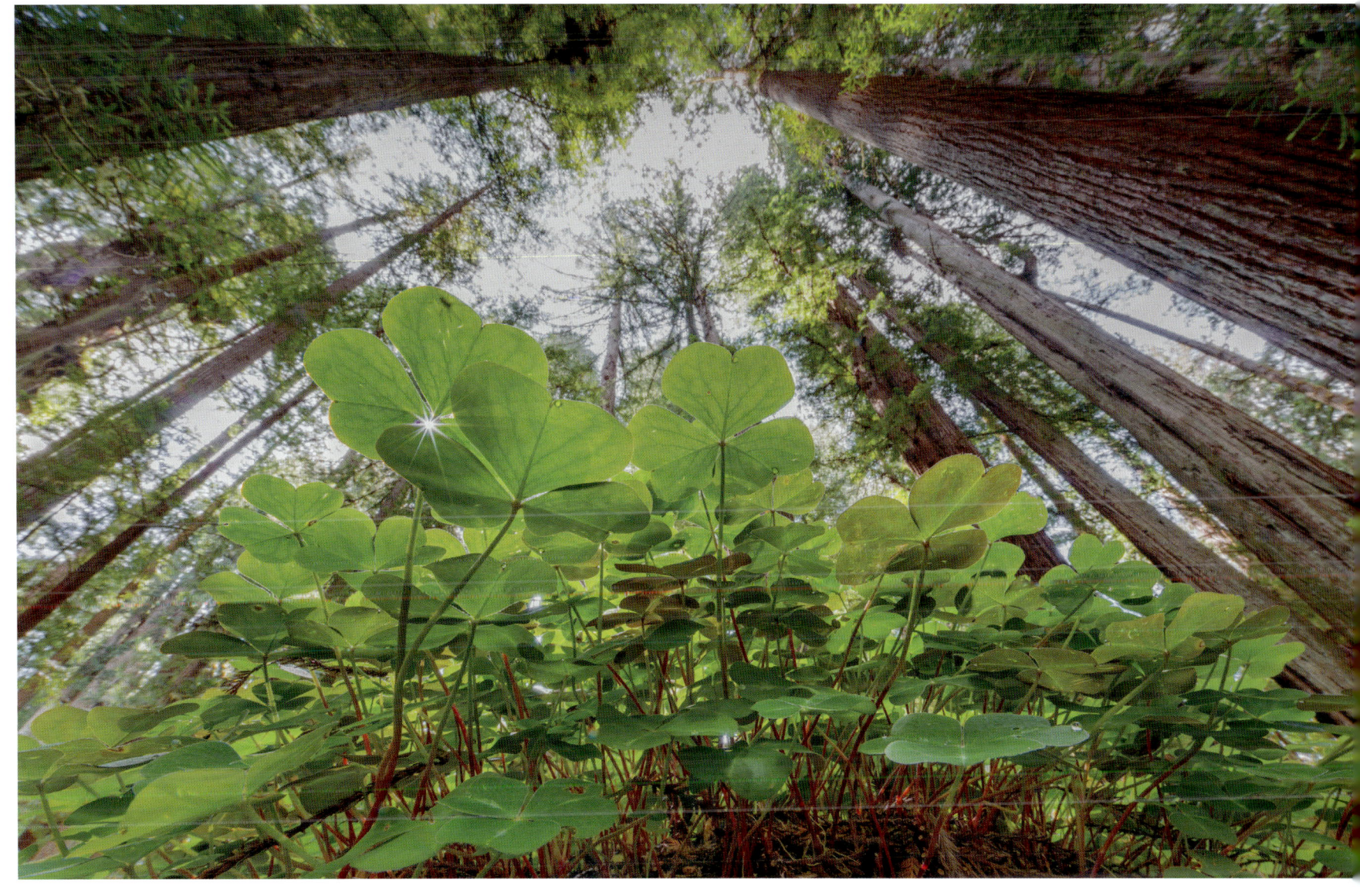

As I got closer to the plants covering the log, I wondered about getting really close and looking up into the gallery forest. I knew I was taking a chance and that failure was the probable outcome, yet I wanted to experiment. So I used my very widest lens: the Nikkor 14–24mm zoom. To get the maximum depth of field, I set the aperture to f-22. One rule broken! Then I pointed the camera skyward into a lightly clouded sky with dappled sunlight streaming down. Another rule broken!

Yet by experimenting and placing the sorrel leaves (now appearing as big as beach umbrellas) so they would reduce the bright sunlight, I was able to make an exposure that might work. By skating on the thin ice of failure, I created an entirely new image.

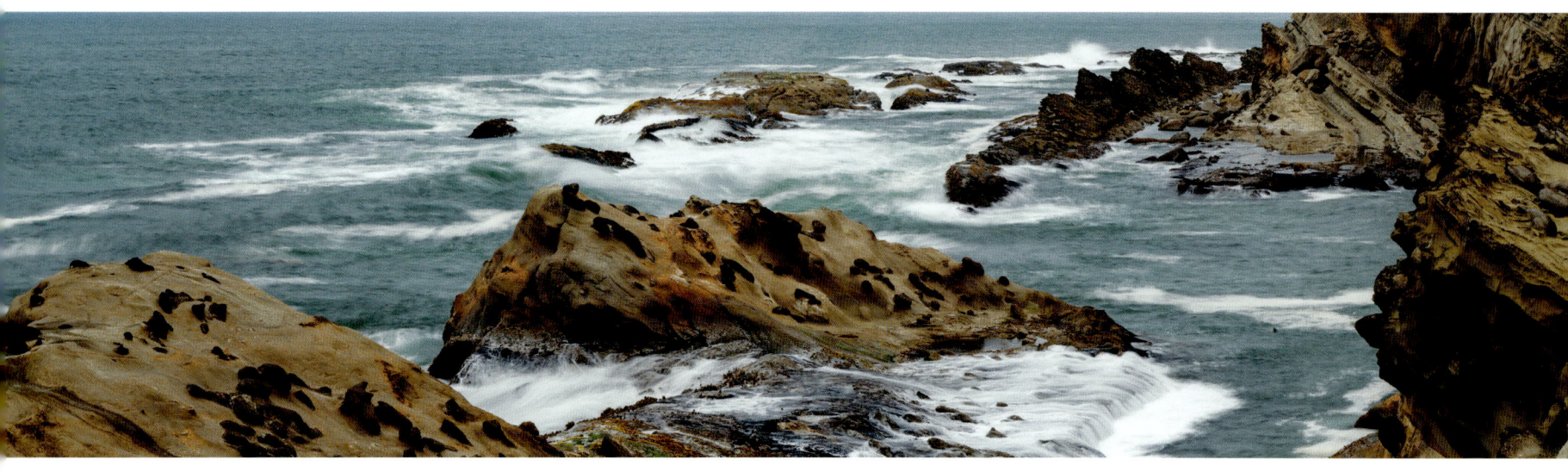

Standing on the high bluffs of Shore Acres State Park in Oregon, with my friends John Shaw and Jeff Foott, we watched the surf from a rising tide pound the sandstone cliffs. I captured the expansive scene before me. My background in journalism taught me to make an "establishing photo"—an image that provides context and a sense of place.

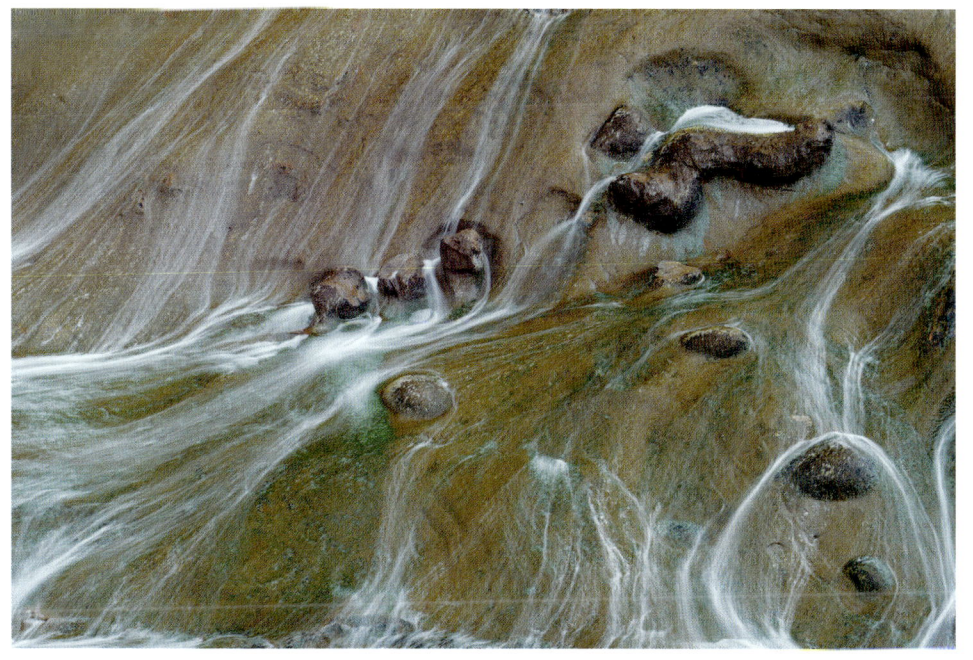

As I studied the scene more closely, I noticed that each wave collided and spilled over the wall, creating a different design with each passing, and I captured a series of images.

Darker concretions embedded into the sandstone protruded from the walls and as each wave hit, the resulting pour-over painted the cliff with streams of moving surf. I noticed that the spillways were somewhat predictable... yet each wave brought a surprise. Some, like the first photograph, didn't have enough water.

At other times, the spillways had too much water and the details and colors of the rock face were lost, as seen in the second image.

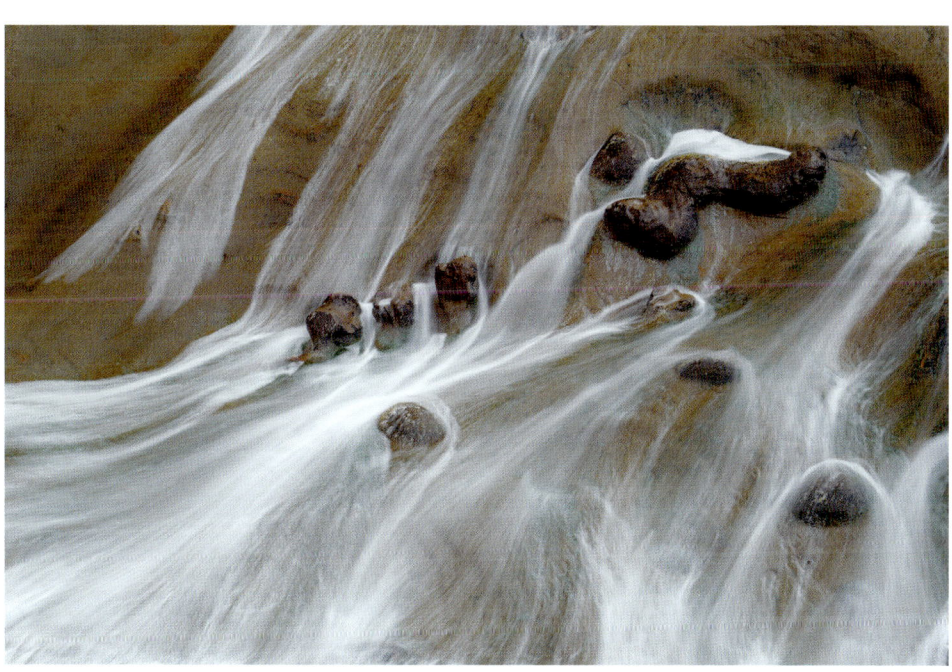

I committed to several hours of waiting for that sweet spot between the right amount of water and the rivulets creating the composition I wanted. Finally, after carefully reviewing each failure, a wave with my name on it arrived. The third image seen here was just right, and the design and the day were complete.

Take the time to experiment.

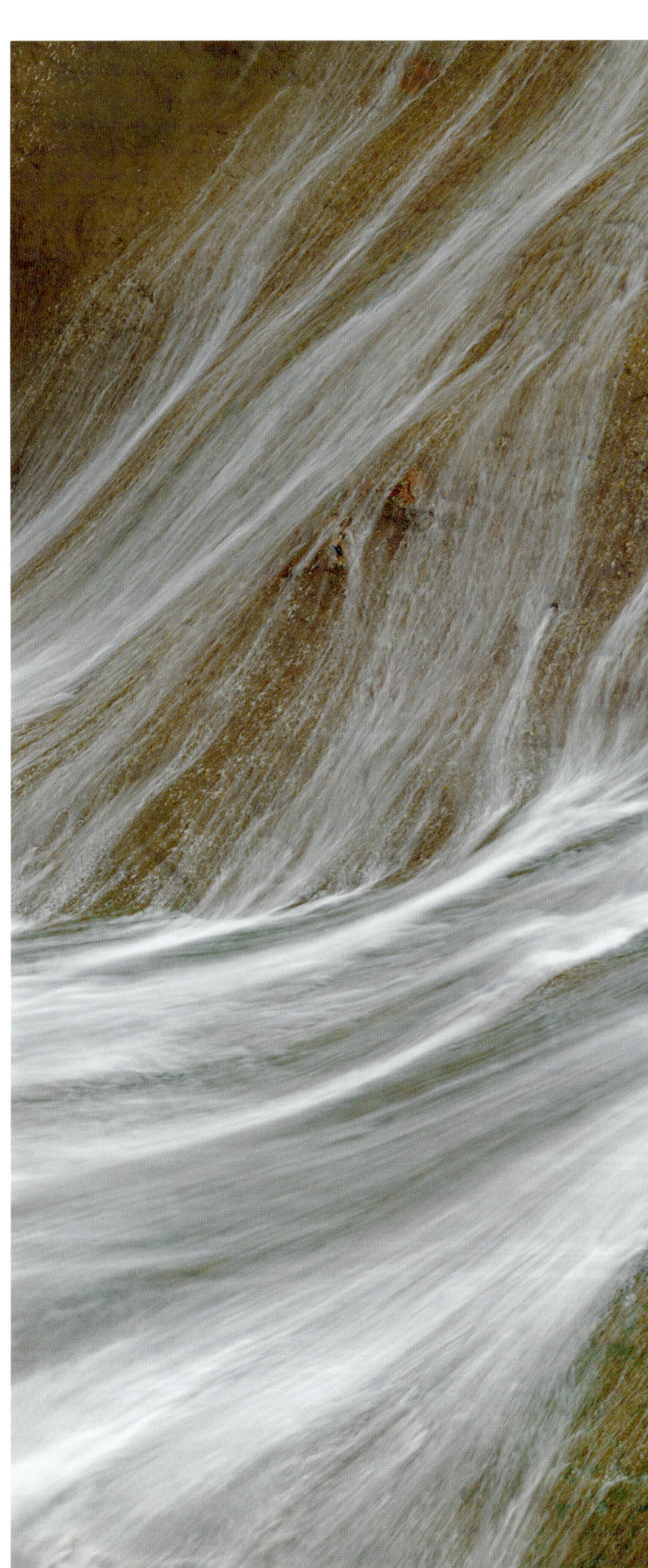

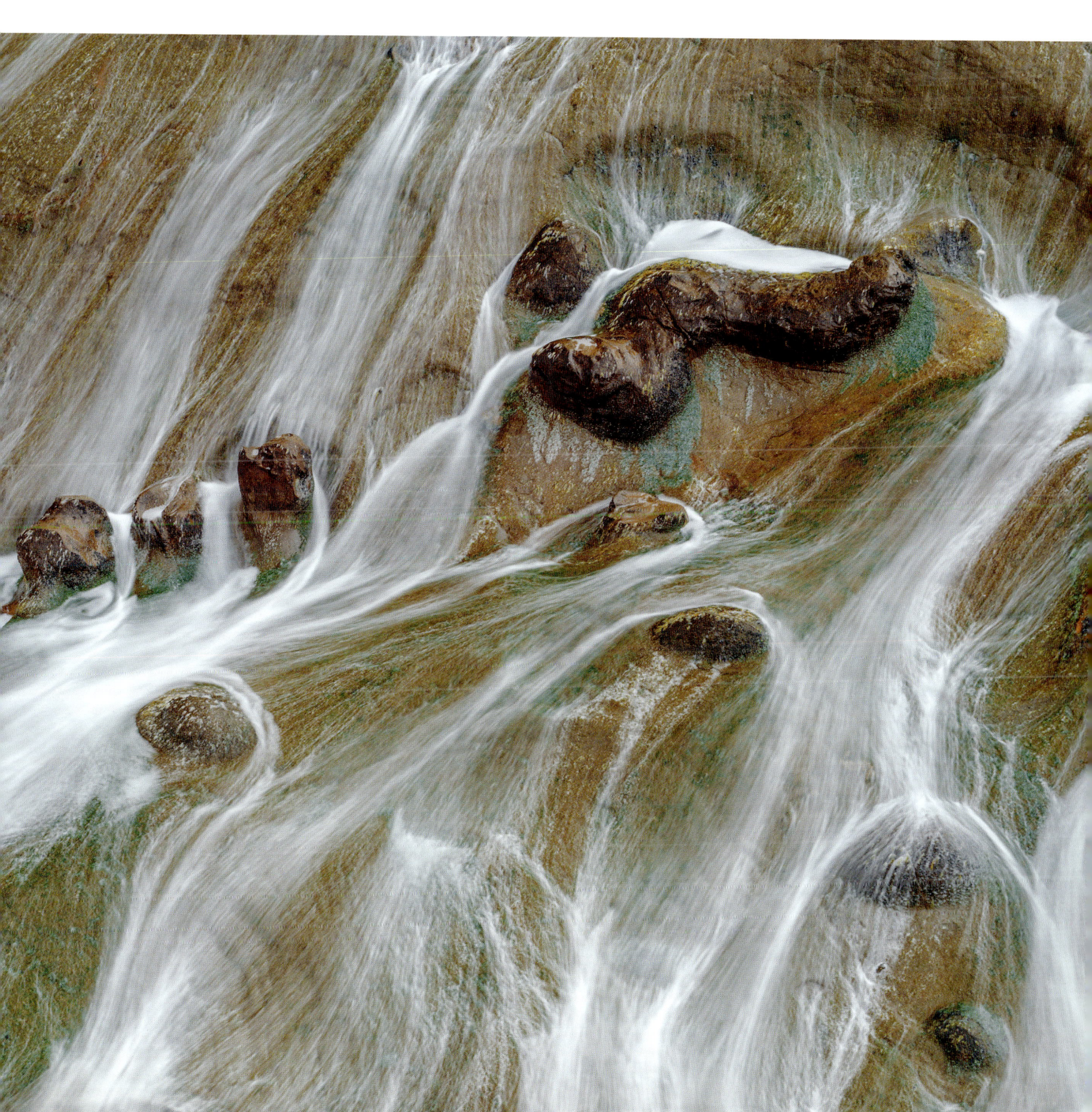

Return

Strong images are like invitations calling us back. I cannot look at my favorite images without feeling that sense of longing. I need to know that place is still out there. I want to know that nothing has changed ... even if I have.

And so I return.

The raging Colorado River is an old friend. Its confluence with the Little Colorado River is sacred to the neighboring Hopi tribe and to me as well. Travertine-colored water mingles with the mighty Rio Colorado. It's both otherworldly and magical.

A few times a year, the angle of the sun is such that it illuminates cliff walls deep into the canyon. Its light brings the rich warm colors, which are in turn reflected in the turquoise Little Colorado River.

My first visit while working as a "swamper" (cooking and leading hikes) in the 1980s netted only unforgettable memories. But in 2000 I returned with a view camera to record the image on the right. My singular attention to the scene planted me in front of another photographer but my arrogance told me I could make the photograph and be out of the way in minutes. Nature had other plans, however. The light proved ephemeral and lasted only minutes. The moment came and went, and years later I was reminded of my transgression. I was a complete jerk, but I hadn't realized it because of my mesmerizing connection to this place.

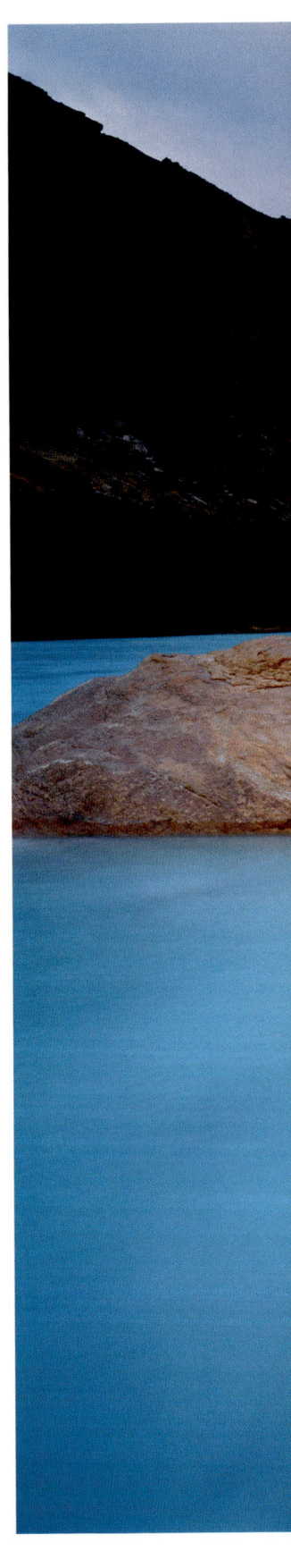

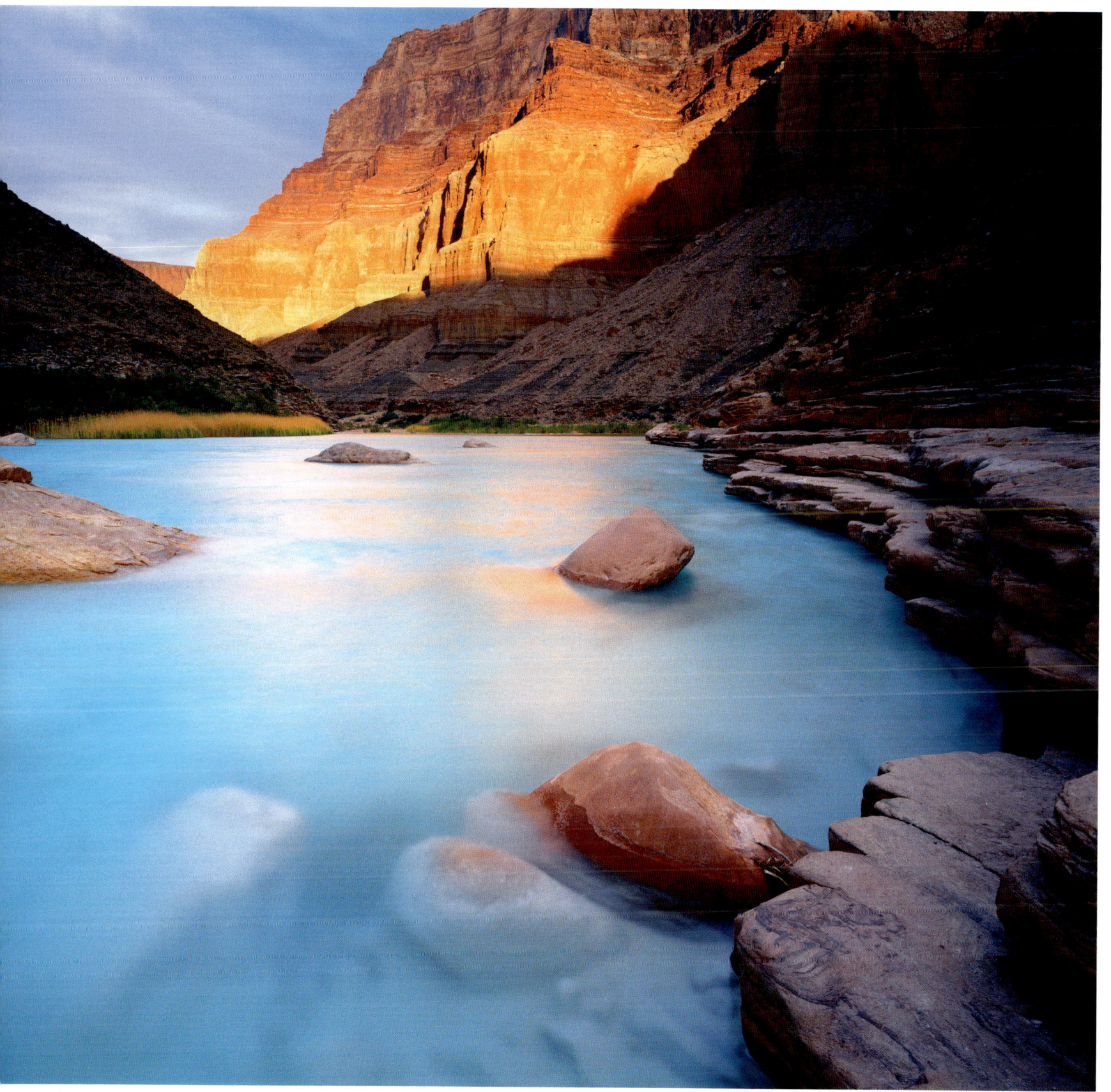

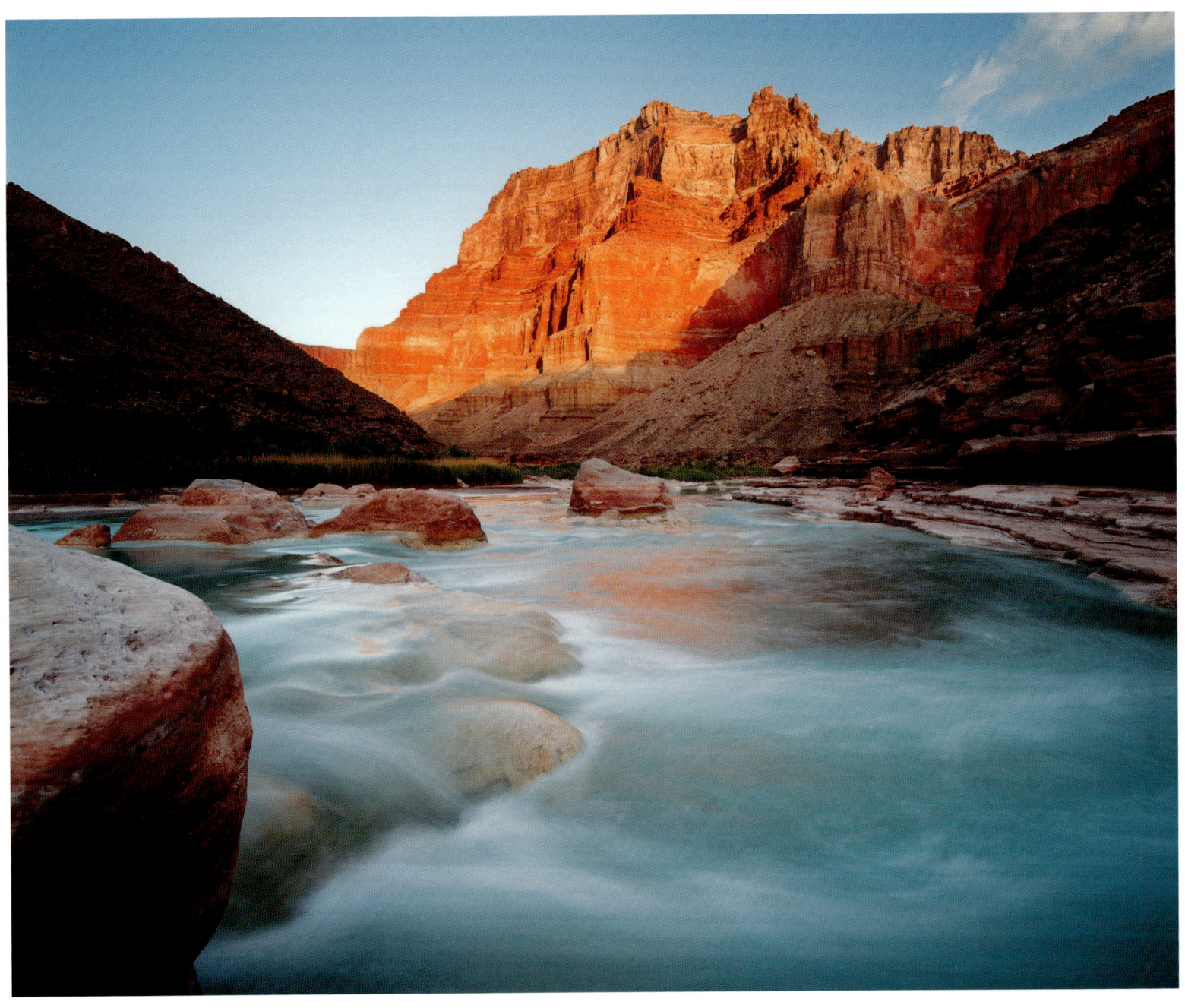

I have returned again and again, but the original conditions with clouds blocking light to the cliff's summit and causing the sun's narrow band of light to vanish so quickly were absent on all subsequent visits. Photographers can never assume that spectacular scenes will reappear. Each visit is another attempt to see a place differently, to observe, and to record honestly and with passion.

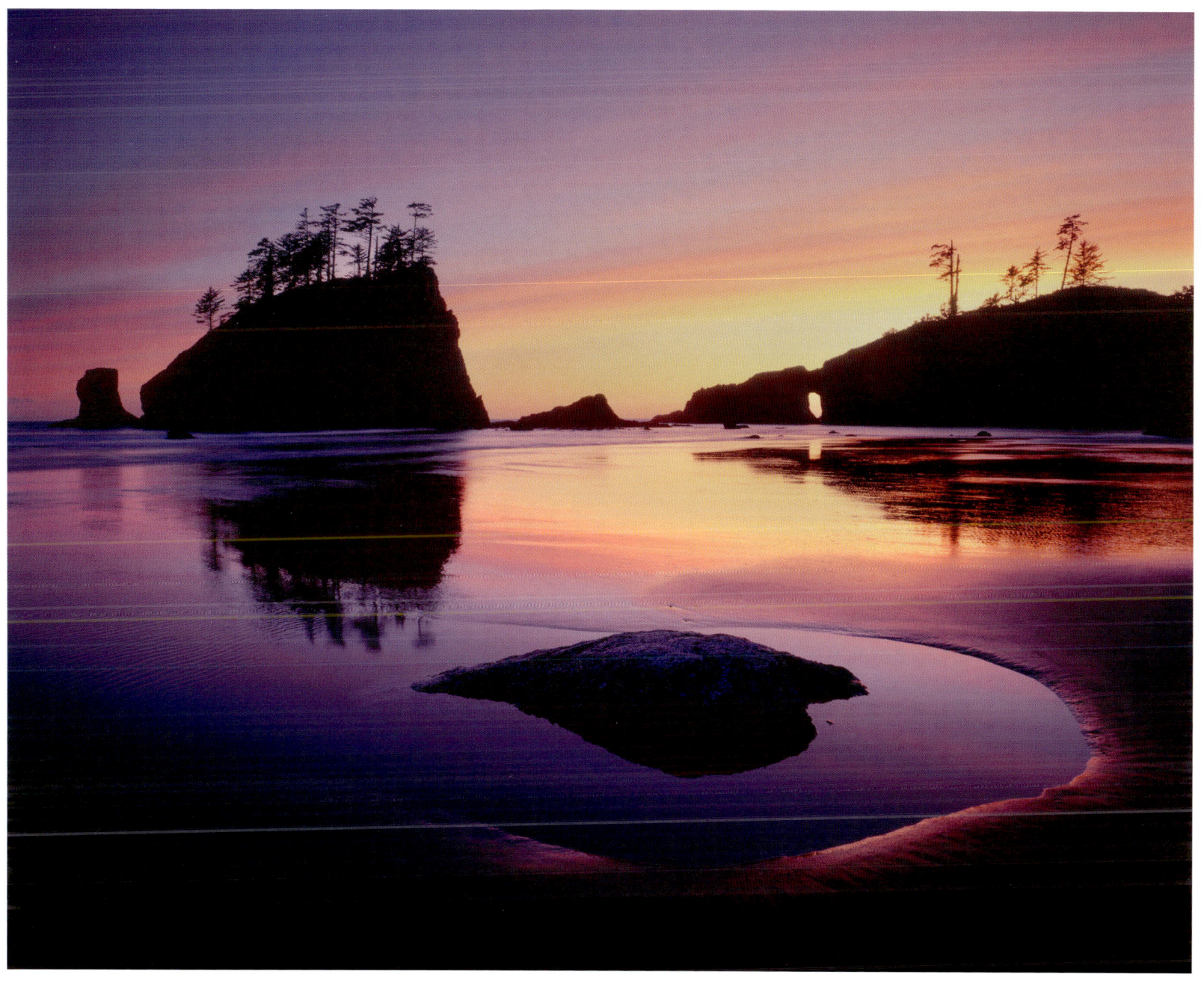

Olympic National Park in Washington possesses a coastline of jagged sea stacks jutting out into the Pacific, with tide pools and shimmering sand in the foreground.

On my first trip to the beach, I arrived well before sunset and enjoyed the time to plan where I intended to be for the last glow of light. The dark, silhouetted monoliths and their reflections became my background, while a coastal boulder in a small tide pool anchored my composition's foreground. The wave action constantly changed the composition as the light ebbed and flowed from the scene. But as you can see in this image, it was worth the wait, as the sky's colorful glow completed the image.

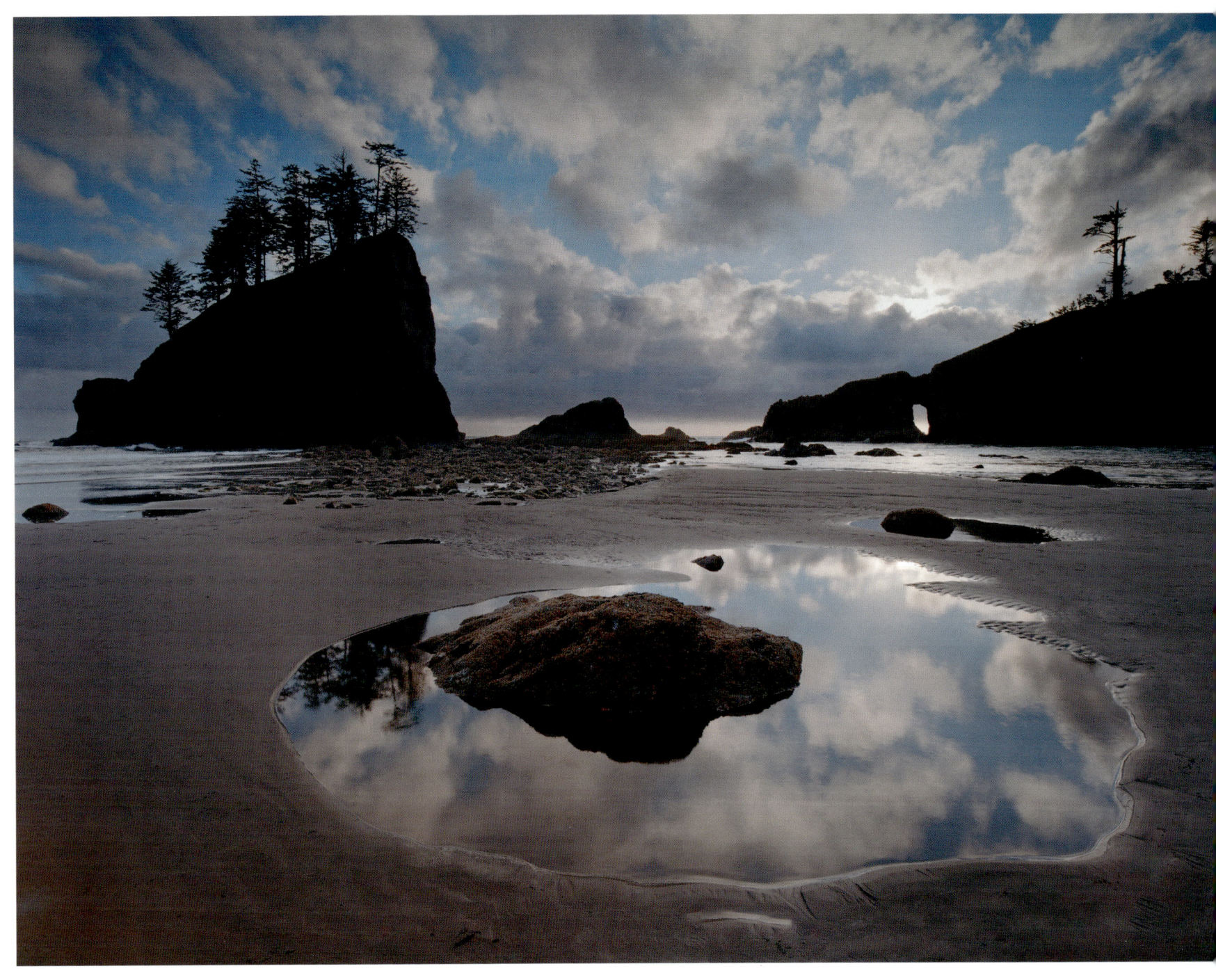

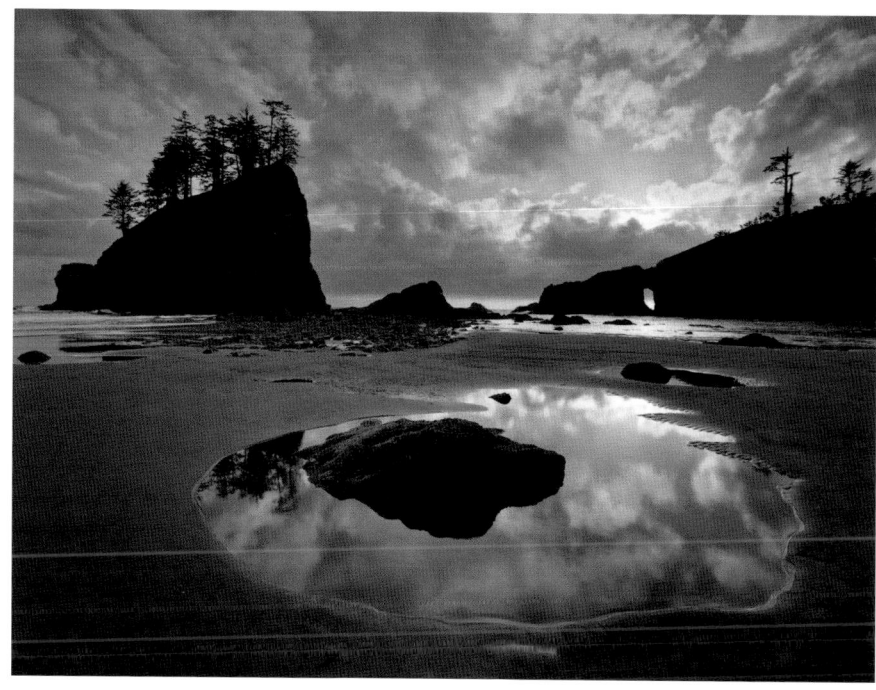

Like a pilgrim, I returned to Olympic National Park years later to find my special place. The rock was there. The pool was there and the sky offered another chance for a similar, yet different, image.

In this attempt, I chose a different focal length and a higher angle to allow for the completion of the tide pool's circle in the foreground. The clouds filled the background and their reflections carried the composition.

To test the strength of the new image (as I often do), I converted it to black-and-white to see if the composition held. It did, as you can here.

Another important reason to return to the same place over and over again is to refine an idea. The image on the next page wasn't simply a refinement; it was a direct result of five previous failures. Each time I hiked into Coyote Buttes, located in northern Arizona, the wind was screaming through the petrified sand dune formations and the reflection pool was a mass of waves. One time the wind was so strong that it caught my focusing cloth and sent my Toyo 4×5 camera on a death spiral down the cliff. So it was with mixed feelings that I left a meeting with a Salt Lake City publisher and made the long drive back to this spot that had challenged me for so long.

Arriving in the pre-dawn light, after three miles of headlamp hiking, I was greeted by not only a calm reflection pool, but also a sun-bleached and twisted root lying at the pool's shoreline. Stubborn tenacity sometimes pays off, as it did with this image.

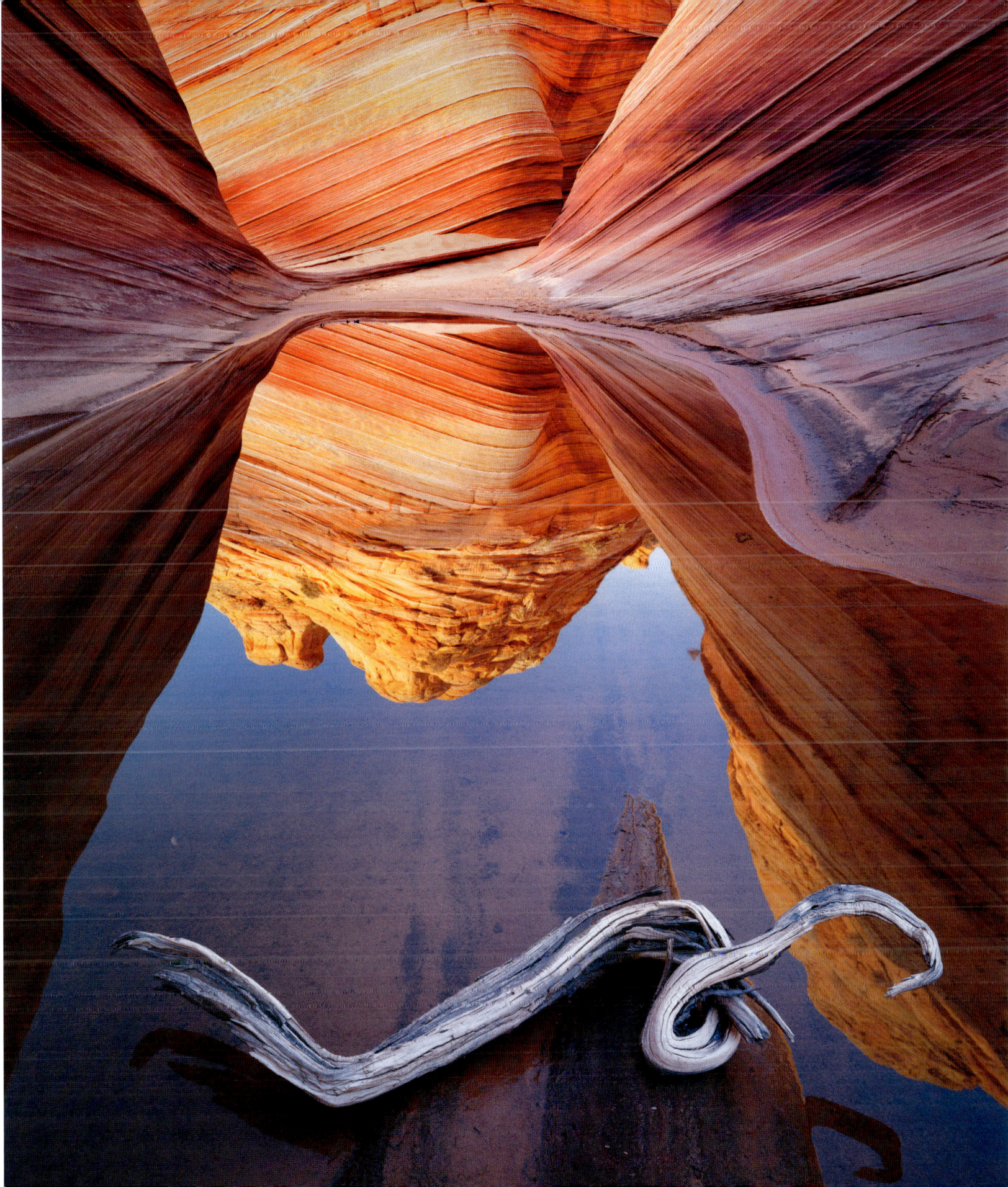

Lessons Learned

I suffer from a love affair with this planet. My camera is my ticket to a front row seat for the spectacle of nature. It has taught me to see with greater intensity, understand more deeply, and appreciate more fully the blue planet we call home.

The images I cherish resulted from being out there, tasting life's offerings, taking chances, doing homework, and reading nature's signs. Collectively, my images represent times when I've never felt more alive, when my pulse was racing, or even when I was full of self-doubt; but all the while, I felt privileged just to be a witness to the visual feast before me.

Here are a few memories.

The sheer drama of the interplay of weather, light, and wild places is what I strive for. I feel that combining these elements represents the mood of the land. Often, I miss the mark. But the harder I work, the luckier I get. So, when the Sonoran Desert near my Tucson, Arizona home comes alive with threatening summer "monsoon" storms, I chase the action. Rainbows are easy to photograph. Lightning is also a simple matter of waiting until the light level goes down and making long exposures directed toward active storm cells.

The challenge in making a photograph like this is how to blend the wonderful rainbows with the momentary burst of electricity. Of course, there's also the problem of being on the wrong end of a lightning strike. I've had several instances when a rogue lightning bolt struck well in advance of a coming storm. So, in the interest of safety, I crawled into the back of my camper amid the violent wind gusts while taking this photograph with a device called the Lightning Trigger attached to my camera. It sensed the coming bursts, allowing my Nikon DSLR to expose for the ambient light while capturing each lightning hit. By recording multiple lightning hits, I was able to combine several hits into a single powerful image against the rainbow background.

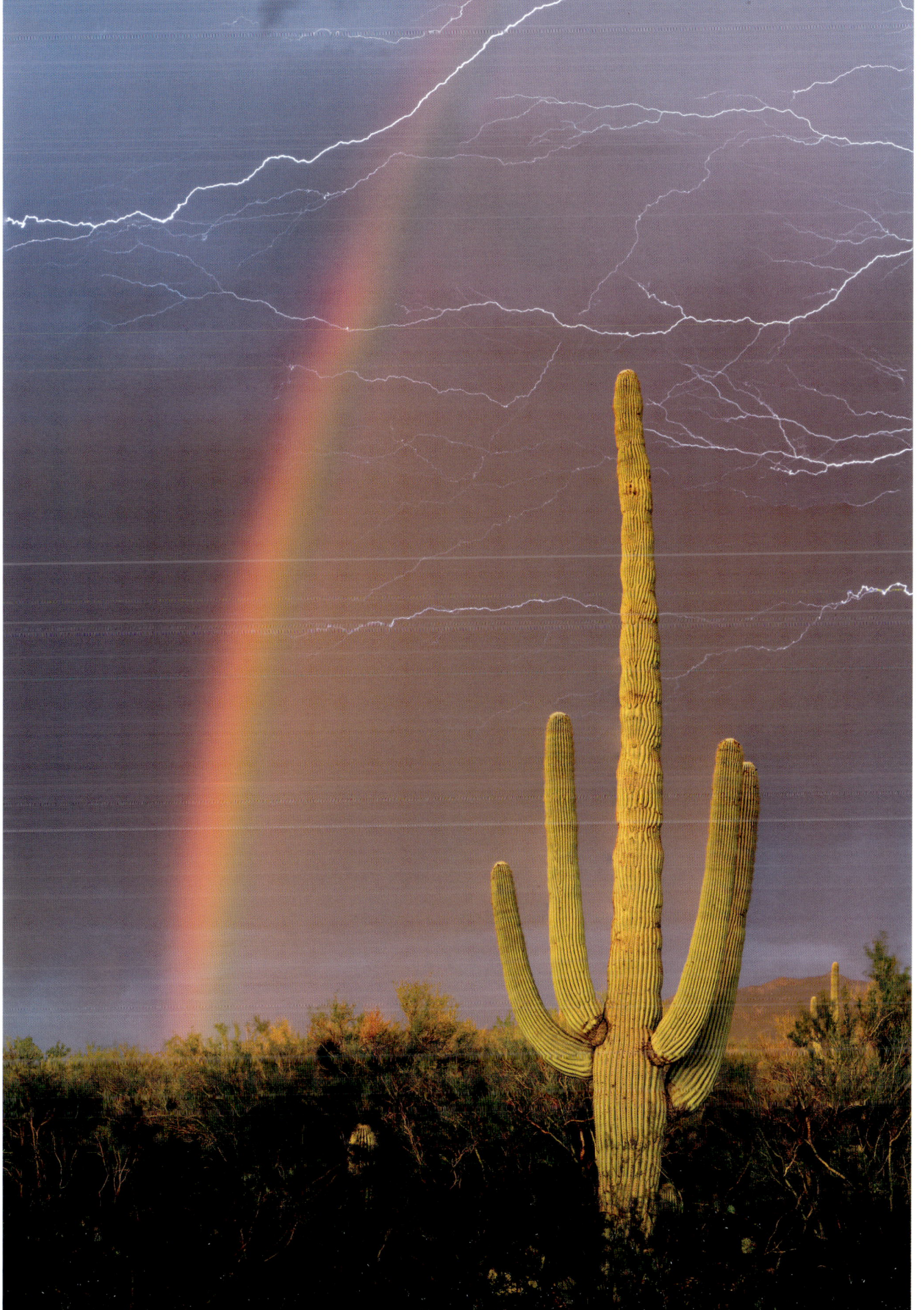

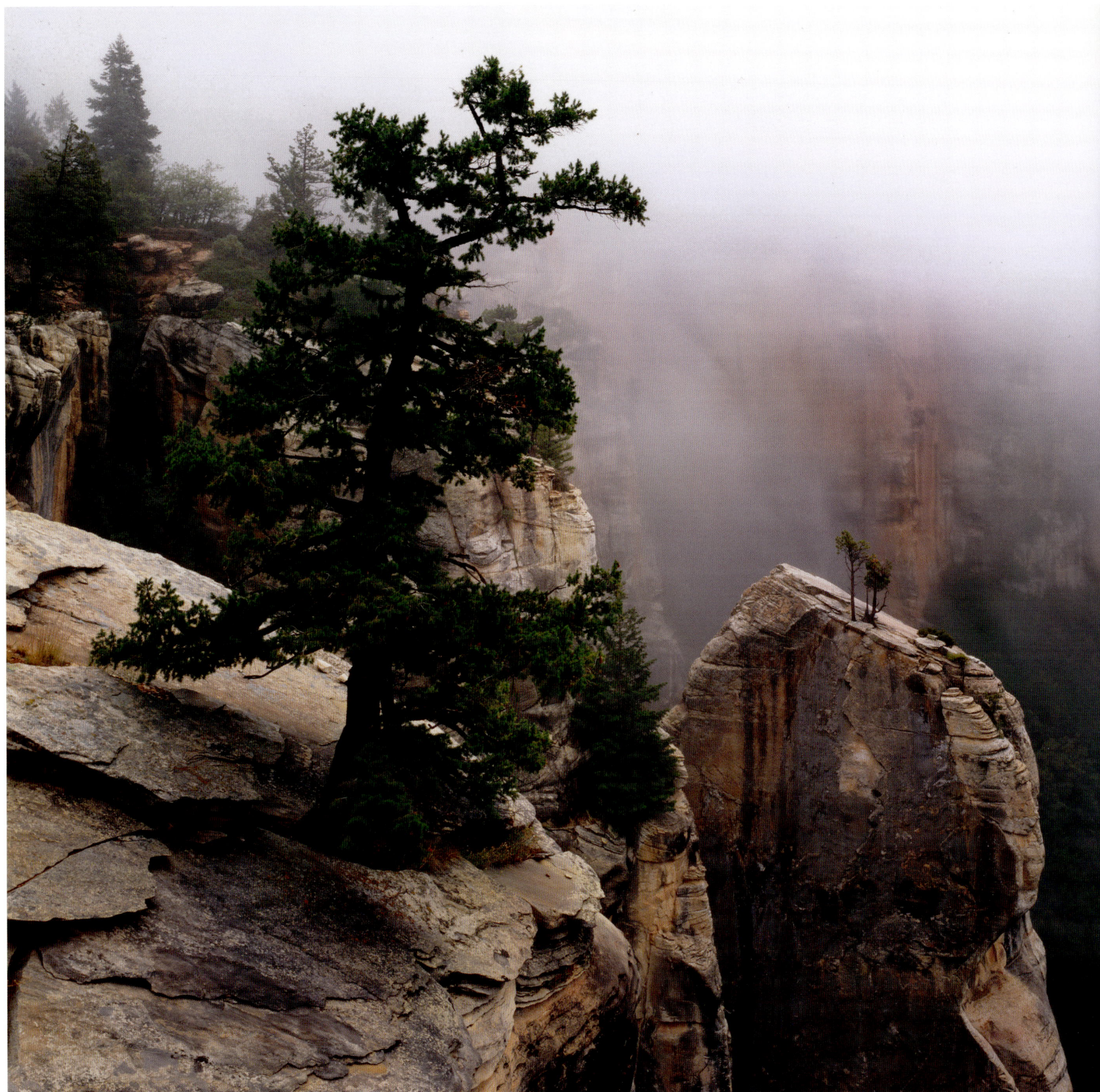

I can recall every image I've ever taken, along with the associated feelings. I had hiked into the Grand Canyon via the North Kaibab trail as rain threatened to cancel my shoot. It's funny how many good images result from walking the fine line between "no picture possible" and "amazing."

As I stood overlooking the rock spires around me, the rain had closed in and the storm clouds lowered, infusing the moment with mystery. My friend Linda Caravello held an umbrella, sheltering my camera and film packs. Even now, when I stare at this image, I feel the freshness of the moment, remembering the fear of failure and enjoying life on the edge of a stony spire.

New digital cameras with sensors that can record anything the eye can see now allow us to capture images that were never before possible. On Kilauea, Hawaii, the glowing Halemaumau crater stood before me as the light level began to fall after sunset. As the darkness closed in, the crater's glow became more pronounced. Fog began to descend, reflecting the glow. I composed and began to make exposures. Because I was shooting digital, I was able to check exposure, composition, and focus. Suddenly, I realized that while the crater anchored the composition, the sky, with the Milky Way high above, was now a very important element in the frame, so I tilted the camera upward and changed to a vertical composition. Several exposures later, I realized a meteor had streaked into the upper left of the frame, producing another magical moment captured with my camera.

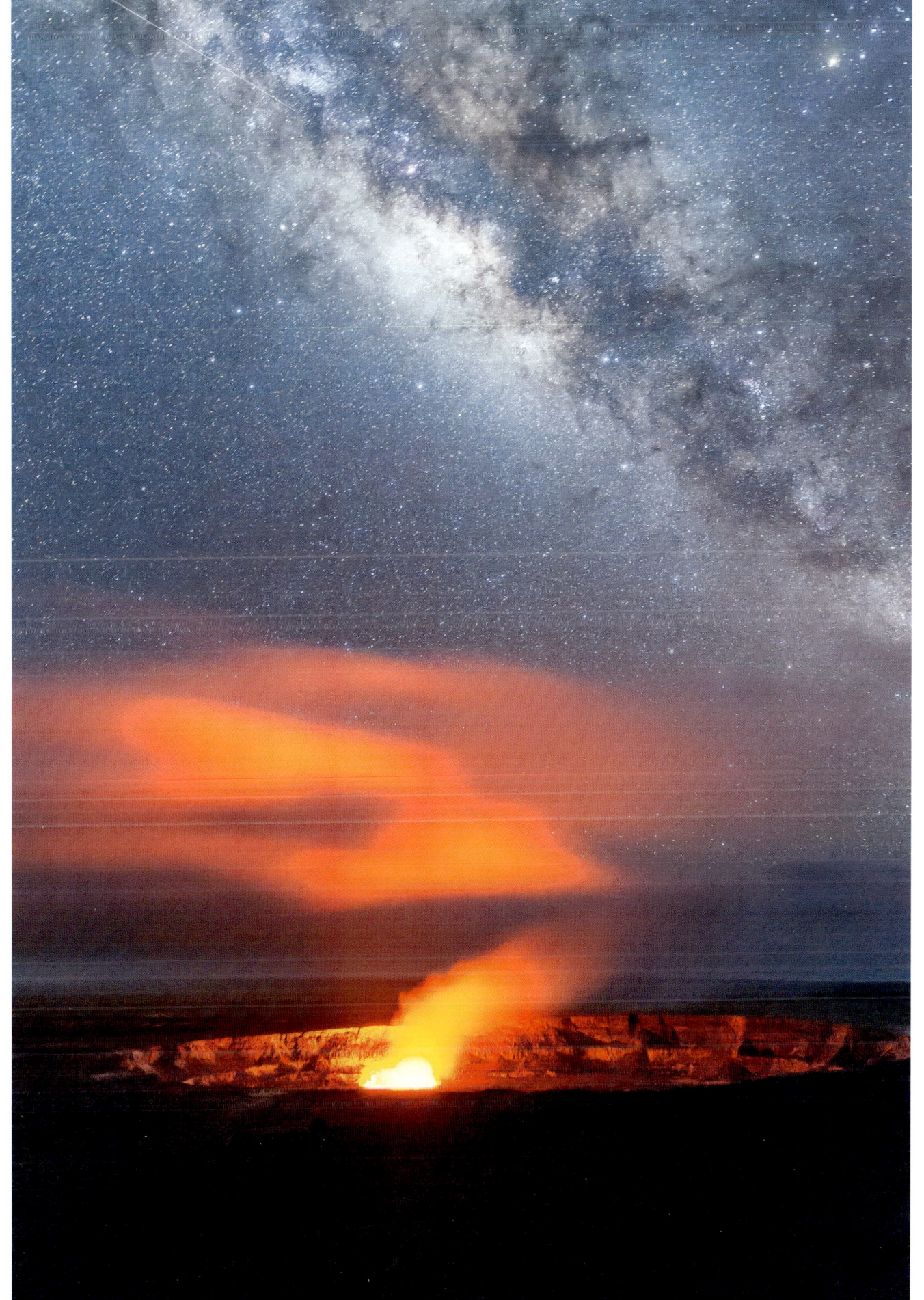

I had made a commitment to photograph at Oxbow Bend in the Tetons at sunrise. I was leading a photography workshop and my entire group of enthusiasts tried to force smiles as we arrived at our chosen location only to find it hidden in a very dense fog bank. People with frantic looks stared at me for guidance as I contemplated the sky. I watched for subtle movements that might point me to another location, or that would encourage us to stay and wait for the eventual lifting of the fog.

Finally, I saw an opening in the fog, showing a drift to the north and perhaps a window of opportunity to the south at the Snake River Overlook. We raced down the road against the oncoming dawn and arrived in time to see the fog beginning to lift below the towering Grand Teton. A rosy cloud flagged the summit, showing us another example of the fine line between utter failure and breathtaking beauty.

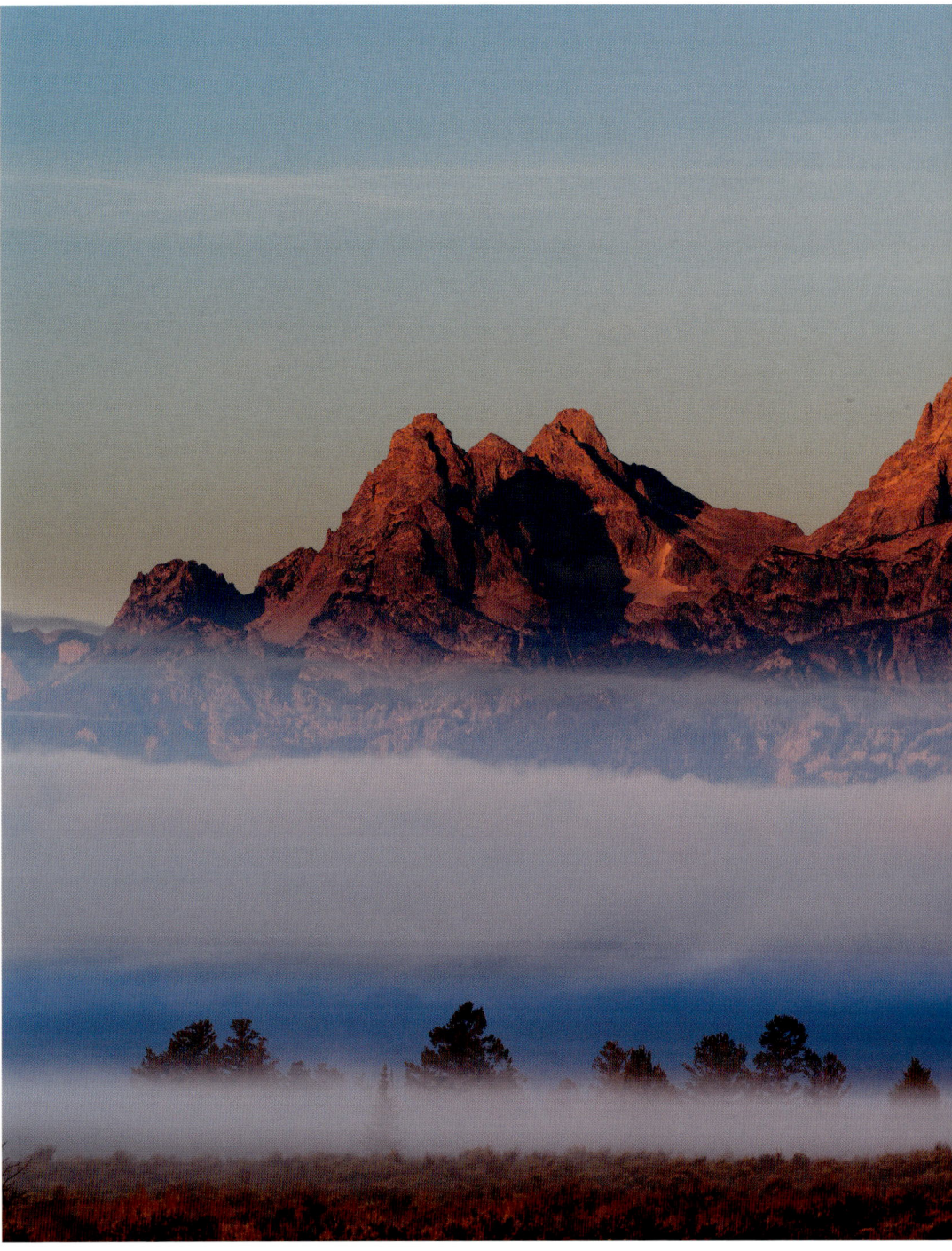

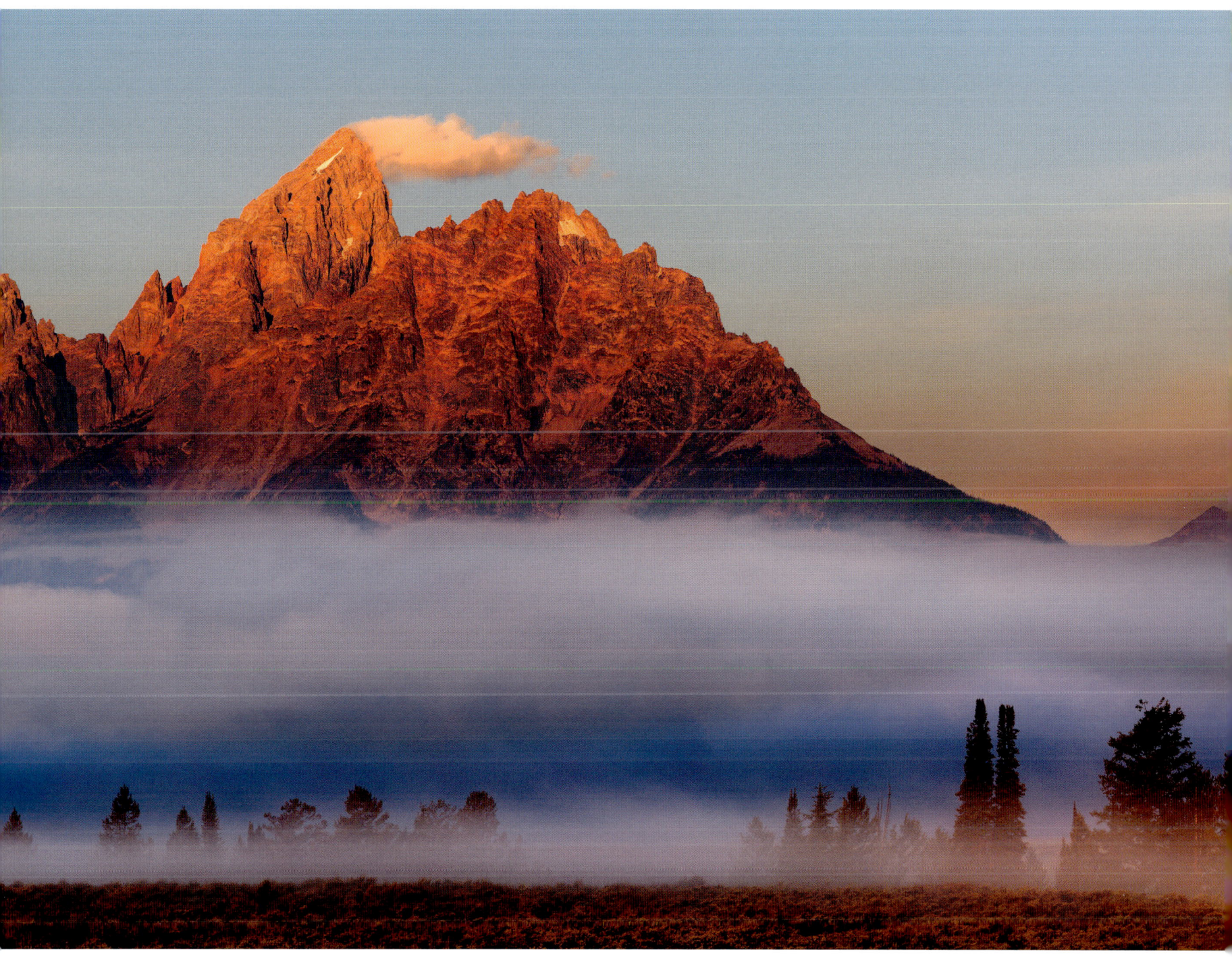

Traveling to California's White Mountains, the plan was to photograph the bristlecone pines in the Patriarch Grove. I intended to photograph through the sunset hours and stay for the opportunity to photograph stars with a full moon rising. I knew the exact pine I wanted to photograph, having been there many times before. But this visit was different. The stars are brilliant at 11,000 feet and after trying a few different compositions, I settled on one that allowed the rising moon to filter through the trees on the background ridgeline. I made several exposures, but felt the tree needed more definition and light on the trunk, so I used my LED headlamp to lightly illuminate the ancient tree's base. Everything was coming into place, but things began to change quickly as an armada of clouds rushed into my frame. I kept making exposures, and the cloud movement made the image.

With great situations, you simply need to keep shooting and "ride the light's ebbs and flows."

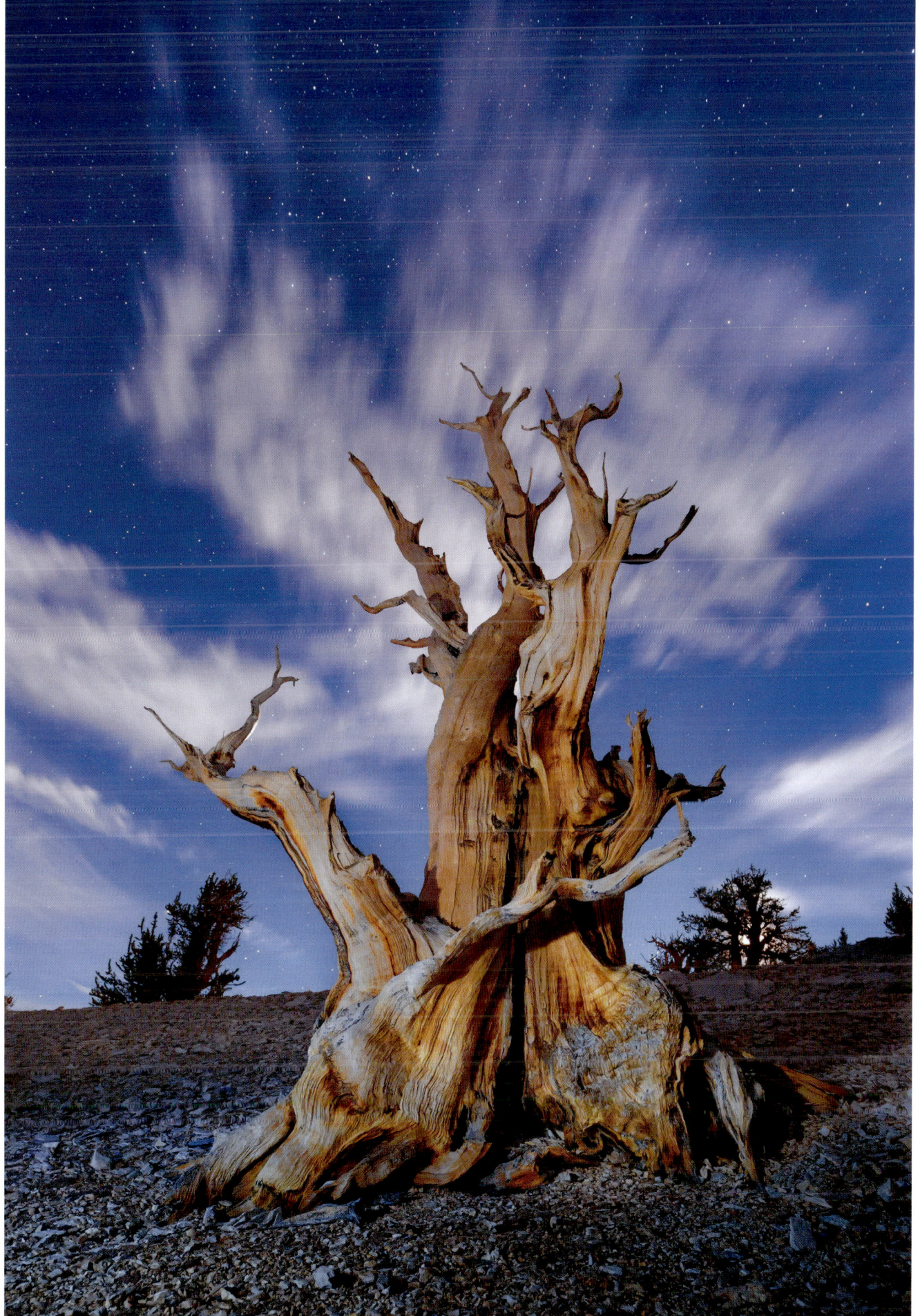

Sunflowers are showoffs. They demand attention and by facing the oncoming sunrise, they glow in the warmth of a new day. But as dawn came, the cloudbank above took on an ominous cast. It was clear in an instant that the contrast between a threatening sky and the bright yellow field at Arizona's Sunset Crater would be my subject. I created a composition that tilted the center of attention skyward to embrace the stunning cloud formation.

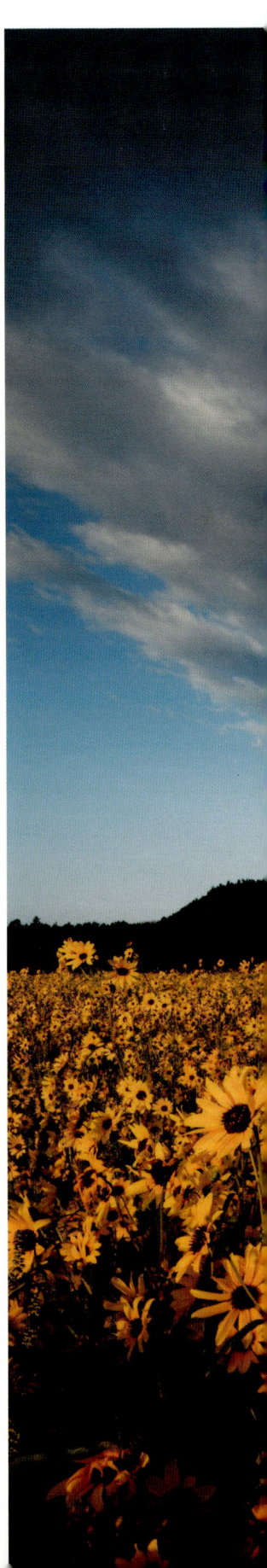

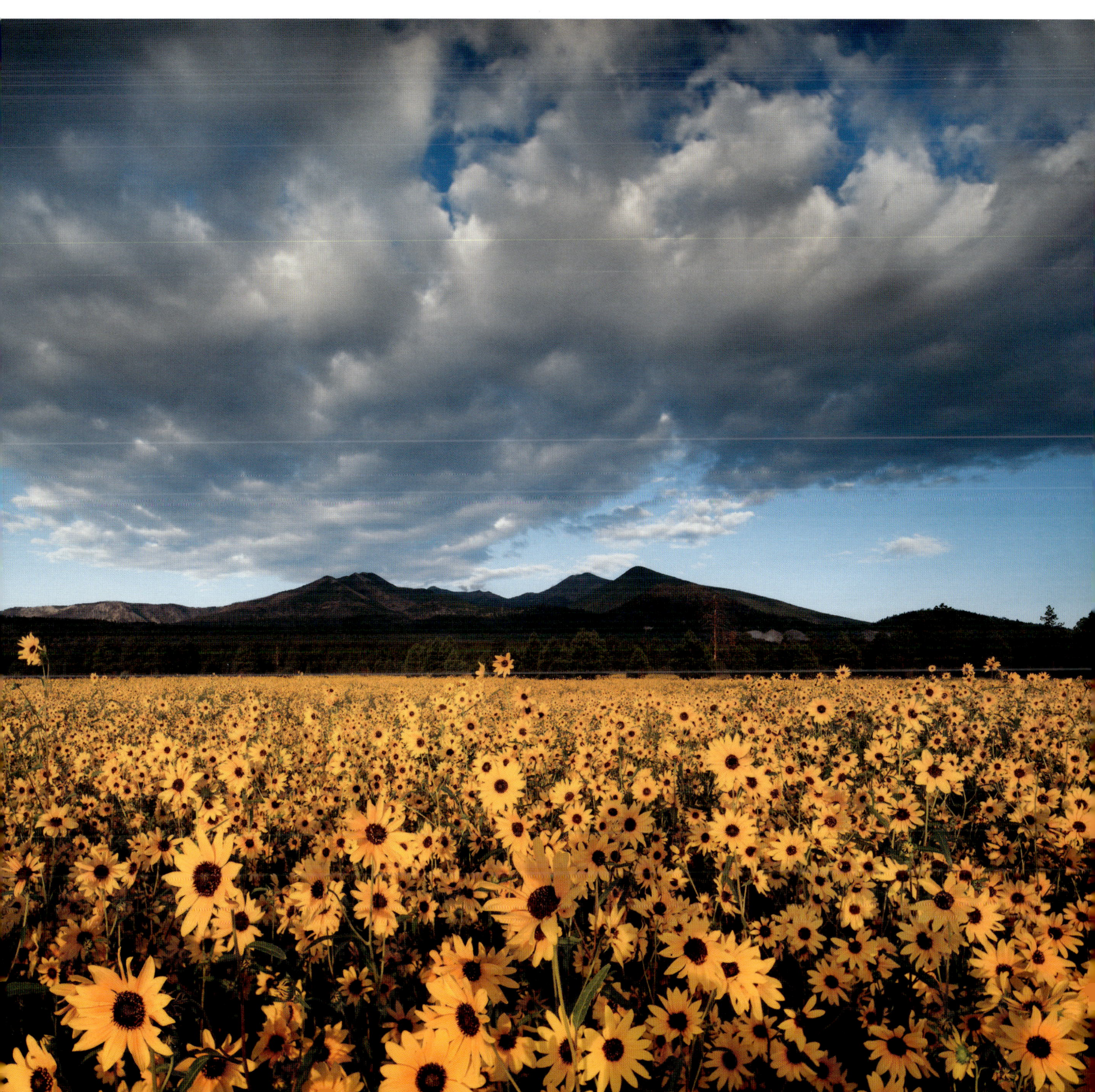

Saguaro cacti are like old friends. I am drawn to their outstretched limbs as they engulf the desert landscape. Together, my workshop students and I witnessed the marvelous example of how the rising sun struck the foreground saguaro and reflected light back onto its limbs. It fairly glowed as the sun's intensity grew and we photographed quickly before the rising sun's light would strike the ground directly behind the subject. I love this image.

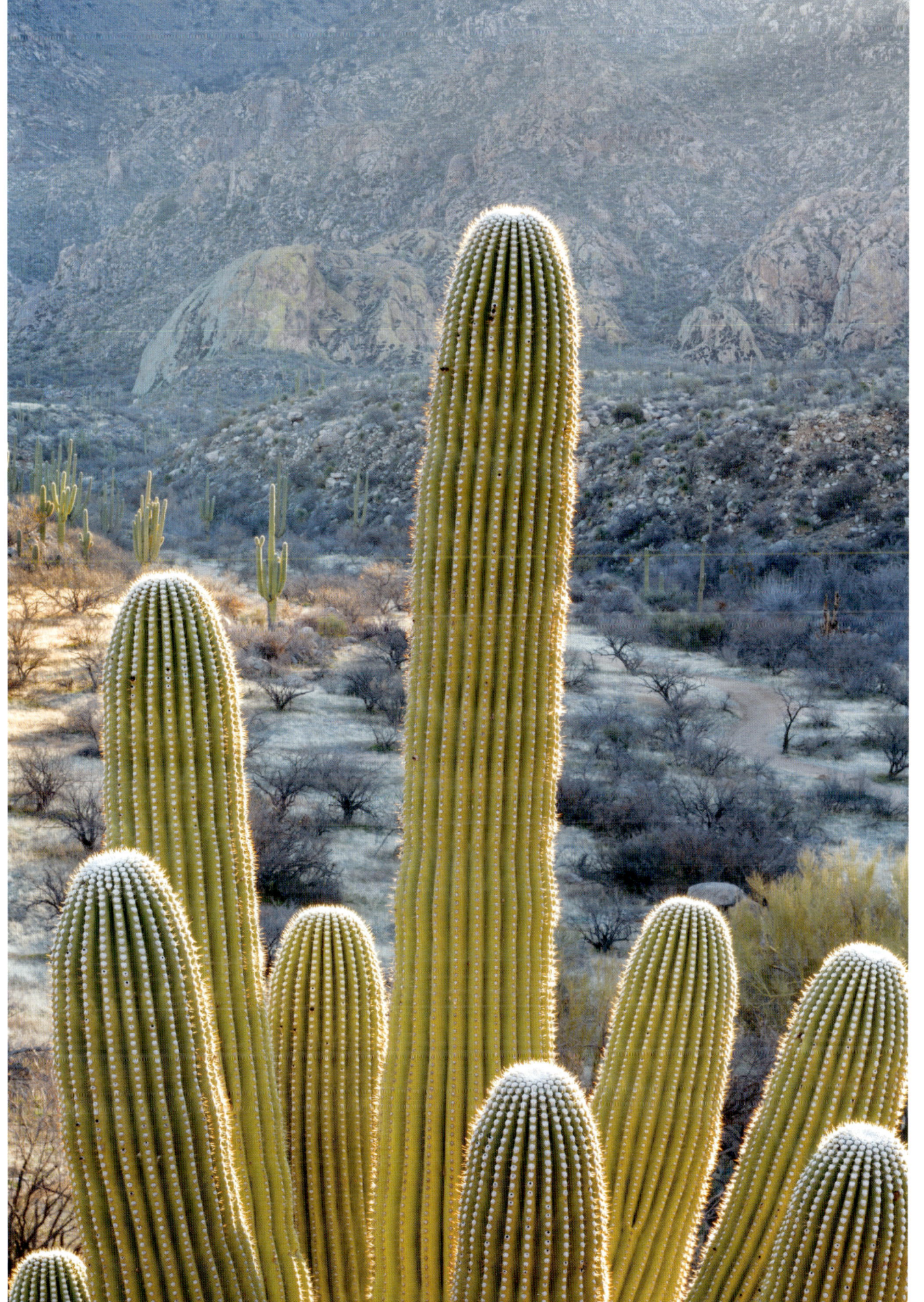

One week later, the mood of the desert had shifted radically. An unseasonal north wind brought a drop in temperature and an extremely rare snowfall. I knew where I wanted to be so, in the early morning, our class climbed to the overlook to renew the connection with my old friend, the saguaro. This time, there was no glow, but spread out before us was a once-in-a-lifetime scene—the Sonoran Desert blanketed in white. Thank you!

The lesson here is when a location or composition is good, make a mental note to return when it becomes GREAT.

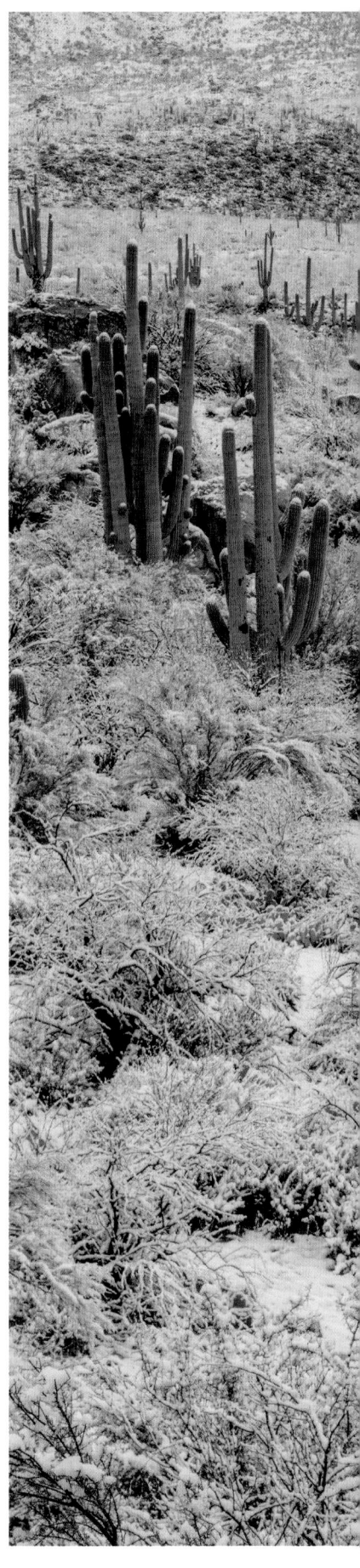

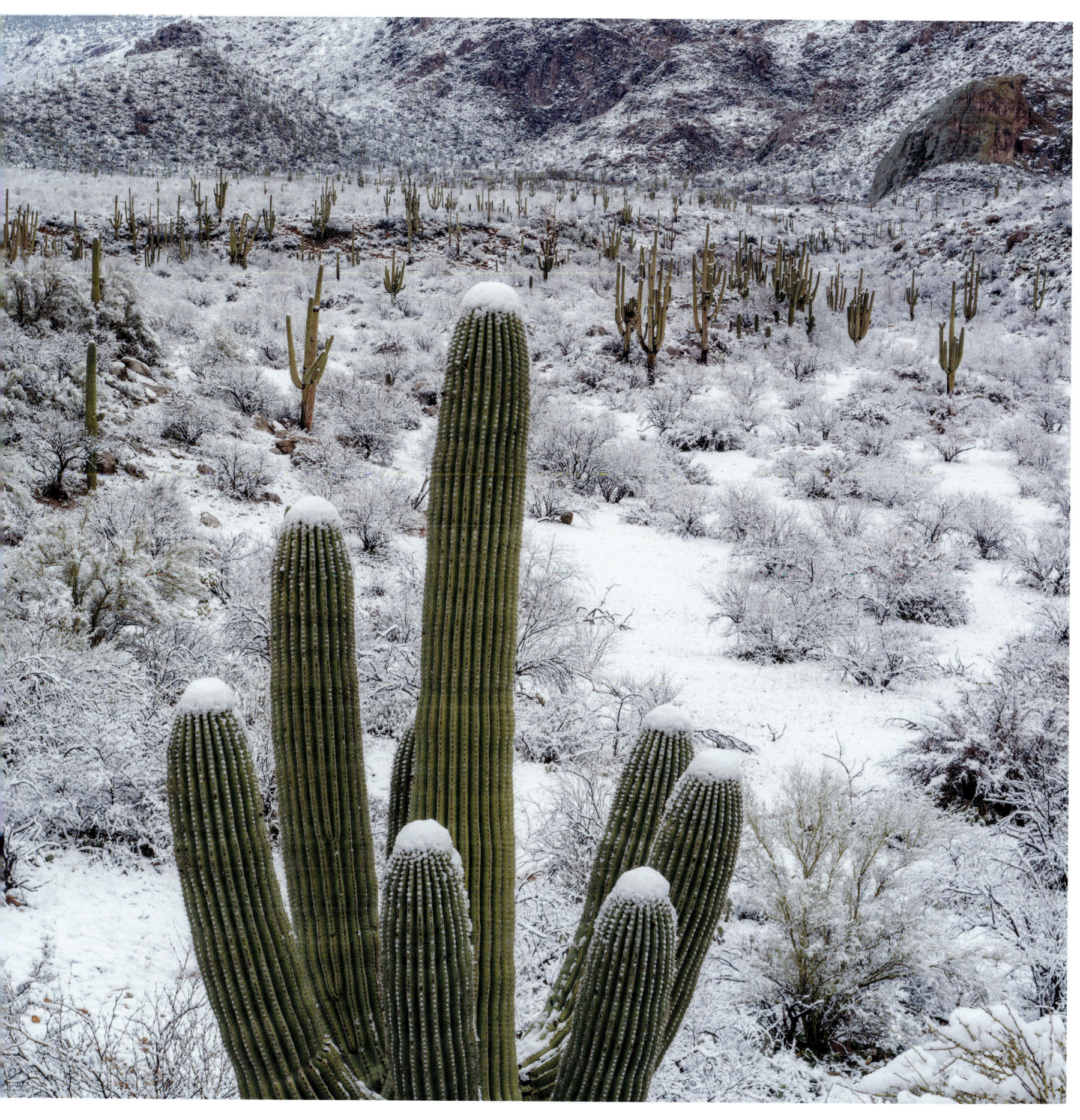

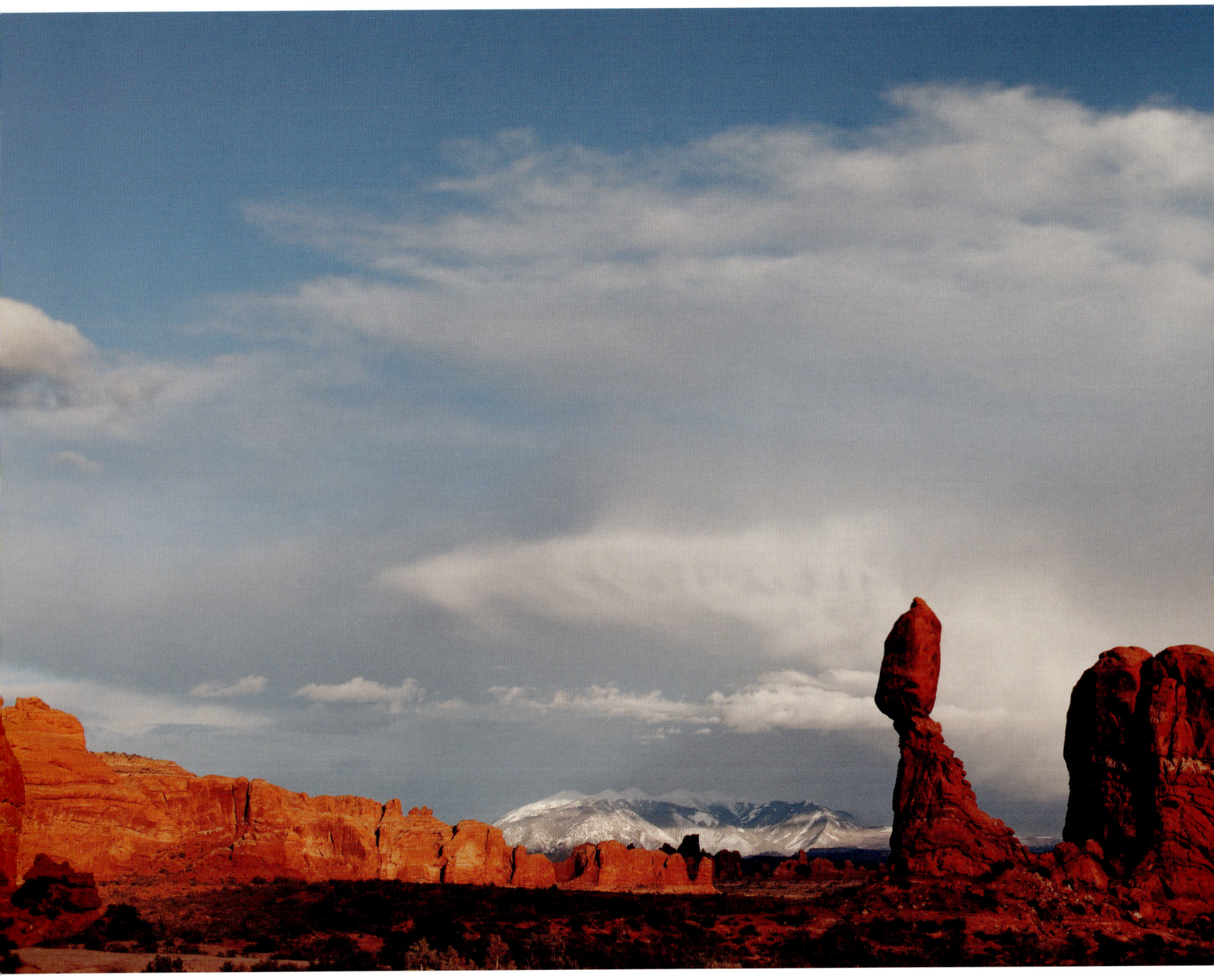

The intensity of seeing defines our photography: watching, waiting patiently, and suffering through miserable weather while optimistically focusing on what may be possible.

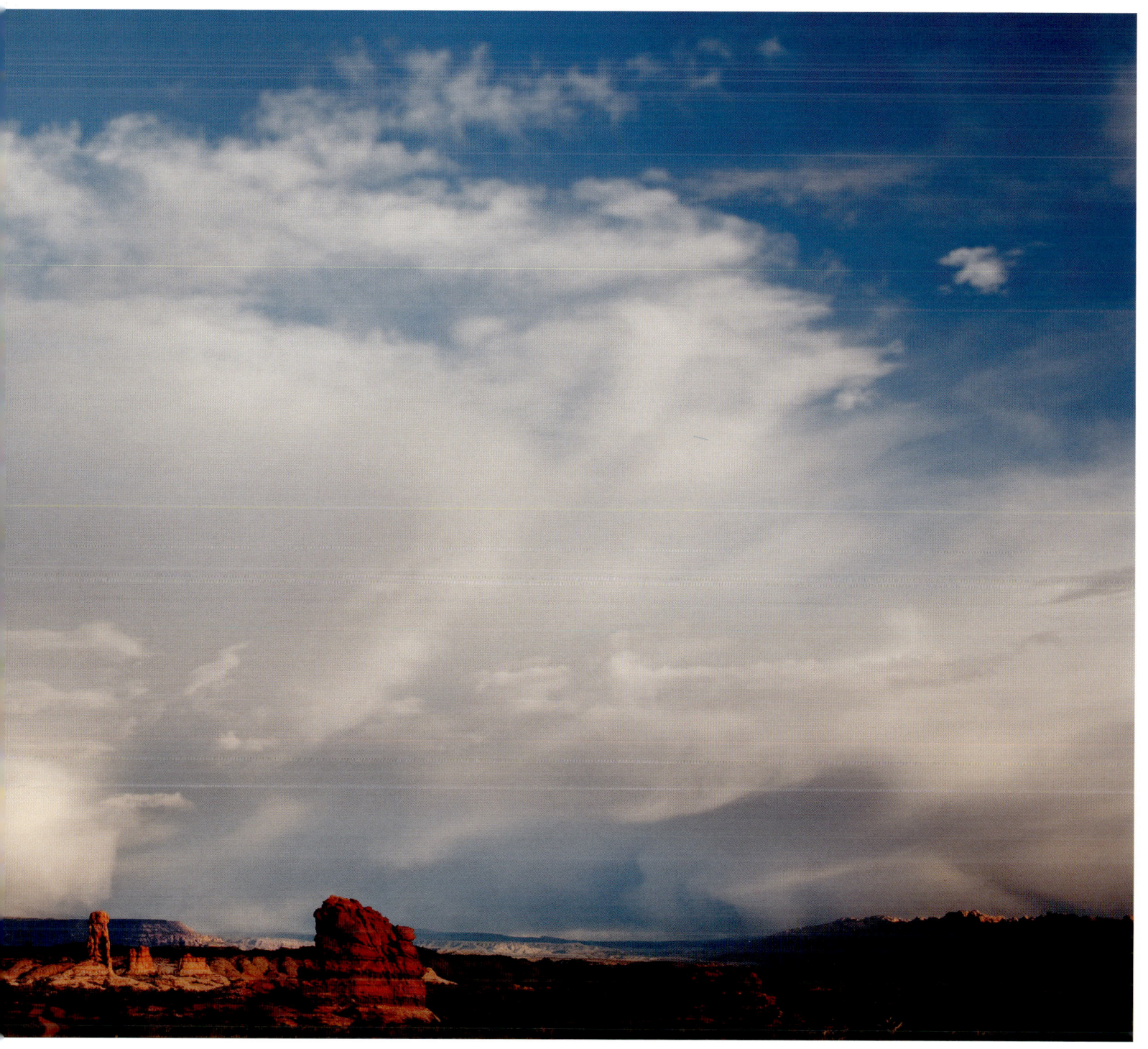

Excitement mounted as the storm before me intensified and the setting sun painted Balanced Rock at Arches National Park in eastern Utah in vivid color. My mind wandered to Ed Abbey, to Bates Wilson, and to all those with the foresight to preserve places like this. I was humbled by the immensity before me, and I wondered: "Who am I to try to capture such a sublime scene?" Yet, I persist.

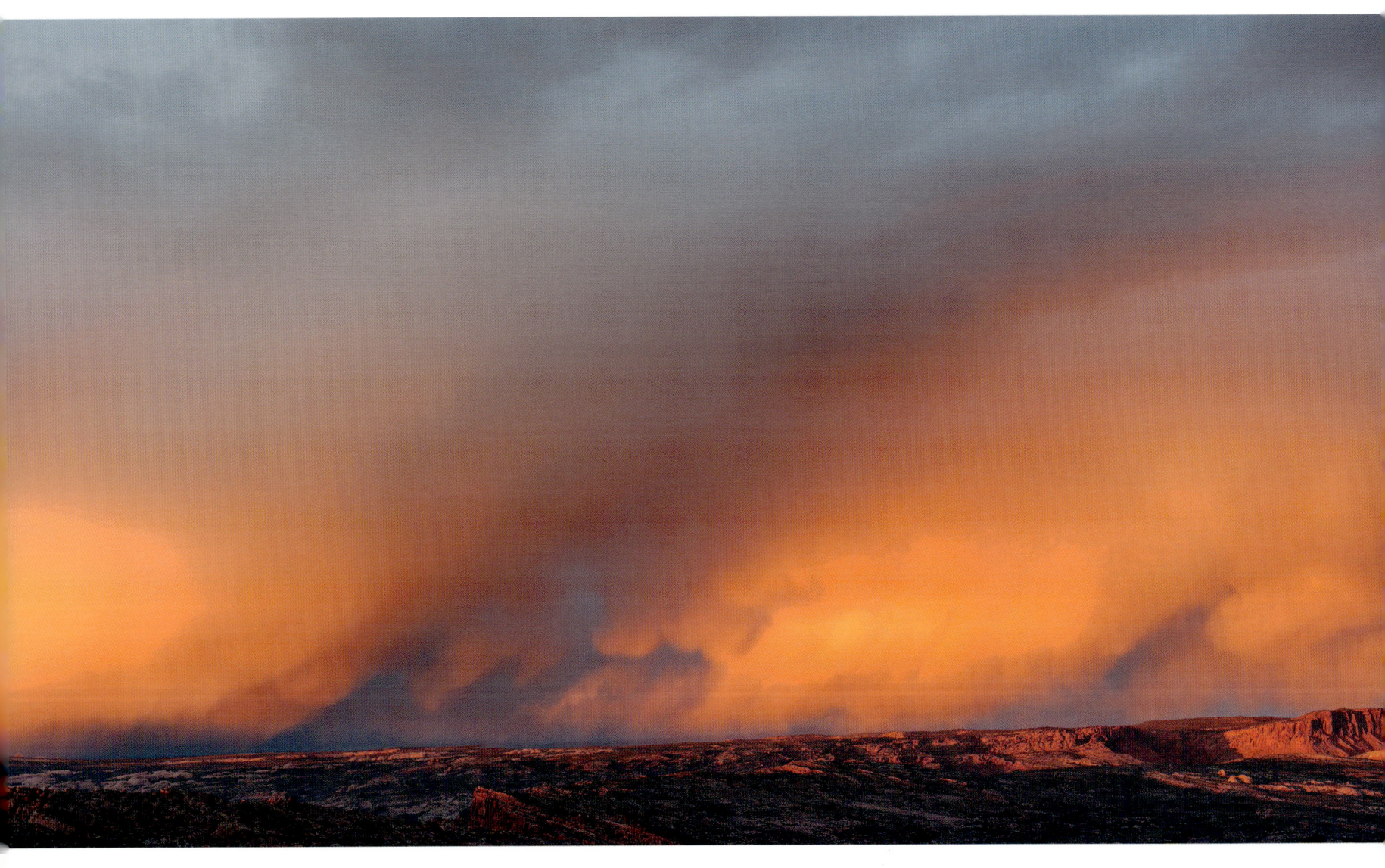

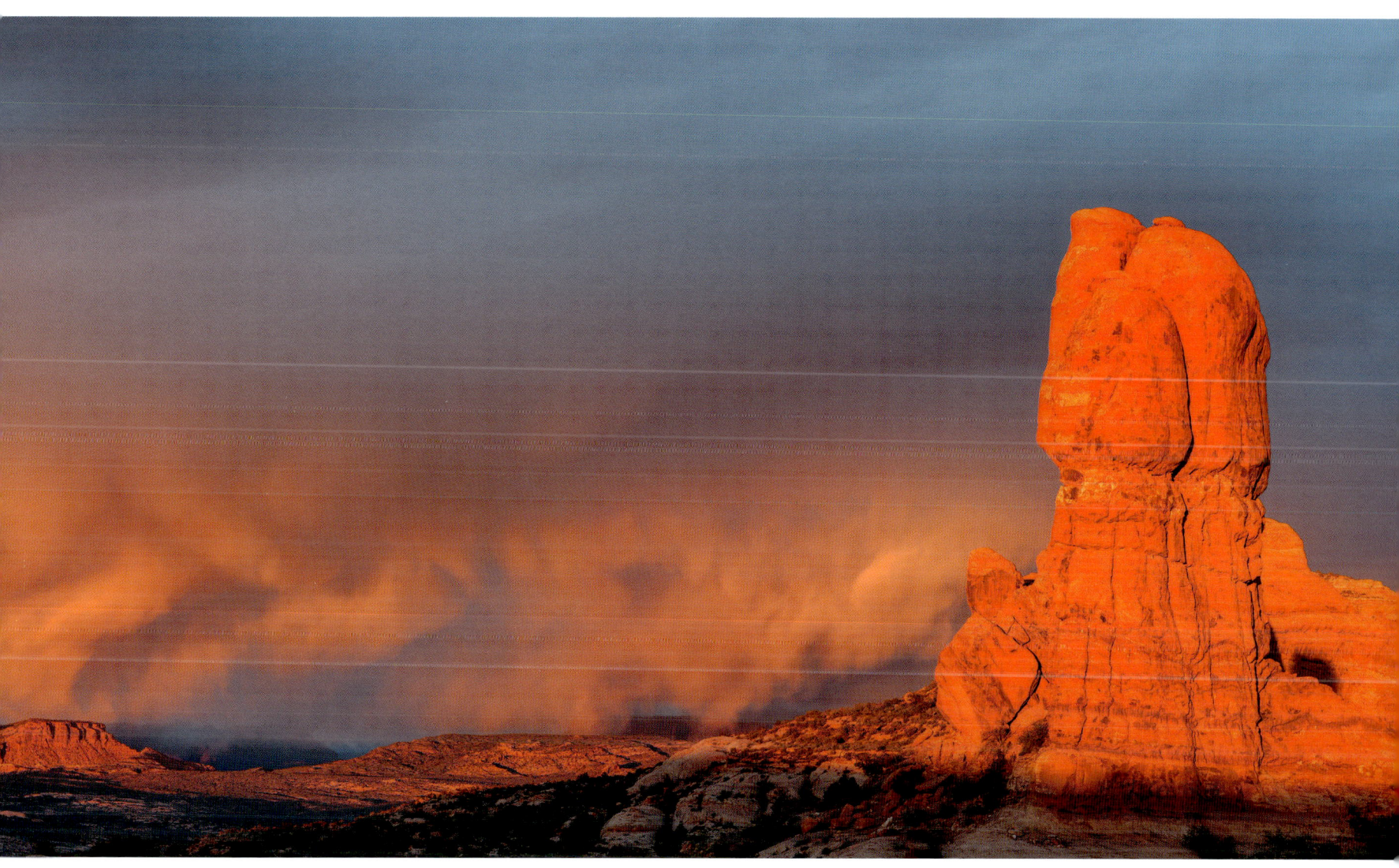

The best image is not always directly in front of us, as I discovered when photographing Balance Rock. I systematically composed a panoramic image as a nuclear bomb-like cloud settled over the sandstone, feeling that nothing could be better than this scene. Then I turned to my left and my jaw dropped. The light, the clouds, and the land were fused into a single molten image of the spirit of the land. My camera recorded a series of vertical images, which I combined to make this large file panoramic.

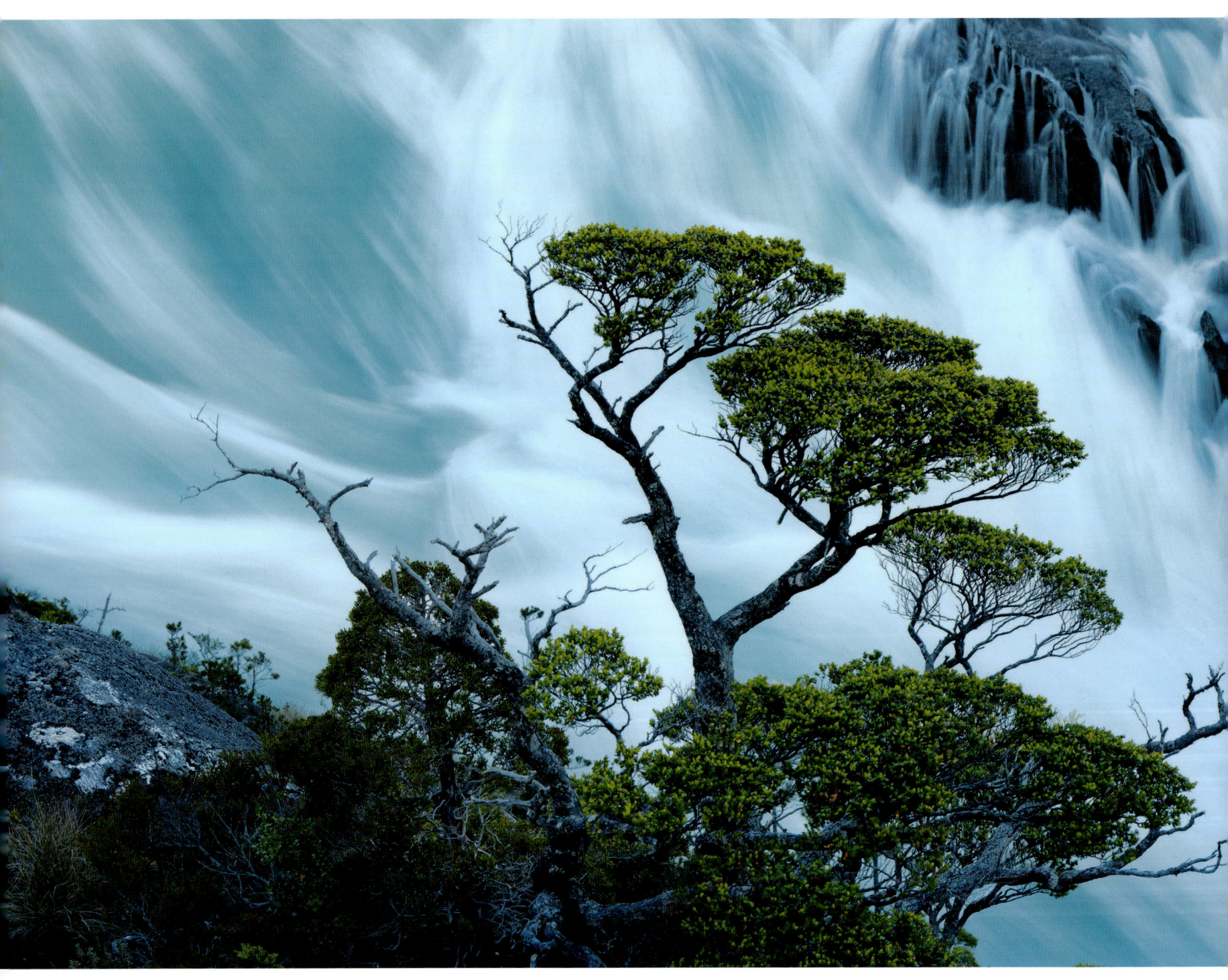

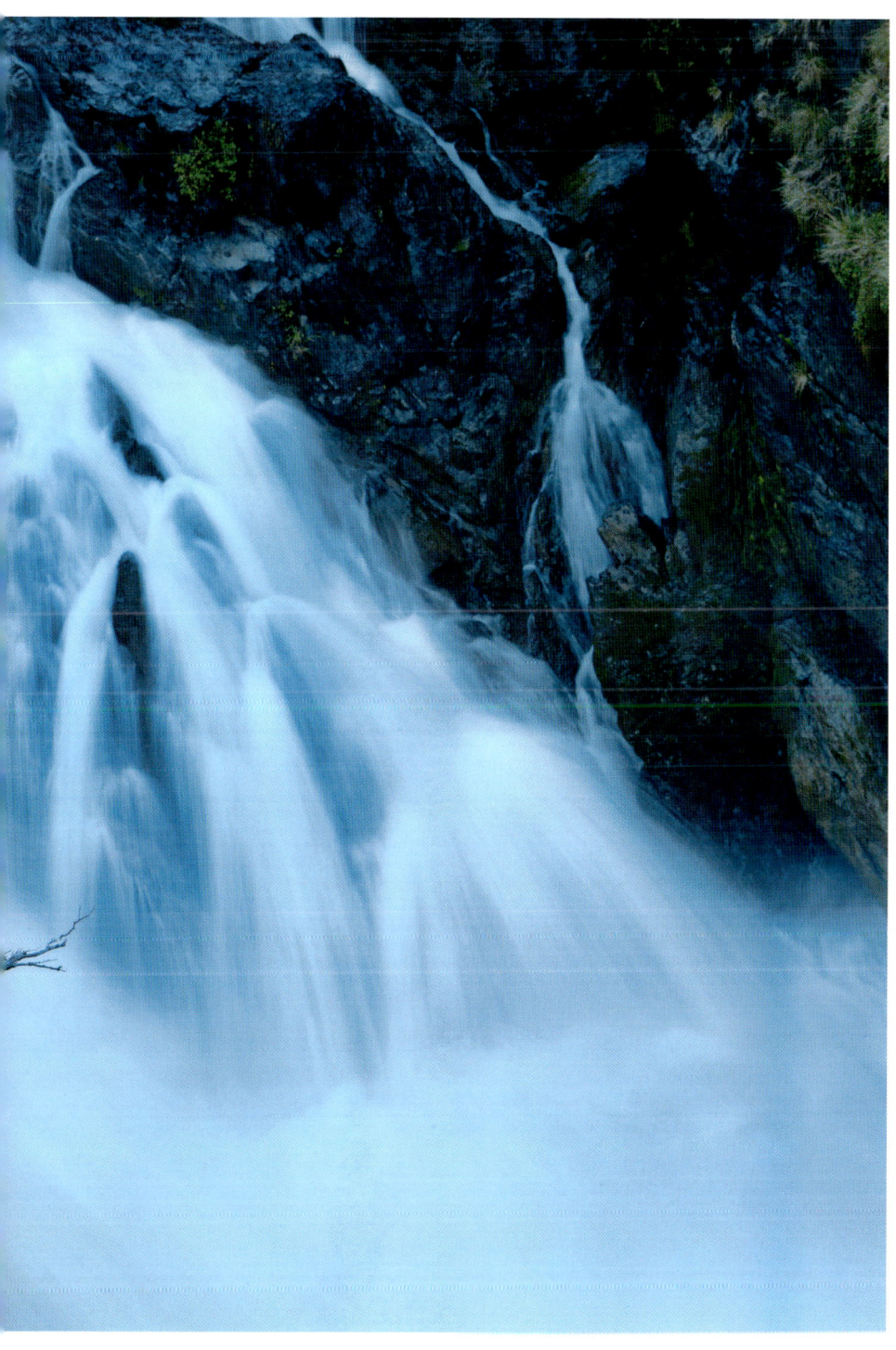

We had come a long way. First flying to the southern hemisphere, then four-wheeling into Chile's Aysén Province. Then we climbed aboard a ferryboat and finally onto yet another boat into Lago O'Higgins. From there we sliced our way through primal beech tree forests to the raging source of the Rio Pascua. I felt scratched, bruised, and battered by thickets when I finally reached the cliffs high above the torrent. But the sheer power of this place erased any feeling of discomfort.

The ground beneath my feet vibrated from the cascading water. My friends all wanted to get closer to the falls. However, I chose another direction and retreated away from the falls. The tenuous beech trees clinging to the shoreline were almost silhouetted against the moving watery background. Their position seemed so precarious against the river's raw power and it was that imbalance I wanted to show and, ultimately, captured.

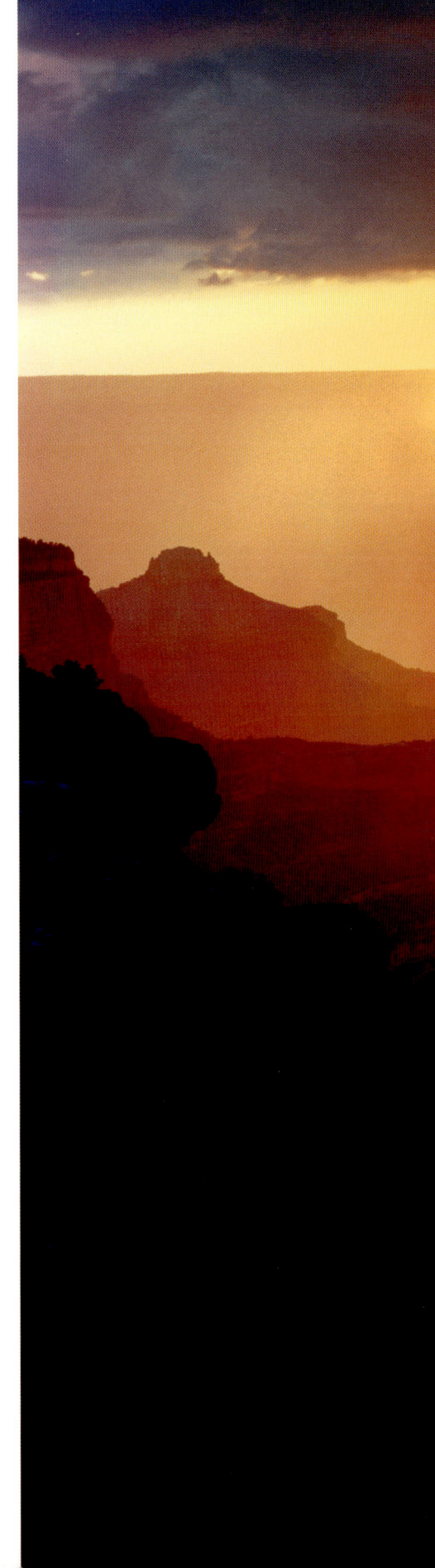

Majesty is a word that's frequently overused. Standing on the end of the Earth at Cape Royal on the Grand Canyon's North Rim is impressive. Yet when describing the potent combination of a backlit rainstorm with "God beams" penetrating the sky of gold, words fail. It is majestic! Isn't this the reason we keep trying to capture the sublime? We try—mostly in vain—to show others what we felt when the landscape spoke to our soul. In the end, we really can't fully capture the moments when the hair on our neck stands on end. But, joyously, we keep trying.

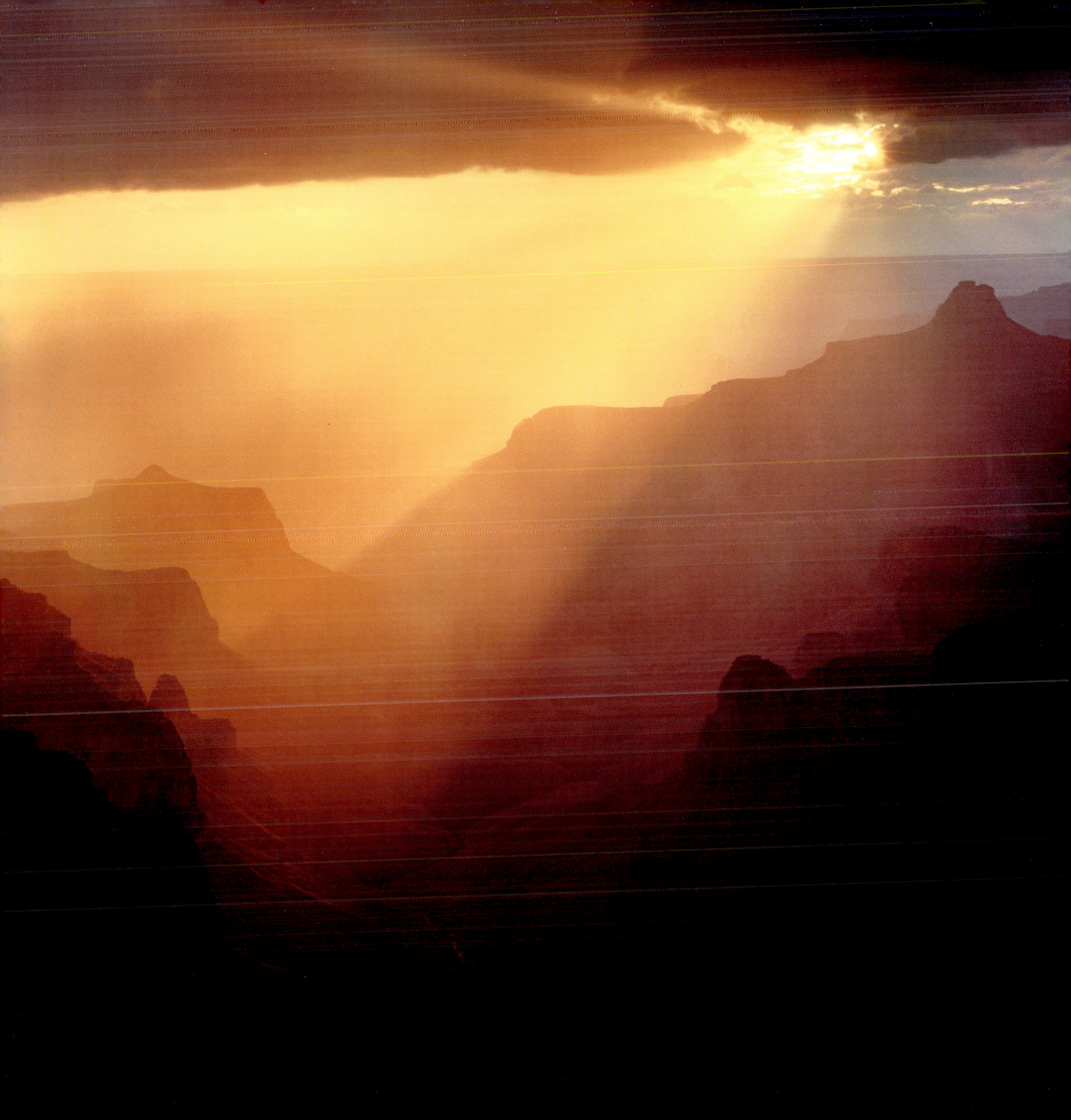

My Equipment

I have been on a long journey with a camera as my passport, allowing me to witness a diverse and spectacular world. I was a photojournalist during Chicago's most turbulent times, with civil rights, the Vietnam War protests, and student upheavals shaping my young life. I marched with Martin Luther King, Jr., covered political conventions, and experienced racial hatred that was also directed at members of the press. My images for the *Chicago Sun-Times,* documenting the Lincoln and Dixon State Schools in Illinois, received the 1971 Pulitzer Prize for Feature Photography.

I was a photo editor and assignments editor for the *Chicago Tribune,* and I directed photography in Tucson at the *Arizona Daily Star.* I freelanced for *Time, Newsweek, U.S. News and World Report,* and *National Geographic* magazines.

All the while, the Sonoran Desert was calling. While still in Chicago, I read an article about Philip Hyde's wilderness advocacy work with the Sierra Club. I decided to model my life after his fine example and work for environmental causes. That decision has taken me to mountaintop vistas, underground sinkholes, the African Savanna and towering dunes, and the most special of all, the deserts of the American Southwest.

I write this in an effort to explain my evolution in photography. The camera is simply a tool, and over the years I have always believed that one must select the proper tool for the job at hand. During my photojournalism days, I worked with two Leicas and two Nikons hung around my neck during long civil rights marches. When I began documenting the landscape, I used the large format Arca-Swiss 4×5 view camera, with lenses ranging from 58mm wide to 720mm telephoto. Then, as film fell away, I returned to Nikon and their amazing digital cameras, which I use today.

I have retained my Arca-Swiss F-Field camera with several of my favorite lenses: the 80mm Super-Symmar, the 120mm Makro-Symmar HM, and the Fujinon 240mm A lenses.

Two Nikon D800E cameras do the bulk of my work today, along with the Nikon D3s for fast action wildlife, and a full complement of lenses. I frequently employ Photoshop to stitch together large images that rival the quality of my earlier work using large format film cameras.

Here are the Nikkor lenses I use:

- 24mm tilt/shift
- 45mm tilt/shift
- 85mm tilt/shift
- 14–24mm zoom
- 24–70mm zoom
- 70–200 f/4.0 zoom
- 80–400 f/4.5–5.6 zoom
- 200mm Micro-Nikkor
- 500mm f/4.0 telephoto
- 1.4x teleconverter
- 2.0x teleconverter

I'm a big fan of Really Right Stuff and use their tripods: TVC 23 and TVC 33 with accompanying BH-55 Pro ball heads and L brackets.

I also use a Gitzo 3540 XLS tripod with a Wimberley head for fast action as well as Wimberly's Sidekick ball head adapter.

My gear is lugged about in several Think Tank Photo backpacks and a Think Tank laptop case. Their sturdy construction keeps my laptop and cameras happy and safe in the field and on airplanes.

I use Mac computers with both Adobe Photoshop and Adobe Lightroom.

My non photographic piece of equipment, which makes much of my work possible, is my Four Wheel Camper, equipped with solar panel electronics and mounted on a Toyota Tacoma. It's my office and home away from home, allowing me to immerse myself totally into the landscape for prolonged periods of time.

Technical Information

Page 3 Harcuvar Mountains, Arizona – March 2005
Arca-Swiss F-Field 4×5 camera, 75mm Nikkor lens, f/45, 2 sec., Fuji Velvia film, ISO 100

Pages 4–5 Badwater Basin, Death Valley National Park, California – March 2010
Nikon D3×, 45mm Nikkor T/S lens, f/13, 1/15 sec., ISO 100, 10 vertical frames combined

Page 6 Escalante Canyons, Grand Staircase-Escalante National Monument, New Mexico – September 1994
Arca Swiss F-Field 4×5 camera, 120mm Schneider HM lens, f/32, 1/2 sec., Fuji Velvia film, ISO 50

Page 7 Grand Staircase-Escalante National Monument, New Mexico – September 1994
Arca-Swiss F-Field 4×5 camera, 180mm Rodenstock Sironar S lens, f/39 at 1 sec., ISO 50, Fuji Velvia film

Page 8 Cheyenne River Sioux Reservation, South Dakota – July 2010
Arca Swiss F-Field 4×5 camera, 80mm Schneider Super Symmar lens, f/16, 1/8 sec., ISO 100, Fuji Velvia film

Page 10 Sands Ranch Conservation Area, Arizona – April 2009
Arca Swiss F-Field 4×5 camera, 110mm Schneider Super Symmar lens, f/45, 1 sec., ISO 50, Fuji Velvia film

Page 13 Hawaii Volcanos National Park, Hawaii – August 2010
Nikon D3X, 24mm Nikkor T/S lens, f/10, 30 sec., ISO 100, 2 frames combined

Page 14 Yucatan, Mexico – January 2012
Nikon D3X, 85mm Nikkor T/S lens, f 18, 4 sec., ISO 100

Page 15 Osa Penninsula, Costa Rica – November 2012
Nikon D800E, Nikkor 200mm Micro lens, f/16, 5 sec., ISO 100

Page 16 Baja California, Mexico – March 2013
Nikon D800E, 85mm Nikkor T/S lens, f/20, 1sec., ISO 100

Page 17 Baja California, Mexico – March 2013
Nikon D800E, 85mm Nikkor T/S lens, f/16, .6 sec., ISO 100

Page 18 White Sands National Monument, New Mexico – January 2013
Nikon D800E, 70–200 f 4.0 lens, f/16, 1/30 sec., ISO 100

Page 19 Red Lake Indian Reservation, Minnesota – October 2012
Arca-Swiss F-Field 4×5 camera, 240mm Fujinon lens, f/45, 6 sec., ISO 100, Fuji Velvia film

Page 20 Valley of Fire State Park, Nevada – March 2012
Nikon D3X, Nikkor 45mm Nikkor T/S lens, f/18, 2 sec., ISO 100

Pages 22–23 Hawaii Volcanoes National Park, Hawaii – August 2010
Nikon D3X, 85mm Nikkor T/S lens, f/16, 1/5 sec., ISO 100, 3 frames combined

Pages 24–25 Boulder Mountain, Utah – October 2012
Nikon D800E, 200–400mm lens at 400mm, f/11, 1 sec., ISO 100, 6 vertical frames combined

Page 27 Kaibab National Forest, Arizona – July 2012
Nikon D800E, 85mm Nikkor T/S lens, 1/6 sec., f/18, ISO 100

Pages 28–29 Death Valley National Park, California – March 2012
Nikon D3X, 70–300mm lens at 240mm, f/18, 1/8 sec., ISO 100

Page 30 Acadia National Park, Maine – November 2001
Arca-Swiss F-Field 4×5 camera, 400mm Schneider Tele-Xenar lens, f 6.3, 1/15 sec., ISO 100, Fuji Velvia film

Page 31 Atascosa Mountains, Arizona – November 2006
Wista DX-2 4×5 Field Camera, 240mm lens, f/8, 1/2 sec., ISO 50, Fuji Velvia film

Page 32 Chacabuco, Chile – February 2010
Nikon D3X, 200–400mm Nikkor lens at 300mm, f/18, 1/13 sec., ISO 100

Page 35 Grand Canyon National Park, Arizona – May 2012
Nikon D800E, 14–24mm zoom at 14mm, f/16, 2 sec., ISO 100

Page 36 Bandon, Oregon – May 2012
Nikon D800E, 14–24mm lens at 14mm, f/18, ½ sec., ISO 100

Page 37 Catalina State Park, Arizona – January 2011
Nikon D3X, 200mm Nikkor Micro lens, f/16, 1/4 sec., ISO 100

Page 39 Big Cypress Seminole Reservation, Florida – August 2010
Arca-Swiss F-Field 4×5 camera, 75mm Nikkor lens, f/45, 2 min., 6 stop ND and polarizing filter, ISO 50, Fuji Velvia film

Page 40 Grand Staircase-Escalante National Monument, Utah – March 2012
Nikon D3X, 14–24mm zoom lens at 14mm, f/9.0, 240 sec., ISO 200

Page 41 Dixie National Forest, Utah – October 2012
Nikon D800E, 24mm Nikkor T/S lens, f/16, 1/3 sec., ISO 100

Page 43 Tamualipas, Mexico – October 2003
Arca-Swiss F-Field 4×5 camera, 75mm Nikkor lens, f/45, 2 sec., ISO 50, Fuji Velvia film

Page 44 Lago Grey, Patagonia, Chile – April 2009
Nikon D3, 24mm Nikkor T/S lens, f/18, 1/80 sec., ISO 200, 5 vertical frames combined

Page 45 San Luis Potosi, Mexico – February 2004
Arca-Swiss F-Field 4×5 camera, 75mm Nikkor lens, f/45, 4 sec., ISO 50, Fuji Velvia film

Page 46 Joseph Creek, Oregon – August 2010
Arca-Swiss F-Field 4×5 camera, 75mm Nikkor lens, f/32, 5 sec., ISO 50, Fuji Velvia film,

Page 47 Zion National Park, Utah – November 2007
Arca-Swiss F-Field 4×5 camera, 75mm Nikkor lens, f/22, 15 sec., ISO 50, Fuji Velvia film

Page 48 Tamaulipas, Mexico – February 2004
Arca-Swiss F-Field 4×5 camera, 300mm Nikkor lens, f/45, 10 sec., ISO 50, Fuji Velvia film

Page 49 Tamaulipas, Mexico – February 2004
Arca-Swiss F-Field 4×5 camera, 400mm Schneider Tele-Xenar lens, f/49, 6 sec., ISO 50, Fuji Velvia film

Page 50 Blue Hen Falls, Cuyahoga Valley National Park, Ohio – October 2006
Arca-Swiss F-Field 4×5 camera, 75mm Nikkor lens, f/39, 6 sec., ISO 50, Fuji Velvia film

Page 51 Blue Hen Falls, Cuyahoga Valley National Park, Ohio – October 2006
Arca-Swiss F-Field 4×5 camera, 240mm Fujinon, f/45, 12 sec., ISO 50, Fuji Velvia film

Page 52 Grand Canyon National Park, Arizona – May 2010
Nikon D3X, 70–300mm zoom lens at 100mm, f/14, 1/3 sec., ISO 100

Page 53 Grand Canyon National Park, Arizona – August 2006
Arca-Swiss F-Field 4×5 camera, 720mm Nikkor lens, f/45, 5 sec., ISO 50, Fuji Velvia film

Page 55 Great Sand Dunes National Monument, Colorado – August 1992
Arca-Swiss F-Field 4×5 camera, 120mm Schneider Symmar HM lens, f/32, 1/2 sec., ISO 64, Ektachrome 64 film

Page 57 Saguaro National Park, Arizona – May 1991
Arca-Swiss F-Field 4×5 camera, Nikkor 75mm lens, f/49, 12 sec., ISO 50, Fuji Velvia film

Page 58 Sonoran Desert National Monument, Arizona – April 2008
Nikon D3, 24mm Nikkor T/S lens, f/22, 1/13 sec., ISO 200

Page 59 Havasupai Reservation, Arizona – May 2007
Arca Swiss F-Field 4×5 camera, Fujinon 240mm lens, f/45, 8 sec., ISO 50, Fuji Velvia film

Page 61 Sonoran Desert National Monument, Arizona – July 2003
Arca Swiss F-Field 4×5 camera, 80mm Schneider Super Symmar lens, f/49, 4 sec., ISO 50, Fuji Velvia film

Page 62 Big Bend National Park, Texas – February 2005
Arca-Swiss F-Field 4×5 camera, 58mm Schneider Super-Angulon lens, f/32, 6 sec., ISO 50, Fuji Velvia film

Pages 64–65 Lago Grey, Patagonia, Chile – April 2009
Nikon D3, Nikkor 24–70mm zoom lens at 44mm, f/8, 1/13 sec., ISO 250, 7 vertical frames combined

Page 66 Baja California, Mexico – February 2013
Nikon D800E, 14–24mm zoom lens at 17mm, f/16, 1/3 sec., ISO 100

Page 67 Olympic National Park, Washington – June 2011
Nikon D3X, 45mm Nikkor T/S lens, f/16, 2 sec., ISO 100, 11 vertical frames combined

Page 69 Prairie Creek Redwoods State Par, California – May 2013
Nikon D800E, 45mm Nikkor T/S lens, f/20, 15 sec., ISO 100, 4 vertical frames combined

Pages 70–73 Grand Staircase-Escalante National Monument, Utah – October 2012
Nikon D800E, 85mm T/S lens, f/16, 1 sec., ISO 100, 6 horizontal frames combined

Pages 74–75 Sonoran Desert National Monument, Arizona – December 2013
Nikon D800E, 14–24mm zoom lens at 14mm, f/14, 1/6 sec., ISO 100

Page 77 Shore Acres State Park, Oregon – May 2013
Nikon D800E, 45mm Nikkor T/S lens, f/16, 1/45 sec., ISO 100, 4 vertical frames combined

Page 78–79 Bosque del Apache National Wildlife Refuge, New Mexico – November 2010
Nikon D3S, 200–400mm zoom lens with 1.4 teleconverter (=550mm), f/10, 1/1000 sec., ISO 1600

Pages 80–81 Torres del Paine, Chile – February 2011
Nikon D3X, 70–300mm zoom lens at 195mm, f/9.0, 1/20 sec., ISO 100, 8 vertical frames combined

Pages 82–83 Death Valley National Park, California – November 2012
Nikon D800E, 45mm Nikkor T/S lens, f/16, 5 sec., ISO 100, 10 vertical frames combined

Page 84 Intertribal Sinkyone Wilderness, California – May 2010
Arca-Swiss F-Field 4×5 camera, 180mm Rodenstock Sironar S lens, f/45, 12 sec., ISO 50, Fuji Velvia film

Page 85 Santa Rita Mountains, Arizona – June 1987
Arca-Swiss F-Field 4×5 camera, 500mm Nikkor lens, f/32, 2 sec, ISO 50, Fuji Velvia film

Page 86 Great Sund Dunes National Monument, Colorado – September 1999
Arca-Swiss F-Field 4×5 camera, 400mm Schneider Tele Xenar lens, f/39, 3 sec., ISO 50, Fuji Velvia film

Pages 88–89 Tucson, Arizona – April 2013
Nikon D800E, 85mm T/S lens, f/16, 1/125 sec., ISO 100

Pages 90–91 Boulder, Utah – October 2008
Arca-Swiss F-Field 4×5 camera, 180mm Rodenstock Sironar S lens, f/39, 4 sec.

Pages 92–93 Tucson, Arizona – September 1996
Arca-Swiss F-Field 4×5 camera, 180mm Rodenstock Sironar S lens, f/32, 1/2 sec., ISO 50 Fuji Velvia film

Pages 95 Yellowstone National Park, Wyoming – July 1991
Arca Swiss F-Field 4×5 camera, 75mm Nikkor lens, f/45, 8 sec., ISO 50, Fuji Velvia film

Page 96 Catalina State Park, Arizona – January 2012
Nikon D3X, 85mm T/S lens, f/20, 1/2 sec., ISO 100, 5 horizontal frames combined

Page 97 Glen Canyon National Rereation Area, Utah – November 2012
Nikon D800E, 14–25mm zoom lens at 14mm, f/16, 1/8 sec., ISO 100

Page 98 Factory Bench, Utah – May 1997
Arca Swiss F-Field 4×5 camera, 110mm Super Symmar lens, f/45, 5 sec., ISO 50, Fuji Velvia film

Page 99 Paria Canyon,Vermilion Cliffs National Monument, Arizona – October 2003
Arca-Swiss F-Field 4×5 camera, 110mm Super Symmar lens, f/39, 8 sec., ISO 50, Fuji Velvia film

Page 101 White Sands National Monument, New Mexico – January 2013
Nikon D800E, 45mm Nikkor T/S lens, f/16, .4 sec., ISO 100, 4 vertical frames combined

Page 102 White Sands National Monument, New Mexico – January 2013
Nikon D800E, 70–200mm f /4.0 lens at 190mm, f/16, 1/13 sec., ISO 100

Page 103 White Sands National Monument, New Mexico – January 2013
Nikon D800E, 70–200mm f /4.0 lens at 125mm, f/16, 1/30 sec., ISO 100

Page 104 White Sands National Monument, New Mexico – January 2013
Nikon D800E, 70–200mm f /4.0 lens at 200mm, f/16, 1/40 sec., ISO 100

Page 105 White Sands National Monument, New Mexico – January 2013
Nikon D800E, 70–200mm f /4.0 lens at 175mm, f/16, 1/40 sec., ISO 100

Page 106–107 Vermilion Cliffs Natiional Monument, Arizona – November 2011
Nikon D3X, 85mm T/S lens, f/16, 1 sec., ISO 100

Page 108 Yellowstone National Park, Wyoming – September 1998
Arca-Swiss F-Field 4×5 camera, 58mm Schneider Super-Anglon lens, f/45, 6 sec., ISO 50, Fuji Velvia film

Page 109 Yellowstone National Park, Wyoming – September 2012
Nikon D800E, 24mm Nikkor T/S lens, f/16, 1/8 sec., ISO 100, 4 vertical frames combined

Page 110 Yellowstone National Park, Wyoming – September 2012
Nikon D800E, 24mm Nikkor T/S lens, f/14, 1/2 sec., ISO 100, 4 vertical frames combined

Page 111 Yellowstone National Park, Wyoming – September 2012
Nikon D800E, 24mm Nikkor T/S lens, f/14, 1/5 sec., ISO 100

Pages 112–113 Yucatan, Mexico – January 2012
Nikon D3S, 200–400mm zoom lens at 400mm, f/10, 1/2000 sec., ISO 1250

Pages 114–115 Torres del Paine National Park, Chile – February 2011
Nikon D3X, 45mm Nikkor T/S lens, f/16, 2 sec., 4 horizontal frames comtined

Page 116 White Mountains, Arizona – August 2001
Arca-Swiss F-Field 4×5 camera, 58mm Schneider Super Angulon lens, f/45, 5 sec., ISO 50, Fuji Velvia film

Page 117 Valley of Fire State Park, Nevada – March 2012
Nikon D3X, 24mm Nikkor T/S lens, f/20, 1/6 sec., ISO 100, 5 vertical frames combined

Pages 118–119 Hawaii Volcano National Park, Hawaii – August 2010
Nikon D3X, 85mm T/S lens, f/16, 1/5 sec., ISO 100, 4 horizontal frames combined

Page 120 Bryce Canyon National Park, Utah – July 2002
Arca-Swiss F-Filed 4×5 camera, 110mm Schneider Super Symmar lens, f/45, 3 sec., ISO 50, Fuji Velvia film

Page 121 El Golfo Biosphere Reserve, Mexico – January 2005
Pentax 6X7, 65mm lens, f/8 , 1/500 sec., ISO 100, Fujichrome 100 film

Note: As a large format landscape photographer, I have always been interested in the detail within the landscape that large format files provide. Since my conversion to digital I apply the same ethos, and my method for achieving incredible detail utilizes tilt/shift lenses for their ability to "shift" side to side on the optical plane. I am then able to combine several images in Photoshop's Panorama mode. In this way I can create files that approach the image quality of my 4×5 view camera.